Confederate Tide Rising

Confederate Tide Rising

Robert E. Lee and the Making of Southern Strategy, 1861–1862

JOSEPH L. HARSH

THE KENT STATE UNIVERSITY PRESS

Kent, Ohio, & London

© 1998 by The Kent State University Press, Kent, Ohio 44242
All rights reserved
Library of Congress Catalog Card Number 97-2635
ISBN 0-87338-580-2

MANUFACTURED IN THE UNITED STATES OF AMERICA

05   04   03   02   01   00   99   98   5   4   3   2   1

Harsh, Joseph L.
    Confederate tide rising : Robert E. Lee and the making of Southern strategy, 1861–
1862 / Joseph L. Harsh.
        p.   cm.
    Includes bibliographical references and index.
    ISBN 0-87338-580-2 (alk. paper) ∞
    1. Confederate States of America—Military policy. 2. Lee, Robert E. (Robert
Edward), 1807–1870—Military leadership. 3. Strategy—History—19th century.
4. Davis, Jefferson, 1808–1889. 5. Confederate States of America—History, Military.
6. United States—History—Civil War, 1861–1865—Campaigns. I. Title.
E487.H34   1997   97-2635
973.7'3013—dc21   CIP

British Library Cataloging-in-Publication data are available.

For Trudy,
with love

We see, therefore, in the first place, that under all circumstances War is to be regarded not as an independent thing, but as a political instrument; and it is only by taking this point of view that we can avoid finding ourselves in opposition to all military history. This is the only means of unlocking the great book and making it intelligible. Secondly, this view shows us how Wars must differ in character according to the nature of the motives and circumstances from which they proceed.

Now, the first, the grandest, and most decisive act of judgment which the Statesman and General exercises is rightly to understand in this respect the War in which he engages, not to take it for something, which by the nature of its relations it is impossible for it to be. This is, therefore, the first, the most comprehensive, of all strategical questions.

Karl von Clausewitz, *On War* 1:25

Contents

Contents · xi

Preface

THIS IS A BOOK I did not set out to write. It wrote itself as I tried to understand why Robert E. Lee crossed the Potomac with his Army of Northern Virginia in early September 1862; and, even more, as I struggled to comprehend why Lee stubbornly clung to his campaign in Maryland long after common sense dictated that he return to Virginia. Persuasive answers to these questions could not be found within the bounds of the Maryland campaign itself.

Ideas never, no more than men, appear from nowhere. Actions are consequences of previous actions, and events evolve from what transpires before them. There is a pattern in history that can only be perceived when the chain of events is untangled and laid end to end, thus allowing the progression from link to link to be revealed. There was a logic in the decisions that Lee made in September of 1862, but it does not emerge until seen in the context of Confederate war aims and grand strategy and until it is viewed as the final step in the arduous journey that carried him to the banks of the Potomac.

Hence, what started as no more than an introductory background chapter in my study of the Maryland campaign ballooned into a reexamination of the Confederate conduct of the first year and a half of the war. The detour was worth the effort. The conclusions resulting from the digression have lead me to view the early Civil War and the Confederate side of the Maryland campaign in a substantially different light. I have come to see Lee's crossing the Potomac as a logical extension of his three-month operations and the battle at Sharpsburg as the finale to his summer's overland campaign to win the war. It was not, of course, that he plotted an expedition into Maryland while still mired in the swamps of the Chickahominy. Rather, it was that opportunities led him forward, from success to success, as he cleared one frontier after another until only the Potomac, the final frontier, remained.

Nor is it true that Lee became so enmeshed in the tactics of defeating his foe that he lost sight of the realities of the war as he perceived them. Critics have sometimes depicted him as a general without an overall strategy, a brilliant practitioner who lacked farsightedness. This has not been my conclusion. It is possible that Lee's perception of the war was wrong and that his prescription for victory was mistaken. But it has not seemed possible to me that Lee acted without serious and constant regard to pursuing the course he believed best suited to bring success to the Confederacy. His words and his actions are too consistent on this point to be denied.

Lee's operations fit comfortably within the war aims of the Confederacy as articulated by its president and Congress and as apparently supported by a large number—if not a majority—of its citizens. In spite of rhetoric proclaiming the struggle to be defensive, the Confederates pursued aggressive goals. Both the desire to incorporate the border states and the need to preserve the vital resources of the upper South yielded offensive aims. Lee understood this, and so too did Jefferson Davis. And it was in partnership that the two evolved a grand strategy for victory.

Critics have pilloried the president for adopting a "perimeter" policy that attempted to defend every square mile of Southern territory and thus squandered meager Confederate resources. Many have also criticized him for meddling in the operations of his field commanders. Yet the evidence suggests otherwise. Except for a brief four-month lapse, Davis labored to concentrate Southern forces into field armies, which he then urged his generals to employ in offensive operations. He recognized that ignorance and the inability to communicate in a timely manner foreclosed the possibility of close control from Richmond. And, although his record on these points is not perfect, it is overwhelmingly positive.

While the view of Davis given here is more favorable than is customary, it is still possible that too much credit is accorded to Lee and too little to the president. Regrettably, much that passed between the two men cannot now be known, and ideas attributed to Lee may have originated with Davis. What can be known is that a relationship grew between the two—one rarely equaled between a chief and subordinate—that allowed the Confederacy to survive longer than it had any right to expect.

Hypotheses about the things that did not happen in history can never attain the status of truth but must always remain at best a matter of educated opinion. Nonetheless, my study has persuaded me of two likelihoods. First, given the unbending determination of the North, the South probably could not have won the war. Second, if the North could have been made to waver in its determination, Davis's policy and Lee's strategy were well suited to achieve Confederate independence.

• • •

These chapters serve as an introduction to a longer and more detailed work entitled *Taken at the Flood: Robert E. Lee and Confederate Strategy in the Maryland Campaign of 1862*. That book and this volume were conceived, composed, and submitted to the publisher as an organic whole. After some thought, it was decided that the first six chapters, because of their general nature in both content and style, would benefit from separate publication. While I have endeavored to make each study stand independently, the structure of the first has inevitably been shaped by its origin and function. Its form is pyramidal. The base is broad, encompassing war aims, military policy, mobilization, concentration of manpower, and related topics. As it progresses, its focus narrows to Lee and the Army of Northern Virginia. Such a format, far from being artificial, reflects the career of Lee. He too moved from the broad to the specific, and the breadth of his early war experiences not only shaped his view of the struggle but also strongly influenced the decisions he rendered in the campaigns of 1862.

This work ends with the Battle of Chantilly on September 1, 1862. Several topics, although belonging chronologically to this volume, are not discussed until the next. The two most important are the origins and vicissitudes of the reenforcing column from Richmond and the development of parallel Confederate offensives on other fronts. These stories are treated as they became known to Lee and had an impact on his thinking and planning on September 2 and later.

The chapters that comprise *Confederate Tide Rising* were written in 1994. Since they were composed, a number of works have appeared that touch upon many of the questions I raise. Among the more important are Steven E. Woodworth's *Davis and Lee at War*; James A. Kegel's *North with Lee and Jackson*; Gary W. Gallagher's *Lee, the Soldier*; Charles P. Roland's *Reflections on Lee*; James M. McPherson's *Drawn with the Sword*; and James I. Robertson, Jr.'s *Stonewall Jackson*. It is, perhaps, a testimony to the unending employment potential for historians that none of these studies reach the same conclusions I offer here. While there are broad areas of agreement among these authors, and between each of them and me, as befits studies based on many of the same sources, there are also wide differences of interpretation, thus keeping unfitting historical studies from ever approaching the certitude of the sciences. Where appropriate I have alluded to several points of agreement and dissent in the endnotes.

The anthology edited by Gary Gallagher now provides convenient access to the memoranda of postwar conversations with Lee; a number of the key articles in Lee historiography, such as those by Thomas Connelly and Albert Castel; as well as several valuable new contributions, especially the one on Davis and Lee by William C. Davis. In the case of previously published pieces, however, I have retained citations to the original printed work.

The obligations I have incurred have proven more resistant to division than the separation of the project into two books. It should be understood, therefore, that my acknowledgments reflect the debts accumulated during the research and writing of both works.

Before any other, I thank Professor Frank Everson Vandiver, mentor and friend, whose early guidance set my professional career on the correct path. Even if I have failed to meet them, I have adopted his high standards.

First and foremost in the present work, I owe gratitude to Dr. Richard J. Sommers of the United States Military Research Institute at Carlisle Barracks, Pennsylvania. Since we were graduate colleagues at Rice University over thirty years ago, Dick has offered friendship, counsel, and prodding, all in abundance, but always in that order. His encyclopedic knowledge is legendary, but his wit and warmth he tries to keep secret. My manuscript benefited immeasurably from his close reading. He would be the first to insist that it would have benefited even more had I possessed the good sense to accept all of his suggestions.

I also greatly appreciate the many contributions of Professor Thomas G. Clemens of Hagerstown Junior College. First as my student and then as my friend and co-instructor in the summer "Battlefields" course, Tom could not escape serving as a sounding-board for my ideas as they developed. He also added many helpful suggestions to the finished manuscript.

I am indebted to John Hubbell, director of The Kent State University Press, for his encouragement, suggestions, and confidence, and to Julia Morton, Linda Cuckovich, and, especially, Joanna Hildebrand, of his staff, for their continuing support; to Jim DuPriest of Richmond Discoveries, Inc., for invaluable help in locating illustrations; and to John Heiser of Gettysburg for his graceful and effective maps.

I am obliged to four friends—John E. Divine, J. Michael Miller, William J. Miller, and John Hennessy—for encouragement and for pointing out sources; also to Bill for reading and commenting on the first three chapters; and to John, the Sage of Loudoun, for leading me to places I had never been. John's death in the autumn of 1996 leaves a "Vacant Chair" that will never be filled. We shall miss him.

I wish it were possible to thank my good friend, the late James V. Murfin, author of the first full-length narrative on the Maryland campaign. Jim was kind enough to dedicate a laudatory paragraph in his book to a young graduate student in whom he saw promise. I believe that Jim would be neither surprised nor displeased to learn that many of my conclusions differ from the ones he drew thirty years ago. We even then disagreed on some points, but we did so in the friendliest and most mutually instructive way.

I would be remiss not to acknowledge the inspiration and information I have gained over the years from National Park Service historians Greg Mertz, Mac Wycoff, Frank O'Reilly, John Heiser, Jimmy Blankenship, Chris Caulkins, Ron Wilson, Tracy Chenault, Will Greene, and especially Dennis Frye. Three who wear the green, Mike Andrus, Jim Burgess, and Ed Rauss, were kind enough to read the early chapters for errors. Two nephews of Smokey, Ted Alexander and Paul Chiles, not only read the entire manuscript but for a long time now have made each of my many trips to Antietam's visitor center welcome and valuable experiences. I thank also my new acquaintance, David Nathanson, at Harpers Ferry library and my old friend Harry Butowsky at the Park Service Washington headquarters, who provided statistics.

Like many before me, it is a pleasure to acknowledge the friendship and invaluable assistance of Mike Musick of the Old Military Records Section of the National Archives.

Dawn Sobol and her staff at George Mason University's Fenwick Library ably and cheerfully located dozens of rare items through interlibrary loan. Lynda Crist and Mary Dix of the Jefferson Davis Association at Rice University answered questions and provided documents. Mike Pinkston of Louisiana State University Press sent a set of unbound pages of volume 8 of *The Papers of Jefferson Davis* so that I might profit from their rich insights in a timely fashion.

I thank Prof. Carmen Grayson of Hampton University for inspiration and support and Nancy Fuchs, reporter and publisher extraordinaire, for reading and critiquing my prose. I am also obliged to Michael Snyder of Pottstown, Pennsylvania, for providing sources.

Some of the present work—and much more so of the forthcoming chapters on the Maryland campaign—benefits from the earlier study by Gen. Ezra Carman. It is due to Dr. William Hugh Johnson, who has diligently transcribed the cramped script of Ezra Carman into legible form, that I have been able to utilize this important source so fully. Will's work will also facilitate the coming publication of the entire Carman manuscript.

In thirty years of teaching, I have been blessed with innumerable bright students whose challenges have kept me young. I must especially thank three undergraduates, Lois Brock, Cora Jacobson, and Sheree Derocher, whose research turned up useful documents; and four graduate students, Leon Tenney, John Allen, John Scully, and Ethan Rafuse, whose interpretations have enriched my own. I also wish to express my gratitude to five wonderful women, whose title happens to be "secretary" but whose specialty has been making the Department of History work over the years: Betty Lockhart, Charlene Calder, Ann McCauley, Jane Constantine, and Betsy Rowe.

Finally, I acknowledge that this book was prepared in a warm and supportive atmosphere. I thank boon companions Joe Hudson and Dick Lemmon, who have listened and at least pretended to be interested. I thank both of my sons, Drew and Greg, for their interest and support in many small ways (such as hauling microfilm readers and building bookshelves). I thank especially my daughter, Laura, my assistant librarian, for the countless hours she saved me in the preparation of cumulative research cards.

To my wife, Trudy, who knows, I dedicate this book.

—— ✤ ——

"The most propitious time"

Fate in Lee's Hands,
September 3, 1862

As the lengthening shadows of the sunny, late summer's eve crept slowly across the northern Virginia countryside outside the walls of his tent, Robert E. Lee spoke distinctly so that Col. Armistead Long, his military secretary, might copy the thoughts onto paper. "The present seems to be the most propitious time since the commencement of the war," he said, "for the Confederate Army to enter Maryland."[1] With these not entirely felicitous phrases, the Confederate commander dictated the opening sentence of the fateful dispatch to Jefferson Davis that launched the Maryland campaign. In spite of its somewhat veiled expression, the momentous idea—fraught with excitement and risk—must have caused the blood of both speaker and listener to course faster. The historical importance of the passing second was self-evident. Indeed, few moments in the brief life of the Confederacy would be so taut with drama and filled with potential. With these words, the general proclaimed that the time had arrived to throw all of his strength behind a blow that would decide the independence of his country.

On this Wednesday, September 3, 1862, from his newly established camp at Dranesville on the Leesburg Turnpike, thirteen miles west from Washington, Lee had good reason to believe the season for decision had come. And he, more than any other man, had caused its coming. He had just completed his second successful military campaign in two months and had all but banished enemy troops from the soil of his native Virginia. Inflicting heavy losses in men and morale on the Federal armies of George McClellan and John Pope in turn, he transferred the scene of fighting from the doorstep of Richmond northward a hundred miles to the backyard of the enemy capital. After barely three months of field command, Lee was already entering upon the time of his great and enduring fame. His troops cheered his appearances among them, and soldiers and civilians alike were collecting and sharing anecdotes about "Mars' Robert."[2] The niggling doubts that lingered after the Seven Days battles had washed away with the tide of Confederate victory at Second Manassas.[3] In ninety-five days Lee had made the Army of Northern Virginia his own, and he and his men shared a trust and confidence upon which great accomplishments could be built. He had forged a powerful weapon in a fiery furnace, and he would not sheath it when final victory seemed so near at hand.

Two blemishes only blighted the bright vista that spread before Lee as he collected his thoughts to compose the dispatch to President Davis. The first was immediate and personal. Both hands throbbed with pain from an injury he had suffered two days before. Near the ruins of the Stone Bridge over Bull Run on the Warrenton Turnpike when his horse Traveller had spooked, Lee grabbed for the reins and tripped heavily onto the ground. He sprained both wrists and broke several bones in his right hand. Now, both hands were bandaged around splints, and his right arm hung useless in a sling.[4]

For a man of simple habits and plain camp routines, the injury created embarrassment beyond the suffering. Lee kept an unpretentious headquarters. He tried whenever possible to avoid occupying houses and inconveniencing civilians. Visitors, especially those familiar with European armies, were amazed to arrive at Lee's headquarters and find only three or four wagons, seven or eight tents, and a dozen or so staff. He usually wrote out the rough drafts of his dispatches, and sometimes, in the case of the most confidential, he copied them himself into his letterbook.[5] But, the unfortunate accident more than inconvenienced Lee; it crippled him. He could not ride on horseback and had to travel in an army ambulance. He could neither hold a pen to write, nor even dress himself.

Frustration compounded Lee's pain. He fretted over the escape the day before of Pope's army, relatively intact, to the security of Washington's forts. Both Pope and McClellan could now repair in leisure their shattered armies, and—reenforced by the host of new regiments pouring in from the North—could plot a new invasion of Virginia at a time and place of their own choosing.

Lee had intended to inflict much more harm on his enemy. He had hoped to crush so thoroughly the Federal forces that the Northern people would begin to question the wisdom of continuing the war. He knew his victories in the Seven Days and at Second Manassas, no matter how complete they may have appeared to naive civilians, had fallen short of the mark. He faced the dreadful prospect that everything his own army had suffered and achieved might be for naught. More than thirty thousand Confederate dead and wounded, the irreplaceable flower of a nation's early enthusiasm, and hundreds of miles of dusty Virginia roads pounded in the choking heat of July and August had brought him to an impasse on the Potomac.

Still, as the long shadows turned to dusk on the evening of September 3, Lee's thoughts probably did not dwell overlong on either his pain or past failures. Crippled though the body might be, the mind roamed over fields where no Confederate army had yet marched: Maryland.

In the more than 130 years since Lee dictated the dispatch to Davis, the Confederate commander's motives for crossing the Potomac and what he intended to accomplish once he left Confederate soil have not been satisfactorily resolved. It has been suggested that Lee wanted to relieve Virginia from the scourge of war and subsist his army off enemy resources; that he hoped to seduce Maryland to secede and join the ranks of the Confederacy; that he aimed to influence Northern politics by encouraging the peace movement in the approaching fall congressional elections; and that he hoped to impress Great Britain and France with the strength and likely success of the Southern effort, so both nations would grant diplomatic recognition and, perhaps, military aid to the Confederacy.

Never have these explanations been sorted out according to their relative importance. They have not been tested against Lee's actions during the campaign, nor have their inconsistencies and improbabilities been addressed. It has not even been determined whether all of them were part of Lee's thinking when he made his decision. Consequently, questions abound.

How could Lee expect both to woo a sister state and at the same time live off enemy resources while in Maryland? Such seduction surely verged on violation. Did Lee have any notion of what was transpiring in foreign capitals? In any case, would he have allowed diplomatic considerations to determine his strategy at a critical moment in the war? And, in the same vein, how much weight would Lee give to political factors, such as Northern elections?

Neither has the nature of Lee's campaign in Maryland, nor his conduct of it, been satisfactorily explained. While most historians have viewed it as a full-throated invasion of the North intended to carry the Confederates to the banks of the Susquehanna deep in Pennsylvania, a few have seen it as a raid across the border. But, with these explanations also, there are serious contradictions.

If Lee intended to undertake either a raid or an invasion, should he not have marched swiftly and directly to obtain his objective in an attempt to forestall contact with the enemy for as long as possible? Why, then, did he ford the Potomac so near Washington when he could have crossed much farther west had he desired? Why did he hold his army idling for five days in the vicinity of Frederick? And, why did he view the Federal garrison at Harpers Ferry as an unacceptable menace to his communications? If Lee engaged in a raid, he did not need to maintain a supply line. If he embarked on an invasion of central Pennsylvania, he could not have expected to maintain an attenuated and vulnerable supply line through the Shenandoah Valley.

Likewise, the appearance of Federal troops at the foot of South Mountain on September 13, which threatened to split the widely separated wings of the Confederate army before Harpers Ferry had been captured, ought logically to have terminated either a raid or an invasion and caused Lee to retire into Virginia. A raid ceases to be viable when the raider suffers heavy losses before obtaining any worthwhile goal. Equally, an invasion becomes untenable once the enemy traps the invader in a box. Yet, Lee did not retire. On the contrary, he made every conceivable effort to protract his stay in Maryland. He stood against heavy odds at South Mountain on the 14th; and he stood against heavy odds at Sharpsburg for four days; and, when he at last returned to Virginia on the 19th, he did so fully intending to recross the Potomac immediately farther up the river.

Is it possible, then, that in Lee's own mind he was engaged in neither a raid nor an invasion? If that is the case, what was he doing in Maryland in September of 1862?

Finally, there are even more fundamental questions that need to be asked. Can the Maryland campaign be fully understood as a spontaneous and isolated military movement? Or, did it emerge from a conscious and comprehensive Confederate strategy for winning the war? How would a mere field commander dare cross a national boundary without permission from his government? Indeed, did not the incursion into enemy territory contradict the basically defensive war aims and military policy traditionally credited to the Confederacy? Beyond the matter of strategic consistency, there is also the question of military wisdom. Should a nation woefully inferior in men and materiel gamble precious resources in high-risk offensives?

The foundation for answering all of these questions—if not the very answers themselves—is to be found in the year and a half of the war that preceded the Maryland campaign. To know—to the extent it can now be determined—why Lee did it, it is necessary to retrace his steps to the Potomac and to the moment he dictated the fateful dispatch to Davis.

— ❧ —

CHAPTER ONE

"He who makes the assault"

Confederate Strategy from Sumter to Seven Pines, April 1861–May 1862

R OBERT E. LEE's dispatch to Davis proposing an expedition into Maryland likely did not reach the president until September 6, 1862, or later, two or more days after it was dictated. Yet Lee ordered Harvey Hill's division to ford the Potomac on the afternoon of the 4th. Hence, no one in Richmond could have known Lee was contemplating crossing the national frontier. Still, if the movement was not expressly authorized, neither was it contrary to the aims the Confederacy sought to achieve in the war, nor did it violate the military policy of the Davis administration. Even more, it was well within the spirit of the grand strategy the South had pursued for the first sixteen months of the struggle. Not surprisingly, no evidence exists that Jefferson Davis ever reprimanded Lee for the undertaking.

Confederate War Aims

Independence was the primary goal of the Confederate States of America, and it came easily, bloodlessly, and virtually without external opposition. Within the remarkably short period of sixty days, seven states of the deep South seceded, adopted a constitution, elected a provisional congress and president, created a cabinet and executive departments, established an army and navy, and designed a national flag. In their own eyes, Confederates established their country two months before the firing on Sumter. Hence, when the war came, they could claim their aim was to defend themselves and to maintain their independence. "We seek no conquest, no aggrandizement, no concession of any kind," Jefferson Davis would explain to the world. "All we ask is to be let alone."[1]

For a century and a third, historians have accepted the official Confederate explanation—part propaganda, part self-rationalization, and part genuine conviction—that Northern aggression forced war upon a country that wanted only to be independent and free from outside intervention. Uncritical acceptance of their aims as officially stated by the Confederates themselves has led to considerable second-guessing of Confederate

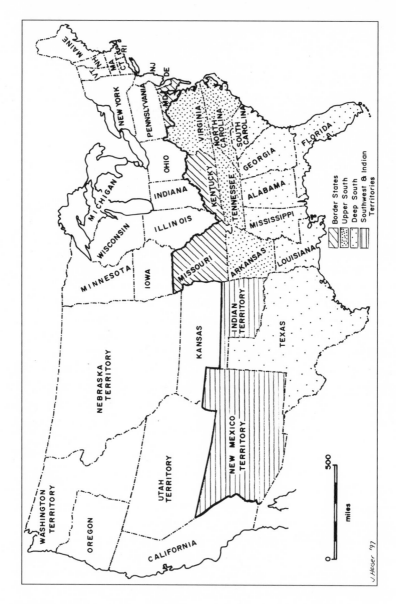

Regions of the United States claimed by the Confederacy. Of the fifteen slave states, only Delaware was omitted.

military policy, strategy, and tactics, all of which frequently seemed to be at variance with the objective. "To be let alone," Confederates needed only to sit at home and swat away invasions by the North. Instead, they conducted the war aggressively, seeming to prefer attacking to receiving attacks, engaging in large-scale offensives, and on two major and several minor occasions invading the soil of the North. Such contrary conduct has caused some critics to conclude that cross-grained Southerners contributed largely to their own defeat.[2]

The contradiction is apparent rather than real, however. The Civil War was not wholly defensive, either politically or militarily, for the Confederate States of America. Never, not from South Carolina's secession on December 20, 1860, was it true that all the South wanted was "to be let alone." From the start, even predating the creation of the Confederate government, Southerners had additional objectives that were essentially offensive in nature. In fact, the Confederates could not adopt an entirely defensive posture, because they *could* not establish independence—as they defined independence—by simple fiat; because they *would* not rely on peaceful political solutions to achieve their ends; and, finally, because the independence of merely half of the slave states was not their objective.

The Confederacy pursued three closely related but distinct war aims: independence, territorial integrity, and the union of all the slave states. For their achievement all three aims mandated, to a greater or lesser degree, aggressive military operations.

In declaring that its object was to maintain its independence, the South, in its rhetoric, confused the difference between an operating government and a sovereign nation. Southerners could not maintain what they had not yet obtained. The Confederate States was not independent so long as no other nation in the world had recognized it; nor so long as the national government had armies in the field to force the states back into the Union. Thus, the primary Confederate war aim was to achieve, not maintain, independence. This objective demanded both diplomatic and political offensives. In military terms, Confederates could pursue a purely defensive strategy only if two conditions prevailed: first, if they started the war with their country intact and secure; and, second, if their armies could beat back invasions without the loss of significant ground. The loss of too much territory would impair, if not thwart, the Confederate attempt to establish independence. Foreign nations would not likely recognize a losing cause. Conversely, Northerners would not likely abandon a winning effort. In addition, the loss of too many resources would lead to the inability to carry on the war with either a defensive or offensive strategy. Hence, even in its primary and simplest aim, independence, there were inherent forces pushing the Confederates toward a generally offensive strategy.

• • •

Beyond independence, a second Confederate goal was, in Davis's words, "the integrity of our territory."[3] None of the seven deep South states achieved total control within its own borders merely by passing an ordinance of secession. Each immediately went on the offensive to expel Federal forces and to capture Federal facilities within its boundaries. By April 11, 1861, Southerners had seized nineteen forts, sixteen ships, eight arsenals and depots, three army barracks, one payroll, one mint, one hospital, and numerous customhouses and post offices. All of these incidents symbolically represented an attack on the American flag, and in four cases there was actual firing on the Stars and Stripes.[4]

Granted, Southerners insisted they were simply reclaiming their own property earned from years of paying Federal taxes and that the seizures were implicit in secession. And, in truth, each of the incidents was of small import when considered alone. Taken collectively, however, the impatient and aggressive manner in which the states captured Federal property was fully offensive and set a pattern for future expectations. The early aggressiveness helped to trigger the war by provoking the North. It not only gratified the current demand of Southerners to seize control of their own fate, it also set a measurement for the conduct of the war. The loss of territory came to be equated with losing the struggle, while holding or retaking territory was seen as winning.

The attack on Fort Sumter on April 12, 1861, was the logical culmination of a three-month-old Southern policy to bypass negotiation and employ military force to achieve territorial integrity. When Jefferson Davis ordered the guns to open in Charleston harbor, the Confederate government took the second aim from the hands of the individual states and made it a national goal. Ironically, by attacking a besieged and heavily outnumbered garrison that had already become heroic in the eyes of its own citizens, the Confederates committed an act of aggression that Americans outside of the South later would rank in infamy with the capture of the Alamo, the sinking of the *Maine*, and the attack on Pearl Harbor.

The Confederates argued that Lincoln committed the aggression when he ordered provisions to Sumter, while their attack on the fort was simply a defensive reaction. According to Jefferson Davis, the South only struck away the arm of the man who had a gun pointed at its breast. "He who makes the assault," he rationalized, "is not necessarily he that strikes the first blow or fires the first gun." The Confederates, with logical consistency, would not view their capture of Sumter as the opening act of the war. They would insist the first step came with Lincoln's April 15 call for seventy-five thousand militia, which they claimed was the announcement by a "foreign power" of its intention to "invade" the South.[5]

• • •

The third Confederate war aim, also present from the start, was the expansion of the national boundaries. The Southern founding fathers envisioned their country stretching north to the Mason-Dixon Line and the Ohio River and west to the Colorado River, including all fifteen slave states and the territories of the southwest. As early as mid-January, the initial four to secede (South Carolina, Mississippi, Florida, and Alabama) sent commissioners to the legislatures of the other eleven states to urge them to join in forming a new nation. By February, the seven states that by then had declared themselves out of the Union (Georgia, Louisiana, and Texas had subsequently gone out) created a provisional government and then immediately set about to induce the remaining eight to join. Lincoln's April call for troops to suppress the insurrection brought in the four states of the upper South (Virginia, Arkansas, North Carolina, and Tennessee), but in Confederate eyes their nation was still incomplete.[6]

Confederates did not see their glass as three-quarters full, nor did they recognize the correlation between a reluctance to secede and the thinning of slavery as it spread northward. Instead, Confederates saw their glass as one-quarter empty and pressed forward to fill it to the brim. In retrospect, it is known that a decisive Unionist majority emerged in all of the border states (Delaware, Maryland, Kentucky, and Missouri). But, in 1861, with a sizable pro-Southern minority in each state, it was possible for the Confederates to believe that all four belonged to them and would become part of their new nation. In addition, the Confederates claimed the southwestern territories (New Mexico and the Indian Territory south of Kansas) as their inheritance from the lands they had helped the Union acquire in the war with Mexico and had held in trust with all of the states.

The vision of fulfilling its natural boundaries, not unlike a Confederate manifest destiny, shaped Confederate policy and strategy. When the Provisional Confederate Congress declared war on the United States on May 6, 1861, it excepted the states of Delaware, Maryland, Kentucky, and Missouri, and the Indian, New Mexico, and Arizona territories.[7] Delaware, distant and detached, never displayed sufficient interest to justify much attention. Almost at once Maryland became a remote hope, when the state was so quickly and heavily occupied by Federal troops that its legislators, some of whom were arrested, could not meet to vote on separation from the Union. Thus was born the myth of Maryland being held in the Union only by the bayonet. Elsewhere, however, the Confederacy moved resolutely to incorporate its missing parts. The government admitted both Missouri and Kentucky to statehood, although neither had a secessionist majority, gave them voting seats in congress, and added them as the twelfth and thirteenth stars to the new national

flag. The Confederacy also created its own Arizona Territory and negoti-
ated treaties and military alliances with the tribes of the Indian Territory,
giving them the right to apply for statehood at a future date.[8]

During the war's first six months, Confederate armies marched north
and west into Kentucky, Missouri, and Arizona to carry the flag to its natural
boundaries. Such progress was made by the end of 1861 that the Confederates had no cause to believe they had overreached their grasp. Indeed, by
December of 1861, Congress would extend and complete the war aims by
declaring that "no peace ought to be concluded . . . which does not insure
to Maryland the opportunity of forming a part of this Confederacy." By
February 1862 Jefferson Davis could clarify and confirm his nation's goals
in instructions to Confederate commissioners abroad. He would insist that
Great Britain and France understand as the basis for any alliance that "no
treaty of peace can be accepted" that did not recognize the independence
of the Confederacy, including the southwest territories, Kentucky, Missouri, and Maryland. The president did allow that the inclusion of the
three named states might be made contingent on a "fair" election in each,
since their citizens had not yet had the opportunity of expressing their
sentiments. In March 1862, in order that there be no possible misunderstanding, Congress easily passed a supplemental resolution (offered by
Senator John B. Clark of Missouri) declaring "no proposition of peace shall
be entertained" until the enemy had been "expelled from every foot of soil"
of the Confederacy. The only opposition voiced to the resolution was that
it was so obvious as to be unnecessary.[9]

When the war winds began to shift, and Kentucky, Missouri, and Arizona slipped from the Confederate grasp, the lost states and territories
became the Confederacy irredenta. It is not likely that the citizens of the
lower and upper South would have abandoned their unredeemed prov-
inces without a struggle. Orphaned congressional delegations, thousands
of civilian refugees, and tens of thousands of volunteer soldiers from the
border states made certain, however, that the goal of an expanded nation would not be forgotten. Thereafter during the war, whenever circumstances permitted, and even in the final months as the military system collapsed, Confederate armies reached northward to reclaim Missouri
and Kentucky.

Hence, when Confederates proclaimed they sought "no conquest, no
aggrandizement," they meant they did not seek to conquer any of the free
states, nor to carve out an unfair portion of the territories as their own.
Movement into the border states would not be invasion and conquest but
liberation. Whatever utility this distinction offered in the political arena,
in military terms the third aim, even more than the other two, determined
that the Confederacy would not adopt a purely defensive posture.

Confederate Military Policy

The Confederacy had no general staff, no civilian coordinating board, nor any similarly modern agencies to translate its war aims into national policy and military strategy. None of its leaders put onto paper a comprehensive plan to serve as blueprint for the mobilization of its human and material resources. Direction came from letters of instruction and war councils between the president, the secretary of war, and prominent generals. Mostly the correspondence and the conferences dealt with discrete situations rather than the general conduct of the war. Not surprisingly, Confederate war policy and grand strategy were often piecemeal, frequently disjointed, and sometimes contradictory.[10] Nonetheless, Southern leaders, considering all of the disadvantages and limitations under which they labored, displayed general consistency, reasonable insight, and considerable determination in mobilizing and applying their resources to achieve their war aims. And it is well they did.

In aiming to secure thirteen of the fifteen slave states, the Confederacy fought to establish its authority over almost exactly one-half of the old Union—nearly 878,000 square miles and the equivalent of a subcontinent.[11] To achieve victory the South needed to mobilize all of its resources to the fullest extent, for in nearly every category important to waging war it was inferior to the North. Even counting the full resources of all thirteen states, only in agriculture, where they produced 42.6 percent of the grain and raised 50.3 percent of the livestock, could the Confederates face the enemy on a roughly equal footing. In the struggle to wrest control of half the country, the South could only draw upon 33.6 percent of the nation's railroads, 27 percent of its banking capital, and 13 percent of its manufacturing. In fact, because the Confederates never controlled large portions of these thirteen states, they could never profit from all of their resources, and the disparity was even greater.[12]

The Confederacy suffered the most critical imbalance in odds, however, in population and human military resources. Even if the Confederates had been able to draw upon all of the 11,441,028 inhabitants living in the thirteen states they claimed, they would still have been at a 1 to 1.7 disadvantage in total population.[13] When that figure is adjusted to approximate the realities of regional loyalties, Confederate population shrinks to about ten million, and the disparity grows to 1 to 2.1.[14] Extract for comparison the six million white population from the adjusted figure, and the ratio soars to 1 to 3.5.[15] Worst of all, in the most crucial category, the military pool of white males aged eighteen to forty-five, the South would face odds of 1 to 3.7.[16]

In the face of such a lopsided balance sheet, the Confederacy performed remarkably well. It not only kept defeat at bay for four years, but it achieved considerable military success during the first thirty-six months of the struggle. To be sure, some of the success can be attributed to enemy bungling and some to simple good luck. But by far the greatest share of the credit belongs to the Confederates and, in particular, to several aspects of their military policy in which they outperformed the Federals.

First, and perhaps most basically, the Confederacy pursued a more determined mobilization of human resources. The South put a considerably larger percentage of its population into the field as soldiers and had the foresight to do it earlier than the North. On March 6, 1861—five weeks before Sumter compelled a reluctant Lincoln to federalize 75,000 state militia for ninety days—the Provisional Confederate Congress authorized an army of 100,000 national volunteers to serve for one year. By May, when both sides recognized the war might be protracted and sought volunteers for three years' service (or the duration of the war if shorter), Lincoln called for 42,000, while Davis was authorized to accept an unlimited number.[17] Then, when the United States Congress significantly increased its forces in July with an act to raise 500,000 volunteers, the Confederates responded with an ambitious call for 400,000 men.[18]

In the spring of 1862, the Confederates faced their first manpower crisis. The initial wave of enthusiasm had crested and volunteering had fallen drastically. Concern grew that the one-year men would not reenlist at the expiration of their terms in April. On March 28 Jefferson Davis proposed, and on April 16 the Confederate Congress passed, the first national conscription act in American history. The proposal originally intended to make every white Southern male between the ages of eighteen and thirty-five, with relatively few exceptions, subject to military service. Subsequent legislation extended the draft age from seventeen and thirty-five, although the youngest and oldest were allowed to remain in their home states as a reserve force. Because politics riddled the draft with a large number of occupational exemptions, including the infamous "twenty nigger rule," conscription succeeded primarily by coercing increased volunteering.[19] Yet, by the end of the war, nearly one million Southerners would serve in the armed forces, a staggering figure that represented 80 percent of its total military pool. By comparison, the North would mobilize only 30 percent of its white males between the ages of eighteen and forty-five.[20]

It would be a mistake, of course, to assume that the odds between the adversaries remained static throughout the duration of the war. Both the total populations and the military pools of each side did remain relatively stable.[21] The number of troops mobilized, however, fluctuated for both the South and the North, and consequently their ratio to one another changed also. From April to July 1861, the Union and Confederate armies were roughly equal (1 to 1), each growing from about 15,000 to about 120,000.

From July to December both sides increased their forces significantly, with the South mobilizing a higher percentage of its manpower but fewer in absolute numbers, so that by January 1, 1862, the 351,000 Confederates were only 61 percent of the 576,000 Federals (1 to 1.6). For three months these odds remained substantially the same, as on April 1, the 401,000 Confederates represented 63 percent of the 637,000 Federals (1 to 1.6).

Then, with Confederate conscription and the Southern enlistment effort in the spring of 1862—which was not met by an equivalent Federal response—the odds changed dramatically. By June 30, the South's 477,000 men represented 76 percent of the North's 624,000 (1 to 1.3), easily the best odds the Confederates would face during the remainder of the war. The favorable balance would not last long, however. Lincoln's call for 300,000 troops in July and August of 1862, combined with heavy Confederate losses in the summer and fall, resulted by year's end in 447,000 Confederates representing only 49 percent of the 918,000 Federals in the field (1 to 2).[22] During the remaining twenty-eight months of the war the Confederacy would face odds ranging from a low of 1 to 1.8 to a high of 1 to 2.2 at the end.

Three points should be extracted and underscored from this mass of statistics. First, except for a brief few months at the start, the North always outnumbered the South in absolute number of men mobilized. Second, never from start to finish did the North's predominance in mobilization come anywhere near realizing its potential of 1 to 3.7 odds. Finally, discounting the opening months, the South enjoyed its most favorable odds in mobilization during the summer of 1862.

The mobilization of manpower is, of course, only the first step in waging war. Military forces are not useful until effectively deployed. The volunteers called into the field need to be applied in a manner appropriate to achieving the country's war aims. Armies must be concentrated in adequate numbers at the right time and place.

It is much more difficult to evaluate a policy of deployment than it is to measure mobilization. A host of subjective factors enter the debate. Nonetheless, it is clear that the Confederacy had to hurdle a series of considerable obstacles before it could concentrate its regiments into effective field armies. It is equally clear that problems of deployment prevented the South from gaining full advantage from its greater proportionate mobilization.

In the first place, predictably, tens of thousands of civilians could not be converted into reasonably trained and adequately equipped soldiers in a very brief period. Fortunately for the South, this lesson applied to both sides, and each had to learn it through experience. Northern impatience precipitated the clash of armed mobs at Bull Run on July 21, 1861, which resulted in the subsequent stampede of demoralized Federals to the safety of Washington. Felix Zollicoffer's ill-considered and disastrously premature attempt to stake out the Confederate claim to eastern Kentucky well illustrated the same point for the Confederates. Not surprisingly, Zollicoffer's outnumbered, green troops, some armed with flintlocks and some without arms, were routed at Mill Springs in January 1862. By itself, the need for training and equipping the volunteer masses meant the war could not be won or lost in 1861.

Training, which was minimal in the Civil War in any case, did not prove to be a long-term problem for the South. The bulk of the Confederate forces were in the field by the spring of 1862; and, as additional volunteers and conscripts became available, they were distributed to the veteran regiments. Greenness continued to plague the North throughout the war because of its piecemeal mobilization and its policy of forming new troops into new regiments. On the other hand, with its wealth to purchase abroad and its vastly superior industry, the North could equip its armies properly by the fall of 1861. The South, through the capture of Federal supplies and its own limited production, did not reach adequacy until mid-1862.

A second factor that inhibited Confederate deployment was unfriendly geography. Because of the overwhelming superiority of the Federal navy, the Confederacy faced the threat of invasion from all points of the compass. Not only could United States armies advance from the north and west with few natural barriers to impede them, but they could also land along the thousands of miles of coastline from the Potomac in the Chesapeake to the Rio Grande in the Gulf of Mexico. Worse yet, fleets of Federal gunboats could penetrate into the interior along a score of major rivers that obligingly flowed to the Atlantic in the east and down to the gulf in the west. If the Confederates had faced no other problems and had wished nothing more than to ward off enemy attacks, they would still not have known where best to concentrate their armies without leaving a myriad of equally strategic points vulnerable.

The North had a much easier task in this respect. Except for the brief concern in December 1861 that the *Trent* affair might lead to war with Great Britain and expose the Canadian border and the north Atlantic coast to attack, and the two day scare in March of 1862 that the CSS *Virginia* might sail up the Potomac, the Union had only to worry about its southern frontier. Hence, the North enjoyed far greater potential for the concentration of its armies.

Organization and administration posed a third obstacle to effective deployment. The Confederacy inherited from the United States a system of military organization by departments. Generals were given responsibility for a geographical region and authority over all of the troops therein. Departmental commanders were independent of one another and reported directly to either the president or the secretary of war, or, when one existed, to a general-in-chief. The system promoted rivalry and narrow vision and frequently stymied both cooperation and coordination.[23] In 1862 the Confederates began to think in terms of theaters of operation, rather than departments, and this gave them an edge—indeed, in the East a very decided advantage—in the concentration of troops during the middle period of the war. On the Federal side, only George B. McClellan among the early leaders seemed to understand the concept of theaters. After his demotion the Union effort again dissolved into a welter of departments, and not even a partial solution was found until the last year of the war.

Logistics was a fourth complication in deployment. An army had to be fed, and during battle its ammunition replenished. The larger an army, the greater the difficulty in supplying it. In logistics the North enjoyed a considerable advantage throughout the war. With superior expertise and resources Federals could build roads, bridges, and railroads wherever needed. The South had difficulty repairing old ones, let alone building new. Confederate commanders soon learned how difficult it was to operate at a distance from their railroads, and, because of their primitive supply lines, they were frequently more vulnerable to maneuver than their Federal counterparts. Sometimes between battles the Confederates had to disperse their armies in order to supply them. They compensated in part by learning to make do with less.[24]

Beyond these problems inherent in the waging of most wars—ones the North also faced to a greater or lesser extent—the South confronted two problems peculiar to its own situation that made it difficult to concentrate effectively those forces it had mobilized.

On the one hand, the Confederacy contained those very states of the old Union that were most committed to the concept of states' rights, most jealous of their state prerogatives, and most parochial in not looking beyond their own state borders. Inevitably, even in the flush of revolutionary rhetoric, such states were slow to share their meager resources and selfish in viewing threats to their territory as paramount. As both Lee and Davis would learn, the time required to educate and persuade local officials in order to pry regiments loose would significantly retard the Confederate effort to undertake offensive operations in the first year of the war.[25]

In addition, the institution of slavery, which had become entangled in nearly every aspect of Southern life, also complicated Confederate mobilization, concentration, and strategy. Slave owners instinctively understood the delicate nature of their institution. They knew an area occupied by Federal troops—even if the occupation were short and even if the area were later reclaimed by Confederates—would never be the same. Most of the slaves would have escaped to enemy lines, never to be regained. As a result, the appearance of Federal forces on its land and water borders threw a Southern state into a panic in which it clung desperately to its own men and equipment, while loudly calling for reenforcements from a national government with none to send.[26]

It is important to note that these problems existed independently of whatever grand strategy the Confederacy adopted, whether defensive or offensive. The same obstacles to concentration had to be surmounted whether the troops collected were used merely to defend against invasions or to undertake offensive operations. The only way for the Confederacy to circumvent the problems was to adopt a policy of dispersal, a variety of guerrilla warfare. And any attempt to wage a guerrilla war would have necessarily sacrificed slavery and the plantation system. Such a notion could only have been born of a desperation that was entirely lacking in the South during the first three years of the war, and that was out of the question for a people convinced not only of their political rectitude but also of their military prowess.[27]

More to the point, in spite of the obstacles, at almost every critical juncture in the first two-thirds of the war the Confederacy outperformed the Union in the concentration and deployment of forces. In virtually every major campaign through the end of 1863, from First Bull Run to Chickamauga, the South brought a higher percentage of its available forces to the battlefield than did the North. While it is true that whenever Federal generals operated in Confederate territory they necessarily had to detail troops to defend their communications; it is also true that significant strength was needlessly lost when the Federals bogged down in garrisons of occupation while there were Confederate armies yet to be defeated.[28]

June 25, 1862, the day before the start of the battles around Richmond, which both sides at the time believed would decide the fate of the war, stands as a concrete illustration of the superiority of early Confederate military policy. On that day one Southern general, Robert E. Lee, commanded all Confederate troops in the Eastern theater from North Carolina to the Potomac. In the same area seven Federal generals held independent and coequal command. In the whole theater the Federals outnumbered the Confederates two to one; but in the armies about to contend for the fate of their countries, there were more regiments in Lee's army than in that of his Federal opponent, George B. McClellan.

It seems likely that had either the Confederates' military policy been less focused or the Federals' more so the North would have won the war in fewer than four years. As it was, with their government's more intense mobilization and concentration, Confederate generals could devise and execute strategies in the belief that final victory might eventually be theirs; without it, it is doubtful any strategy could have forestalled earlier defeat.

Confederate Grand Strategy

As in the case of military policy, it would be easy to conclude that the Confederacy lacked a grand strategy for winning the war. No leader ever committed to paper a comprehensive plan for coordinating Confederate military operations, and the inconsistencies in the employment of troops during the war could be seen as proof that Southerners possessed no controlling vision for the use of the impressive manpower they called into the field. On the one hand, some of the time the Confederates seemed to engage in a "perimeter defense" and attempt to contest every inch of Southern soil; a strategy that critics claim led to a fatal dispersal of force. On the other hand, Confederate armies launched several ambitious invasions of the North; a strategy that critics charge was bound to fail and frivolously squander scarce resources. In between extremes, Confederate commanders on the field so frequently preferred to attack rather than stand on the defensive that one pair of critics has suggested the influence of Celtic chromosomes.[29]

In truth, the Confederacy did not possess a grand strategy in the modern sense of a highly detailed and unified program, nor even in the sense of the more primitive plans proposed by Winfield Scott and George McClellan for the North to restore the Union.[30] Nonetheless, the Confederacy did evolve a grand strategy for victory. It can be found scattered throughout the words and actions of two men, a general who would not take center stage until after a year of the war had passed and the president of the Confederate States.

Jefferson Davis was an exceptionally strong war president. It could be argued that he shouldered a combined burden equal to that carried by George Washington and Abraham Lincoln. Davis had both to create a nation and its government out of whole cloth and at the same time fight a titanic struggle to determine its fate. Periodically, historians join in a survey to rank the presidents of the United States from best to worst. Judged by many of the criteria applied in this poll, if Davis were included, he ought to be ranked among the great and very near the top of the list.[31]

During his four-year presidency, there was no doubt that Davis ran his administration, nor that he exerted considerable influence over the entire Confederate government. He was more active than most nineteenth-century presidents in submitting proposals for legislation, and, on the reverse side, he sent thirty-three veto messages to Congress.[32] He was master of his cabinet and, although he did not always make happy choices, he was not so slow as some presidents to replace ineffective secretaries. He also set the framework and the tone for Confederate grand strategy.

Davis seldom put on paper specifics of strategy. He understood the impossibility of detailed control over the war at a distance from Richmond. Whether his insight derived from experiences in the Mexican War, his term as secretary of war during the 1850s, or simply from common sense, cannot be known.[33] In any case, he recognized he would always be deficient in knowledge of geography and timely intelligence of troop dispositions. He acknowledged the need and with but few exceptions granted his commanders the "discretionary power which is essential to successful operations in the field."[34] He aimed to select generals with the ability to design their own strategy and the willingness to accept the responsibility. As president, he labored to provide the men and the means and to protect his commanders from the ill-informed and contradictory crosscurrents of public opinion. He attempted—and usually succeeded—in confining himself to proposing "general purposes and views" for the guidance of his commanders.[35]

Davis nonetheless did provide a firm strategic framework within which his generals in the field could work. Throughout most of the war, he expected them to undertake offensive campaigns whenever circumstances permitted. More than any other individual, Davis was responsible for the aggressive grand strategy of the Confederacy. Except for a brief hesitation in the winter of 1861–62, he operated on the belief that the South could only win the war by seizing and pressing the military initiative. He rejected the defensive because he understood the theoretical superiority of the offensive. "The advantage of selecting the time and place of attack was too apparent to have been overlooked," he proclaimed as early as March 1862.[36] He also recognized that if the enemy were allowed to penetrate too deeply into the interior the "resources of our country will rapidly decline to insufficiency for the support of an army."[37]

Davis believed the offensive grand strategy needed to be applied in three distinct but related ways. First, in order to maintain territorial integrity, Confederate armies must aggressively foil enemy invasions. They must seize "the opportunity to cut some of his lines of communication, to break up his plan of campaign; and defeating some of his columns, to drive him from the soil. . . ."[38] Second, offensive campaigns were required to claim the Confederacy irredenta. The president believed that Missouri and Kentucky belonged in the South and that Kentucky especially was essential to the viability of the new nation.[39] He would also, at least on one occasion, enthusiastically support military intervention in Maryland.

Finally, and perhaps most controversially, Davis supported the idea known popularly as "carrying the war into Africa." Harking back to the Punic Wars, this term expressed the Roman belief that Carthage could not be defeated in Italy but only on its home ground in northern Africa. It also reflected the military thinking of the nineteenth century that "carrying the war into the heart of the enemy's country is the surest plan of making him share its burdens and foiling his plans."[40] It represented as well the views of a vocal segment of the Confederate citizenry who, once Southern soil had been violated, demanded vengeance be visited on the North.[41]

Davis himself sought less to avenge the South than he did to weaken the North. From the start, he wanted the Northern people to feel the destructiveness of the war, and he sought to increase its cost to them and to sap their will. In June 1861, a month prior to the battle of First Bull Run, when Federals had gained no more than a toehold at Alexandria in northern Virginia, he lamented that lack of military preparedness compelled Southern troops to be "retiring from the Potomac," rather than "contending for the banks of the Susquehanna."[42] Even at the depths of the black Confederate winter of 1861-62, he would deny that he had ever lapsed into a "purely defensive" strategy.[43] Then, on the eve of the anniversary of First Bull Run, he would disparage any doubt "as to the advantage of invading over being invaded" by the enemy. "My early declared purpose and continued hope," he wrote to a critic, "was to feed upon the enemy and teach them the blessings of peace by making them feel in its most tangible form the evils of war." He insisted "the time and place for invasion has been a question not of will but of power."[44] And in September 1862, when the possibility arose that Confederate armies might march into Pennsylvania and Ohio, he prepared a proclamation to be issued to the Northerners that declared the "sacred right of self-defense demands that, if such a war is to continue, its consequences shall fall on those who persist in their refusal to make peace."[45]

After the war, Davis seemed to deny that the Confederacy had ever undertaken purely offensive military operations. As near as he would come to admitting this would be to confess that they had on occasion employed "offensive-defensive" operations, a phrase he borrowed, consciously or otherwise, from the Swiss military theorist Baron Henri Jomini.[46] With this apparent circumlocution, Davis was able to maintain his claim that the Confederacy was the injured party engaged in a defensive war, and, when it went on the attack, it was simply following accepted military theory that the best defense is sometimes a good offense.

In truth, Davis gave away more of his argument than he may have realized by paraphrasing Jomini. The acknowledged interpreter of Napoleon did indeed provide the theoretical foundation for the Confederate grand strategy, but not in a way that furthered Davis's political rationale. In his most famous work, *Summary of the Art of War,* Jomini divided all wars into two simple categories according to a single aspect of their war aims. If a nation sought to conquer all or part of another, its war was offensive. If not, it was defensive. According to this broad—and not very helpful—definition, the Confederacy clearly engaged in a defensive war.

Logically, Jomini labeled any strategy for invasion and conquest an offensive strategy. With less logic and with confusing consequences, he called any strategy that did not aim at invasion and conquest a defensive strategy. He then proceeded to subdivide defensive strategies into alternative and substantially different categories. He described the first option as the "passive defense," an updated version of the strategy of delay employed by Roman General Fabius Cunctator against the military genius of Hannibal of Carthage. In the passive defense a general attempted to frustrate his opponent with feints and minor engagements, bait him into exhausting pursuit far away from the enemy's base of supplies, all the while avoiding pitched battles. In principle Jomini opposed the passive defense because he believed that only initiative—when correctly applied—could win wars.[47] He advised against the use of this first strategy unless a nation were hopelessly outnumbered or outgeneralled.[48]

Jomini believed the best course open to a nation engaged in a war not aimed at conquest was the "active defense" or—as he unhappily insisted on calling it at times—the "defensive-offensive." Herein, the general, even though he operated within a defensive political framework, seized the initiative to defeat the enemy, either by maneuvers that forced the enemy army to retreat or by combat that destroyed it. Jomini believed the side that maintained and pressed the initiative would eventually win, while the side that merely reacted would inevitably lose.[49]

Whether consciously or coincidentally, Jefferson Davis's thinking ran parallel to Jomini's theories. In political terms, Davis needed to argue to the world that the Confederacy fought only in its own self-defense. But, in the military realm, he believed he must adopt the offensive, the only grand strategy that would lead to victory. Where Davis and the Confederates stretched Jomini's theory—if indeed they did not exceed it—was by including invasion as appropriate in their conduct of a defensive war.

Davis's term, the "offensive-defensive," may well be adopted to designate Confederate grand strategy, but it must be understood that offensive was much the greater element in the alloy. From the attack on Fort Sumter in April 1861 to the assault on Fort Stedman in March 1865, the Confederates consistently—albeit not invariably—used the offensive, on both the strategic and tactical level, to try to gain their war aims. It is especially appropriate to note, as a prelude to Lee's campaign in September 1862, that it was the Confederates who first set foot across the Potomac. In May 1861 they seized Maryland Heights opposite Harpers Ferry three weeks before the Federals occupied Alexandria and Arlington Heights.[50]

Although obscured by the telescoping effect of history, the first eighteen months of the war divided into three distinct and drastically different phases for the Confederacy. In the opening six months, from April to October 1861, the Confederates pursued a straightforward program for asserting control over the border states and territories. Southern armies achieved a string of stunning successes that carried their standards far toward their final intended boundaries.

A disastrous six-month period followed, from November through April 1862, in which the Confederates relied upon a largely defensive posture to hold onto their gains. In this second phase, the Confederacy suffered a staggering reversal of fate that plunged its citizens into despair and raised considerable doubts over its ultimate ability to win independence. By the anniversary of the fall of Sumter, the brief experiment with a strategy of defense had nearly lost the war for the South.

The third phase opened in April and May of 1862 and witnessed the Confederacy's most determined attempt to mobilize its manpower, concentrate its armies, and press forward with the offensive. Coincident with the start of this third phase there appeared at the right time and place the second central figure in Confederate grand strategy. Robert E. Lee assumed command of the army in Virginia, and during the summer that followed he put flesh onto Jefferson Davis's framework for the offensive. Lee's strategy to demoralize the North and, for the most part, his execution of that strategy gave the Confederacy the best chance it would ever have to win its independence.

The First Phase of the War, April–October 1861

Certainly the offense—in both desire and deed—interwove a dominant design throughout Confederate strategy during the first half-year of the war. Including the attack on Fort Sumter, Confederates mounted a dozen offensive operations of varying size and results in the following six months. They also won two important battles, Bull Run and Ball's Bluff, by counterattacking against Federal initiatives. During the same period, Southern generals proposed three additional major offensive campaigns, which were turned down for reasons having nothing to do with their being offensives. Indeed, the factors inhibiting the Confederacy from launching even more aggressive operations during the war's opening months derived from the chaotic military situation and not from political punctilio or philosophical caviling.

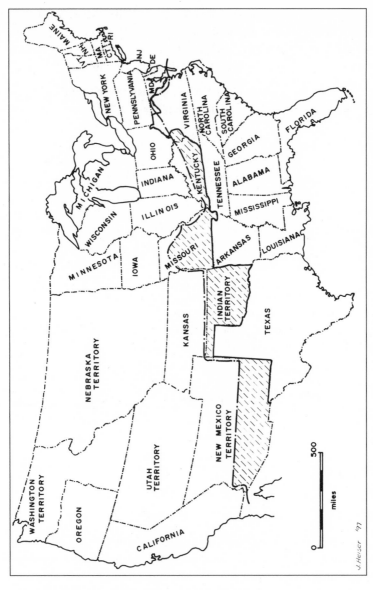

Phase one, April–October 1861. In this phase of the war, the Confederacy pursued mobilization, concentration, and offensive operations to obtain its greatest territorial domain. The shaded portions depict the areas gained by offensives.

In adopting the offensive-defensive the South faced a fundamental predicament. Undertaking aggressive operations imposed greater burdens of preparation than standing on the defense. The offense required both a larger force and one composed of better-trained and better-equipped troops. Hence, even without the complications of geography, states' rights, and slavery, the Confederacy would have been hobbled in launching an effective offensive-defensive strategy at the very start of the war. The South needed time to concentrate its forces, discipline and arm its volunteers, and exert the authority of the newly created government over the still emerging military establishment.

During this first phase, from April through October, Confederate forces operated with little coordination and with negligible guidance from the national government. Local commanders frequently acted on their own with barely a nod of approval from Richmond—a nod that sometimes came before and sometimes after the fact. In this initial period, the commitment to offensive war aims and the pursuit of the offensive-defensive strategy derived more from the Southern peoples' instinctively shared perception of the nature of the conflict than from direction from above. Indeed, this spontaneous popular aggressiveness strongly suggests Jefferson Davis was piloting a natural current when he followed the offensive-defensive.

If the early offensives were premature, their timing was nonetheless fortuitous. Had the Confederates waited for planning and preparation, they would have missed a window of opportunity. While the enemy, a lumbering Goliath, still rubbed sleep from its eyes, the South jumped to the attack. The North suffered from the first of several stages of delusion over the time and cost needed to restore the Union and tried to get by with a meager effort, minimal mobilization, and spasms of armed activity that passed for military campaigns. Never again would the South experience such favorable odds, nor such ineptness in its foe. The circumstances justified the Confederate gamble in taking precipitate offensive action.

In all three subtheaters of the west, Missouri, Kentucky, and the southwest, spontaneous and nearly autonomous efforts erupted to plant the Confederate flag at the farthest boundaries of its proclaimed manifest destiny. In Missouri, where the conflict was truly a civil war between neighbors, fighting broke out as early as May. By July the prosecessionist Missourians had collected their forces into an army, received supporting troops from Arkansas, Texas, Louisiana, and Tennessee, and prepared to take aggressive action. Ben McCulloch of the Confederate army and Sterling Price of the Missouri State Guard, after conferring to settle the command question, decided on their own authority to launch an offensive to retake the state of Missouri. On August 10 they defeated a Federal army under

Nathaniel Lyon at Wilson's Creek. By mid-September, Price had besieged and captured Lexington on the Missouri River and "liberated" nearly two-thirds of the state.[51]

Kentucky presented a unique and complicated case. Both Northern and Southern factions within the state supported an official policy of neutrality as a cover to gain time to strengthen their respective positions. For a while, the Federal and Confederate governments respected Kentucky's anomalous status and refrained from sending troops across its borders in the hope of winning its allegiance in the political realm. Not surprisingly, it was Confederates who broke the peculiar stalemate by taking the offensive. Using the Federal threat to occupy the mouths of the Tennessee and Cumberland rivers as pretext, Gen. Leonidas Polk crossed the border from Tennessee and occupied Columbus on September 4. Polk acted not only without prior authorization, he violated the expressed policy of both Jefferson Davis and Tennessee Governor Isham Harris.

Neither Davis nor Harris opposed entering Kentucky eventually, but they were waiting for political developments to mature. On September 5 Harris urged that Polk be withdrawn, and Davis at first agreed. But, within hours of directing the secretary of war to send a telegram recalling Polk, the president changed his mind. On a brief telegram from Polk explaining a few details of the military situation, Davis wrote the endorsement: "The necessity justifies the action." Although he would place the burden for further explanation on Polk by telegraphing that "The necessity must justify the action," Davis thereafter pursued a straightforward policy of supporting the occupation. He later wrote to Polk, "We cannot permit the indeterminate quantities, the political elements, to control our actions in cases of military necessity."[52] The incident well illustrated the president's policy and style. He both supported his commanders' offensive operations and deferred to their superior information.

Six days later Davis named Albert Sidney Johnston to an expanded Western Department that included not only Kentucky and Missouri but also Kansas and the Indian Territory. A week later Johnston advanced to establish a defensive line in southern Kentucky, which ran from Columbus on the Mississippi River through Bowling Green in the center to Cumberland Gap in the Allegheny Mountains. Hence, Confederate occupation of Kentucky not only came before that state had been admitted to the Confederacy but even two months before the rump convention at Russellville would declare for secession.[53]

Nor were the Confederates unmindful of their interests in the remote southwest. On July 8, 1861, the War Department authorized the invasion of the New Mexico Territory. On July 23 a small force under John Baylor entered the territory, captured a Federal garrison, and established a Confederate civil government for Arizona. Thereupon, Henry H. Sibley began to organize a brigade-sized force to occupy the entire territory and, according to some evidence, had as his ultimate—if unrealistic—goal the conquest of California.[54]

In the Eastern theater—where the scanter interest of Maryland and Delaware in secession circumscribed Confederate war aims and where the vast Federal forces gathered to defend Washington circumvented Confederate policy—Confederate strategy was, under the circumstances, more circumspect. When the first commander of Harpers Ferry, Col. Thomas Jonathan Jackson, ordered his Virginia troops across the Potomac to occupy the towering heights that dominated his position, he was quickly ordered to withdraw lest he offend Maryland.[55] As Union regiments continued to flow into the armies of Irvin McDowell at Washington and Robert Patterson at Chambersburg, the Confederates decided they could not hold the line of the Potomac, and they evacuated Alexandria on May 23 and Harpers Ferry on June 15. Confederate troops pulled back only about twenty miles, however. Joseph Johnston's army took up position in the Shenandoah Valley in front of Winchester behind Opequon Creek; and in the east Pierre Beauregard's forces occupied Manassas Junction behind the Bull Run River.[56]

Beauregard soon became dissatisfied with the Confederate defensive posture in Virginia. He opposed standing on the defensive and permitting the North the advantage of choosing the time and location of military action. During June and July he twice earnestly pressed on Davis plans to force the issue by assuming the offensive. On June 12 he proposed that Johnston be transferred from the valley to unite the two armies for a march on Arlington. Davis accepted the idea of the advance without the slightest demur, but he rejected abandoning the valley as unnecessary. He counseled Beauregard to await the reenforcements that would allow the offensive to be undertaken without Johnston's transfer.[57]

By mid-July the Federal forces around Washington had increased in greater proportion than the Confederates around Manassas, and intelligence indicated that McDowell was preparing to advance into northern Virginia. Beauregard, on July 14, sent a military aide to Richmond with a new, even more ambitious, strategy for the government to consider. After a hurried trip by rail, Col. James Chesnut met that same evening with Davis, Adj. Gen. Samuel Cooper, and Virginia military advisor Robert E. Lee to present Beauregard's plan. Once again Johnston was to come to Manassas, but this time he was to leave five thousand men to hold the valley temporarily. Johnston's twenty thousand men and Beauregard's twenty thousand were to fall upon and destroy the separate columns of McDowell as he advanced from Washington. Johnston was then to return rapidly with his own and half of Beauregard's army to defeat Patterson on the upper Potomac.

It was at this point that Beauregard's plan lost firm touch with reality, and Chesnut's recounting of its concluding details may have caused his audience's eyes to widen in wonderment. While Beauregard's men returned to Manassas, Johnston was to proceed to the far reaches of mountainous western Virginia and join with the small army of Robert Garnett to defeat the invading force from Ohio under George McClellan. Thereafter, Johnston and Garnett would return east to cross into Maryland and threaten Washington from the rear, while Beauregard attacked from the front.

As Chesnut later recollected the meeting, the brunt of the reply fell to Lee, with Davis assenting to the points as the general put them forward. This in itself is revealing, suggesting that Davis and Lee had not only previously held extensive strategy discussions but that they had already found themselves in substantial agreement. Lee said the plan "might be brilliant in its results, if we should meet with no disaster in details"—a tactful way of saying the scheme was far too complicated. As for the heart of the plan—the combination of Johnston with Beauregard to defeat McDowell—Lee said "that the time for its execution had not yet arrived." McDowell must first be drawn sufficiently far from Washington to be vulnerable before the combination took place. Otherwise the Federals would simply fall back to their entrenchments and defeat the Confederate strategy. It is worth noting that, so far as is known, no one raised any objection either to attacking Washington or to entering Maryland.[58]

Ironically, on the very day of the meeting in Richmond, McDowell's army set out from Washington on its own offensive, and on July 18 occupied Centreville four miles from the Bull Run River. With timely warning from Southern spies in Washington, Beauregard alerted the Confederate capital. Davis now set in motion the strategy exactly as Lee had sketched it and ordered Johnston from the Valley to Manassas Junction. While McDowell reconnoitered the Confederate position, Beauregard planned a flanking movement to the east. But McDowell moved first and on the 21st successfully turned the Confederate left flank. Late in the day, the opportune arrival of one of Johnston's brigades tipped the scales, and the Federal army broke in rout for the safety of Washington.

The chaotic condition of the Confederate army, which was nearly as disorganized by victory as the Federals were by defeat, prevented effective pursuit, nor was there any serious discussion of it at the time. Later, looking back with regret, some Confederates would believe they had missed their best chance of the war to mount an offensive across the Potomac.[59] At the time, when weeks of summer turned into months of autumn, impatience grew with the inactivity of the army. It was common knowledge that the North had been compelled to start virtually from scratch in replacing its ninety-day militia with green volunteers and was engrossed in training and refitting its armies.

The feeling became widespread that an irretrievable opportunity was slipping away. Davis felt it, when he wrote to Johnston on August 1, "We must be prompt to avail ourselves of the weakness resulting from the exchange of new and less reliable forces of the enemy . . . , as well as the moral effect produced by the late defeat."[60] Robert Toombs, who had resigned as secretary of state to command a Georgia brigade at Manassas, felt it with some exaggeration, when he assured the president that were the Confederates "to enter Maryland between Leesburg and Martinsburg" and "cut off the enemies communication with the north, Washington would necessarily fall without a blow."[61] Even a military professional such as Thomas Jonathan Jackson (who had acquired both a major-generalcy and the nickname "Stonewall" after Bull Run), before leaving to command in the Shenandoah Valley, is alleged to have argued for "an active campaign of invasion" that makes "unrelenting war amidst their homes" and forces "the people of the North to understand what it will cost to hold the South in the Union at the bayonet's point."[62]

Nor was the general who would lead the invasion immune from this feeling. In the weeks following Bull Run, Joseph Johnston, who had been given command of all the Confederate forces in northern Virginia, advanced his main body to Centreville, established a strong forward post at Fairfax Court House, and extended his pickets to Munson's Hill, within four miles of the Potomac, where it was said his flag was visible from the White House. His line ran in a fifty-mile arc from Leesburg in the west to Dumfries in the east, with both flanks resting on the Potomac.

Johnston "had assumed this advanced position" in late August, as soon as railroad repairs had made it logistically feasible, for two reasons: first, to remove his men from the "unhealthy atmosphere" of Bull Run Valley; and second, "to be ready to turn the enemy's position and advance into Maryland whenever the strength of this army would justify it." But the passage of time brought Johnston no appreciable increase in strength, while the enemy, under its new commander, George B. McClellan, daily grew more numerous. With a line so long, so thinly held, and so near the enemy, Johnston correctly believed his army was unwarrantably vulnerable. On September 26 he wrote to the new secretary of war, Judah Benjamin, summarizing his plight and suggesting that Davis, or someone who could speak for the president, visit northern Virginia for a conference.[63]

Benjamin replied on the 29th that Davis would visit the army and confer on "the possibility of a prompt offensive movement."[64] The prospect must have excited Davis, for he left Richmond by train at six in the morning of

September 30 and arrived at Fairfax Station late in the afternoon. He traveled by carriage four miles to Beauregard's quarters in a brick house on the outskirts of Fairfax Court House. At eight o'clock the following evening, he held a lengthy conference with Johnston and his two ranking subordinates, Beauregard and Gustavus W. Smith.[65]

After an hour spent discussing details of army organization, Smith opened the subject of launching an offensive. The generals emphasized the vulnerability of their defensive line and noted indications that McClellan was assembling a massive army that might prove invincible once it was ready to take the field. They agreed the best Confederate strategy would be to cross the Potomac in a turning movement to force the Federals out of their fortifications and strike them before they were prepared.

Davis listened with interest and apparently with approval. He had, in fact, been predisposed in favor of a movement into Maryland and had brought maps of the crossings at the Potomac Falls with him from Richmond. Such a readiness was not surprising from one who had three months earlier fretted that the war could not be carried to the banks of the Susquehanna.[66] Unfortunately, the generals insisted they would require a large addition of *seasoned* troops before they could undertake the campaign. Johnston and his subordinates, aware of the need for disciplined forces for an offensive, demanded that the new men must be as well trained as the ones already at Manassas. Davis answered that they were asking an impossibility, because the only reenforcements available were those just being organized across the South. Nothing in the accounts of the meeting suggests that Davis would not have approved the offensive, if the generals had been willing to undertake it with the troops available. He even proposed as an alternative that they mount raids across the Potomac to break up enemy batteries posted there, although Johnston dismissed this option as a risk greater than its potential worth.[67]

After this war council dashed his hopes for an offensive, Johnston adopted a defensive posture. He pulled his advanced pickets back almost fifteen miles to Fairfax Court House.[68] He also devised a contingency plan for meeting a Federal advance from any direction, one that would give him the option of the tactical offense. He improved existing roads and built new ones behind his lines to facilitate the rapid concentration of troops, and he withdrew his artillery from his Centreville fortifications, concentrating them in a central location behind the Bull Run. He replaced them with "Quaker Guns," the wooden logs painted black, which would cause such a stir in the Northern press when discovered.[69]

The only bad news for Confederate strategy during the first six months came from the far reaches of the Eastern theater, the mountainous counties of western Virginia. Not only did the rugged terrain here render the movement of troops and supplies difficult, but the majority of the citizens held pro-Union sentiments. Although the Confederates mounted several small offensives and sent one of their highest ranking generals, Robert E. Lee, to command operations, by the late autumn they had been compelled to abandoned two-thirds of the region and held only the southwestern counties below Charleston.[70]

All in all, therefore, October 1861 represented an early high-water mark in Confederates' progress toward achieving their war aims. In the West their expanded boundaries ran through New Mexico, Missouri, and Kentucky, and in the east, save for the mountains, their line was only twenty miles south of their frontier. Their vigorous mobilization and concentration of troops at the war's start had allowed them to win victories by either outnumbering or roughly equalling their foes on the battlefield, in spite of the imbalance of odds portended by the census returns. And, their success had come through a willingness to pursue the offensive-defensive.[71] President Davis could boast to his new Congress that instead of the enemy's "threatened march of unchecked conquest, they have been driven at more than one point to assume the defensive," and "the Confederate States are relatively much stronger now than when the struggle commenced."[72]

Yet, in retrospect, it can be seen that the Fairfax War Council was the high point of the first phase. If the strategy under discussion had been adopted, Confederate forces would have crossed beyond the national boundaries of the Confederacy in a preemptive strike. Nothing in surviving documents indicates that giving aid to Marylanders was a consideration, nor that impressing foreign powers entered the discussion. The question was broached, discussed, and decided in purely military terms.

If consideration of an invasion of the North marked the high point of the first phase of the war, the decision against invasion revealed the limitations in the first phase and that the thinking that led to a new phase had already started. Most of the blame for the shift must probably fall on Davis's shoulders. It was not unrealistic for the generals who would command the operation to ask for an army of fifty to sixty thousand seasoned troops. The only reasonable explanation of Davis's refusal to concentrate even thirty thousand troops from the Peninsula, North Carolina, Pensacola, and elsewhere for a campaign—one that might decide the fate of Confederate independence—is that he had begun to slip into a defensive or perimeter mode of thinking.

Although the Confederates had not gained all of the territory they believed belonged to them, by October 1 they had achieved such success in Arizona, Missouri, and Kentucky that Davis was perhaps unwilling to imperil their gains by withdrawing and concentrating forces in one theater at the expense of others. The president had come to Fairfax excited at the prospect of the forces in northern Virginia undertaking an offensive. When he discovered that those present for duty totaled scarcely more than half the aggregate force sent from Richmond—one in a long line of instances when politicians and generals on both sides would be appalled by the staggering absenteeism in Civil War armies—his enthusiasm cooled. In a little more than three months, when the bitter fruits of a defensive posture had begun to ripen and bad news was pouring in on all fronts, Davis would remember only that his fall-back plans for a raid against the Potomac batteries had been rejected by his generals. In his mind the inactivity had therefore become the generals' responsibility. But, of course, no raid, no matter how successful, would likely have tipped the scales in the first phase.

It is possible that the best chance the Confederates would ever have to establish their independence came and went in the fall of 1861. It is possible that a really smashing victory in Maryland or Pennsylvania, on the heels of Bull Run, Wilson's Creek, and Ball's Bluff, coming while Federal armies were yet unformed in the west and when McClellan had only just begun to organize the Army of the Potomac, might have convinced Northerners to let go the tiger they had by the tail. On the other hand, it is reasonable to ask what Joe Johnston, Pierre Beauregard, and G. W. Smith—considering the military record they would compile in the war—would have accomplished with a moderately sized army in offensive operations beyond the borders of the Confederacy. The odds against cautious generals leading barely seasoned troops and supported by an immature logistical system achieving a decisive victory are long indeed.

In Davis's defense, although it is unclear he raised these points during the Fairfax council, it should be noted that as president he was compelled to grapple with other serious problems at this time. The Confederacy was on the verge of confronting a number of hard questions raised by a war stretching longer than anticipated and a foe reacting with more determination than expected. Not only was more money required and too few arms available, but the term of the twelve-month volunteers was half over and recruitment had slowed to a trickle. The Confederacy had invested heavily in men, generals, and materiel in the army in northern Virginia. Elsewhere there were fewer men, weaker leadership, and less equipment. Albert Sidney Johnston, although appointed, had not yet left Richmond to take command in the West.

"The cause of the Confederacy is staked upon your army," Davis had written to Joseph Johnston three weeks before the conference. At that time Davis acknowledged that "time brings many advantages to the enemy" and wished it were possible to "strike him in his present condition." Nonetheless, until the Confederacy had another army or a second line of defense,

Davis believed it unwise to hazard its only effective force in an offensive without a "reasonable assurance of victory," or an unavoidable necessity. "It is true that a successful advance across the Potomac would relieve other places," Davis had continued, "but, if not successful, ruin would befall us."[73]

It is likely that this was still the president's thinking when he met with his generals at Fairfax. It was not an unreasonable position; indeed, it resembled the North's determination after Bull Run to perfect the organization and discipline of its army before undertaking another offensive. Davis failed, however, to give due regard to his own insight that time brought far greater advantages to the enemy. Thus, in part, because it paused to gather its strength, the Confederacy would slip from its pinnacle of early success.

The Second Phase of the War, November 1861–April/May 1862

While many Confederates celebrated the approaching end of the short war that political rhetoric had promised and early success now seemed to confirm, many of their leaders, including Davis, Lee, and both Johnstons, recognized final victory lay at the end of a long and perilous road they had only just begun to travel. In truth, November 1861 witnessed the close of the war's first phase and the opening of a new and drastically different period in the history of the struggle. Even as the Confederates shed their provisional government and elected Davis to a full six-year term on November 6, a Federal fleet and army appeared off the coast of South Carolina to augur that the permanence of the Confederacy was far from a settled fact. Indeed, the second phase of the war, the six months that ran to May 1862, would bring a chain of defeats, retreats, and setbacks to manacle Confederate optimism and scar Confederate hopes ever after.

Reversal of Southern fortune came not from coincidence. In part, it came from the failure to continue the very policies that had yielded the early successes. In the second phase the South lost the roughly balanced odds it had enjoyed in troops in the field. To a degree this was the South's own fault. As volunteering fell off and as troops whose terms ended refused to reenlist, the Confederate ratio of men mobilized as compared to its enemy's fell to three to five. But also, the government slackened its commitment to concentrating forces in field armies in the three main theaters. In July of 1861, the active armies in Virginia, Tennessee, and Missouri comprised almost 80 percent of Confederate troops, but this relatively high concentration slipped to 63 percent by January 1862, as units were scattered to protect distant points.[74] Finally and not least in importance, the Confederacy pursued a less aggressive strategy, mounting only three offensive campaigns during the period—all of which ended in disaster.[75]

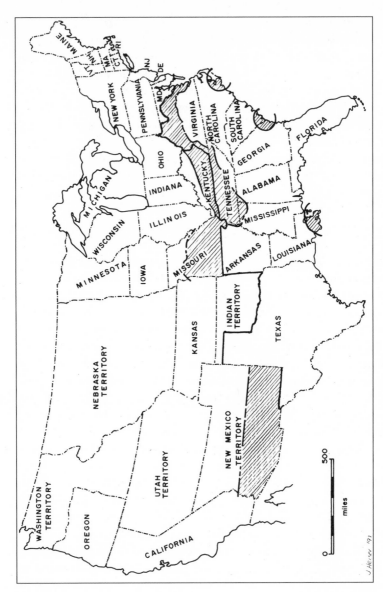

Phase two, November 1861–April/May 1862. In this phase of the war, the Confederacy pursued a "perimeter" defensive policy and, as indicated by the shaded areas, lost considerable territory.

In equal or greater part, however, Federal success caused Confederate failure. November 1 coincided with the start of a major Union effort to concentrate its forces and to implement a coordinated strategy for overwhelming the Confederacy by bringing pressure to bear simultaneously on several fronts. Massive Federal offensives were undertaken in both the West and the East, while three combined army-navy amphibious expeditions established enclaves at widely scattered points on the south Atlantic and Gulf coasts.

In Kentucky in the Western theater, Albert Sidney Johnston had been assigned the impossible task of holding a protracted frontier with an inadequate force among a population of mixed sympathies. When Felix Zollicoffer on the right flank attempted to advance in the eastern part of the state, he was routed at Mill Springs on January 19. While Johnston thereafter remained on the defensive, he could only hold his long, exposed line at the sufferance of the Federals. In mid-January, he sent an aide to Richmond to plead with the president for reenforcements. Johnston proposed that Confederate strength be concentrated into two main armies, one in Virginia and one in Kentucky. Both would then be large enough, he argued, to undertake effective offensives. Davis apparently agreed with the strategy in principle, but the president stated flatly and somewhat enigmatically that no troops could be spared because the timing was wrong for the concentration.[76]

Actually, even had Sidney Johnston been reenforced by troops idling elsewhere in the West—perhaps all or part of the 18,000 men in Alabama and west Florida, stationed mainly at Pensacola—it is doubtful much good would have come of it. He already commanded 101,000 men, aggregate present and absent, in Kentucky and Tennessee, about 30 percent of the entire Confederate army, but he had to spread them so thinly that his main force at Bowling Green totaled less than 50,000. Johnston at this point suffered more from his own "perimeter" mentality than from a dispersal policy of the government. His house of cards needed only the slightest push to collapse.[77]

In early February, a Federal army under U. S. Grant trailed gunboats under Andrew Foote up the Tennessee River and confronted little opposition in capturing Fort Henry. Grant then lay siege to nearby Fort Donelson on the Cumberland River, which capitulated on the 16th. With the surrender of the 15,000-man garrison, a large portion of Johnston's left wing evaporated, and the Confederates necessarily abandoned their center at Bowling Green. In fact, Johnston lost not only Kentucky but decided he could not hold middle Tennessee and evacuated Nashville on February 23. In searching for a secure location to reorganize his shattered army and acting at last on his own recommendation to concentrate, Johnston did not stop until he reached Corinth in northern Mississippi.[78]

The South fared no better in its bid to retain Missouri. In spite of amateurish leadership, the Confederates held on to the southwestern corner of the state until February 1862, when they were compelled to withdraw to Arkansas. Earl Van Dorn, commander of the Trans-Mississippi Department, ignoring orders to join Johnston's concentration at Corinth, instead united the Missouri State Guard with his forces from Texas, Arkansas, Louisiana, and the Indian Territory to launch an offensive to retake Missouri. But his army was stopped short of that state's borders at the Battle of Pea Ridge by a Federal force half its size commanded by Samuel Curtis on March 7 and 8. Within a month another Federal army under John Pope completed the conquest of Missouri with the capture of New Madrid and Island No. Ten. For the next two years, most of the troops of Van Dorn and Sterling Price were employed east of the Mississippi, and the Confederates were unable to mount an offensive to retake Missouri until 1864.[79]

Nor would the winter and spring bring good news to the Confederacy from the far west. In January, Henry Sibley's invasion of New Mexico met with some initial success. After defeating Edward Canby in a modest victory on February 21 at Valverde outside of Fort Craig on the Rio Grande, Sibley marched overland and occupied Santa Fe, the territorial capital, on March 4. But his undermanned, poorly equipped, and weakly led expedition made progress only because of confused and timid opponents. Colorado volunteers and U.S. regulars defeated the Confederates at Glorieta Pass, well short of the Colorado River, on March 28, and Sibley fled for the safety of Texas. By May 4, 1862, the southwest was safe from all but Indians.[80]

At the very outset of the second phase the South was made to feel the disadvantage of having a long coastline in a war against an enemy who possessed overwhelming naval superiority. The interest in amphibious coastal operations originated in the need of the Federal fleet for refueling and supply stations for ships engaged in its 3,500-mile blockade. George McClellan expanded the concept into coastal enclaves and incorporated it into his grand strategy for overwhelming the South. With minimal cost in Federal manpower, these expeditions swooped down on unsuspecting Southern coasts, frustrating Confederate leaders, terrorizing civilians, and pinning down Confederate troops whose absence from their main armies could be ill afforded.

In the first week of November, the rich Port Royal area of South Carolina fell to the combined forces of army Gen. Thomas Sherman and naval Capt. Samuel DuPont. Sherman then established an enclave that threatened Charleston and on April 11 captured Fort Pulaski on Tybee Island, closing the port of Savannah to blockade running. In late January an army-navy expedition under Ambrose Burnside moved down the North Carolina coast and on February 8 captured Roanoke Island with its brigade of defenders. Burnside moved to the mainland, seizing New Berne on March 9, and took up position to break Richmond's rail communications with the south and also to move on the Confederate capital itself from below Petersburg. Federal movement against the Gulf Coast commenced with the capture of Ship Island, Mississippi, on December 3, which served as a stepping-stone for the movement on New Orleans. A Federal fleet under David Farragut, followed by an army under Benjamin Butler, captured the Confederacy's largest city and the third busiest port in the prewar country on April 25.[81]

The Eastern theater, in spite of Joseph Johnston's fears, remained relatively quiet after the Confederate war council met at Fairfax Court House on October 1. The Federals, busy constructing an offensive machine to coerce the South back into the Union and fearful of premature engagements that might result in another fiasco such as Bull Run, had carefully avoided aggressive actions before their preparations were complete. Their new commander, George McClellan, had successfully pursued this policy save for one major lapse. An ambitious subordinate, Col. Edward Baker, crossed the Potomac with a brigade on October 21 at Ball's Bluff opposite Leesburg. Baker's expedition was inadequate in numbers, leadership, and conveyances for retreat, a catastrophic triple fault. Nathan Evans's Confederate forces surrounded the Union troops on three sides and drove them over the steep Potomac cliffs. The Federals lost 900 of their 1,700 men on the bluffs or trying to swim the river.[82]

As the winter passed, Confederate spies informed Johnston the enemy was collecting a large fleet of transports in the Washington area, and the Confederate commander became convinced that McClellan would not attack the entrenched position at Manassas but was planning a large-scale amphibious turning movement. On March 7, in order to give himself more time and space to react, Johnston fell back to a new line behind the Rappahannock River. In what was not unlike a giant military chess match, McClellan responded by expanding his turning movement and carrying his Army of the Potomac to Fort Monroe at the tip of the Yorktown peninsula between the York and James rivers. This move forced Johnston to abandon all of northern Virginia and carried the scene of fighting away from Washington and eventually to the vicinity of the Confederate capital.

In early April Johnston hurried to Yorktown to reenforce John Magruder's Army of the Peninsula and to try to stop McClellan's advance toward Richmond. On April 13 Johnston arrived ahead of his troops and conducted a thorough survey of the Confederate entrenchments erected in front of Yorktown and along the Warwick River. Johnston immediately concluded that the Yorktown line could not be held, because the engineers had constructed faulty fortifications and because both of its flanks were vulnerable to turning by the Federal navy on either the York or James River. Convinced it would be a mistake to commit his army from northern Virginia to the Peninsula, Johnston hastened back to Richmond the same evening.

Very early on the morning of the 14th, he visited Jefferson Davis in the executive office on the third floor of the Treasury Building. Johnston told the president that not only could Yorktown not be held, but Richmond could not be successfully defended against siege operations. He urged that the Confederates effect a massive concentration of forces by stripping troops from elsewhere, draw McClellan toward Richmond and away from the Federal supply base at Fort Monroe, and then attack and destroy the Federal army. Davis listened "with apparent interest" and suggested a brief recess so that new secretary of war, George W. Randolph (the third to hold the office), and Robert E. Lee, who was now general-in-chief of Confederate forces, might attend. Davis wanted to hear the case argued before he made a decision. Johnston requested that Generals James Longstreet and Gustavus Smith be permitted to join the group.

The six men met—in what was perhaps the most impressive war council ever held in the Confederacy—at Davis's office at 10:00 A.M.[83] In the meanwhile, Smith had drawn up a strategy memorandum, which Johnston presented as embodying both of their ideas. After arguing the necessity for abandoning the Peninsula and for the maximum concentration of strength, Smith's paper presented an alternative to fighting McClellan in front of Richmond. Apparently both Johnston and Smith preferred to leave an adequate force to garrison Richmond and drive with the remainder of the army "rapidly across the border, and make an active campaign beyond the Potomac, striking Baltimore and Washington, if not Philadelphia and New York, before McClellan could take the works around the Confederate capital."[84]

An extraordinarily long discussion ensued, which at times grew "very heated." The men talked until six o'clock, when they took an hour's dinner break, and then reconvened at the executive mansion, where the conference dragged on until one in the morning. During the fourteen hours, Longstreet said next to nothing, although he would later claim he intended to support the offensive into Maryland, until Davis misinterpreted his prefatory remarks as underestimating McClellan. The president himself, until near the end, played his favorite role of listening and asking occasional questions.[85] The council grew into a debate between four men, with Johnston and Smith arguing against a Confederate concentration on the Peninsula, and Lee and Randolph arguing in favor of it. Randolph, who had held office for only a month, had served in the old U.S. Navy and then as chief artillerist under Magruder on the Peninsula, devoted most of his remarks to the points that the Confederacy could not afford to abandon the naval yards at Norfolk and that the fortifications at Yorktown were not so weak as portrayed by Johnston.

Once again, as it had the previous July at the conference over Beauregard's plan, the burden of playing devil's advocate fell to Lee. Curiously, in view of the reputation he would earn for aloofness, on this occasion he was voluble and contentious. Lee raised three major objections against the plan of Johnston and Smith. In the first place, he was not yet convinced of the impossibility of stopping McClellan on the Peninsula, arguing that the restricted space between the two rivers made it a particularly conducive field for a delaying type of defensive operations.[86] Second, Lee relied upon the ironclad CSS *Virginia* at Norfolk to protect Johnston's right wing on the James, and the Confederate artillery at Yorktown and opposite at Gloucester Point, where the York River narrowed, to protect his left. Finally, Lee argued that, if troops were to be stripped from South Carolina and Georgia as Johnston requested, Charleston and Savannah would almost certainly fall to the enemy.[87]

Although none of the firsthand accounts attest to it, at some point someone must have raised a question about the assumptions undergirding the strategy of Johnston and Smith. At this stage of the war, there was as yet no persuasive reason to believe that a Confederate offensive against Washington would cause McClellan to retrace his steps or would even induce the Federal general to detach a significant force for the protection of the Northern capital. After all, the Confederates would have farther to travel, and they might find Richmond captured before they had even started siege operations against Washington. It is doubtful either Davis or Lee was prepared to exchange capitals, or to "swap queens" as Lincoln would later put it.[88] Finally, around midnight, Davis accepted the arguments of Lee and Randolph and rejected all parts of the proposal. He ordered Johnston to march the divisions of Longstreet and Smith to the support of Magruder and to hold the line at Yorktown.

Hence, for the second time Johnston was denied permission to undertake an offensive and compelled to defend a position he believed indefensible. Davis did enlarge Johnston's command to include Magruder's army on the Peninsula and Benjamin Huger's division at Norfolk.[89] Also, Lee did start the concentration of troops by ordering J. R. Anderson's brigade from North Carolina and Maxcey Gregg's from South Carolina to Richmond. These reenforcements from the Carolinas were not given directly to

Johnston, however, but sent to the Rappahannock to watch Irvin McDowell's force at Fredericksburg, although Lee assured Johnston they were still under his nominal authority.[90] In April, therefore, Johnston's strength did not increase beyond the troops he could have anticipated all along would be his. When he discovered that McClellan had over a hundred heavy siege guns in place to demolish the Confederate batteries on the York River, he felt he had no choice but to withdraw. Not only would his line be breached at Yorktown, but the river would be free for Federal troops to turn his flank. On April 29 Johnston informed Lee that he intended to abandon Yorktown before McClellan's batteries were ready to open and that he would order the evacuation of Norfolk at the same time.[91]

The following day, April 30, Johnston sent his longtime friend Lee a remarkable dispatch that pleaded and lectured in equal parts. He opened with a stark admonition, "We are engaged in a species of warfare at which we can never win." It was "plain" McClellan would "depend for success on artillery and engineering," he went on. "We can compete with him in neither. . . . We can have no success while McClellan is allowed, as he is by our defensive, to choose his mode of warfare." Bluntly Johnston told Lee, "We must therefore change our course, collect all the troops we have in the East and cross the Potomac with them, while Beauregard, with all we have in the West, invades Ohio." Concluding with a plea more emotional and political than military, he observed, "Our troops have always wished for the offensive, and so does the country."[92]

Johnston's dispatch must have received Richmond's immediate attention, for Lee replied on the following day, May 1. Writing for the president, Lee regretted that the idea of the Western army invading Ohio, "however desirable," is "at this time impracticable." On the other hand, the "feasibility" of "advancing a column to the Potomac with all the troops that can be made available" had been under consideration for some time. According to Lee, Davis concurred in Johnston's views of "the benefits to be obtained by taking the offensive," and he was "very desirous of being able to carry it into effect."[93] The government's philosophical approval of a bold northward offensive meant little in the short term. Such a move was predicated on the concentration of Confederate troops in the East, and Lee had already made clear on April 23 that, "it would require some time to assemble a sufficient force."[94] In the meanwhile, Johnston would have to make the most with what he already had in the Richmond area. Both Lee and Davis did, however, redouble their efforts to collect troops from North and South Carolina, Georgia, and Florida, although none would arrive in time to help on the Peninsula.[95]

On the night of May 3 the Confederate army slipped away from its Yorktown entrenchments with campfires burning. On May 5 Johnston fought a successful delaying battle at Williamsburg, and on the 7th stopped a Federal amphibious division at Eltham's Landing at the head of the York River. Johnston then took up position about twenty miles from Richmond, with his right on the Chickahominy and his left stretching northward toward the Pamunkey. On May 14 he learned that the evacuation of Norfolk and the destruction of the CSS *Virginia* had given the Federal navy control of the James far enough inland to attack Drewry's Bluff, less than six miles from Richmond. Once again, Johnston's flank had been turned by water, so he crossed to the right bank of the Chickahominy and fell back to the suburbs of the capital, entering its minimal defensive works on May 17.[96]

Thus, at the close of the war's second phase and after a year of fighting, the Confederacy now faced critical prospects on every front. Kentucky was lost to the enemy, and Tennessee was nearly gone. One Northern army had pierced the state of Mississippi, and another held New Orleans. Virginia west of the Alleghenies was a lost province, having in March officially announced its intent to secede from the Old Dominion and seek statehood. While Burnside nibbled up pieces of the North Carolina coast, David Hunter's forces in South Carolina threatened Charleston. But the direst threat came from McClellan's army, by far the largest and best organized the North had in the field, as it advanced slowly—but inexorably, it seemed— toward the Confederate capital. A quiet desperation settled over the city, and in the dark of night, to avoid igniting panic, the Confederate government loaded its archives onto railroad cars to be ready for instant flight.[97] By mid-June McClellan's soldiers would be able to see the spires of Richmond's churches.

The Confederacy had began to suffer the consequences of abandoning the initiative to the enemy. As Jomini had warned: "He who awaits the attack is everywhere anticipated."[98] Northern columns had snatched up isolated Confederate garrisons, captured weakly defended Southern cities, and driven major Confederate armies deeper and deeper into the heartland. Unfortunately, it was a fact of political geography for the South that it could not afford to abandon its frontiers to the enemy, for it was in Virginia and Tennessee that the major human, industrial, and financial resources lay. By late May 1862 the South had nearly lost the war.[99]

Publicly, Jefferson Davis admitted that "the tide is for the moment against us." And he granted that "events have demonstrated that the Government had attempted more than it had power successfully to achieve." Privately, he was blunter, conceding that "Recent disasters have depressed the weak and are depriving us of the aid of the wavering." More to the point, he confessed, "I acknowledge the error of my attempt to defend all of the frontier, seaboard and inland."[100]

The Start of Phase Three, April–May 1862

Instead of hunkering down behind its fortifications to lick its wounds, the Confederacy gathered its strength and redoubled it efforts. While the second phase was running its dismal course, a new period in the war was beginning. Even as Federal armies advanced across Tennessee and Virginia, the third stage—the stage on which the brightest passages of Confederate arms would be acted out—was rehearsing behind the scenes. Yet the third phase opened so darkly illumined that it has been difficult for later generations to distinguish its overlapping beginning from the string of reverses that had plagued the Confederacy since November.

By March Jefferson Davis had determined that the government must undertake extraordinary measures or lose the war, and he acted accordingly. First, he moved to mobilize more men in an attempt to bring the odds against Confederate forces in the field to nearer balance. Since both the efforts to increase the flow of volunteers and to induce men whose one-year terms were expiring to reenlist had fallen short of expectations, he resorted to drastic actions. On March 28 he submitted a conscription bill to Congress, and by April 17, although weakened by political loopholes, it became law with considerable bipartisan support.[101] Second, the administration made renewed attempts—gradually at first but with increasing vigor—to concentrate the regiments scattered around the country into field armies of respectable and effective size. With Federal forces now either on the soil or threatening the coast of every state in the Confederacy, this effort to centralize met with even more resistance than before. Third, the Confederacy recommitted itself to an aggressive stragegy with such troops as it could concentrate, although this time the offensives were undertaken to drive enemy armies from the heartland, rather than to stake out claims to new territory.

None of the new policies yielded quick success. All three met with initial failure. If more time had been allowed for the new mobilization and concentration policies to take effect, the early offensives in the new phase might have had a better chance to succeed. But Davis and his generals viewed the Confederate situation as so dire that aggressive operations were initiated almost immediately—before conscription had a chance to add new men and even before there was much opportunity to effect further concentration of the forces already in the field.

Unfortunately for the Confederates, only one of the major offensives that launched their third phase, and it the smallest, succeeded. When Joseph Johnston withdrew from Manassas in early March, he left Stonewall Jackson's division in the Shenandoah Valley to retard the advance of Nathaniel Banks's Federal army and to protect the Confederates' distant left flank. Jackson had liberally interpreted Johnston's instructions to include the possibility of assuming the offensive if a promising opportunity presented itself. On March 23, under the false impression he was attacking an inferior force, Jackson assaulted James Shields's division at Kernstown, near Winchester, and suffered a severe defeat. Jackson retreated with his small army up the Valley to Mount Jackson, some thirty miles south of Winchester.[102]

About the same time, Johnston had moved the bulk of his army to the Peninsula to confront McClellan's advance from Fort Monroe, leaving behind Richard Ewell's division at Gordonsville and a brigade under Charles Field to watch McDowell at Fredericksburg. Johnston instructed Jackson and Ewell to join forces if they perceived the chance to strike the enemy.[103] Prodded by dispatches from Lee urging an offensive to relieve the pressure on Richmond, Jackson responded with a four-week campaign that justly became famous in military annals. Although surrounded by superior forces, he used speed and maneuver to confuse and defeat his foes. Feinting first to the west to hold the troops from John C. Frémont's Mountain Department at bay, Jackson then joined with Ewell and drove down the Valley, defeating Banks at Front Royal and Winchester and, finally, by May 30 chased the hapless Union general across the Potomac. Federal forces almost immediately began to close in behind the Confederates' dangerously advanced force at Harpers Ferry, and Jackson had to hurry back up the Valley to escape the trap. But he had achieved his goal.

Although small in size, Jackson's Valley campaign yielded large results. As Stonewall neared the Potomac fifty miles northwest of Washington, panic gripped the Lincoln administration and a large number of troops that should have been sent to McClellan to complete his investment of Richmond were diverted instead to snare Jackson. Although no troops were actually withdrawn from McClellan's army, that Federal commander was denied the use of thirty thousand men under McDowell who were to have joined him overland from Fredericksburg. Moreover, the Army of the Potomac was put in a strategically vulnerable position astride the Chickahominy. McClellan was required to retain part of his army north of that river and to draw supplies from White House on the Pamunkey because of his continuing expectation of the arrival of McDowell. Thanks to Jackson, McDowell would never come. And, thanks to Jackson, Lee learned of the Lincoln government's overweening fear for the safety of Washington.[104]

If Jackson's campaign showed the promise of what the new aggressive Southern policy might achieve, the two major offensives the Confederates undertook in the early spring of 1862 with their main Western and Eastern armies demonstrated the failure that might as easily result. In the West

Albert Sidney Johnston, belatedly reenforced by orders of the Davis administration and aided by the arrival from Virginia of a new chief lieutenant (Pierre Beauregard), began to collect an effective field army at Corinth. The regiments of Leonidas Polk from west Tennessee were formed into a *corps d'armee*, while those from central Kentucky under William J. Hardee were combined into another. The two newly arrived divisions from Mobile and Pensacola under Braxton Bragg were combined with a small division under Daniel Ruggles from Louisiana to form a third corps; and the remnants of Zollicoffer's force from east Tennessee, now under former U.S. vice president John C. Breckinridge, constituted the reserve.[105]

To be sure, it was something of a pathetic attempt at concentration that collected at Corinth only 50 percent of the paper strength of Johnston's sprawling department, which stretched from Arkansas to east Tennessee. And yet his newly christened Army of Mississippi, numbering some 50,000 present for duty, might hope to contend successfully with any one of the three enemy armies arrayed against it in the West.[106] On the other hand, if the forces of John Pope, Ulysses Grant, and Don Carlos Buell were to combine, the Confederates would be heavily outnumbered. As early as March 26 Robert E. Lee, now operating as general-in-chief, wrote to Johnston urging him to strike one of the three before they could combine. Finally, when it became clear on April 2 that Buell's Army of the Ohio was on its way to join Grant at Pittsburg Landing in west Tennessee, Sidney Johnston decided he could not afford to await the arrival of Van Dorn from Arkansas to complete his organization; let alone bide time while new levies were raised and trained.[107]

On April 3 the Confederates set out from Corinth, and three days and twenty miles later they attacked a surprised Grant in his camps on the Tennessee River. As the assault swept forward in successive lines by corps, the ranks became commingled. Near the end of the day—after Grant's army had been beaten back to the banks of the Tennessee, but Johnston had been mortally wounded—Beauregard called a halt to the attack and pulled his front lines back to regroup. Ever after, controversy would rage over whether the Confederates might have destroyed Grant if they had pressed forward on April 6. Overnight, in the breathing time and space allowed them, the Federals crossed over more than twenty thousand troops from Buell's Army of the Ohio, which had arrived just in time. Grant's counterattack on the 7th drove the Confederates back over their hard-won ground. With a combined total of nearly 24,000 casualties, Shiloh became the first of more than three score excessively bloody battles fought before the fate of the Union was decided.

Beauregard drew all the way back to Corinth to reorganize the shattered Army of Mississippi. Within a week he was reenforced by the arrival of the tardy Van Dorn from Arkansas, while troops raised by (or from fear of) conscription began to fill his ranks. In the meantime, Henry Halleck, the Federal general who had translated the textbooks on strategy, left his desk in St. Louis to take field command of the united armies of Grant, Buell, and Pope and to lay siege to Corinth. On May 30, unable to withstand the superior engineering and artillery of so large an enemy army, Beauregard abandoned Corinth and retired south to Tupelo, forty miles deeper into the interior of Mississippi.[108] In the West, it was difficult to distinguish the new phase of the war by its results.

In the East, the other Johnston faced equally serious problems. Joseph E. Johnston had fallen back to the suburbs of Richmond not because he intended to fight the enemy there or because he believed he could withstand a siege. Instead, he wanted to draw the Federals as far as possible from their base of supplies, in order to attenuate their line of communications and give them the opportunity to make a mistake. He watched carefully for any opening McClellan might give him. Johnston's strategy added pressure to the increasingly taut relationship between himself and the president. Davis wanted desperately to avoid the evacuation of Richmond, but neither did the president want the army to become entrapped in a siege. On May 17 he wrote to Johnston, "The defence must be made outside of the city, the question is where and how?"[109] Johnston agreed, but he could not answer with specifics, as he was waiting for McClellan to determine the "where and how." In addition, Johnston was becoming less and less inclined to tell Davis anything, and, as a result, the president grew suspicious that the general would not make a wholehearted defense of Richmond.

A week later Johnston thought he saw his opportunity. Two of the Union army corps crossed to the south bank of the Chickahominy and advanced slowly to Seven Pines in the direction of Richmond, while the remaining three corps moved along the north bank toward Mechanicsville.[110] As the spring had been one of the wettest in memory, the ground was already soaked and the streams swollen. In the event of more rain, McClellan would find it difficult, if not impossible, to cross the Chickahominy with reenforcements to support either wing should it be attacked. The separation of the Federal army also afforded Johnston the chance to overcome Confederate inferiority in numbers by focusing his strength against a fraction of the enemy. This was a critical advantage, because, in spite of Davis's repeated suggestions that Johnston take the offensive, until late May the army under Johnston's immediate command had benefited little from the new Confederate commitment to mobilization and concentration.

In January, while still headquartered at Centreville, Johnston had roughly 62,000 men (present for duty) to defend his Department of

Northern Virginia, which stretched from the Shenandoah Valley east to Fredericksburg.[111] In early April he had taken about two-thirds of this force with him to the Peninsula, leaving Stonewall Jackson's division in the Valley, Richard Ewell's division on the upper Rappahannock, and a brigade under Charles Field opposite Fredericksburg. By late April, after losing several brigades sent to North Carolina to confront Burnside, but gaining Magruder's Army of the Peninsula, the 56,000 men (present for duty) under Johnston's immediate charge represented a net loss of about six thousand.[112] Nor, during most of May, did Johnston receive more than a few of the regiments from the new forces arriving in Richmond. Lee halted Benjamin Huger's division—available after the evacuation of Norfolk—at Petersburg, and he sent the three brigades pried loose from the south Atlantic states northward to create a force to oppose McDowell at Fredericksburg and to replace Ewell at Gordonsville. At one point, the administration even tried to persuade Johnston to give up Longstreet or G. W. Smith to command this force, which was informally called the Army of the North. Johnston refused to release either general and requested instead the troops be added to his army.[113]

So long as Lee and Davis viewed McDowell's overland advance from the north to be nearly as serious a threat as McClellan's movement up the Peninsula, they refused to collect all of the forces in the Richmond area into Johnston's immediate army. This unwillingness to unite in the face of the enemy's closing pincers caused much discussion among the general officers, and on April 21 Daniel Harvey Hill wrote to his former comrade-in-arms George Randolph, now secretary of war, to urge the combining of Confederate forces. Noting a Northern newspaper article "boasting of the greater concentration of their forces," Hill warned that with the Federals focusing their strength against Corinth and Yorktown, "We must do the same, else we will be beaten at both points, and the Southern Confederacy will cease to exist." A month later, having observed no progress toward concentration, Hill once again appealed to Randolph, promising him, "The desire for this is universal with our officers."[114]

Davis and Lee did not relent, however, until the end of May, after McClellan had crossed the Chickahominy and approached even nearer to Richmond, and after Jackson's advance to the Potomac caused McDowell's forces at Fredericksburg to be diminished. Still, as Johnston decided to move against McClellan's separated army, he finally knew that he would be able to utilize Huger's division and the four brigades from the north, which were now united as a division under Ambrose Powell Hill. With this increase of some 13,000, Johnston would be able to bring about 69,000 thousand men against McClellan's army of 98,000. While he would still only have 57 percent of the Confederate troops in the Eastern theater, fortunately for Johnston the Federals suffered even more from the policy of dispersal and would have only 46 percent of their theaterwide forces available to resist his attack.[115]

On May 27 Jeb Stuart's cavalry reported that McDowell's army had started its march southward from Fredericksburg. This news, combined with intelligence of an expedition by a portion of McClellan's army north to Hanover Court House, convinced Johnston that the joining of the two Federal armies was imminent. He determined to strike at once before they could unite. According to his plan, G. W. Smith and A. P. Hill would attack McClellan's three corps north of the Chickahominy, and Longstreet and D. H. Hill would assault the two corps south of the river, while Magruder and Huger punched through the gap in the center. That night, however, later cavalry reports revealed that McDowell had turned back and that the enemy juncture was no longer an immediate threat.

Johnston thereupon abandoned his desperately concocted plan and returned to his preferred strategy of concentrating his forces against the two Federal corps isolated south of the river. On the morning of the thirtieth, he decided that a sufficient gap had developed between the Chickahominy and the two Federal corps to invite attack. He drew up new plans for the following day. With only A. P. Hill watching the main body of the enemy north of the river, Longstreet and D. H. Hill were to assault the front of McClellan's exposed left wing. After the battle had started, Huger was to turn the enemy's left flank, while Smith and Magruder were to oppose any reenforcements McClellan might try to bring across the river and also to fall on the right flank of the vulnerable left wing.[116]

Heavy rain on the night of the 30th increased Confederate hopes that McClellan would not be able to pass reenforcements over the river to support his isolated corps. Although plagued by delay and miscoordination, the main Confederate attack on the 31st met with impressive success. At two o'clock Longstreet decided to wait no longer for Huger to get in position on the right flank and launched D. H. Hill against the front of Erasmus Keyes's Fourth Corps. Hill drove Keyes out of his entrenchments and back several miles, before the Federals stabilized on Samuel Heintzelman's Third Corps. Huger never did get into the battle. Without knowing it, Smith had been unable to prevent McClellan from crossing Edwin Sumner's Second Corps south of the river. When Smith moved to attack Keyes's right flank, his march brought him across the front of Sumner's position at Fair Oaks Station, thereupon causing a secondary battle to develop.

As night fell and the Confederates regrouped to renew their attack on the following morning, a shell fragment severely wounded Johnston, whose life was in doubt as he was carried from the field. On June 1 the Federals counterattacked and regained most of the ground they had lost, and the

Confederates fell back to their camps in the outskirts of Richmond.[117] Johnston's long-awaited countershot had ricocheted.

Curious similarities marked the two major early spring offensives undertaken by the Confederate armies to recoup their drooping fortunes in the Eastern and Western theaters. At both Shiloh and Seven Pines the Confederates achieved surprise and gained striking victories on the first day of fighting. But in each case the Federals reorganized overnight, brought up reenforcements, counterattacked to regain all of their lost ground, and forced the Confederates back to where they had started.

Neither battle gained the initiative for the South, nor did either compel the enemy to change its strategy. Ironically, Shiloh and Seven Pines were worse than failures, for they cost the South the life of Sidney Johnston and the long absence of the severely wounded Joseph Johnston. At the moment of its greatest crisis and at the time when its strategy desperately needed revision, the military establishment of the Confederacy lost its most experienced leadership and the two generals popularly believed to be the best in the country. In the dark dawning of the third phase of the war, Confederate fortunes receded to their lowest ebb.

CHAPTER TWO

"It would change the character of the war"

The Ascent of Lee, to June 1, 1862

STARTLED BY THE unexpected sound of heavy artillery firing on the eastern horizon, Jefferson Davis rode out from the capital on the late afternoon of May 31 to discover if Joseph Johnston had at last chosen to attack McClellan. As the presidential party approached the general's headquarters on the Nine Mile Road, Johnston departed so hastily in the opposite direction as to give the impression he intended to avoid Davis. The president did find General Lee present, but, in spite of having spent the last three hours with Johnston, Lee could give no explanation for what was occurring. The two men listened for several moments to a swelling rattle in the distance—which they identified as musketry—before mounting and riding toward Fair Oaks Station on the Richmond and York River Railroad. Along the way they found abundant evidence of a battle in progress and indications of considerable Confederate success. Confusion commanded, however, and no one could tell them either what was happening or what was supposed to be happening. Finally, after coming under small arms fire, Davis sensed opportunity escaping in the failing light and started to issue orders to units in the area. But even had the president known what he was doing, there was too little time left to accomplish it. Davis was on hand, though, when litter-bearers stumbled down the road and loaded the barely conscious Johnston onto an ambulance.

In that moment of gathering dusk, Davis likely experienced sharply conflicting emotions. The day's tactical success showed promise of being as overwhelming as that at First Manassas. Yet, the victory was far from complete, and the loss of Johnston's coordinating hand endangered all that had been gained. The appearance of Gustavus Smith, the army's second-in-command, did little to allay the president's concern. Although Smith knew the plan for the day, so much had gone awry, and he knew so little of affairs on Longstreet's front on the right at Seven Pines that Smith was unsure even whether or not the Confederates might be forced to retreat.

Great indeed must have been Davis's unease, as late that night he rode back from the battlefield in the gloomy darkness with a lone companion. A fiasco this near to Richmond would be fatal. There was no margin for further confusion or hesitation, and the responsibility for decisive action rested squarely upon his shoulders. Smith did not seem up to the job, nor had any other commander of division yet marked himself for higher command. If there were time to bring someone from afar, who was there to bring? At some point before they reached Richmond, Davis turned to Lee and asked him to take temporary command of the army defending Richmond.[1]

Davis's choice of Robert E. Lee was logical and would turn out to be one of the wisest he would make as Confederate president. Yet, at the time, it seemed more curious than wise.

Lee's Running Start

Clearly, Davis had for many years respected and trusted Lee. Just as clearly, the president must have harbored some doubts, for he had found it difficult to know how best to utilize Lee's talents at the start of the war. The Confederacy inherited the general with the admission of Virginia, as Lee at that time was major-general and commander of the land and naval forces of the Old Dominion. His demotion to brigadier-general in the Confederate army can scarcely be considered a slight, since that rank was the highest then recognized by law. Nevertheless, the failure to appoint him to an important field command was peculiar, at the very least. After all of the assignments had been parceled out to others, Lee found himself at Richmond in an ambiguous position. With no specific orders, his role evolved into one akin to advisor on Virginia affairs.[2]

Eventually, Davis had settled on the use of Lee as something of a troubleshooter when various disasters threatened. In late July he sent the general to northwestern Virginia when the Confederate effort there verged on collapse. Later in 1861, after a Federal invasion force threatened Port Royal, the president dispatched Lee to command the Department of South Carolina and Georgia. In these assignments Lee had demonstrated some ability both as an administrator and an engineer but absolutely none as a warrior chieftain. Indeed, his one venture in actual field command had been an abortive campaign in the Upper Gauley Valley that had ended in failure even to bring his enemy to battle.

Yet, not only Davis but seemingly the Confederate Congress possessed faith in Lee. In August 1861, when five full generals were commissioned to head the army, Lee was named third most senior, outranking Joseph Johnston and Pierre Beauregard, the heroes of the recent battle at Manassas. Then, in the winter of 1862, when the string of reverses had begun to sour Confederate hopes, Congress passed an act permitting the president to appoint a military officer as secretary of war and a week later created the office of commanding general of the army.[3] The assumption was wide-spread that Lee would fill one or the other of the positions.[4] Davis signed the first legislation into law but did not act upon it. He vetoed the second on the grounds that the bill infringed on his constitutional prerogatives as commander-in-chief by authorizing the commanding general to supersede field commanders.[5] The congressional initiative was undoubtedly aimed at ridding the War Department of the unpopular Judah Benjamin, who was blamed for the loss of Roanoke Island, but it was not necessarily unfriendly to Davis. Both houses not only sustained the veto but also supported the reorganization proposed by the president.

Davis accepted fully the need for changes, although he insisted on mak-ing them on his own terms. By March 17 he had worked out a transfer that sent Benjamin to the State Department and appointed George Randolph, who resigned an army commission, as the new secretary of war.[6] As early as March 2, however, the president summoned Lee from Savannah back to Rich-mond.[7] To what extent Davis believed he could satisfy the political demand for change with a pliant advisor who would not threaten his control of the war, and to what extent he honestly sought Lee's sage advice, cannot now be known. In any case, on March 13 a presidential order "charged" Lee "with the conduct of military operations in the armies of the Confederacy."[8] Taken at face value, Lee's assignment should have made him general-in-chief in a position similar to that of Winfield Scott and George McClellan in the North. But Jefferson Davis's preemptive view of the constitutional role of the com-mander-in-chief precluded that possibility, and Lee functioned simply as the highest-ranking military advisor to the president.[9]

It was in this ambiguous capacity that Lee oversaw the writing of the proposal for conscription; sporadically coordinated operations in the West and more consistently affairs in Virginia; and attended the April 14 war council, which debated concentration on the Peninsula versus an offensive thrust northward. In spite of the vagaries of his position, Lee apparently grew considerably in the president's eyes. On May 30, the day before Seven Pines, Davis would write to his wife, "General Lee rises to the occasion . . . and seems equal to the conception." That Davis was referring only to Lee's administrative abilities, however, is revealed in his subsequent sen-tence, "I hope others will develop capacity in execution."[10] In turning to Lee as Johnston's temporary replacement, Davis for the fourth time used the general to stanch a hole in the dike.[11] It is a safe assumption that no one, not even Davis, could have predicted what the results would be. Lee's record in the war would not have justified the prediction.

In spite of the inauspicious omens surrounding Robert E. Lee's posting to field command—of which historians have made much—Lee enjoyed from the start a combination of advantages no other Confederate general would ever realize. Undoubtedly, his greatest assets grew from the strength of his own character. Although he possessed a broad vein of playful humor and was subject to periodic fits of temper, Lee was able to suppress these human traits and project an aura of aloofness that protected him from intrigue and jealousy.[12] Within months of joining the army he began to attract loyalty and devotion in an intensity which Civil War soldiers awarded only to two other leaders, Stonewall Jackson and George McClellan.

Lee's two most useful qualities as a Confederate general, however, derived from his pragmatic acceptance of the hand dealt him by fate. In the first instance, he resigned himself to incomplete and contradictory information and still—on an extraordinary number of occasions—found a way to impress his will on confusion around him. In the second, he exhibited the inherent, sanguine confidence to confront the most serious problems with a positive attitude. He would be able to devise solutions to tangled strategic situations with a "best-cases" optimism based on his ability to perceive the enemy's problems almost as plainly as he saw his own.[13] Lee also brought to his new position maturing ideas on policy and strategy, and he possessed—although his Civil War career had certainly not yet demonstrated it—a sharp eye for strategic opportunities. Lee's qualities contrasted sharply with the prickly Joseph Johnston, the ambitious Pierre Beauregard, and the malleable Sidney Johnston.

Beyond his personal attributes, Lee also enjoyed important advantages in situations that increased greatly his ability to reverse the course of the war for the Confederacy in the East. These circumstantial benefits resulted first from the fortuitous timing of his new assignment, which came at exactly the right moment to capitalize on the Confederacy's new commitment to mobilization and concentration, and, secondly, from the unique working relationship Lee developed with Davis, which allowed the general to harvest so fully the fruits of the spring's revivified efforts.

Lee possessed the uncommon ability to serve well as both subordinate and chief simultaneously. He was as good a follower as he was a leader. The day after the appointment to field command, Davis was too ill to ride out to the army, but he wrote, "Please keep me advised as frequently as your engagements will permit of what is passing before and around you."[14] And thereafter, Lee wrote both frequently and fully to the president, asking his advice and often discussing the most trivial details of administration, as well as important questions of policy and strategy. Always he employed a tone both confidential and deferential; as on June 5, when he forwarded a letter to Davis on the merits of several brigade commanders, he concluded, "I thought you ought to know it. Our position requires you should know everything & you must excuse my troubling you."[15] By the close of his first week in the field, Lee had established with Davis a working partnership with few parallels in military history and none in the Civil War. On June 7, at the end of an afternoon visit by the president to army headquarters, military secretary Armistead Long would note in his private journal that the relations between the two "are very friendly. The general is ever willing to receive the suggestions of the President, while the President exhibits the greatest confidence in General Lee's experience and ability, and does not hamper him with executive interference."[16]

That Davis did in fact quickly evolve a relationship of exceptional trust and respect with Lee is certain. By June 19 Davis would write to his wife, "Lee is working systematically, cooperating cordially and the army is said to feel the beneficial effect of it."[17] After the war, with obvious exaggeration but nonetheless revealing emphasis, Davis would proclaim, "I repeat, *we never disagreed.*"[18] Throughout the war Davis insisted on his right to overall control, but he sought generals who would assume responsibility. The president wanted to be consulted, but he was almost always willing to acknowledge Lee knew best what to decide in particular situations.

Because of his surpassing rapport with Davis, Lee would realize the best command conditions his government could provide. First, he was given a larger, more coherent theater of operations than his predecessor, Johnston. Second, he was allowed to concentrate the largest army ever fielded by the South, one so large that he would outnumber his foe in his first campaign. And, finally, he was permitted to devise and pursue—with considerable support and little interference from above—a grand strategy so broad it bordered on national policy. And Lee benefited not only from having these advantages, he profited almost equally from facing enemy generals who lacked them. From March of 1862 until March of 1864, the Lincoln administration had insufficient confidence in its commanders in the East to give them theater command, to concentrate their forces adequately, or to provide them effective support in pursuing the strategy the generals deemed militarily best.

When Lee left his desk in the War Department to take the field, he did not simply take over the post vacated by the wounded Joseph Johnston. Had that been the case, he would have relinquished his role as quasi-general-in-chief and assumed command of the Department of Northern Virginia. He did neither. When Davis wrote the official letter on June 1, notifying Lee of his new responsibilities, the president made it clear the new assignment would "interfere temporarily" with his duties "in connection with the general service, but only so far as to make [him] available for command in the field of a particular army." In other words, while Lee would no longer be able to devote his full attention to all Confederate operations, he would retain this larger responsibility and authority.[19] For several weeks he continued to receive and answer dispatches and reports from eastern Tennessee and even as far away as Mississippi. In practice, he soon became so preoccupied with his new field command that he ceased to exert control over operations at a distance. The point is, Lee's authority to command the "armies of the Confederacy" was never revoked, and this made his position much stronger than Johnston's had ever been.[20]

Secondly, the command vacated by Johnston, often shifting and frequently confused, had narrowed in scope and authority with the passing months. Technically, Johnston still commanded the Department of Northern Virginia, but for several reasons that official assignment had become meaningless. In practice, he exercised direct control over only one—albeit the major one—of the forces defending Richmond. Upon its creation in October 1861, Johnston's department had consisted of the Valley District of Stonewall Jackson, the Potomac District of Pierre Beauregard, and the Aquia District of Theophilus Holmes and had extended from the eastern slope of the Allegheny Mountains to the mouth of the Potomac River.[21] When Johnston transferred most of his troops to Yorktown in April to confront McClellan, his authority had been temporarily increased to include Magruder's Department of the Peninsula and Huger's Department of Norfolk.[22]

While this arrangement seemed to give Johnston control over northern, central, and eastern Virginia, it did not work out that way in practice. Ironically, from the moment Johnston moved closer to the capital, the administration assumed he could not keep in direct touch with his scattered command, and communications from his various subordinates were funneled through Lee in Richmond. Some dispatches went astray, and all were delayed; and as a result Johnston forfeited control of everything except the army in his immediate presence. He lost direction of Jackson as early as April, and except for the order to abandon Norfolk, he exercised little authority over Huger until May 30, the day before Seven Pines. Likewise, the forces Lee built up in the Gordonsville–Hanover Junction area to oppose McDowell were not given to Johnston until late in May. Johnston exerted some influence over the Drewry's Bluff and Chaffin's Farm garrisons on the James River, but he was denied his request for command of the Department of Henrico, which included Richmond, its fortifications, and its defenders.[23]

The order assigning Lee to command did not name the Department of Northern Virginia, nor did it mention any department for that matter. It said that Lee "will assume the immediate command of the armies in Eastern Virginia and North Carolina." Hence, even Lee's field command was considerably broader than Johnston's had been, as it included both North

Carolina and the Shenandoah Valley; and, as the summer progressed, Lee would extend his influence to William W. Loring's troops in distant southwestern Virginia. In effect Lee came to control the middle Atlantic as his theater of operations. This was an advantage that he enjoyed and that Johnston had not, nor would any of the Federal commanders Lee faced in 1862 or 1863.

The freedom to develop theaterwide strategy might have meant little to some generals. Such was not the case with Lee. Almost from the moment he left his office in Richmond, he set in motion the preliminary maneuvers of a grand strategy to coordinate Confederate efforts in the Eastern theater toward winning the war.[24]

Every Victory Should Bring Us Nearer

On June 3, just one full day after taking command in the field, Robert E. Lee called his generals to conference at "The Chimneys," a house on the Nine Mile Road near Fair Oaks Station. He wanted to canvass the ideas and gauge the mood of his new subordinates, most of whom he knew previously and upon whom his success now depended. It quickly became apparent the generals shared the conviction—often repeated by Johnston—that Richmond could not be successfully defended against a large, well-equipped enemy who employed engineering and siege techniques. Even though Lee wholly agreed with the premise, the pessimism evinced by some of the officers dismayed him. When Gen. William H. C. Whiting, a career engineer, took pencil and paper to demonstrate how regular approaches and successive parallels would lead to inevitable defeat, Lee interrupted him with, "Stop, stop, if you go to ciphering we are whipped beforehand."[25]

Lee understood the gloomy probabilities, but he insisted on operating on the basis of possibilities. He thus promptly exhibited one of his most useful character traits. He would tackle problems with a positive attitude, and he would plan solutions in light of the best outcome that might result. This optimistic or "best-cases" approach well suited a cause facing heavy odds and long-shot chances of success. In speaking to the generals, Lee likely used words very similar to those penned by Davis to Johnston two weeks before: "It is needless to say that the defense must be made outside of the city. The question is, where and how?"[26]

On this important point, Lee's new subordinates provided little help. Some advised retiring nearer to the capital, especially withdrawing from the high ground opposite the Chickahominy, which was subject to Federal long-range artillery fire from north of the river. Once again Lee rejected the pessimism and passive defense mentality displayed by such thinking.

In recounting the episode, he would remark to an aide, "If we leave this line because they can shell us, we shall have to leave the next for the same reason, and I don't see how we can stop this side of Richmond." Although Lee divulged nothing of his own plans at the council, he also opposed withdrawing farther—and he particularly disliked abandoning the ground near the Chickahominy—for a different reason. He had already decided to go on the offensive to pry Richmond loose from the enemy's tightening grip. He knew his present position, with his left nearly touching the Chickahominy, hindered McClellan in uniting the two wings of the Army of the Potomac which were still split by the river. Lee wanted to retain the option of striking the enemy so vulnerably situated.[27]

In the midst of the meeting, Jefferson Davis appeared at the door. The president had been on a visit to the front lines, when he spied Traveller, Lee's distinctive dapple gray, among a large number of horses outside the house. Davis soon perceived the despondency among the generals and voiced his "marked" disappointment. Lee asserted control over the meeting by mentioning that he had already remonstrated against pessimism, and shortly thereafter the president withdrew.

After the conference broke up, Lee displayed a fine sense of diplomacy by riding after the president and pointedly asking what suggestions *he* proposed. Davis replied that he "knew of nothing better than the plan" Lee "had previously explained" to him as the strategy Johnston intended to follow on May 28 to stop the reported junction of McClellan and McDowell. Recalling the Johnston plan in abridged form, the president mentioned only that part which called for A. P. Hill's division to fall on the flank and rear of the Federals north of the Chickahominy. Since the enemy had subsequently strengthened their defenses in that quarter, Davis speculated, a stronger attacking column would be required; it would be necessary to bring Stonewall Jackson's army from the Valley. There is no record of any response by Lee.[28]

Although the president's permission to order Jackson from the Valley must have intrigued Lee, it did not satisfy him. Even during these first days, while he was still immersed in the details of learning his new command, and while the imminent threat to Richmond necessarily occupied most of his attention, Lee's strategic thinking probed well beyond his immediate problems. Two days after "The Chimneys" conference, he wrote to Davis urging troops be stripped from the south Atlantic states to reenforce Stonewall Jackson for an offensive into Maryland and Pennsylvania. "After much reflection," he told the president, "I think it would change the character of the war."[29]

Admittedly, as a desk-bound military counselor, Lee's record in support of coordination, concentration, and aggressive operations had been mixed.[30] Apparently, viewing the war from a tent in the field focused his thinking and sharpened his commitment to all three. Contrary to the ordinary progression, the closer Lee got to the trees, the more clearly he saw the forest. Once in command of an army, he better appreciated the need to relate battles and campaigns to a larger scheme and to avoid barren victories and the squandering of blood and resources in meaningless fighting. After eight months in his new command, he would insist, "The lives of our soldiers are too precious to be sacrificed in the attainment of successes that inflict no loss upon the enemy beyond the actual loss in battle. Every victory should bring us nearer to the great end which it is the object of this war to reach."[31] It was a truth, in fact, that he acted upon from the start. During his entire three years of command—from the Seven Days to Appomattox—Lee would try to implement a coherent grand strategy that promised the Confederacy at least a chance to win the war.

It is likely that Lee's understanding of the nature of the contest and what it would take to achieve Confederate victory had evolved gradually during the war's first year, during the time when his job had been to administer but not originate policy. In addition to his stints in the field in western Virginia and South Carolina, he had spent twelve months, off and on, organizing troops and national resources and viewing the war from the presidential level. He had also apparently paid close attention to Northern newspapers. This had given him the opportunity to think in broad terms, to recognize the strengths and weaknesses of the Confederate position, and to observe early tendencies displayed by the North.

It also put him in an unusual, if not unique, position. With the absence of policy-planning agencies and the parade of three different secretaries through the War Department, only Jefferson Davis paralleled Lee's grasp of the Confederate war effort from top to bottom. The general understood Confederate war aims and policy, and—through almost daily contact with Davis—he better than any other individual understood the president's views. No one, except Davis, was better situated than Lee to devise a grand strategy for the South. In more recent times, of course, it would be presumptuous if not an outright usurpation of authority for any general to assume responsibility for devising overall strategy for a war, especially one with national policy ramifications. Probably, it was somewhat presumptuous even during the Civil War.

On Lee's behalf, it can be noted that he frequently explained at least specific parts of his strategy in dispatches to the president, and he may have explained the whole in private conversations now lost. Also, periodically he asked flatly to be overruled if his actions ran contrary to policy. Even more, nothing in Lee's strategy ran counter to the known ideas and inclinations of the president, although Lee did expand them, harmonize them, and move into areas where presidential views are not known. Lee's strategy did not contravene Davis's concepts; it transcended them. In the end, Lee's ultimate justification must be that if he had not elaborated the president's generalized strategic philosophy, as a general his operations would have lacked coherence and purpose.[32]

No strategy in any war can be successful unless it is grounded in the realities of the struggle. It is for this reason that textbook examples cannot be applied directly to life, and some generals, well educated in their profession, never succeed in practice. There can be no guarantee that a reality as perceived is a reality in fact. A general's genius is nowhere better tried than in distinguishing between what he desires and what is real.

Robert E. Lee believed that certain basic truths about the war had been established by June of 1862. Some had been known from the start, while others had only emerged during the thirteen months of fighting. A few were hopeful, but most meant grim tidings for the Confederacy. All were so fundamental that they shaped Lee's thinking before he spread a map to ponder the movement of troops. Each was sufficiently important in itself that if removed from the equation Lee's solution does not prove. From Lee's overall view of the realities of the struggle, it is possible to see the assumptions that undergird his strategy.

Foremost, Lee understood that the Confederacy faced overwhelming statistical disadvantages in its bid for separation. He never shared the popular delusion that independence could be achieved rapidly or cheaply. He recognized the "United States Government is one of the most powerful on earth," and he assumed that the people of the loyal states would make formidable opponents. As early as May of 1861, while he still commanded Virginia militia, he acknowledged that Northern "resources are almost without limit." The North inherited "nearly all the workshops and skilled artisans of the country" and possessed the capital and credit to "draw upon the resources of other nations to supply any deficiency." At this time, Lee believed the South would "not succeed until the financial power of the North is completely broken," and that would "occur only at the end of a long and bloody war."[33]

Thirteen months of warfare convinced Lee the prognosis was even grimmer. By the time he took field command in June of 1862, or shortly thereafter, he had concluded the North possessed the men, money, and materiel to defeat the South, regardless of any military program the South might undertake, whether offensive or defensive. "Conceding to our enemies the superiority claimed by them in numbers, resources, and all the means and appliances for carrying on the war," he bluntly acknowledged, "we have no right to look for exemptions from the military consequences of a vigorous use of these advantages. . . ."[34] And on another occasion he referred more succinctly to "the natural military consequences of the enemy's numerical superiority."[35] In other words, Lee came to see the raw mathematics involved. No matter that Southern losses resulted from Southern victories, the Confederacy would exhaust its manpower and supplies while the Union was still calling forth its reserves. In purely military terms the South could not defeat the North.

It is true that such a prediction also could have been forecast for the American colonists, who had faced even steeper odds in their bid for independence. The colonists had been fortunate, however, in gaining substantial aid from France and in having Great Britain distracted by war with half of Europe. Lee did not expect aid from any foreign nation, nor did he believe the North would engage in war with other countries. Even at the height of the *Trent* affair—the crisis between Britain and the United States resulting from American seizure of Confederate emissaries James Mason and John Slidell from a British mail steamer—Lee wrote, "We must make up our minds to fight our battles and win our independence alone. No one will help us."[36] Viewing foreign affairs realistically, he did not "expect the policy of any Government toward us to be governed by any other consideration than that of self interest."[37]

Lee knew something of the European antipathy toward slavery, and in 1861 he predicted the North would "be shrewd enough to make the war appear to be merely a struggle on our part for the maintenance of slavery; and we shall thus be without sympathy, and most certainly without material aid from other powers."[38] The diplomatic history of the contest did not surprise him as it unfolded. Near the end, he wrote to Davis, "As far as I have been able to judge, this war presents to the European world but two aspects. A contest in which one side is contending for abstract slavery and the other against it. The existence of vital rights involved does not seem to be understood or appreciated. As long as this lasts," he confessed, we "can expect neither sympathy or aid." He concluded, "Our safety depends upon ourselves alone."[39]

Believing, on the one hand, that the South could not conquer the North and, on the other, that the South would receive no help from outside, brought Lee to the verge of concluding the Confederacy could not win the war. How close he came was revealed in his cry of despair on the eve of Appomattox, "A few more Sailor's Creeks and it will all be over—ended—just as I have expected it would end from the first."[40] Still, in spite of these fatalistic words, Lee did not succumb to hopelessness until the closing days of the war. For three years he planned and executed campaigns as if the Confederacy had a chance to win. That the chance was slender Lee knew, and the knowledge shaped both his planning and his execution. From his desperation evolved his willingness to take great risks.

· · ·

The opportunity Lee saw for Confederate victory was precarious, because it rested in Northern hands just as certainly as did Confederate defeat. The North's preponderant odds would only decide the war, Lee reasoned, if Northerners "continue united in their efforts to subjugate us" and made "vigorous use of these advantages."[41] Conversely, the Confederacy could gain its independence if the United States lacked the determination and endurance to apply its full resources to preserving the Union. "It is plain to my understanding," Lee wrote to Davis, "that everything that will tend to repress the war feeling in the Federal States will inure to our benefit."[42] The best Southerners could do was to pursue the course most likely to discourage the North and to foster such dissatisfaction that "the war would no longer be supported" by the Northern people. "That, after all," Lee wrote to Davis, "is what we are interested in bringing about."[43]

During the opening two years of the war, the period in which Lee formulated and first attempted to apply his strategy, there were indeed signs from the North that the South's cause was not without hope. According to Lee's aide-de-camp, Charles Marshall, one of the most critical observations Lee drew from his study of enemy newspapers was that the North "dreaded the effect of protracted hostilities." The general noted the short terms of the initial volunteers, the concern of the business community over the enormous expenses being incurred daily, the rabid impatience of many editors and politicians for a hasty advance of their armies, and the Lincoln administration's need for good news to feed its people to counteract waning enthusiasm. It was not unreasonable to question how long the North would support a costly war merely to keep the South in the Union. If the struggle could be prolonged, and if its cost in money and blood were to escalate sharply, the North might abandon the effort. For the South to win, wrote Marshall, Lee believed it was necessary to "encourage the belief that the war would be of indefinite length" and would require the North to make "great sacrifices of life and treasure," and—after all that—the Confederacy might still prove unconquerable.[44]

Because he viewed Northern demoralization as essential to Southern victory, Lee developed a surprisingly modern appreciation of the relationship between politics and the military in the conduct of war. This is especially striking, since, as a career soldier, he had never evinced much interest in politics in his private life. During the war, he would frequently take the temperature of Northern patriotism by watching closely the enemy's success and failure in recruiting new troops, by observing the results of Northern elections and the progress of the peace movement, and even by monitoring the fluctuations of gold prices on the New York market.[45] During the course of the war, he would on several occasions suggest to Davis political actions the Confederate government might take to nurture anti-war sentiment in the North.[46]

Of course, Lee's main focus from first to last was on military affairs. No one understood better than he that he was no more than a soldier. He could operate only in the military realm, and—after he was appointed to field command—the Army of Northern Virginia was his only effective weapon for discouraging the North. The most he could contribute would be to design and execute a strategy that caused the Northern people to question the cost they found themselves paying. First, he must undo their successes and make them start over again. Then he must consistently "frustrate," "embarrass," "baffle," and "mystify" Northern offensive plans and deny them the kinds of successes that would feed their expectations for early or easy victory. He must create a string of Federal defeats that would sap Northern morale.[47] It would take "revolution among their people," he believed, and "nothing can produce a revolution except systematic success on our part."[48]

At the same time, Lee recognized another stark truth that necessarily governed any strategy he might adopt. The same raw mathematics meant the South itself could not wage an overly protracted contest. Once the war had started, a logistical hourglass had been set on end, and its sands ran relentlessly against the Confederacy. So heavy was the imbalance against the South that the Federals could lose three soldiers to every Confederate lost and still gain in the pure arithmetic of the war. Eventually, Confederate resources in men and materiel would diminish to the point they could not carry on the war while waiting for the North to tire of the struggle. "While making the most we can of the means of resistance we possess," Lee confessed to the president, "it is nevertheless the part of wisdom to carefully measure and husband our strength, and not to expect from it more than in the ordinary course of affairs it is capable of accomplishing."[49]

For this very reason Lee believed he could not afford the "positive loss" that must result from "inactivity."[50] He concluded the South's "constantly diminishing" resources in "disproportion" to the North's compelled him to force the issue.[51] He had to control the tempo of the war by inflicting maximum damage on the enemy in a series of victories won in rapid order. Northerners must be made to return again and again in quick succession to their wells of manpower and their coffers of money until it hurt to draw more from either. Victories on paper would not be enough. The North must be made to suffer the serious losses that could only result from battle. Nor would partial victories suffice. Lee believed it would be necessary not merely to defeat the Federals but to "destroy," "crush," "ruin," and "wipe out" the enemy army.[52] When he wrote, "If we can defeat or drive the armies of the enemy from the field, we shall have peace," he did not mean he believed it possible to annihilate the Northern people or exhaust Northern resources.[53] He meant the South would win when the North no longer had the will to replace its shattered armies.

Thus, Lee was left to design a strategy to frustrate and hurt the enemy, while simultaneously sparing Confederate manpower and preserving the South's physical resources for feeding and equipping its armies. In the long summer months that lay just ahead, Lee would find an aphorism to express his goal: he wanted "easy fighting and heavy victories."[54]

Easy Fighting and Heavy Victories

As Lee translated his personal views on the realities of the war into an offensive grand strategy, he seems to have given no thought to adopting what Jomini had called the passive defense. Lee chose instead to employ the Jominian offensive-defensive, or, as he himself termed it, "active" or "aggressive" operations.[55] It is possible, of course, that the idea of skillfully withdrawing in front of superior forces and fortifying strategically important points in the hope of inducing the enemy to do all of the attacking ran counter to Lee's character. After the war, no less an admirer than Jefferson Davis confessed a belief that Lee was by nature "combative." And one of his subordinates, Maj.-Gen. Henry Heth, asserted that the "determination to strike the enemy" was a "leading characteristic of the man," and that the general "was the most aggressive man in his army."[56] If true, however, it is certainly curious that Lee would possess a personality trait that exhibited itself only in the carefully deliberated decisions he made during the phase of his life when he consciously held his greatest responsibilities. Nothing in Lee's life before or after the war, nor in his war career beyond his conduct of grand tactics, suggests he suffered from a compulsive quirk that caused him to attack when he ought not to have.

Yet, even if true, explanations of Lee's strategy in terms of his personality are at best only part of the truth, and considerably the lesser part. The greatest weakness of psychological interpretation is its immunity from historical proof, and its greatest danger is that it shuts out further inquiry into legitimate historical motives. Even if a passive defense did run counter to Lee's nature, it also ran counter to the best military thinking of the Civil War generation; it contradicted the policy of the Confederate government and the expectations of the Southern people; and, if adopted, it would have ignored the lessons that Lee believed the first year of the struggle had incontrovertibly taught.

Lee did not invent the offensive-defensive, of course. Not only had it been around since the beginning of warfare, but the offensive in any form—

from limited counterthrust to full-scale invasion—had been the preferred option in military thinking since Napoleon had so ably demonstrated its effectiveness. Henri Jomini, Napoleon's "interpreter," described the passive defense as "always pernicious." And Henry Halleck, Jomini's "American interpreter," condemned the strategy in even stronger language: "To merely remain in a defensive attitude, yielding gradually to the advances of the enemy, without any effort to regain such positions . . . , or to inflict on him some fatal and decisive blow on the first favorable opportunity" could result only from "ignorance, stupidity, and cowardice."[57] More to the point, Lee did not even introduce the offensive-defensive into Southern thinking. It had already played a prominent if inconsistent role in Confederate grand strategy from Sumter to Seven Pines. In deciding to employ aggressive operations, Lee merely adopted the approach that reflected Confederate war aims and that had gained impressive successes in the early months of the contest.

Nor did Lee's choice of strategy run counter to the wishes of his government. On June 8, 1863, after summarizing to Secretary of War James A. Seddon the many advantages to be gained from an offensive into Pennsylvania, Lee concluded, "Still, if the Department thinks it better to remain on the defensive, and guard as far as possible all the avenues of approach, and await the time of the enemy, I am ready to adopt this course. You have only . . . to inform me." Two days later, Seddon replied, "I concur entirely in your views of the importance of aggressive movements by your army. Indeed, in my present judgment, such action is indispensable to our safety and independence, and all attendant sacrifices and risks must be incurred. I steadily urge and sustain this view."[58]

Most decidedly, the offensive was also the strategy consistently urged and sustained by the Confederate president. Lee knew, when he entered field command, that Jefferson Davis expected him to go on the offensive to save Richmond and to reclaim Virginia. He also knew Davis was ready for even wider applications of the offensive, if the opportunities presented themselves. Whatever was said between the two in conversations in the spring of 1862, when their offices had been within easy walking distance of each other, cannot now be known. Davis's steady support of aggressive campaigns, however, throughout the Confederacy and throughout the war, as well as his unvarying sustenance of Lee's own offensives, strongly suggests the two agreed on the question from the start.

"I readily perceive the disadvantage of standing still," Davis wrote to Lee on the eve of the Gettysburg campaign, "and sorely regret that I cannot give you the means which would make it quite safe to attempt all we desire." The same letter makes clear that Davis's commitment to the consistent use of the offensive derived from a view similar to Lee's of the necessities arising out of severely imbalanced odds. "That any advantage,"

Davis went on, "should have been lost by delay is sad enough where the contest at best was so very unequal as to give little room for the exercise of what General Charles Lee called 'that rascally virtue,' prudence."[59]

Lee's choice of the offensive also reflected what he—and other Southern generals as well—believed to be the realities of the war that had emerged by early 1862. The passive defense, no matter how skillfully conducted, forfeited initiative to the foe, or, in other words, it allowed the enemy to control the time, the place, and the manner of the fighting.[60] Whatever that might mean in the abstract theory of the textbook, in this war and against McClellan, it meant Southern defeat by siege techniques constructed by the enemy's superior engineering and supported by its unmatchable heavy artillery. As Joseph Johnston had warned exactly one month before his wounding, the Confederates could "compete . . . in neither" and could not hope to win the war "while McClellan is allowed . . . to choose his mode of warfare."[61] This precisely was Lee's view. In his June 5 letter to Davis in which he wrote favorably of Jackson's offer to enter Maryland and "change the character of the war," Lee went on to warn, "McClellan will make this a battle of posts. He will take position from position under cover of his heavy guns, & we cannot get at him without storming his works, which with our new troops is extremely hazardous." To Lee the conclusion was obvious: "It will require 100,000 men to resist the regular siege of Richmond, which would probably only prolong not save it."[62]

Lee chose the offense because he wanted to win the war, and he thought it offered the only chance. He believed the defensive was the sure path to defeat.

On first consideration, it may seem curious that Lee dismissed out of hand a defensive strategy. After all, the few advantages commonly conceded to the defense were of the very sort to yield the "easy fighting" that Lee sought. Almost always, the army on the defensive needed fewer troops, suffered lighter casualties, and consumed fewer supplies. Because the husbanding of Confederate resources was critical to protracting the war, it might seem that Lee ought to have been attracted to any system of operations that promised such benefits.

The fatal flaw in this thinking is the confusion between strategic and tactical operations. Without doubt, the tactical defense is superior to the tactical offense under certain conditions. If the defender is allowed to choose strong ground and is able to induce the enemy to attack prepared positions, the defense will either win the battle or, at the least, inflict severe punishment on the offense. Even here, however, the enemy must be willing to play an assigned role. If the offense refuses to make open field assaults, and instead resorts to siege operations, then the advantages of the defense dwindle to insignificance. If, in addition, the offense possesses superiority in engineering and artillery, then the tactical defensive, as Lee perceived, actually becomes a disadvantage.

On the level of strategy, the defensive offered no benefit whatsoever in husbanding resources. On the contrary, in the absence of a Maginot Line or a Chinese Great Wall to confront the foe along the entire frontier, the strategic defense could not avoid abandoning large chunks of territory to the enemy. Lost with the territory would be all of the defender's resources in manpower, food, and raw materials. For a nation successfully to pursue a strategy of defense it needed a large, rich heartland into which it could withdraw. Unfortunately for the South, its heart was located on its frontier.

When Lee took field command, defensive operations on both the tactical and strategic levels were bankrupt. By June 1, 1862, McClellan had already made the Civil War "a battle of posts," and his offensive strategy was utilizing Federal naval, artillery, and engineering superiority to their full advantage. The Union armies were steadily and not all that slowly driving the Confederates beyond their resources for sustaining a protracted war.

Once Lee became the commander directly responsible for the Eastern theater, he believed that two immediate objectives were clear and inescapable. First, he must prevent the capture of Richmond. Second, he must restore Confederate control over as much of Virginia east of the Alleghenies as possible. There was no way to accomplish either goal save going on the strategic offensive. Implicit in his decision was the assumption that once victorious he would need to continue to defend Richmond and the heart of Virginia for as long as the enemy continued its efforts against either. That aim would form the backbone of his strategy for three years.

Lee's intense concentration on Virginia has earned him the criticism of being parochial in outlook and blind to the importance of the Western theater.[63] This accusation is unfair. In the first place, the East unavoidably occupied nearly all of Lee's time and attention. Not only did he need to create and maintain an army and its support systems, but, because of the lack of useful maps, he also needed to learn the geography of his theater. On top of that, a series of Federal commanders made certain that Lee—even had he undertaken no initiatives of his own—received constant employment. Secondly, Lee had not found it possible to control the West from Richmond, and it is hard to imagine how he might have done so from the field. He knew—and could know—far less about the geography, conditions, and enemy strength and dispositions in the West than in his own theater. While in Richmond he had been able only to offer general advice and urge activity, and he continued to do this, although less frequently, from the field. He could do nothing more, short of crippling his own army by sending off reenforcements, or by taking field command in the West himself.[64]

The question as to whether the Eastern or Western theater was the most important is misdirected. Both Virginia and Tennessee were vital to the continued existence of the Confederacy, and each, if lost, opened the back door for the capture of the other. Nonetheless, it seems likely—as much as any such hypotheses can be—that the loss of Virginia would have led more quickly to the collapse of the Confederacy than the loss of any other area.

Conversely, no state was so vital to the prolonged existence of the Confederacy as the Old Dominion. Although Virginia was but one of the eleven states that made up the core of the Confederacy and covered less than 8 percent of its land surface, it held nearly one-third of its industry and nearly 20 percent of its population, banking capital, railroad mileage, and grain production. Virginia, particularly its north, east, and central regions, was both Ukraine and Ruhr River basin to the Confederacy.[65]

If manpower, food, manufactures, railroads, and wealth were not enough to make Virginia indispensable to the Confederacy, the state was also ideally located to derive maximum benefit from aggressive Confederate strategy. No other part of the Confederacy was so well situated to serve as a fulcrum for the support of military operations to frighten, frustrate, and exasperate the North.[66] First, the Northern capital perched precariously and vulnerably on Virginia's northeastern border. Second, the Shenandoah Valley—with its northeast to southwest axis tilting it away from Richmond—pointed directly toward the upper Potomac, Washington's flank, and the rich fields of central Pennsylvania that lay just beyond Maryland's narrow neck. So long as a Confederate army capable of taking the offensive operated in Virginia, the Federals were compelled to deploy a substantial portion of their troops to defend these two points.

Third, Lee knew and appreciated the strategic significance of the extreme sensitivity displayed by the Lincoln administration to any threat to the security of the Northern capital. All that was necessary in order to seize the initiative and force the enemy onto the defensive was to exert pressure on Washington, either directly in its front or on the upper Potomac. What Lee referred to as the "well known anxiety of the Northern Government for the safety of its capital," gave the Confederates a powerful lever in the Eastern theater.[67]

At the same time, Lee recognized that the absolute necessity to protect the Confederate capital was a millstone around his own neck. Richmond, as did Washington, held great symbolic importance for its nation. Although the seat of national government for only twelve months, the Virginia city on the James just as fully represented Confederate pretensions to nationhood as its counterpart on the Potomac reflected Federal determination to preserve the Union. Powerful political symbols impact on public morale in wartime and therefore exert a strong influence on military decisions. Jefferson Davis understood this when he wrote to Joseph Johnston in mid-May, "There is much manifestation of a determination that the ancient and honored capital of Virginia, now the seat of the Confederate Government, shall not fall into the hands of the enemy." To impress upon his army commander the political importance of the city, Davis added, "Many say rather let it be a heap of rubbish."[68]

Lee, too, appreciated Richmond's significance for morale. When the situation became so dire that Davis felt compelled to consider what options existed after the fall of the capital, the president called the general to speak at a cabinet meeting on where a new defensive line might be formed. After discussing military technicalities and naming the Staunton River for the next line, the usually reserved Lee went beyond his appointed topic to assert—with moistening eyes—"Richmond must not be given up; it shall not be given up."[69]

Unlike Washington, Richmond was much more than a symbol, and its reduction to a rubbish heap would have been a heavy blow to the Confederate ability to carry on the war. The loss of Washington would have embarrassed the North, especially with foreign nations, but the Federals could have enacted laws and directed military operations from Baltimore, Philadelphia, Harrisburg, or a dozen other cities. Had Richmond been merely the Confederate seat of government, its loss also could have been absorbed, and the capital shifted from town to town, as the colonists had done in the American Revolution.

Richmond, however, was important in ways that could not be shifted. It was the key to Lee's army's continued access to supplies.[70] No other city possessed its rail connections with the rest of the state or the remainder of the Confederacy—save Petersburg, and that town could not have been held had Richmond fallen. Lee testified to Davis and the cabinet that the next defensible line after the James was the Staunton (Roanoke) River, almost one hundred miles to the southwest.[71] The South had neither the materials or the expertise in the time available to convert Danville or Lynchburg, the two most likely options, into adequate rail centers.[72] Any substitute supply base would have been, in any case, just as susceptible to the siege methods of the enemy.

Even more, evacuation would have meant the sacrifice of Richmond's considerable manufacturing capacity. The factories of Henrico County, in which the city was located, excelled half of the eleven states of the Confederacy. Compared to Tennessee, it produced three-quarters as much flour and machinery and more iron products.[73] Richmond was as vital to Virginia as Virginia was to the Confederacy.

Unfortunately for Lee and his strategy, Richmond was as vulnerable as it was vital. The city was relatively secure only from the west. Although any overland threat from the north had to cross two major river systems, those same rivers were avenues for the Federal navy. From the south, Richmond was exposed to a hostile force based in North Carolina that could cut its communications with the rest of the Confederacy and move on Petersburg. And from the east three broad and almost indefensible approaches were open to a foe who controlled the water. First, the enemy could navigate the York River to West Point, within thirty-five miles of Richmond, where a railroad obligingly ran to the Southern capital. Or, using their established base at Fort Monroe, the Federals could advance up the Peninsula. Finally, the best approach of all was the James River, whose course carried it almost to the back porch of Jefferson Davis's White House.

McClellan had, of course, already availed himself of most of these opportunities. He had sent Burnside to North Carolina to pinch Richmond from the south, while his own army had moved up the Peninsula until it had uncovered the head of the York, from which river he now drew his supplies. From mid-May onward, after the evacuation of Norfolk and the destruction of the ironclad *Virginia*, Lee's greatest fear had been that McClellan would switch the Federal line of communications to the James. It was the enemy move that Lee most dreaded, and it would continue to haunt him through 1862 and 1863, until finally in June 1864 Grant's overland campaign hammered its way to City Point and turned his fear into reality. Until that time much of Lee's strategy was aimed at keeping the Federals away from the James.[74]

Lee made the offense the keystone in the grand design overarching his strategy to win Confederate independence. To him it must have seemed a choice so plain and obvious as not to be a choice at all. Only by going on the offensive could he seize and retain the initiative; could he control the time, place, and manner of the fighting; could he inflict maximum punishment on an enemy determined to use siege warfare; and could he hope to preserve Richmond and most of Virginia to sustain his army long enough for the enemy to tire of the war. McClellan's demonstrated intention to bring Federal superiority in engineering, artillery, and the navy fully to bear had robbed the strategic defense of any chance for success.

Lee's use of the offense was neither unique, nor even original in the Confederate conduct of the war. His contribution came in his understanding of what it would take to apply the offensive successfully to win independence. In the first instance, he became the warmest and most constant advocate of the concentration of Confederate forces into the two main field armies of the East and the West. Both armies needed the strength to undertake aggressive operations and to inflict severe punishment on the enemy. Troops scattered across the South in isolated garrisons contributed nothing beyond a false sense of security to local residents. In addition, Lee believed that Confederate concentration would compel the Federals to consolidate their own armies and thus relieve areas of the South away from the main theaters of fighting.[75]

Secondly, Lee consistently avoided planning too far in advance. In fact, he knew he could not. His operations must aim to take advantage of opportunities that the enemy provided or which he could create for himself, and neither could be foreseen. None of Lee's campaigns would be planned more than a month in advance, and some would be decided in hours. In consequence of his policy of flexible response, his success would be closely tied to the quality of his information about the enemy and the ability of his army to respond quickly.

Finally, Lee recognized the Confederacy possessed strengths that could overcome Federal superiority in navy, artillery, and engineering. He would change the character of the war by turning it away from these points of enemy preeminence and toward operations in which he stood a chance to compete on leveler ground. For two years, infantry, cavalry, and maneuvering would be Lee's trumps. He would carry the war into the open fields of Virginia and away from navigable rivers, labyrinthine fortifications, and the heaviest caliber of the enemy's guns. He would rely on his cavalry to screen his own movements and pierce the intentions of his opponents. He would demand that his infantrymen outmarch and outfight their foes.

The disparity in resources between the contestants predetermined that Lee would have scant margin for error in applying his grand strategy. It remained for him to find operational or campaign strategies that would accomplish all of his intricate aims and to execute them at a high level of proficiency.

They Ought Always to Be Turned

Although Robert E. Lee neither invented the offensive-defensive, nor inaugurated its use into Confederate strategy, his determination to pursue a consistently aggressive policy in which he seized and held the initiative and controlled operations in the war's main theater would indeed "change the character" of the contest. It also marked a turning point in the third phase of the Confederate struggle to gain independence. It may be doubted whether the South's renewed effort to mobilize and concentrate its military forces would have ever yielded more impressive results than Shiloh and Seven Pines, unless a field commander had emerged who had the skill to apply the strength at the right time and in the right places. In Lee's hands, the Army of Northern Virginia would come close, perhaps as near as it could come, to achieving protracted stalemate against the imbalanced odds it faced.

For the next two years, the Eastern theater would witness a remarkable contest of wills between Lee and a series of Federal commanders to determine whose offensives would dominate. The Federals would always possess a considerable theaterwide numerical edge. However, their inability to concentrate their forces sufficiently or, during most of the period, to achieve effective coordination would virtually nullify their advantage. There was a substantial difference in nature, moreover, between the offensives each side was trying to wage that inured to the benefit of the Confederacy. The Federals could not avoid undertaking a full-scale offensive of invasion. This meant they must operate in hostile country, protect a vulnerable supply line that lengthened with each mile advanced, and pin down and defeat the enemy's armies—all the while defending the hundred-mile front along the Potomac in their rear.

In his pursuit of the offensive-defensive, Lee clearly enjoyed certain advantages over his opponents. With but two exceptions, he would operate in his own country with easier access to supplies and information and with no worries about guerrilla activities threatening his lines of communication. Thus, he would be able to concentrate a larger proportion of his forces on the battlefield. He would also be able to undertake concealed movements with much greater likelihood of achieving surprise. Lee would not, on the other hand, invariably possess the advantage of interior lines, a benefit that almost always accrued to the passive defense. Strategically, he would possess interior lines so long as he continued to operate within his own country, but tactically, whether he possessed interior or exterior lines would depend entirely upon the configuration of the two armies at the time of battle.[76]

Relative strength would, of course, still be a concern. Yet, to carry out the offensive-defensive, Lee did not need the theaterwide superiority required by the Federals for their invasion. He needed only to achieve near equality, if not superiority, on the tactical level of the battlefield. Probably the greatest benefit of the initiative was that it allowed Lee to select the time and point of attack. Possession of this knowledge—which naturally was denied to the enemy—would permit him to use speed and maneuver to concentrate his strength against weak points of his foe. "It seems to me that we cannot afford to keep our troops awaiting possible movements of the enemy," Lee insisted, "but that our true policy is, as far as we can, so to employ our own forces as to give occupation to his at points of our selection."[77]

Lee's abstract description fits perfectly the definition of the campaign strategy commonly known as the turning movement. In this maneuver a commander sent all or part of his army on a wide sweep around the enemy to threaten a point so vital that the enemy had to respond to the danger. When successfully executed, the turning movement achieved exactly what Lee wanted. It compelled the foe to abandon a prepared position, which, entrenched or not, had been carefully selected for its topographical strength.

The progress of the war would make clear that Lee preferred maneuvering the enemy out of a chosen position over a frontal assault on prepared enemy lines. He frequently referred to the need to "bring out," "draw out," or "force out" the Federals into the open, where they might be struck while unprepared and off-balance.[78] "You are right in not attacking them in their strong positions," he would lecture Jackson in August of 1862. "They ought always to be turned as you propose, and thus force them on more favorable ground."[79] It is revealing that Lee's first recorded comments on campaign strategy, which came during the Richmond war council of July 14, 1861, alluded to the necessity "to draw the enemy further from his entrenchments, and, by lengthening, to weaken his line, which would give us a better chance of success."[80]

In theory, the turning movement could be employed to achieve three ends. Its sole purpose might be to compel the enemy to retreat and thereby forfeit whatever territory had been gained. Such a campaign could be virtually bloodless and certainly offered Lee the best prospect for "easy fighting." Lee rejected this use of the turning movement, however, because he believed it would not lead to the "heavy victories" he thought necessary to damage Federal morale. In another version, the object of the operation could be to seize and hold a threatening position and thus force the enemy to do the attacking. This option offered the advantages of the tactical defense. In effect, McClellan was currently employing this strategy before Richmond. The Confederates had the choice of either suffering the consequences of siege operations or of attacking entrenched lines. Lee would not reject this strategy, and, in fact, there are strong indications that this would be his aim for at least part of the Second Manassas campaign. The weakness of using the turning movement to go on the defensive was—as McClellan was about to discover—that it opened the door for an aggressive opponent to reclaim the initiative.

Lee would prefer to use the turning movement, whenever he had the opportunity and the resources, in its third form to press the offensive to its logical conclusion. He would want to retain the initiative by doing the attacking himself. His object was to render the enemy vulnerable and then to deliver the killing blow. Clearly, as friends and critics alike have perceived,

Lee never shied from battle. In fact, he believed giving battle necessary to inflict the maximum punishment on the Federals and to nurture their desire to quit. To create and sustain the impression of Confederate indomitability, Lee believed he must attack. Nonetheless, he wanted to give battle only under conditions favorable to his own army, conditions that would allow him to minimize his own losses. No strategy offered Lee more promise for "easy fighting and heavy victories" than the turning movement that ended in a crushing attack on the enemy.

During the war, two glaring contradictions in Lee's application of his turning strategy would appear: the bloody and futile frontal assaults on Malvern Hill during the Seven Days and on Cemetery Ridge at Gettysburg. Neither attack, however, was the object of its campaign, both of which were indeed turning movements. Nor was either attack even the opening gambit of battle; both were attempts by Lee to bring an ongoing battle to successful closure. In both instances, he believed the time to achieve a crushing victory was rapidly expiring and that the Federal army was vulnerable. In each case, he misjudged both the weakness of the enemy and the capabilities of his own army. In other words, Malvern Hill and Cemetery Ridge were tactical, not strategic mistakes.

After opposing armies became entangled and strategy gave way to tactics, a commander had but two ways to retain the initiative without making a frontal assault. He could break off the engagement and withdraw to start a new turning movement. This option did not appeal to Lee, although he did briefly contemplate it on the final day at Second Manassas. His wartime operations indicate he believed that once significant battle had occurred and substantial success had been obtained it was imperative to finish the fighting on the same field. If this practice sometimes got Lee into trouble, there were also instances, such as Second Manassas and Chancellorsville, to vindicate his belief in pressing his momentum.

The second way for an aggressive commander to avoid making a frontal assault was to launch a flank attack. At its most basic this operation involved nothing more complicated than attacking the enemy line on the side or in the rear at a point where it was unprepared for an assault. If the enemy obligingly exposed its own flank, as Pope would at Second Manassas, the flanking force would not even have to leave the position it held. Ordinarily, however, a flanking column marched in a narrow arc to a point where the enemy was vulnerable. Lee executed this tactic in its classic form to open the battle of Chancellorsville. He also attempted it on so many other occasions when the enemy foiled his execution, especially during the summer of 1862, as to demonstrate his partiality to the maneuver.

Although sometimes confused in identification, the turning movement and the flank attack have important differences. The turning movement was a strategic maneuver, and it might end successfully in an offensive battle, a defensive battle, or no battle at all. It needed to begin in stealth, so that the enemy would not have time to take countermeasures. But once the turning operation was launched, secrecy was not only unnecessary but self-defeating. The enemy needed to know a vital point was threatened in order to come out in the open and be attacked.

The flank attack was a tactical operation, which when successful always ended in battle. It needed to be concealed from the enemy until the moment the attack was launched. Also, it offered somewhat less promise for either "easy fighting" or "heavy victories." Although the attack was delivered against a weak point of the opponent, the remainder of the enemy army was near at hand and in a strong position.

Alone or in unison, the turning movement and the flank attack would provide the basis for all of Lee's greatest victories. These, and not his rare lapses, define his offensive-defensive strategy and tactics.

It is not certain, and probably can never be known, to what extent and in what combination, Lee's military operations were shaped by his education and reading, his past military experiences, and his personal character and predilections. Occasionally he made revealing comments about his aims and methods, but he never spoke or wrote, and perhaps he never asked himself, about where his ideas originated. Even Charles Marshall, Lee's amanuensis, was silent on the subject.

It is easy to recognize that Lee's ideas on strategy and tactics closely paralleled the teachings of Henri Jomini. The Swiss theorist had summarized his advice to generals into what he called the "fundamental principle of war," and which he expressed in four maxims. Two dealt with strategy and two with tactics. First, Jomini admonished, the general should maneuver to "throw" the "mass" of his army "upon the decisive points of a theater," and by that he meant those points where the most decisive results could be gained. He recommended as his prime example an operation against the communications of the enemy. Jomini recognized the simple truth that large armies consume huge quantities of food and other materials daily, and if their supplies are interrupted, or even threatened, an opposing commander has no choice but to react. Hence, an army occupying a strong, well-fortified defensive line, which would be costly if not futile to assault, could be forced to abandon its position by threatening its supply lines.

Second, once the enemy had been forced into the open, then the general should "maneuver to engage fractions of the hostile army with the bulk of one's forces." Third, after the armies closed for fighting, the commander should apply the same principles in tactics: he should direct his masses against both the decisive point on the field of battle and against fractions of the enemy. And, fourth, the general should undertake all of his operations "at the proper time and with energy."[81]

Clearly, what Lee attempted diverged little from what Jomini taught. Since there is no evidence that Lee ever referred to Jomini, however, it is impossible to know for certain whether he was influenced by Jomini's writings. After all, Jomini's lessons derived from an analysis of the campaigns of Napoleon, Frederick the Great, and other masters of military strategy, and anyone, including Lee, might read military history and independently draw similar conclusions. Moreover, even Jomini recognized that his advice incorporated obvious common sense.[82] No general need be a profound student of military science to appreciate the value of having favorable odds on his own side or to prefer open-field maneuvering to attacking an entrenched enemy or to expect that victory would more often result from attacking a weak position than a strong one.[83]

In addition, shaping Lee's life were influences larger than anything he might have read in books. In his case both experience and tradition were probably mightier than the printed page. How could he not have learned from his experiences in the Mexican War? As an engineer on Winfield Scott's staff, he had witnessed the success that might be gained by maneuvering, especially the effective use of the turning movement to neutralize superior enemy forces. In fact, Lee had personally scouted and discovered the routes for Scott's turning movements that led to the American victories at Cerro Gordo and Contreras. It was likely not coincidence that in his one offensive Civil War campaign prior to June 1862 Lee had attempted at Cheat Mountain a turning movement similar to the one at Cerro Gordo.[84]

As well, any explanation of Lee must also make allowance for the power of tradition. He was, after all, the son of Revolutionary War general Henry "Light Horse Harry" Lee. Although his father's life ended tragically in debt-enforced exile, the paternal legacy was more positive than otherwise. Against heavy odds, Henry Lee successfully led the cavalry of Nathaniel Greene's army in the southern campaign, he served as governor of Virginia, and he uttered the most famous of all epitaphs for George Washington. Son Robert, during the last year of his own life, would write a brief introductory biography for the reprinting of his father's military memoirs.[85]

Connections there were also with the most revered American general, he who had perservered through enemy superiority and numerous defeats to become father of his country. It was impossible to walk the streets of Alexandria, Virginia, where Lee spent much of his youth, without encountering the ghost of Washington at every corner. Later, Lee married Mary Custis, the great-granddaughter of Martha Washington and the heiress of the Arlington plantation.

On April 23, 1861, the dual strands of the tradition came together in a strikingly dramatic moment. John Janney, president of the Virginia secession convention, tendered the command of the state's forces to Lee in an address that paraphrased the famous epitaph by Henry Lee: "'First in war' your fellow citizens hereby make you. Now it is your charge to become 'first in peace' and 'first in the hearts of your countrymen.'"[86] The words were from Robert's father, and the summons was to take Washington's mantle.

Education, experience, and tradition contributed to Lee's molding. Napoleon, Scott, Washington, and Henry Lee stood as models. But in the end, the whole was something very different from these parts. Robert E. Lee was sui generis.

It is ironic that Lee had to be demoted to gain a position from which his great talents could influence the course of the war. From his eyrie as general-in-chief he nudged and prodded far-flung subordinates who frequently ignored his suggestions. From the back of Traveller—or, in the case of the Maryland campaign, from an ambulance—he carried the Confederacy as near to final victory as the stubborn, unrelenting determination of the North would allow.

CHAPTER THREE

— ✤ —

"How do we get at those people?"
Lee's Strategy in the Seven Days Campaign,
June 1–July 2, 1862

O N JUNE 2, Lee's first full day in the field, he found the time to write to his daughter-in-law, Charlotte, to reassure her that her husband (and his own son) Rooney had survived the Battle of Seven Pines unharmed. There is more than a tinge of pathos to the letter, which reveals how keenly Lee felt the strain of his personal situation. All three of his sons were now in Confederate uniform, and at the moment he had heard nothing about the well-being of his wife, who remained behind enemy lines at Marlbourne plantation on the Pamunkey River. The letter also makes clear Lee grasped that the fate of his country had descended directly on his shoulders. Alluding to the wounded Joseph Johnston, Lee wrote in a much-quoted phrase, "I wish his mantle had fallen on an abler man."[1]

Less often quoted is the remainder of the same sentence, "or that I were able to drive our enemies back to their homes." Lee was displaying not merely modesty, therefore, but equally determination. While he had not sought the heavy burden, neither did he shy from the full dimensions of the role now his. If the Confederacy were to survive the summer, he must turn back the military tide that ebbed so perilously low. What is most impressive is the rapidity with which he devised and executed a campaign that did just that. Twenty-six days after taking command, he launched his attack. And, in exactly one month, he wrote a new chapter in Confederate military history on the gathering of intelligence, the concentration of troops, and the coordination of divided columns. That Lee did not accomplish all he intended derived from his attempting too much.

Lee Plans to Turn McClellan, June 1–16

There was close agreement among Confederates on how *not* to respond to the quandary posed by McClellan. It was obvious, as Jefferson Davis wrote forcefully to his wife, "We must find if possible the means to get at him without putting the breasts of our men in antagonism to his heaps of earth."[2] And none dissented from cavalry commander Jeb Stuart's plaintive appeal to "Let us fight at advantage before we are forced to fight at disadvantage."[3] On these points Lee needed no advice. He was among the first to record the view that McClellan's use of siege techniques would likely result in the capture of Richmond but that "storming his works . . . with our new troops" would be "extremely hazardous."[4] When it came to a specific plan to escape the dilemma, however, the little that he heard was contradictory. While Stuart urged an attack on the enemy's southern flank, James Longstreet recommended the northern. Some, such as the reserve artillery chief, William Pendleton, feared it would be necessary to choose between "protecting Richmond and beating McClellan, because it would not be possible to accomplish both."[5] In the end, the new commander was left to find his own solution.

From the start of his search, Lee sought a plan that would force the Federals out into the open where he could destroy them but that would not at the same time expose his own army to the risk of unacceptable losses. Once he had gathered sufficient information, as might be expected, he would look to a turning movement, rather than a flank attack, to accomplish this aim.

Lee recognized two weaknesses in the Federal position that he might develop to advantage. The more obvious but less important was the split in the Federal forces occasioned since mid-May by McClellan's approach to Richmond with his army astride the Chickahominy River. It was this fracture of the enemy that Johnston had tried to exploit by assailing the left wing of the Army of the Potomac at Seven Pines and Fair Oaks. Johnston had attacked frontally, however, relying for victory on surprise and McClellan's inability to bring reenforcements across the rain-swollen river. Lee was not dissuaded by the failure, which he somewhat sharply referred to as the "experiment" at Seven Pines. He believed that battle had been fought in the wrong way and at the wrong place. He did not like frontal assaults at any time, but he especially thought it wrong to initiate a battle by attacking the enemy lines directly.[6]

Moreover, Seven Pines had proven Federal engineering equal to the challenge presented by the Chickahominy. Under the worst circumstances, enough men and guns had been crossed over the river to meet the crisis. The separation of the Federal army was a weakness in its position, but it did not mean that either wing was cut off or isolated from the other. The river was more than an annoyance but less than a crippling disability for McClellan. Still, Lee was sufficiently interested in keeping the enemy's forces split that one of his first actions was to move Confederate lines somewhat farther out from Richmond and to strengthen his position near New Bridge so that McClellan could not easily unite the Federal army.[7]

More to the point, Lee believed Johnston had tried to pick up the wrong end of the stick. Lee was much more interested in the situation north of the Chickahominy, which he recognized constituted the greatest weakness in the Federal position. He did not not think that the enemy's northern wing was either weaker or more exposed than the southern, and indeed it was neither. The Federal right wing ran at nearly a ninety-degree angle north from the river and was heavily entrenched at Beaver Dam Creek with strong outposts thrown forward to Mechanicsville. McClellan had, in effect, refused the flank of his line, and until June 19 it was manned by a division of William Franklin's Sixth Corps as well as Fitz-John Porter's entire Fifth Corps, or about 30 percent of the Army of the Potomac.[8] Nor did Lee have any reason to believe that the Chickahominy isolated the Federal right wing to any great Confederate tactical advantage. In order to attack Porter and defend Richmond at the same time, Lee's own army would be divided by the same river. He would also have to operate on an exterior and longer line. McClellan would be able to shuttle troops back and forth across the Chickahominy quicker and more easily than would Lee.

The weakness Lee saw was not tactical but strategic. McClellan's supply line ran by water up the York River to West Point—where the river became the Pamunkey—and thence to the plantation owned by Rooney and Charlotte Lee, the White House. At this point the ships were unloaded and the supplies hauled by wagon or rail fifteen miles to field depots in the immediate rear of the army. Exposed to attack from the northwest, the Federal supply line was made doubly vulnerable by the wretched roads that Lee knew rendered McClellan almost wholly dependent on the Richmond and York River Railroad. By operating north of the river, therefore, the Confederates could undertake a turning movement that would "bring McClellan out" into the open to defend his communications. In addition, any move made from the west would be the most efficient way to employ Jackson's army from the Shenandoah Valley. Here Lee benefited inestimably from his expanded, theaterwide command. It is difficult to imagine what plan he could have evolved had he not enjoyed broader authority than had ever been granted Joseph Johnston. Unlike his predecessor, he was able to apply Jackson to the equation in solving the problem of relieving the capital.[9]

Lee knew also that he must complete his plans and launch his campaign as soon as possible, because the Federals could take a number of counteractions that would diminish the usefulness of a turning movement, if not render it altogether impractical. First, McClellan might extend his entrenchments northward and more fully cover his communications. In particular, this might occur if McDowell or other reenforcements arrived overland for his support. Second, McClellan might cross his entire army to the south bank of the Chickahominy, and Lee had personally observed Federal engineering operations that made him believe this likely.[10] This move—which in fact McClellan was planning—would actually lengthen the exposed Federal supply line, but it would also greatly increase the miles that any turning column from the main army in front of Richmond would have to travel to threaten, let alone break, the Federals' communications. Even if Lee were to rely wholly on Jackson, the Confederate forces would be more dangerously split than McClellan's.[11]

Third, McClellan might abandon the line to the York River and start to draw his supplies from the James. This was Lee's greatest fear; for if McClellan switched to the James, the Federal army might march directly into the heart of Richmond with virtually invulnerable communications. Lee, Davis, and Johnston had been sorely aware of the danger from this direction since mid-May, when Federal gunboats first appeared at Drewry's Bluff.[12] In response the Confederates had been able to spare only a small brigade under Henry Wise, augmented by a few troops from Holmes's Department of North Carolina, and to start construction of river batteries. No adequate defense could be prepared in the foreseeable future. To compound the danger, Lee came to worry that the Federals would bring Ambrose Burnside's corps from North Carolina to advance on the south side of the James.[13]

Hence, understanding the need for relative haste, Lee determined the basic elements of his first campaign—a turning movement against McClellan's communications that would in some manner make use of Jackson's forces in the Valley—as early as June 5, three days after he took command. The tactical details of the operation would not come so easily, however, and would have to evolve through several phases during the next twenty days.

Even while Lee was in the preliminary stages of developing his turning movement, a tantalizing option diverted him. On June 4 a civilian emissary from Jackson arrived with an enticing suggestion. According to Congressman Alexander Boteler, Jackson would undertake to cross the Potomac and invade Maryland and Pennsylvania, if the Valley army's 16,000 men could be strengthened to 40,000.[14] Lee immediately understood that such a move might compel the Federals to suspend or even abandon their offensive operations against Richmond. He also may have liked the plan because it promised to deliver battle at a distance from the Confederate capital and thereby minimize the consequences of a defeat. Interestingly, the plan was a land-based, reverse-image reflection of McClellan's Peninsula strategy. It was also at least the fourth time a serious plan was proposed to cross the Potomac.

Jefferson Davis's initial response to an interview with Boteler, which may have come before conferring with Lee, was skepticism. On the 4th, the president wrote to Jackson, "Were it practicable to send to you re-enforcements it should be done."[15] Nonetheless, Davis never had and did not at this time entertain any qualms about setting foot on enemy soil "to teach him the pains of invasion and to feed our army on his territory."[16] Thus he would be open to persuasion from Lee.

"After much reflection," Lee wrote to the president on June 5, "I think if it was possible to reinforce Jackson, it would change the character of the war."[17] Considering the panic created by Jackson's approach to Harpers Ferry just two weeks before, it was reasonable to assume that his entering Pennsylvania might cause such terror as to compel the Lincoln administration to recall many of its far-flung forces to defend its capital. Lee argued that Georgia and North and South Carolina should be stripped of troops to support Jackson's offensive, because "it would call all the enemy from our Southern coast and liberate those states."

Lee did not offer to send Jackson any troops from the army at Richmond. Indeed, he did not see Jackson's proposed offensive as a substitute for his own turning movement. He viewed it only as an alternative use of Jackson's force to help relieve pressure on Richmond. Lee could not assume that Jackson's movement alone would be enough to force the enemy to abandon its position on the Chickahominy. Hence, he continued to plan for his own "diversion to bring McClellan out" of his entrenchments. Unfortunately, the full burden of dislodging McClellan would now fall entirely on Lee's Army of Northern Virginia. His army must provide both the turning column and the force to defend Richmond, and its strength would also be diminished by not receiving the reenforcements from the deep south sent to Jackson instead.[18]

Lee's advocacy apparently persuaded Davis, because the War Department set about the task of trying to find the 24,000 troops to send to the Valley. To Lee's regret, it was quickly discovered that such a large force for such a distant mission could not be raised in the requisite period of time, unless it were detached from his own army. There were enough regiments in the south Atlantic states, but some, such as those in the Charleston area, would take time to pry from the grip of local authorities; others, such as those from Holmes's Department of North Carolina, might be nudged as far as Richmond for the defense of the capital, but they were not available for more distant fields so long as the threat from Burnside continued. In the end, only a large brigade of Georgia troops under Alexander Lawton could be found to send to Jackson.[19]

In any event, Jackson's offer to cross the Potomac—which he had conceived on May 30, while at Harpers Ferry and within three miles of that river—did not stand very long. By June 6 the Federals had chased him ninety miles south to Port Republic, deep in the Shenandoah Valley, and the armies of Frémont and Shields were closing in on his front. On that date, Jackson reported to Richmond he had for the present exhausted his opportunities in the Valley. He intended to rest and drill the troops and offered to come east to cooperate against McClellan. When Lee saw Jackson's letter on June 8, he realized the window of opportunity for a thrust into Maryland and Pennsylvania had closed and endorsed it with the observation, "If General Jackson . . . cannot undertake offensive opera-tions . . . re-enforcements will be lost on him."[20]

Returning perforce to his original plan, Lee wrote to Jackson on the 8th, "Should there be nothing requiring your attention in the Valley so as to prevent your leaving it a few days, . . . please let me know, that you may unite at the decisive moment with this army near Richmond." Neverthe-less, as Lee made clear, Jackson was not to pass up an opportunity "for striking the enemy a successful blow."[21] On that very same day, of course, Jackson had started the maneuvering that would lead to his double victory over Frémont and Shields at Cross Keys and Port Republic. The next morn-ing, June 9, a telegram reporting Jackson's preliminary success restored Lee's hope that Stonewall would still be able to undertake a limited offen-sive to hurt the enemy before marching east against McClellan.[22]

Impelled by an increasing sense of urgency, Lee did not wait for the mili-tary situation in the Valley to become clearer before he crystallized his own thinking. On June 10 he sent an outline of his campaign strategy to the president for approval. He would send "two good brigades" from the Army of Northern Virginia, which with Lawton, would make Jackson "strong enough to wipe out Frémont." While this was occurring, Lee could "hold McClellan in his present position for a week or ten days," and addi-tional troops could be collected from the South. Then, Jackson "would move rapidly to Ashland," a station on the Richmond, Fredericksburg, and Potomac Railroad about twelve miles northwest of the enemy's entrench-ments at Beaver Dam Creek. Here Jackson would be joined by fresh reenforcements from Richmond and, wrote Lee, would "sweep down north of the Chickahominy, cut up McClellan's communications and rear, while I attack in front."[23]

Although the maneuver Lee described resembled a pincer movement, by including a column from the Army of Northern Virginia and by aim-ing to threaten the enemy's communications it was still a classic turning movement. "I think this is our surest move," he wrote; "McClellan will not move out of his intrenchments unless forced, which this must ac-complish." And, as if it were a truth that could not too often be repeated, he added, "it will hazard too much, with our inferior numbers, to attack him in them."

Two observations can be made on Lee's campaign strategy when viewed in its embryonic stage. First, if the second wave of reenforcements were to join Jackson at Ashland, then Lee was seemingly content at this early phase of his thinking for the turning column to be out of touch with the main body for the entire operation. Second, his statement "while I attack in front" is enigmatic. Lee probably wanted to weaken McClellan's response to the threat from the rear and also to prevent the Federal commander from seizing the initiative by moving toward Richmond. Still, it is not clear at this point how Lee believed he could accomplish this without storming the much-dreaded Federal entrenchments, as he had repeatedly stated he did not wish to do.

Lee made one point in particular very plain, however: the need for haste. "Please consider this immediately and decide," he urged Davis. "It must be commenced tonight." If the president approved, he was requested to order the railroad transportation for Lawton's brigade at once.

Lee received nearly instantaneous approval.[24] The following day, June 11, he took three decisive steps to set his campaign in motion. In language that closely paralleled that of his proposal to Davis, he sent general instructions to Jackson to "crush" the Federals in the Valley and then hasten secretly to Ashland and "sweep down between the Pamunkey and the Chickahominy" to cut the communications of the enemy, while the Richmond army attacked from the front.[25] Lee also selected W. H. C. Whiting with two brigades to reenforce Jackson by rail via Charlottesville.[26]

Then, turning to another pressing problem, Lee decided the time had come to gain more precise information about the right wing and rear of McClellan's army. He had just received news the night before that suggested "there is a stronger force on the enemy's right than was previously reported."[27] He needed to know how far north toward the Pamunkey the enemy line extended and the strength of any forces McClellan had posted in the rear to protect communications with White House.

Lee issued orders, therefore, for his cavalry chief, Jeb Stuart, "to make a secret movement to the rear of the enemy . . . with a view of gaining intelligence of his operations, communications, &c.," which would provide "guidance of future operations." Lee apparently intended the reconnaissance to penetrate to the vicinity of Old Church on the Mechanicsville Turnpike, some five miles in McClellan's rear, and his instructions abounded in cautionary advice. Stuart was to leave sufficient cavalry behind to protect the main army; he was to take only the strongest men and horses and "to save and cherish" those he did take; and, he was to guard carefully the secrecy of his movements. Curiously, considering the need to avoid alerting McClellan to Confederate interest in Federal communications, Lee ordered Stuart to attack wagon trains and collect grain and cattle, and he did not limit in number the size of the cavalry force to be employed.[28]

On June 15 Stuart returned from an excessively noisy raid in which he had carried twelve hundred troopers within three miles of the White House, cut the Richmond and York River Railroad, and ridden a complete circle around McClellan's army. His written report contained no intelligence information of value and made the somewhat naive and counterproductive boast that his "success . . . will no doubt cause 10,000 or 15,000 men to be detached from the enemy's main body to guard his communication. . . ." Stuart's conduct raises the question of whether Lee had made clear and whether Stuart had understood the true aim of the mission. Nevertheless, Lee must have received orally the valuable information he sought. After Stuart's ride, he seems to have been satisfied that the Federal line did not extend too far to the north, and there were no substantial forces in the enemy's rear to protect the supply line to the White House.[29]

Lee received other information on June 15 that caused him to modify his evolving plans, but on the whole simplified his situation. In a dispatch from Jackson, which was a week-old response to Lee's first proposal of joint action, Lee learned that Stonewall advised against further offensive operations in the Valley for the present, but the current inactivity of his opponents would enable him to slip away to join in the move against McClellan.[30] On June 16 Lee acknowledged to Jackson there was probably no longer time for a new offensive in the Valley and that "the sooner you unite with this army the better." Lee knew that part of McDowell's corps had joined McClellan, and he also reported it as fact that Burnside had arrived. This news reawakened Lee's fears that McClellan might increase protection of Federal communications and, as well, be preparing a move on Richmond from the James River. He closed by suggesting a meeting with Jackson.[31]

By June 16, therefore, Lee possessed the general outline of a plan for a turning movement that would force the enemy out of its entrenchments to defend its communications. Having also gained new reasons for quickly launching the plan, Lee turned to filling in its tactical details and completing preparations in two other areas necessary to make his strategy more likely to succeed: the security of Richmond and the accumulation of maximum strength for his army.

Lee Concentrates His Army

Lee's campaign strategy courted many risks, but its greatest weakness came from its simplest problem: Lee did not have enough men. The field army he inherited from Johnston was too small to undertake simultaneously all that he hoped to accomplish. He could not—all at once—send reenforcements to Jackson in the Valley; augment Jackson's column for the turning movement after it reached Ashland; mount a frontal assault south of the Chickahominy; and provide adequate defense of Richmond against any possible countermoves McClellan might make, especially from the James River. Hence, even before he had settled the details of time and place, or decided upon the units he would use in his offensive, he set about finding ways to increase the size of his army.

Where once Lee had been a tepid supporter of concentration, he now became its warmest advocate. His perspective from the field convinced him the Confederacy could not fight the war only with pawns or it would lose them all, one by one. Seeing no alternative, he confronted this politically sensitive issue squarely, and he achieved one of his most remarkable victories. By using his dual position as general-in-chief and commander of the armies in North Carolina and eastern Virginia and by exerting all of his influence with Davis, he was able to achieve what Joseph Johnston had desperately wanted but failed to obtain. Lee successfully collected a vast force for the defense of Richmond, including the largest army the Confederacy ever put into the field. Although Lee's success owed much to his own determined actions, it came also in part because the timing was right.

Joseph Johnston had called repeatedly for concentration throughout his tenure of command, and, as late as the middle of April, his bid to gather troops from other regions of the South lay at the heart of his strategy for launching a column north across the Potomac to relieve pressure on the capital. For several reasons, the government had all but ignored his request. For one thing, it was too early to take advantage of the new men the April Conscription Act was just beginning to bring into the service. For another, both Davis and Lee at that time viewed McClellan's army before Yorktown as but one of the serious threats posed by the Federals in the Eastern theater. They were paying considerable if not equal attention to McDowell at Fredericksburg, Burnside in North Carolina, and Hunter on the South Carolina coast. Lee had even rationalized that the confined boundaries of the Peninsula afforded Johnston opportunities for a smaller force to bottle up a larger one. Not until the first of May did Johnston finally convince his superiors that he could no longer hold Yorktown against the artillery, engineering, and navy of the enemy, and, furthermore, that McClellan would successfully employ the same siege techniques to capture Richmond.

Only after the fall of Yorktown, the evacuation of Norfolk, and Johnston's retreat to the outskirts of Richmond, did both Davis and Lee finally make an effort to obtain troops from the south Atlantic coast. At first they could shake nothing loose from states panicked by invasions of their own shorelines and already demanding reenforcements. On May 12 and 13 Lee wrote to the Department of South Carolina and Georgia and to the Department of North Carolina, "Such is the pressure in Virginia that it has become necessary to concentrate our forces as much as possible, in order to be enabled successfully to meet the heavy columns of the enemy in their attempt to advance on Richmond. . . ."[32] In spite of the urgency of Lee's language, his appeal yielded the limited net result of but one brigade that arrived in time for the attack at Seven Pines.[33] Small wonder Johnston would still complain to Lee on the very eve of the offensive, "I have more than once suggested a concentration here of all available forces."[34]

On May 31, when Johnston opened his attack to save the capital, the Confederate field army comprised the divisions of Longstreet, Smith, and D. R. Jones from the Department of Northern Virginia; the divisions of McLaws and Magruder from the Army of the Peninsula; Huger's division from Norfolk; and A. P. Hill's newly constituted division from the forces in the Hanover Junction area, which had been watching McDowell at Fredericksburg. These seven divisions contained, in rounded figures, 129 regiments of all arms and represented only 22 percent of the 577 regiments the Confederacy then had in the field.[35] Thus constituted, Johnston's army totaled about 74,000 men present for duty.[36] In confronting the 92,000 men of the Army of the Potomac, he faced odds of 4 to 5.[37] Although this ratio was significantly better than the 3 to 4 overall odds the Confederacy would be able to achieve in its renewed mobilization efforts during the third phase, it did not give Johnston even the slight edge that an attacking army was supposed to enjoy over its opponent.

Jefferson Davis would do everything within his power to ensure that Lee's odds would be more favorable. His June 1 order giving Lee command of the "armies in Eastern Virginia and North Carolina" meant the general would have immediate and direct control over the thirty-three regiments and 22,048 men present for duty in Holmes's Department of North Carolina, as well as the nineteen regiments (11,288) in the Department of Henrico for the defense of Richmond and the thirty-five regiments (15,904) of Stonewall Jackson in the Shenandoah Valley.[38] In case any question existed about Lee's authority over the latter, on June 3 the president had specifically recommended to Lee that Jackson be brought to Richmond.

Nor did Davis limit his efforts to the mid-Atlantic theater. On June 2, in a telegram to John Pemberton in Charleston that trumpeted, "General Lee is in the field," he exerted the power of the presidency to shake troops loose from South Carolina and Georgia. "Need re-enforcements," the telegram continued, "Can you give them? Decisive operations pending here. . . ."[39] The appeal, which was seconded by Secretary of War Randolph and Lee himself, met with even more than the customary resistance. The governor and council of South Carolina passed an official resolution declaring that only "extreme necessity will justify a further withdrawal of any more troops from this State." The acting mayor of Savannah begged the president not "to leave us at the mercy of the enemy." And Pemberton, who commanded the Department of South Carolina and Georgia, magnified each movement of the enemy on his coast into a major offensive about to be launched against him, warning Davis at one point that further reduction of his force would compel him to abandon either Savannah or Charleston.[40]

Such resistance necessarily caused delay, and far fewer troops from the two states reached Lee in time for his offensive than should have. Still, eight Georgia and two South Carolina regiments would arrive in time; and, just as importantly, the machinery for concentration was set in motion, so that reenforcements would continue to come forward in July and August.[41] Also, in the next several weeks, Davis, Randolph, Lee, and Adj. Gen. Samuel Cooper carried the search for regiments as far away as Florida, Alabama, and Mississippi. Their efforts gathered only two regiments immediately, but four others would soon follow.[42] And, naturally Lee used his direct control over the Department of North Carolina to shift as many troops from that state as he safely could in view of the continuing threat from Burnside. He accomplished this by moving Holmes's regiments in several stages to Petersburg and Drewry's Bluff, where they were centrally located to guard the James, to return to North Carolina in an emergency, or to be rushed to the Chickahominy at the last moment. In this way, Lee was able to utilize three brigades of seventeen regiments, or almost half of the forces in Holmes's department.[43]

As a result of these efforts, by June 26 Lee commanded the largest army ever assembled in the Confederacy. He achieved this by integrating the defensive forces in the Department of Henrico into Johnston's army; by calling Jackson from the Valley; by transferring half of Holmes's men from North Carolina; and by scraping together a division-sized force from South Carolina, Georgia, Alabama, and Mississippi. More regiments were on the way from these states, and Florida as well, but he chose not to wait for them, fearing the favorable opportunity to strike McClellan might slip away in the meantime.

Nonetheless, as a result of less than a month's work, a Confederate force of 112,220 present for duty in 215 regiments of all arms could now be brought to bear on McClellan's 101,444 men. And this time, when the offensive was launched, the odds would favor the South 11.2 to 10.1.[44] If the edge were not great, the change in balance was certainly impressive. Even more remarkable, for this great battle to determine the fate of Richmond and whether the war would be short or long, the Confederacy gathered 9.4 percent of its total pool of white males aged eighteen to forty-five for Lee's army—a proportion more than four times greater than the 2.3 percent assigned by the North to McClellan's Army of the Potomac.[45]

Lee Wrestles with Grand Tactics, June 4–24

Lee adopted the strategy of a turning movement within days of assuming field command, but he took nearly three weeks to decide finally on the grand tactics of the operation that determined which forces he would employ and where and how they would be used. During the period, he apparently changed his mind several times. In his original version, which amounted almost to a double turning movement, he considered using Jackson to mount a major offensive in the Shenandoah Valley to panic Washington into weakening McClellan's army by detachments. At the same time, Lee intended to employ part of his forces at Richmond to pin down the Army of the Potomac and with the other part to create a diversion to force McClellan out of the entrenchments where he could be destroyed. It was during this earliest phase of his thinking that Lee recognized the value of field entrenchments for his own army and set Confederate soldiers to digging.

As early as June 3 Lee ordered his chief engineer, Walter Stevens, "to make an examination of the country in the vicinity of the line which" the Confederate army occupied, "with a view of ascertaining the best position in which we may fight a battle or resist the advance of the enemy." Lee further directed "the commanding points on this line" be prepared for artillery and "the whole line strengthened by such artificial defenses as time and opportunity may permit. My object," he continued, "is to make use of every means in our power to strengthen ourselves and to enable us to fight the enemy to the best advantage." But he made clear he did not intend "to construct a continuous line of defense or to erect extensive works." Having started this first set of entrenchments, Stevens was ordered "to resume the examination and see what other positions can be taken nearer Richmond in case of necessity."[46]

Manual labor was new to the Army of Northern Virginia, and it was unwelcome to many who viewed such work as beneath their station and entirely outside their duties as warriors. Lee had to create a "pioneer corps" of three hundred men and nine officers from each division to "throw up earthworks, dig rifle pits, and construct lines of abatis." It was also necessary for him to collect the spades, shovels, picks, and axes for their use.[47] Clearly, Lee only intended to create light field works of the kind that both armies later in the war would instinctively throw up each night when camped near the enemy. He was not digging in for a prolonged defense or to resist a siege. Jefferson Davis understood "that reviled policy of West Pointism and spades," as he put it sardonically, was necessary to Lee's success.[48] Many in and outside of the army misperceived this, however, and referred disparagingly to the new commander as "Granny" or "Spades" Lee.[49]

History has more correctly recognized that Lee's primary aim was to be able to hold Richmond with a minimum force and make available additional troops for his "diversion."[50] But Lee set his army to digging for another reason as well. It was a means to introduce a greater degree of discipline into the Confederate army. Lee appreciated, as did Jomini, the value of "inuring armies to labor and fatigue" in order "to maintain a high military spirit." Lee observed "the enemy working like beavers," both "day and night," and it worried him that "our people are opposed to work." He wrote to Davis, "Nothing is so military as labour, & nothing so important to an army as to save the lives of its soldiers."[51]

Lee's comments on discipline underscore a point sometimes forgotten. After the war, Lt. Col. Robert Chilton would claim with manifest exaggeration that Lee had inherited an "armed mob." Chilton was nearer the mark when he characterized the Army of Northern Virginia as a collection of *"undisciplined individuality."* In describing the condition of the army after Seven Pines, he recalled, "It was extremely wasteful, little observant of the relations which should exist between commanders and the commanded, and absenteeism without proper authority, prevailed largely amongst both officers and soldiers, which greatly reduced effective strength."[52]

Lee soon stamped his own character on the Army of Northern Virginia. Wasteful behavior gave way to habitual hoarding during the lean days of hard campaigning that lay ahead. The informal relations between officers and men—which perhaps was rooted in the democratic culture of the volunteers—never entirely disappeared, but it was brought under control and became a strength rather than a weakness of the army. Absenteeism in its various guises was endemic in the volunteer forces of both sides, and it would continue to plague Lee throughout the war. While Lee hardly wrought the three-week miracle remembered by Chilton, he did effect a change of tone that was noticeable to outsiders.[53] If the army failed to achieve all that Lee demanded of it in their first campaign together, it nevertheless maneuvered and fought better than it ever had before.

While Lee worked to increase numbers, entrench, and improve discipline, he continued to mull over the tactical details of his turning movement. By June 10 he had reconciled himself to the idea that Jackson for the present could accomplish nothing more in the Shenandoah Valley. He had decided the most efficient role for Stonewall would be to create the diversion that forced McClellan out into the open. Lee would reenforce the Valley army at Ashland before it moved against the Federal line of communications. Then Jackson would sweep down on McClellan's rear, as Lee wrote Davis, "while I attack in front."[54]

It was this final piece of the plan that dissatisfied Lee. He accepted the fact that the army in front of Richmond could not stand idly by and permit McClellan to focus exclusively on the threat from Jackson. At the same time, he wanted to avoid a frontal assault on the Federal entrenchments in which he could find no significant weaknesses. For nearly two weeks he wrestled with this dilemma.

This is where matters stood on June 16, when James Longstreet, the army's senior divisional commander, dropped by headquarters to make a proposal. Prior to this, Lee had divulged his developing strategy only to Davis and Jackson, while Longstreet, who knew of no plan, may have doubted there was one. After Longstreet innocently suggested that Jackson be brought from the Valley to attack McClellan's right wing, Lee revealed that he had already ordered "Jackson to march down and attack McClellan's rear, while he simultaneously made an attack on his front." Longstreet liked the first part of the plan, but the second part troubled him. He pointed out the obvious truth that the strength of the Federal position made any attack in front "hazardous." He went on to argue further that a failed attack would "leave Jackson in perilous condition."[55] In calling attention to the fact that Jackson's isolation was the hub of the problem, Longstreet may have helped Lee start searching in the right direction.

On the same day, June 16, and probably as a result of his talk with Longstreet, Lee made another reconnaissance of the Federal position north of the Chickahominy. His observations were not heartening, however. And, as he gazed at the formidable enemy works, he mused rhetorically to his military secretary, "Now, Colonel Long, how can we get at those people?"[56] Although he was no more anxious to attack the strong entrenchments at Beaver Dam Creek than those at any other point along McClellan's line, he was now focusing on the connection between Jackson and the Army of Northern Virginia as the key to solving his problem. Yet, so uncertain did Lee remain on this point that the letter of instruction he wrote to Jackson on the 16th made no mention of the role to be played by the Confederate troops around Richmond.[57]

Sometime during the week that followed Lee decided upon a solution to his tactical dilemma. On June 23, with Jackson's army already on the march toward Ashland, he summoned four of his generals to a council at his headquarters at the Dabbs House. Lee's invitation to just those generals who were to be engaged in the offensive indicates he hoped to continue to guard the secrecy of his operation by revealing its full details only to those who needed to know. After the arrival of D. H. Hill, A. P. Hill, James Longstreet, and Stonewall Jackson (whose sudden appearance from the Valley surprised his fellow division commanders), Lee closed the door to his office and explained the details of his revised turning movement.

There is no evidence that Lee discussed the evolution of his plan, so the generals had no way of knowing that much of it was quite new. No longer were reenforcements to be sent to distant Ashland, nor would Jackson act as a detached column to threaten White House on the Pamunkey, relatively far in McClellan's rear. Instead, Jackson was to come south on the Pole Green Church Road, which would bring him into the immediate rear of the enemy entrenched at Beaver Dam Creek. At this closer distance, Lee could afford to reenforce Jackson with three full divisions from the Army of Northern Virginia.[58]

Lee's revised plan promised to solve three important problems. First, it offered greater security for Jackson. Second, it utilized Lee's own army without requiring it to attack entrenchments. And, third, it provided an overwhelming force to crush the Federals when they came out in the open to defend their communications. The three divisions from the Army of Northern Virginia would number 45,000 men present for duty, which combined with Jackson's nearly 22,000, would give Lee about 67,000 men in his turning column. The Confederates would thus initially enjoy odds of better than 2.6 to 1 against Porter's augmented Fifth Corps, although it was assumed that McClellan might rush reenforcements north of the river.[59]

Still, one serious obstacle would have to be overcome. All of the bridges across the Chickahominy were in enemy hands. The divisions of Longstreet and both the Hills might be delayed in crossing the river, and until their arrival Jackson's right flank would be unprotected. Lee's solution to this problem was rather complicated. Jackson was to start his march toward Pole Green Church at three o'clock on the morning of June 26. Lawrence Branch's brigade of A. P. Hill's division—after receiving word from Jackson of his approach—was to ford the Chickahominy above Mechanicsville and take up position to protect Jackson's flank. After the enemy had "discovered" the movements of Branch and Jackson and had moved out of their works either to retreat or to fight for their communications, the remainder of A. P. Hill's division was to ford the Chickahominy near Mechanicsville and drive away the enemy outposts established there. This would uncover Meadow Bridge for the use of Longstreet and D. H. Hill. All four divisions were then to form en echelon, with Jackson in the lead and their right flank, the one nearest the enemy's works, refused. In this manner, using different roads "if practicable," they were to "sweep down the Chickahominy, . . . General Jackson bearing well to his left, turning Beaver Dam Creek and taking the direction toward Cold Harbor." And, finally, "they will then press forward towards the York River Railroad, closing upon the enemy's rear and forcing him down the Chickahominy."[60]

Two obvious objections might have been put forward to the plan by the generals, but apparently neither was raised. It could have been suggested that McClellan might not fight to reestablish his communications with the York, but abandon them and change his base of operations to the James. It may have been assumed, however, that such a move was too risky to be attractive to McClellan, as he would have to march the Army of the Potomac across the front of the entrenched Confederate forces defending Richmond, while Jackson's column pressed him from the rear.

It might also have been objected—as Jefferson Davis himself had pointed out when Lee told him of the plan—that McClellan might respond by attacking the weakened wing of the army left to defend the capital. But thanks to his successful efforts at concentration, Lee was now able to leave a substantial force south of the river to guard against this possibility. In his front line of defense he had available the divisions of McLaws, D. R. Jones, Magruder, and Huger, which with the reserve artillery and cavalry numbered some 25,000 men present for duty. Theophilus Holmes's division of 9,000 was on alert to move forward at the first sign of danger, and one of Holmes's brigades (Ransom's) was already on the Nine Mile Road. If these forces should be compelled to retire to the inner defenses of Richmond, another 10,000 were available from its garrison. In all, Lee had close to 45,000 men to defend Richmond.[61]

In addition, if indeed the Federals did abandon their entrenchments north of the Chickahominy and thereby uncover New Bridge, Jackson's column would then be free to cross over in their rear. As Lee put it to Davis, "If you will hold [McClellan] as long as you can at the intrenchment, and then fall back on the detached works around the city, I will be on the enemy's heels before he gets there."[62] Lee understood perfectly well that McClellan could not simply make a headlong dash for Richmond. Once the communications of the Army of the Potomac had been broken, the enemy was in check. McClellan could make no other move until he had first reestablished the flow of supplies to his army.

The Seven Days, June 25–July 2

Lee demonstrated excellent strategic insight in planning his first campaign. All of McClellan's bridge building, earthworks, and abatis rendered the Northern army secure in position, but none of the Federal precautions provided any defense against a turning movement against its supply line. The tactical plan Lee devised for carrying out his strategy, however, was

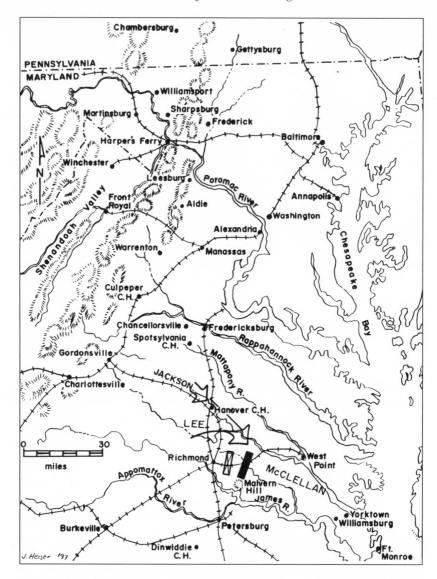

Lee's first turning movement, June 1862. The aim was to force McClellan to "come out" from his fortifications and fight to reestablish communications with the Pamunkey River.

unworkable and even naive. His instructions were both unnecessarily complicated and at the same time ambiguous and vague. He brought the key force in his operations a distance of one hundred miles to operate in a region unknown to its commander—indeed, virtually unknown to Lee, even after Stuart's reconnaissance. He expected his commanders—one new to the division level and another unused to the other three—to perform intricate maneuvers in the presence of the enemy *after* their movements had been "discovered." He ordered 67,000 men to "sweep" forward en echelon where he did not know for certain that more than one road existed. He did not name a wing commander to coordinate the operation on the field. Jackson would seem to have de facto control, since the other divisions were supporting him; but Longstreet, whose division was last in line, held the senior commission and would be *de jure* in command if a disagreement arose.

Most critically of all, nowhere did Lee build into his plan a way to assess and respond to McClellan's reaction to the threat to Federal communications, and this in spite of the fact that the whole point of the operation was to strike McClellan after the Army of the Potomac had been brought out of its entrenchments.[63] Even after McClellan was in check he would still have a number of different options open to him, and Lee needed to shape the ongoing offensive to take into account his opponent's responses. Lee's plan did not even specifically address the question of how long it would take McClellan to come out into the open. Apparently, Lee believed he possessed effective communications and would receive timely intelligence to fine-tune a sweeping movement from his headquarters behind the lines.

All in all, there is small wonder the tactical operation failed. How it failed, however, was both curious and ironic.

It is usually asserted that Lee's plan went awry before it had even started. By the evening of June 25 Jackson had reached only as far as Ashland, about five miles short of the point on the Virginia Central Railroad where he was supposed to have camped. The next morning Branch did not receive word of Jackson's arrival at the railroad until 10:15. Thereupon, Branch immediately crossed the Chickahominy and marched east, paralleling and protecting Jackson's flank.[64] Still, Jackson did not reach Pole Green Church until about five o'clock—about twelve hours late—and by that time Lee's plans for the opening of the campaign were allegedly in ruins. The sluggishness of the famed "foot cavalry," combined with its commander's apparent lack of concern over his slow progress, have occasioned endless historical speculation over causes ranging from misunderstanding to fatigue. And it is undeniable that it would have been better had Jackson been on time.

Yet Jackson's delay did not in itself ruin Lee's strategy. And, to the extent that Jackson understood his role, he had no cause for serious concern until he reached Hundley's Corner (on the Mechanicsville Road just beyond Pole Green Church) and discovered no sign of either of the Hills or

Longstreet, who were to have lined up behind him for the sweeping attack. He had not forfeited the benefit of surprise, because, once he had crossed the railroad and Branch was protecting his flank, Jackson was no longer aiming for surprise. Indeed, according to the plan the enemy was supposed to know of his threat, in order to feel threatened. The battle was not intended to start until Jackson encountered the Federals moving out of their entrenchments to protect their communications. But, when Jackson reached Hundley's Corner, not only did he discover that his supports had not arrived, but he heard the sounds of a heavy battle occurring to the south, near the Chickahominy. Something had now gone seriously awry—but it had gone awry on Lee's end of the field.

At three hours past noon, Ambrose Powell Hill, who had been in command of a division for less than a month and who would on a number of occasions during the war show he valued action over thought, tired of waiting. Although Hill had no reason to believe that the Federals had "discovered" the approach of Jackson and Branch—let alone that the enemy was responding to the threat of their approach—he crossed the Meadow Bridge and advanced on Mechanicsville. Eighteen months later, Hill reported he acted spontaneously "rather than hazard the failure of the whole plan by deferring it."[65] Evidently, he either forgot in the interval, or he had never understood in the first place, the whole point of Lee's strategy.

Still, A. P. Hill's first hasty action need not have been fatal to Lee's plan. His division easily cleared the Federal outposts from Mechanicsville and uncovered the Mechanicsville Bridge so that Longstreet and D. H. Hill could cross. But then Powell Hill irretrievably wrecked the program for the first day. Instead of making an attempt to find Jackson and fall into line behind him, and in spite of positive orders from Lee not to advance until he had heard from Jackson, Hill advanced straight ahead and hurled his regiments against the strong Federal line at Beaver Dam Creek.[66] Thus, the first day of the campaign ended with exactly what Lee had worked so hard to avoid.[67] The opening of the Seven Days was not only not a turning movement, it was not even a flank attack. It was a frontal assault on well-prepared enemy entrenchments. Not surprisingly, it was bloodily repulsed. Lee must share part of the blame for the failure. Although he cannot be held responsible for a subordinate's disobedience of a direct order, Lee could have done more—especially since he had already ridden north of the river— to prevent Hill's premature action from turning into a full-scale assault. On the contrary, having been unable to prevent it from starting, Lee tried without success to support Hill's attack.

In the absence of conclusive evidence, it is only possible to speculate as to why Lee contributed to the derangement of his own plan. First, he may have simply believed that the only thing worse than an untimely attack was not supporting any attack once it had started. He would later demonstrate on a number of occasions his belief in the necessity of following through even with a bad beginning. Secondly, he may have felt the need to distract the enemy from the vulnerability of Jackson's detached column, which was supposed to have been supported by three divisions but now had only Branch's brigade on its flank. Finally, Lee may have pressed Hill's assault because he feared McClellan would counterattack south of the river before New Bridge had been uncovered and a direct route opened for Confederate communications with Richmond.[68]

Certainly, this latter concern was prominent in Lee's mind on June 26. In spite of his earlier bravado to Davis about being on the "heels" of a Federal thrust at Richmond, first-battle jitters may have affected him as he witnessed his plans unravel. After receiving Jackson's note in the morning acknowledging the late arrival at Ashland, Lee wrote to Davis, "I fear . . . our plan of operations has been discovered" by the enemy.[69] Lee's "fear" was not that Jackson had been discovered—which was an integral part of the plan—but that premature discovery would encourage McClellan to attack south of the river before New Bridge was in Confederate hands.

That Lee felt the delay did compel changes in his tactical arrangements is attested by three actions he took during the day. He ordered Theophilus Holmes to prepare to move all of the remaining field forces in North Carolina to Richmond; he ordered John Walker to leave one regiment at Drewry's Bluff and march with the remainder of his brigade to support Benjamin Huger's division in front of Richmond; and he ordered Huger to "hold your trenches tonight at the point of the bayonet if necessary" and to call on Henry Wise's brigade at Chaffin's Bluff and forces from the inner defenses of Richmond if required.[70] Curiously, for all of his concern about gaining access to the New Bridge, Lee does not seem to have considered the possibility that the Federals would destroy it as they pulled back.

In the report he submitted almost two years after the battle, Lee passed over Jackson's delay as "unavoidable," and he censured no one for the frontal assault.[71] After the war, however, he somewhat unfairly placed the entire blame for the Beaver Dam Creek fiasco on Jackson, telling his cousin Cassius Lee "of the delay of Jackson in getting on McClellan's flank, causing the fight at Mechanicsville, which fight . . . was . . . necessary to prevent McClellan from entering Richmond, from the front of which most of the troops had been moved."[72]

Still, in the search to explain Confederate failure on the first day a key figure has been overlooked. In all of the controversy over blaming Jackson, A. P. Hill, and Lee, virtually no attention has been paid to the Federal side of the question. McClellan had learned from a deserter on the night of

June 25 of the approach of Jackson. Although the determination to retire to the James was a separate and later decision, by the next morning the Federal commander had already decided that he would not come out of his entrenchments to defend his communications with the York. Hence, nothing any of the Confederate commanders did or did not do would have brought success to Lee on the first day in the way he had planned.

Confederate tactical failure has also obscured the fact that Lee's strategic success was only delayed on June 26, it was not denied. Jackson's position at Hundley's Corner rendered McClellan's communications untenable, and in that sense Lee had achieved his goal in spite of the useless attack at Beaver Dam Creek. McClellan now had to move, and he would have to move quickly to ensure the continuing flow of supplies to his army. The Federal commander had to change his mind and fight to regain his communications with the York River, change his base to the James, or retreat down the Peninsula to Fort Monroe. In any of these cases, he would be in the open and vulnerable to attack. All that Lee had to do was wait and strike his enemy once in motion.

On the morning of June 27, Lee's enemy still refused to cooperate. Instead of coming out of his entrenchments to fight, McClellan abandoned the Federal works along Beaver Dam Creek and retired southeast to a position nearer Duane's Bridge over the Chickahominy. This was good news for the Southerners, because it uncovered New Bridge and gave Lee direct communication with the forces of Magruder and Huger south of the river. But the problem still remained of how to get at McClellan. Lee assumed his opponent would make a stand behind Powhite Creek, a tributary of the Chickahominy and a strong natural defensive position. With the lesson of the first day giving fresh reason to avoid a frontal assault, Lee sent D. H. Hill's division to support Jackson and met with Stonewall himself about noon at Walnut Grove Church. Lee ordered Jackson, whose command was now increased to four divisions, to march to the southeast to Cold Harbor to turn the flank of the enemy's new position. In the meanwhile, Longstreet and A. P. Hill continued eastward to confront the Federals at Powhite Creek, but they were not to attack until Jackson had arrived.[73] Once again, however, the general who had gained repute for his lightning speed responded sluggishly. And once again, it was A.P. Hill who did not wait for Jackson.

The enemy was discovered as expected at Powhite Creek, but the Federal force was so small that it was easily swept aside. Fitz-John Porter had chosen to stand a little farther east behind Boatswain's Swamp, an even stronger defensive position. Although A. P. Hill initially restrained his lead brigade, he apparently did so only to await the remainder of his division. As soon as all of his troops were at hand, Hill launched repeated frontal assaults, each attended with heavy losses. Jackson was late in reaching Cold Harbor, because of a misunderstanding with his guide. When he did arrive he fronted the right-center of Porter's line and not the flank. Finally, only a general Confederate assault along the entire front—which Lee approved, if he did not direct—compelled the Federals to fall back before nearly twice their numbers. Darkness and a reformed Federal line ended Confederate pursuit.

In back-to-back days of bloody fighting, Lee made little strategic progress. As early as the evening of June 25, Jackson's arrival in Ashland sufficiently imperiled McClellan's supply line to ensure that the Federal commander must react in some manner. Two days of savage assaults had not changed that strategic situation. Tactically, Lee had pushed McClellan's right wing back to a tight semicircle around the Chickahominy bridges. This achievement cost the Confederates in excess of 10,000 casualties, while inflicting losses of about half that number on the enemy.[74] Judged by his own grand strategy to hurt the North so severely it would tire of the war, while husbanding Southern resources, Lee could scarcely yet claim success.

On the morning of June 28, Lee learned that during the night McClellan had withdrawn his right wing south of the Chickahominy. Finally, Lee and his impetuous army had no choice but to await the enemy's action, since, with the bridges destroyed there was no way to get at him immediately. Lee spent the entire day trying to find out what McClellan would do next. Apparently, Lee believed the Federals had three options, which he ranked from most to least likely as follows: (1) to recross the lower Chickahominy and reestablish communications with the White House; (2) to retreat down the Peninsula and use Fort Monroe as base; or, (3) to switch rivers and open a base at some point on the James.[75] Lee probably continued to discount the third option for several reasons. The Confederates held the James as far east as Chaffin's Bluff, and for McClellan to establish his base farther downriver would create a supply line more exposed than the one had been to the York. If McClellan decided to operate from the James, therefore, he would have to fall back with his entire army to the new base, an intricate and risky movement with the enemy on one of his flanks and in his rear. It was this latter course, in fact, that McClellan had decided to pursue.

At last, on the morning of the twenty-ninth, Lee recognized he had finally achieved half of his strategic goal. The Army of the Potomac was in the open and on the move. Confederate pursuit began at once and continued through two days of sporadic and sometimes heavy fighting. As McClellan's army passed over narrow roads through the valley of a creek called White Oak Swamp, Lee attacked his rear and tried unsuccessfully to get in his front. In the end, McClellan reached the banks of the James, where, under the protective fire of Federal gunboats, he threw the Army of the Potomac into a nearly impregnable semicircle.

Lee's final thrust, a fruitless and perhaps futile frontal assault on Malvern Hill, ended the campaign on July 1. It was the third straight-on attack of the campaign that should never have been made. Perhaps Lee underestimated the topographical strength of the Federal position; perhaps he believed the enemy too demoralized and off balance to defend even an incredibly strong position; or, perhaps Lee was simply so frustrated at his inability to catch McClellan in the open, he chanced a desperate final roll of the dice. In any case, the attack at Malvern Hill contradicted everything the Confederate commander had been trying to achieve in his first campaign. The next day McClellan moved his army down the James several miles to better portage at Harrison's Landing.[76]

Lee's first campaign failed to achieve its main tactical objective, the destruction of the enemy army. But Lee had probably demanded too much from the resources at his disposal in expecting to destroy the Army of the Potomac in his very first operation. He had required largely unseasoned troops and their inexperienced commanders to undertake an intricate offensive. He had necessarily to use the chief subordinates already in place, and some of them were not up to their responsibilities. Not surprisingly, his army had responded clumsily and inefficiently to his complicated and sometimes ambiguous orders. In addition, he discovered his foe to be well trained and led by an able if deliberate commander.

Lee's accomplishments were nevertheless considerable. He had driven McClellan twenty-five miles south and east and ended the siege operations against Richmond. He had forced the main Federal army in the East at least temporarily to assume the defensive, and he had given a badly needed boost to Southern morale. Just as important, Lee had demonstrated in his first campaign that strategy could "baffle" his foe's well-laid plans and "frustrate" its superiority in navy, engineering, and artillery. Granted, he did hold a slight numerical advantage in the immediate vicinity of Richmond after the junction with Jackson. It is not clear that Lee knew this, however, and, even if he did, he could not expect to sustain such an edge. It is also true that he had at least three times permitted costly frontal assaults that had wasted Confederate resources without commensurate results. In fact, his 20,135 casualties represented a loss of 1.68 percent of the Confederate military pool of whites of military age, while the 15,849 casualties he inflicted on the enemy amounted to only 0.36 percent of their pool. He could not afford many victories that drained his resources nearly five times faster than the North's.[77]

Nonetheless, in spite of his first campaign's many tactical failures, Lee's use of concentration, initiative, and the turning movement had completely dominated his enemy. The experience suggested his grand strategy for achieving Confederate independence could succeed. With personnel changes, tighter organization, simpler plans, and more reliance on maneuver, he might neutralize overall Federal superiority in numbers and protract the war sufficiently long that the North would quit the struggle. By far the happiest result of the Seven Days campaign was the hope for victory that it restored to the South.

CHAPTER FOUR

— ❧ —

"The enemy is congregating about us"
Lee in Strategic Stalemate,
July 2–August 9, 1862

Tʜᴇ ᴛᴇʟᴇsᴄᴏᴘᴇ ᴏꜰ history has focused on the triumphs of Confederate arms during the late summer of 1862 and obscured the dire strategic straits that continued to paralyze Confederate forces through June and July. In the West, after the fall of Corinth, Henry Halleck divided his massive Federal army to consolidate gains in north-central Mississippi, while sending a column under Don Carlos Buell through northern Alabama toward Chattanooga. Braxton Bragg, who replaced the ailing Beauregard, could not decide where or how to stem the seemingly inexorable enemy tide.

In the East, Lee's victory before Richmond brought impasse rather than release. With his army sorely weakened by its first campaign and Federal columns converging against him, Lee could find no way to sustain the offensive-defensive. As the summer days dragged into weeks, it began to appear as if the supreme exertion by the Confederacy to mobilize and concentrate its manpower and to seize control of the war would end still-born.

Lee Loses the Initiative, July 2–5

If not while the guns still reverberated from Malvern Hill, then very soon thereafter, Lee realized how limited was the victory he had achieved. He had gathered most of the Confederacy's strength in the East into his army, seized the initiative, broken McClellan's communications, and forced the Federals to abandon their entrenched position. He had then pursued the enemy with a determination and persistence heretofore unmatched by any commander on either side. Yet, in the end, he had accomplished little more than to push his foe aside.

On the evening of June 30, as the Army of Northern Virginia emerged from the White Oak Swamp in pursuit of the Army of the Potomac, Lee had fretted over his inability to deliver the coup de grace to his opponent. "He will get away," he had muttered in despair, "because I cannot have my orders carried out!" And McClellan did get away—with the organization, the trains, and, so far as Lee knew, the morale of the Northern army intact.

"Our success has not been so great or complete as we could have desired," he confessed to his wife. And in his final report, his disappointment still rankling, he stated flatly, "Under ordinary circumstances the Federal army should have been destroyed." He knew full well the Confederacy did not have the resources to spend heavy casualties on limited victories, nor the time to waste on missed opportunities.[1]

What compounded Lee's frustration and sharpened his anger was the dawning realization that his victory had worsened the Confederate strategic position. The Army of the Potomac had been driven from the outskirts of Richmond, but it remained less than twenty miles from the Confederate capital. While those twenty miles gained breathing space for the Confederacy, ironically McClellan now posed an even greater potential threat. So long as the Federal army had approached Richmond from the north, its communications necessarily ran overland for some distance and were vulnerable to a turning movement. Now McClellan was based on the river that flowed directly into the heart of Richmond. With his vastly superior navy controlling the James, the Union general would be free to approach the Confederate capital along either bank with a water-based and secure supply line. Until he chose to resume his offensive, McClellan could sit at his impregnable position on the James—refitting, resupplying, and accruing new strength—and Lee could do little about it. In short, once McClellan reached Harrison's Landing, the initiative in the Richmond area slipped from Lee's grasp. The Confederate commander was now compelled to wait and watch for the movement of the enemy.

In addition, so far as Lee knew, his victory had not improved the overall situation in the East. Notwithstanding a week of Confederate attacks around Richmond, the Federals remained on the strategic offensive, and the Confederates were still on the defensive in the grand strategic scheme of the Eastern theater. Before Beaver Dam Creek, Lee had been encircled by enemy forces in South Carolina, North Carolina, western Virginia, northern Virginia, and on the Chickahominy. According to information available to him during the first week of July, the situation remained materially unchanged, except that the army on the Chickahominy was now on the James and the scattered departments in northern Virginia were being united into a field army for active service. Neither of the changes were good news.

All in all, Lee understood the remaining dangers too well to share in the euphoria that swept Richmond after the retreat of McClellan's army. As a result of the Seven Days, Lee and the Confederacy had simply emerged into a lighter shade of darkness.

On July 4 Lee arrived at Harrison's Landing and, accompanied only by Stonewall Jackson, undertook on foot a close examination of the entire

Federal line. Both generals reluctantly agreed that an assault was out of the question.[2] The following day, Lee acknowledged he had lost the initiative, when he bluntly admitted to Davis that his only course of action was to withdraw his army to the vicinity of Richmond to await McClellan's next move. He had been able to find no weak spot in the Federal position at Harrison's Landing. And, even if one had been discovered, he wrote the president, the enemy's gunboats "would prevent us from reaping any of the fruits of victory and expose our men to great destruction."[3]

In the July 5 dispatch to Davis, an incisive strategy document that succinctly summarized Lee's direst concerns, the Confederate commander also acknowledged that McClellan on the James posed a greater danger to the Confederate capital than had McClellan on the Chickahominy. Observing the arrival of seven "large-size New York Sound steamers" crowded with reenforcements and the presence of a "New York ferry-boat," he worried the Federals were preparing to cross the river and launch a new offensive from the south side.[4] Lee could parry such a thrust only from a more central position nearer Richmond. Hence, however much he might dislike the moral effect of withdrawing after a victory, he believed he had no alternative.

Since the mid-May appearance of enemy gunboats at Drewry's Bluff, Lee (as well as Davis and Johnston) had worried about a Federal advance up the James. Efforts to fortify Drewry's and Chaffin's Bluffs with river batteries had made little progress due to lack of time, laborers, and skilled supervisors.[5] Lee's fear of this new and greater threat would dominate his thinking throughout July and early August. His attention would be riveted on McClellan, and for the next five weeks all of his major strategic decisions would be shaped—if not dictated—by the looming enemy presence at Harrison's Landing.[6]

Concentration and Estrays

In the same revealing letter to Davis, Lee alluded to the second greatest concern that occupied his mind in early July, the alarming weakness of the Army of Northern Virginia. "Our ranks . . . are much reduced," he wrote, and "I beg that you will take every practicable means to re-enforce" them. Finding himself for the moment stalled in his strategy to pursue the offensive, Lee renewed his attempt—which the fighting had interrupted—to concentrate idling Confederate regiments into field armies for active service. In this effort, he would continue to enjoy the energetic support of the president and the War Department, and the results, although less dramatic than the yield in June, would add 19.7 regiments and approximately 13,800 men to his ranks.[7]

Nearly eleven regiments, the bulk of the new units, came from the recalcitrant Department of South Carolina and Georgia, which had contributed so grudgingly to the June concentration. Richmond's manner of prying loose these reenforcements revealed the sometimes comic opera nature of Confederate command problems when compounded by states' rights and the immutability of human nature. Responding to civilian complaints, Jefferson Davis had determined to replace the department commander, Maj. Gen. John C. Pemberton. The president had also decided that the threat from Federal forces along the South Carolina and Georgia coast would be minimal during the coming summer season and that most of the mobile forces of the department would be free for operations elsewhere. On July 5, in an adroit move to accomplish both aims in one stroke, Adj. Gen. Samuel Cooper ordered Pemberton to push completion of his coastal fortifications, concentrate his artillery in garrisons, and concluded, "The residue of your troops you could then bring here with the least delay for operations in the field."[8]

Visions of glories gained while leading a division in the field under Lee worked a magical transformation. Pemberton ceased to magnify the threat from the enemy and began an energetic search for available troops he could take to Virginia. By the end of July he had dispatched the brigades of Thomas Drayton and Nathan Evans, as well as several independent regiments.[9] But for Pemberton it was never to be. G. W. Smith, who was Davis's first choice to replace him, continued too ill for active duty, and by the time Beauregard was named at the end of August, it was too late. Pemberton would miss his chance to serve with the Army of Northern Virginia and instead travel down the path that carried him to personal ignominy as the "defender of Vicksburg."[10]

Only five regiments were available from North Carolina and for a simple reason. By July 1 nearly 60 percent of that department's troops were already in Virginia. After the arrival of James Martin's brigade at Petersburg on July 5, only 4,882 men present for duty remained in the state.[11] When Holmes was relieved and sent to the Trans-Mississippi and D. H. Hill was named as his replacement on July 17, the department was downgraded to the status of a district.[12] It was probably inevitable that stripping the state would offend and alarm its political leaders, and on August 4, Gov. Henry T. Clark wrote to Lee detailing depredations by enemy raids, protesting the handful of green regiments that remained in the state, and demanding the return of seasoned troops.

Lee replied with firmness and sensitivity. He pointed out to Clark that the Confederacy did not have enough troops "to pursue the policy of concentrating our forces to protect important points and baffle the principal efforts of the enemy and at the same time extend all the protection we desire to every district." Cutting to the heart of the dilemma, Lee observed, "The safety of the whole state of North Carolina . . . depends in a measure upon the result of the enemy's efforts" in Virginia. After the Federals succeeded in Virginia, they "would make your State the theater of hostilities," and that would be "far more injurious and destructive to your citizens than anything they have yet been called upon to suffer."[13]

The War Department recognized from the start that the already shorn south Atlantic states would not be able to provide enough new regiments to make good Lee's twenty thousand battle losses. On July 4 Secretary of War Randolph telegraphed to recruiting officers in Virginia, North Carolina, and Georgia to bypass the time-consuming step of forming new regiments. Instead, they were to send the conscripts in groups of one or two hundred directly to Richmond, where they would be assigned to existing regiments. "We have no time now," Randolph added dolefully, "to prepare them for the field as carefully as we wish."[14]

Davis informed Lee the following day of the expedient the department was taking to fill his ranks quickly, and Lee not only approved but took his own steps to speed the process. He sent personal appeals to South Carolina, Tennessee, and Texas for reenforcements. In the case of the two Western states, he wrote to Gov. Isham Harris of Tennessee and Sen. Louis T. Wigfall of Texas, appealing to state pride, to obtain enough additional units to form a full Tennessee brigade and two Texas brigades in the Army of Northern Virginia. He also requested the addition of individual soldiers to fill the depleted ranks of the six regiments from those states already with him, and he went so far as to detail officers from Tennessee to return to their home state to seek recruits for the three Volunteer State units.

The results of these efforts are difficult to assess, but an unspecified number of South Carolina soldiers did arrive in August and were assigned to Joseph Kershaw's brigade. In September replacements from North Carolina would join the army in Frederick, Maryland. It is not likely that Lee received more than several thousand troops in this manner. Moreover, since most of these men were conscripts forced into the army by the April law and none had received the rudiments of drill or discipline, not only is their usefulness in question, but it is uncertain how long many remained with the army.[15]

Unfortunately for the Confederacy, even if ample new regiments had existed, their concentration would not have solved Lee's problem entirely. Battle casualties were only part—and a somewhat lesser part—of the cause of the emaciated Confederate ranks. In early July Lee discovered that more than one-third of the men who should have remained after the deduction of fighting losses were unaccountably missing. Instead of the 86,000 who should have been present for duty, only 56,000 were with their colors.[16] Lee thus confronted a predicament that would hobble his military operations for the remainder of the war. On any given day, thousands of officers and men who had been assigned to his army and who should have been available for duty were not. They would be absent for a variety of causes, but most of the explanations were unacceptable.

Lee correctly understood that the overall problem of "estrays" was "one of the evils resulting from the laxity of discipline in the army."[17] Not only did officers approve leaves for trivial reasons, but a large number of the citizen-soldiers of the Confederacy assumed the right to leave and return to their regiments of their own volition. Unauthorized absence from the ranks, usually referred to as "straggling" even when the army was not on the march, was probably inevitable in a volunteer army. The problem was exacerbated when "conscripts," men held to service against their will, were brought to the front by the intensive concentration in June. Lee recognized he could never achieve the same high level of discipline with amateurs that might be reached with professionals.[18] Still, he also knew that something must be done to stop the hemorrhaging from the ranks.

Lee had first addressed this problem in General Orders issued just four days after taking command of the army. "To prevent straggling" he had created a special provost guard composed of a lieutenant, a sergeant, and ten men from each regiment, which, along with a company of cavalry detached from Stuart's force, was to visit Richmond "to pick up all parties absent without authority."[19] This system had proven woefully inadequate during the hard marching and severe fighting from Beaver Dam Creek to Malvern Hill, and Lee turned to sterner measures.

Beginning with the Special Orders of July 8, which detailed the withdrawal of the army to the vicinity of Richmond and called on each division commander to "use every effort to reorganize his command, in securing the return of stragglers and all effective men," Lee tried a series of measures to correct the problem.[20] General Orders, No. 77, issued on July 11, prohibited leaves of absence "under any circumstances" and required that the sick and wounded be put on report and under supervision of medical authorities who would return them to duty at the earliest possible time. It also required division commanders to post guards around their camps, to institute "regular roll calls during the day" to "determine the presence of the men, and when absent" to "adopt immediate measures for their return to their companies."[21]

In General Orders, No. 94, issued a month later, Lee ordered the provost guard, accompanied by a medical officer, to follow behind each division on the march. When men who were legitimately sick fell out of ranks, the surgeon was to "give them a ticket for transportation in the ambulances or train of the wagons," so that they might still keep up with the army. Those adjudged not to be sick were to "be marched into camp under charge of the guard." In the same orders, Lee tried to correct another prevalent "evil." During a battle many unwounded men—some from genuine compassion and some from a desire to avoid fighting—dropped out of the ranks to help wounded comrades. Lee directed that hereafter two men from each company would be assigned to assist the fallen: each would be provided with written authority signed by both the company and regimental commanders and "no other will be permitted to leave the ranks for this purpose."[22]

Lee also cast about for other ways to net the estrays. He ordered the military commander of Richmond "to arrest all deserters and absentees without authority from the army, and to cause them to be reported to the commands to which they belong."[23] He tried to limit the practice of War Department bureaus of transferring his soldiers for details in the quartermaster, subsistence, ordnance, and signal corps.[24] He also urged that General Orders be published requiring recently exchanged prisoners of war to report "at once" to their former commands.[25] And, in perhaps his most extreme measure, when John B. Hood's division was ordered to Hanover Junction to meet a threatened advance of the enemy from Fredericksburg, Lee ordered the brigadier to carry along his less seriously sick so that they might rejoin their regiments at the earliest possible moment.[26]

The Confederate commander wrote stern lectures to his subordinates that "Examples should be made of the delinquents." And on two occasions he rebuked his two chief lieutenants for their laxity. On July 27, noting that Jackson reported fewer men than he should have had, Lee asked, "What has become of them? . . . Do not let your troops run down. . . . This will require your personal attention." On August 1, in response to Longstreet's complaint of a large number of absences in Micah Jenkins's South Carolina brigade, Lee observed that "an exceedingly lax state of things" existed in the command, and he ordered Longstreet to "take every necessary step to enforce discipline."[27]

In a more positive approach, recognizing that ignorance of military procedures and boredom in camp were two roots of the problem, Lee tried to instill pride and discipline by increasing drill and daily instruction.[28] His measures worked—at least as long as the army remained relatively stationary—as 13,473 men were reported to have returned to the ranks in the period from July 10 to July 20 alone.[29] When he undertook energetic operations in the heat of August and September, however, Lee would discover that the problem of "estrays" had returned unabated.

As Lee contemplated the wreckage a victory had wrought in his ranks and how little it had netted him strategically, there is no indication his intention to pursue the offensive lessened. Still, the experience must have reawakened his commitment to rely on maneuver and to avoid frontal assaults, or, put in his own terms, to emphasize the use of "easy fighting" to gain the "heavy victories." This determination would be another key element in shaping Lee's strategy for the remainder of the summer.

Threat from the North: Strategy, July 6–13

No matter how much Lee may have wished to rely on maneuver, during the first week in July he had neither the opportunity nor the freedom to pursue the strategy he deemed best. McClellan's snug encampment at Harrison's Landing both forestalled assault and nailed the Army of Northern Virginia to the defense of Richmond. On July 6, leaving only cavalry in McClellan's immediate front, Lee started to pull his divisions back to a line near the Confederate capital from which he could respond to an enemy advance along either bank of the James. He established a thirty-mile semicircle that began on the Mechanicsville Turnpike due north of Richmond and ran east and south until it crossed the James and anchored on Falling Creek on the south side. He also advanced a division into Prince George County across the river from Harrison's Landing to preempt an enemy move along the south bank.

The orders for the withdrawal and the realignment of the divisions revealed the fluid structure of the army. The shifting organization of the Army of Northern Virginia resulted from the polyglot origin of its forces and from Lee's ongoing search for effective formations and efficient commanders. In the early months of his field command, Lee was slow to formalize structure above the division level either because he liked the flexibility of smaller groupings or because he was unsure of which subordinates merited greater responsibilities, or, perhaps, from a combination of both reasons.

On June 1 Johnston's army had been temporarily organized into two wings of three divisions each, but Lee quickly abandoned the wing formation and required each division to report directly to him.[30] For the Seven Days campaign, Lee regrouped seven of the eleven divisions of his expanded army into three "commands" under Jackson, Longstreet, and Magruder.[31] Now, in pulling back to Richmond, Lee reshuffled the army again, this time into two "commands" and four independent divisions.[32] He sent Jackson with three divisions to the Mechanicsville Turnpike; on Stonewall's right was McLaws; next right was D. H. Hill; Longstreet (with A. P. Hill) then filled the interval to the James behind Chaffin's Bluff; Huger extended the line across the river and along Falling Creek; and Holmes's division was advanced below the Appomattox to watch McClellan more closely.[33]

Changes came not only in command structure but also in personnel. During July four of the most senior generals associated with the Army of Northern Virginia disappeared from its ranks forever. Benjamin Huger was appointed inspector general of artillery, and his division was given to Richard H. Anderson.[34] William H. C. Whiting left his division to John B. Hood to go on sick leave, and when Whiting returned he was assigned to the engineers.[35] Both John B. Magruder and Theophilus Holmes were transferred to the Trans-Mississippi Department. LaFayette McLaws inherited the bulk of Magruder's command, while D. H. Hill took over the redesignated "district" of North Carolina.[36] Lee's role in removing Huger, Whiting, Magruder, and Holmes may have been minimal, but he certainly seized the opportunity to replace them with superior field commanders in Anderson, Hood, McLaws, and D. H. Hill.[37]

On July 9 Lee reestablished his headquarters in the Dabbs House near Richmond on the Nine Mile Road.[38] Here, for the first time in two weeks, he found the time to survey the overall situation in the Eastern theater. Sifting through the "conflicting and exaggerated" intelligence coming in to him was a frustrating exercise. Imperfect and obsolete information necessarily clouded his perception of the strategic situation. As he would complain to Davis, "The reports are so conflicting and sometimes opposing, and our people take up so readily all alarming accounts, which swell in their progress, that it is difficult to learn the truth till too late to profit by it."[39] With the impact of the steamship and the railroad on rapid military movements not yet fully understood, it is not surprising that dramatic rumors abounded about enemy troop shifts. In particular, Lee would be plagued the entire summer by reports of the Federals transferring massive forces from the Western theater to support McClellan, and some of the stories he believed, at least temporarily.[40]

Doubtless, the news coming in to Lee at this time was not appreciably different from the general run of Civil War intelligence. But for the first time in his role as a field commander, Lee was dealing with muddled information where he needed accurate intelligence to plan for operations. Behind the desk in Richmond he had been able to make general suggestions and be insulated from their direct consequences. This was no longer true now that he was charged with executing not only strategy, but logistics and tactics as well. It was hard to see the forest, when standing in the midst of the trees, especially while the trees kept changing size, shape, and location.

Even through the garbled intelligence, however, it was clear enough to Lee that "from every quarter the enemy is congregating around us."[41] He knew that Federal forces under David Hunter held the Port Royal region of South Carolina and threatened Charleston. He knew also that Ambrose

Burnside's corps at New Berne, North Carolina, not only imperiled Richmond's communications with the south but also posed a potential danger to Petersburg. Union troops under Jacob Cox occupied nearly all of the mountainous western counties of Virginia, and heavy garrisons held the key towns at the head of the Shenandoah Valley, Martinsburg, Winchester, and Harpers Ferry.

In addition, the North had now fielded a second full army in the Eastern theater, one almost as big as McClellan's. This new force, designated the Army of Virginia, came from a consolidation of the units under Banks and Frémont that had fought Jackson in the Valley with portions of the Washington garrison and Irvin McDowell's corps, which was supposed to be but never quite became a part of McClellan's Army of the Potomac. Abraham Lincoln brought John Pope from a winning reputation in the Western theater to command this patchwork army and instructed him to defend Washington and cooperate with McClellan, in that order. Ironically, Pope and his new army were announced on June 26, the first day of Lee's assault on McClellan.[42]

No direct evidence indicates whether Lee knew that the North had already begun to raise 300,000 more volunteers to replenish the depleted Union ranks. Yet, the chronology of the event makes his knowledge highly likely. Lincoln's memorial to the loyal governors of July 1 was known to the Northern public by the following day; and by July 8 the War Department had issued quotas, and the states had started recruiting.[43] This unwelcome news must have reached Lee by July 10 or shortly thereafter. It could only have been disheartening to hear that the Lincoln administration's first response to defeat had been to call for increasing its armies by nearly 50 percent. The new troops would not be ready for the field for several months, but their imminence increased immeasurably the pressure on Lee— within the concept of his own grand strategy—to act quickly. Once equipped and trained, the new Federal regiments would nullify the relative gain in odds the Confederacy had made since the spring. Lee may have been wise enough to delay judging just how bad this news was until he could gauge by the response to the call whether the Northern public shared the determination of its political leaders.

There was much, after all, that Lee did not and could not know during the first two weeks of July. He did not know the extent of the dismay his victories had caused in the North, nor the extensive military movements ordered by the Federal administration that even now were altering the strategic situation. He did not know that both Hunter and Burnside had been instructed to strip their departments for reinforcements for McClellan, nor that Burnside's men had already arrived and lay in transports off Fort Monroe. Nor could he have known that in Lincoln's mind the decision may have already been made to withdraw McClellan's army from the James and return it to the defenses of Washington.[44]

Because Lee assumed that McClellan's army continued to be his major and most immediate threat and would remain so in the foreseeable future, he seems at first to have paid little attention to John Pope and the Army of Virginia. With one hundred thousand enemy troops on Richmond's doorstep, Lee could spare little time for worry about another force of indeterminate size, location, and intentions. Still, the withdrawal of Jackson from the Valley—although yielding significant short-term benefits—had put Lee in an anomalous position. Stonewall's forces on the Shenandoah had not only threatened Washington and pinned down considerable enemy troops that would have otherwise been sent to McClellan, they had also protected Richmond's lifeline with its western granary in the Valley.

The Virginia Central Railroad, which ran from Staunton through Gordonsville to Richmond, provided a major portion of the subsistence for Lee's huge army, as well as the swelling wartime population of the Confederate capital. The need to protect this source of food and its delivery system had been a primary reason Joseph Johnston had not been allowed to concentrate all of the forces in eastern Virginia at Yorktown to oppose McClellan. According to Lee, in late March Jefferson Davis declared, "The loss of the Central road and communication with the Valley at Staunton would be more injurious than the withdrawal from the Peninsula and the evacuation of Norfolk."[45] After Jackson left for Richmond in mid-June, both the Valley and its rail link had been protected by fewer than two thousand cavalry. But, by July 10, naught but a company of cavalry and a handful of administrative troops remained in the north to watch and report on the Federals.[46]

Lee must necessarily have recognized the risk he took in continuing to expose one of his major lines of communication. One obvious solution would have been to send Jackson, perhaps with a greatly augmented force, back into the Valley, hoping not only to guard the western supply line but also to raise once again Northern fears for the safety of Washington. Either the idea did not occur to Lee—which is not likely—or he considered McClellan's new position on the James so much more dangerous than his previous one on the Chickahominy that he hesitated to divide his forces to send a column to a distant theater.

It was John Pope who forced Lee's hand by advancing a portion of the Federal Army of Virginia far enough south to probe a sensitive point in the Confederate supply line. On July 12 Maj. Cornelius Boyle reported from Gordonsville that at 11 A.M. Federals had occupied Culpeper Court House, about twenty-seven miles to the north. This immediately caught Lee's attention, as Gordonsville was the important railroad junction where the north-south Orange and Alexandria joined the east-west Virginia Central. Federal occupation of Gordonsville would interrupt the flow of supplies from the Valley via Charlottesville and Lynchburg and pose a serious threat to Lee's ability to subsist his army.[47]

Although Lee did not feel he could lightly spare troops from Richmond, neither did he believe he could ignore this threat to his communications. Hence, on July 13 he ordered Jackson with his own and Ewell's divisions and the Laurel brigade of cavalry—about 15,000 troops—to Louisa Court House. The selection of Jackson was logical, as he had a proven record in independent command and still technically commanded the Valley District. In sending such a small force, Lee intended to show the Confederate flag in the region and to gather more information about the nature of the threat posed by Pope. But he also made it clear that Stonewall was to take up position so that he might strike the flank of any enemy move on Charlottesville to the west or on Richmond to the east.[48]

Pope's advance severely complicated the strategic situation. Lee was now compelled to contend with both Pope and McClellan and potentially to confront a situation even more dangerous than the one he had just escaped. If Pope advanced on Richmond from the north, while McClellan resumed his offensive from the southeast, Lee would either have to abandon the Confederate capital or be crushed between the prongs of a pincer. If all of this were not enough, Lee learned on the same day, July 13, that Burnside had withdrawn most of his independent corps from North Carolina. Although the destination of this new threat was yet unknown, Lee assumed Burnside was on the way to reenforce McClellan.

The Army of Northern Virginia would be heavily outnumbered by the combined forces of McClellan, Pope, and Burnside, and Lee would need even more than before to neutralize Federal strength by maneuver. He had no recourse but to try to prevent the trap from closing too tightly. Unfortunately, at the moment he could not see how he might accomplish this. He temporized by ordering Theophilus Holmes, still the commander of the Department of North Carolina, to leave garrisons in the Cape Fear region and to shift the remainder of his troops to Virginia, concentrating them between Drewry's Bluff and the Appomattox River. This was a hollow order, however. Except for the three thousand men in the green regiments of the brigades of Samuel French and Thomas Clingman, Holmes had no more troops to bring.[49]

Lee Marches in Place, July 14–August 4

Lee passed four frustrating days in near strategic paralysis.[50] Then on Friday, July 18, he received dispatches from Jackson and Stuart with news that even worsened his predicament. According to Jackson a "large force" of Federals had left Fredericksburg for Orange Court House, eight miles north of Gordonsville, while Stuart reported "a large force assembling at Winchester," at the head of the Shenandoah Valley. Lee did not know that these troops belonged to McDowell and Banks, respectively, and were corps in Pope's Army of Virginia. He saw them instead as new and independent threats. Although he did "not credit" the idea of massive Federal concentration at Winchester, he believed the combined reports might indicate the enemy intended to "secure possession of the Valley," cut his critical supply route, and endanger Richmond's western approaches. Hence, he approved Jackson's decision to march west to Gordonsville "in the hope of striking a blow" against the enemy's flank should the opportunity present itself. He also ordered Stuart to send a force to Hanover Junction, where the Virginia Central joined the Richmond, Fredericksburg, and Potomac Railroad and which would be uncovered by Jackson's shift.[51]

Still, Lee treated the new intelligence skeptically. He did so not only because the quality of the information he was receiving at this time upset him, but also because he was convinced the enemy's primary focus remained on the James. He wrote to Davis that "heavy re-enforcements are reaching McClellan." He was certain "they will leave no stone unturned to capture Richmond," and repeated his fear that troops would be transferred from the West to the Army of the Potomac. Concerned that none of the promised Confederate reenforcements had yet reached his own army, he also appealed to Davis in unusually strong language to hasten the transfer of troops from South Carolina and to hurry forward the conscripts to fill his depleted regiments. "We must," he concluded starkly, "endeavor to arouse our people."

Another five days passed in agonizing slowness without resolution of the strategic imbroglio and with minimal new information for the Confederate commander. On July 23 Lee's attention remained fastened on the James River, and he continued in his belief that "General McClellan is being re-enforced to the extent of the means of his Government and that he will continue to be so." He noted with concern the increased activity of the Army of the Potomac and its "daily demonstrations to deceive us or test our strength." He speculated that McClellan was under political pressure and "no doubt feels the necessity to advance upon Richmond." Under these circumstances, Lee felt an even greater need for the foe on the James to be

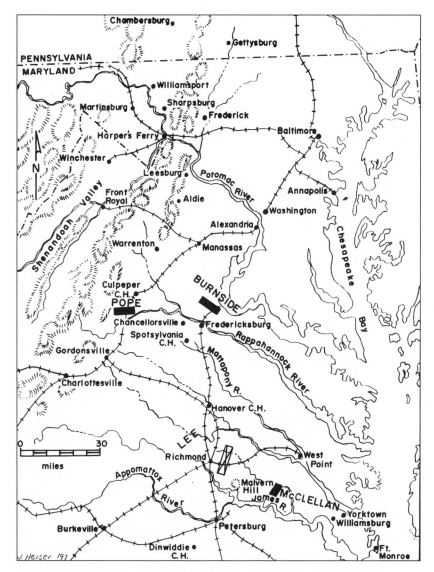

Lee "spread-eagled," July–August 1862. Threatened by Pope on his left flank, McClellan on his right, and Burnside in the center, Lee went through a period of strategic paralysis.

"watched and restrained." After increasing Longstreet's command with Wise's brigade from Chaffin's Bluff, he ordered Longstreet to advance a force eight miles down river to New Market for closer observation of McClellan. He also instructed D. H. Hill, who had replaced Holmes, to use artillery and sharpshooters from the right bank "to annoy and arrest, if possible," Federal supply transports on the river.[52]

At the same time, Lee's fears had abated somewhat in regard to the enemy's threat from northern Virginia. Although he could "get no clew" to Pope's intention, Lee "inclined to the belief" that the Army of Virginia was to be nothing more than a covering force for Washington during McClellan's offensive. He suspected Pope, whom he was already beginning to dislike, was based at Manassas and that his "scouts and skirmishers are sent out for plunder, provisions and devastation." Viewing matters in this light, Lee naturally refused to weaken his own army to send additional men to Jackson until Pope came "within striking distance." He told Stonewall, however, that he was "ready to re-enforce" him "as soon as that prospect is apparent."[53]

One occurrence of the 23d did provide a narrow shaft of light to pierce the gloom for Lee. William W. Loring, commanding the Department of Southwest Virginia, who apparently was still considered under Lee's authority as general-in-chief, had written suggesting an offensive into the Kanawha Valley of western Virginia. Lee not only approved the idea, but, significantly, he encouraged it, "particularly at this moment, as the enemy seems to be tottering in his various positions." No doubt he was pleased by the chance to bring a new force into the strategic stalemate. A Confederate army operating in the Kanawha Valley would be on Pope's flank—albeit his distant flank—and might relieve some of the pressure on Richmond. Still, Lee made it clear that there were no reenforcements available to send to Loring.[54]

Friday, July 25, would bring Lee even greater cause to worry about the Federal force on the James and to downplay the threat from Pope. He learned that Stevens's division from Port Royal, South Carolina, had joined McClellan. And, by this date, he seems to have known that Burnside was at Fort Monroe. As a result Lee reported he was "feeling weak, uncertain which side of the James the enemy will advance, and being obliged to watch both."[55] From amid conflicting reports on northern Virginia, he seems to have believed that virtually all of the column at Fredericksburg had gone overland to join Pope, who was now based at Warrenton with about 43,000 men, including those in the Washington garrison. If true, this meant that Pope's main force was fifteen miles farther south than Lee had previously believed, but it was also farther west. Pope's new line indicated an approach to Culpeper and Charlottesville and removed pressure from the direct overland route to Richmond via Fredericksburg and Hanover Junction.[56]

In spite of this, July 25 is the date on which Lee first displayed a strong desire to strike at Pope's army. It may or may not be more than mere coincidence that this is also the date on which Lee first expressed personal disdain for John Pope. Apparently, he had read in the newspapers of General Orders, No. 11, which Pope issued from Washington on July 23, and which were the culminating and most drastic of a series of orders intended to end mollycoddling of traitors. Commanders in the Army of Virginia were ordered to arrest all disloyal males "within their reach" and offer them the choice of swearing an oath of allegiance or being expelled beyond Federal lines. Any citizen who took the oath and then violated it could be shot without benefit of trial, and his property forfeited to the government.[57] The Confederates considered these orders license for "indiscriminate murder," and Jefferson Davis declared Pope and his officers to be beyond the pale of protection usually extended to prisoners of war. When captured, they were to be held in close confinement and not be eligible for parole; and, if any Confederate civilians were executed, a like number of Pope's officers were to be hanged.[58]

Unquestionably, Pope's orders also outraged Lee and triggered in him an uncharacteristic dislike for an individual opponent.[59] To what extent Lee would permit personal repugnance to influence his strategic thinking must remain conjecture. But whatever the cause of his changed thinking, Lee wrote to Jackson on the 25th that he was "extremely anxious" to send him reenforcements "to suppress Pope."[60] At the same time, he did not want Jackson—or any additional forces that might be sent to him—to get beyond reach of a sudden recall to Richmond in case of an advance by McClellan. "If Pope goes far enough," Lee asked Stonewall, "could you swoop down north of the Rappahannock, suddenly uniting with Stuart, and clear the left bank opposite Fredericksburg?"

Within twenty-four hours Lee received a three-day-old dispatch from Jackson which in effect answered his question. Apparently, Jackson felt "too weak" to resist Pope's advance, let alone undertake an offensive against the Federals. Swallowing hard, no doubt, Lee told Jackson reenforcements were a "difficult question," but he would "endeavor to send" a division to him. As Lee put the dilemma succinctly to Davis, because "Pope is too strong to be allowed to remain so near our communications . . . , I feel that it will be necessary to reenforce [Jackson] before he can do anything and yet I fear to jeopardize the division of this army, upon which so much depends." The inconvenience of Jackson's weakness annoyed Lee to the extent that he lectured him on gathering in his stragglers and tightening his procedures for counting his men. He concluded by temporarily lowering his expectations and advising Jackson to "take a strong position and resist the advance of Pope."[61]

After sleeping on his dilemma, Lee made up his mind. On July 27 he ordered A. P. Hill's division and Starke's Louisiana brigade to Gordonsville to report to Jackson. Lee believed the new forces would double Jackson's size to about thirty-six thousand. He advised Stonewall to "Cache your troops as much as possible till you strike your blow and be prepared to return to me when done. . . ." He added, "I will endeavor to keep General McClellan quiet till it is over, if rapidly executed." Clearly, Lee changed Jackson's mission when he sent the reenforcements. No longer was Stonewall simply to resist Pope or even to await an opportunity to strike. Now, he was ordered to go on the offensive. Jackson must create his opportunities, if necessary, and do so speedily. And, at least as late as the 27th, Lee had no intention of sending further troops, nor of going north to supervise the operation himself.[62]

The next day, July 28, Lee undertook to keep his end of the bargain. He ordered Harvey Hill to put together an expedition from forces south of the James, including picked infantry and cavalry, to which were added five batteries from the Artillery Reserve and a number of long-range pieces, totaling forty-three guns. Under cover of night, Hill was to seize a point across from Harrison's Landing, open fire on the Federal ships, and cut off McClellan's water-based communications.[63] Lee hoped this would compel McClellan to move downstream to a broader part of the James, or at least "anchor him in his present position from which he would not dare to advance, so that I can reinforce Jackson without hazard to Richmond, and thus enable him to drive if not destroy that miscreant Pope."[64]

Hill did not launch his surprise attack until the night of July 31. A thirty-minute shelling from Coggins Point caused the Federals to douse their lights, stirred considerable confusion among the tents, and yielded a handful of casualties. It did not for a moment cause McClellan to consider moving his base. Three days later the Federal commander did send a force across the river to seize Coggins Point to prevent a recurrence of the attack. Lee was so disappointed in the failure that he eventually replaced Hill as district head and sent him back to command his old division in the field.[65]

Harvey Hill's expedition accomplished nothing, except to divert Lee's mind during another frustrating week of enforced inactivity. But the relative quiet ended on August 3 when McClellan once again called the Army of the Potomac to Lee's attention forcibly by crossing troops to the south bank of the James, which "seemed to threaten an advance on Petersburg." The next day Federal gunboats steamed upriver and anchored off the old battlefield at Malvern Hill, "as if to sweep the ground preparatory to its occupation by a land force," which seemed to foreshadow a move along the north bank. While Lee puzzled over these contradictory actions by the enemy, a letter he received from Jackson deepened his perplexity.[66]

If the Confederate commander had expected Jackson to commence an offensive against Pope immediately upon receiving reenforcements, he was to be disappointed. Stonewall continued to act with cautious watchfulness for several reasons. First, he had apparently heard of a Federal buildup at Fredericksburg, which if true would not only threaten his communications with Richmond but would also threaten Richmond itself, since the Confederates had only a portion of Stuart's cavalry in the Ashland-Hanover area. More pointedly, Jackson reported his offensive delayed because he had yet to find a promising way to turn Pope's strong position north of the Rapidan River.[67]

Lee replied with patience, considering the developing pressure in his own front. He discounted the threat from Fredericksburg, although he noted he had the day before ordered Stuart to reconnoiter the area. And he warmly approved Jackson's approach. "You are right," Lee wrote, encapsulating his own strategic philosophy and likely reflecting on the costly frontal assaults of the Seven Days, "in not attacking them in their strong and chosen positions. They ought always to be turned as you propose, and thus force them on more favorable ground." Lee even held out the hope that additional reenforcements might be sent north.[68]

The Crisis Crests, August 5–9

Lee's patience would be short-lived, however, for the next day, August 5, it must have seemed that both time and luck had run out on him. First, Stuart sent him the startling news that two Federal brigades of some six thousand men were advancing south on the Telegraph Road from Fredericksburg against Hanover Junction, the center of his line of communications with Jackson.[69] Pursuant to Lee's orders of the 3d to reconnoiter as near as possible to Fredericksburg to discover the enemy's size and intentions, Stuart had coincidentally encountered a Federal raid to destroy the Virginia Central Railroad at or near Hanover Junction. John Gibbon's brigade of western regiments, supported by John Hatch's brigade, both of Rufus King's division of McDowell's corps, reached Thornburg, fifteen miles south of Fredericksburg, before encountering Stuart. After skirmishing with what the Federals believed to be a superior Confederate force, Gibbon broke off the raid and returned to camp.[70]

Lee, of course, had no way of knowing the affair was simply a raid and not the vanguard of a new campaign against Richmond based on Fredericksburg. Indeed, Stuart encouraged the gloomier view by reporting that "Burnside is at Fredericksburg, with 16,000 men, to follow on the same route."[71] It is likely that Lee had known for about a week that Burnside's force from North Carolina lay in transports off Fort Monroe

without disembarking and that the Confederate commander had anticipated Burnside's ultimate destination—which he expected to be McClellan
or Pope—would reveal which of the two armies would be the major thrust
in a new Federal offensive.[72] Now, it appeared the Federals had decided to
use Burnside as an additional, independent column from the north to pierce
Lee's weakly held center between Jackson and the Army of Northern Virginia on the James.

The worst tidings of August 5 were yet to come, however. Even as Lee
pondered his response to this new and unexpected threat from
Fredericksburg, word arrived later the same night that McClellan had
marched up the James with a large force and reoccupied Malvern Hill. To
the Confederate commander, "it looked like" the long-dreaded "general advance of McClellan's army" up the James had begun.[73]

From all of the information available to him, Lee must have believed he
now confronted the most critical moment of his brief career in the field. He
scrambled to protect himself as best he could from these multiple threats.
He ordered Hood's division to move some five miles to the northwest to a
point on the Brooke Turnpike, where it would be centrally located to march
on either Ashland or Hanover Junction.[74] But it was toward McClellan—
from whom he always expected the greatest danger—that he directed his
full attention. He massed five divisions—his entire remaining force north
of the James—at the foot of Malvern Hill, while he hurried to New Market
to take personal charge of the defense against the Army of the Potomac.[75]
He also ordered Anderson's division at Drewry's Bluff to be ready to march
at a moment's notice to join the main army north of the river.[76] And he
wrote to D. H. Hill to "spare no effort in urging on the works at Drewry's
Bluff to a speedy conclusion," as it might soon be necessary to order into the
field the three brigades on loan from North Carolina.[77]

When Lee arrived at Malvern Hill, he found "the enemy appeared in
considerable strength. . . . His troops were drawn up in line of battle, his
artillery in position, and he apparently was prepared to deliver battle in as
strong force as he did" a month earlier. Because the day was "intensely hot"
and the troops moved slowly, darkness fell before Lee had time to do more
than advance a force east to Willis Church to threaten Federal communications with Harrison's Landing. Whether Lee—remembering the bloody
and futile assaults of July 1—was laying the groundwork for a turning
movement, or whether he would have waited to develop McClellan's intentions will never be known. The next morning, much to Lee's surprise
and confusion, the Army of the Potomac had disappeared, slipping back to
its base at Harrison's Landing.[78]

The enemy's sudden departure suggested to Lee that McClellan must
have had ulterior motives for the move upriver, and the Confederate
commander's attention reverted back to the new threat from the north. As

he wrote to Jackson, "I have no idea [McClellan] will advance on Richmond now, but it may be premonitory to get a new position, reconnoiter, &c. I think it more probable to cover other movements, probably that of Burnside from Fredericksburg. . . ."[79]

It is clear that among his many speculations, Lee did not yet suspect that McClellan was actually preparing to withdraw the Army of the Potomac back to Washington, as had been ordered over the Federal commander's protests four days earlier. Nor did Lee perceive there to be a strategic pattern uniting all of the Federal movements that would redound to the immense benefit of the Confederacy. He could not know that the hand of Henry Halleck, the new Federal general-in-chief, was already at work concentrating virtually all of the Union field forces in Virginia in front of Washington. Abiding by his own writings, which elevated concentration above maneuver, Halleck was preparing to duplicate his successful spring campaign against Corinth.

Ignorant of the true meaning of the enemy moves, it is also clear that Lee was shaken by the crisis. On August 7 he wrote to Jackson, "[I]t seems at present . . . too hazardous to diminish the forces here"; Stonewall should plan to act without waiting for reenforcements. Lee then proceeded to critique a proposal Jackson had put forward in a letter of the 6th.[80] Apparently, Jackson believed the force at Fredericksburg was merely part of Pope's army and not Burnside's North Carolina contingent. Stonewall suggested that if he advanced against the Federal base at Warrenton he would draw all of Pope's forces after him into Fauquier County and thus relieve the pressure on Richmond. Lee agreed the plan might work, if the Fredericksburg column were a detachment of Pope's. But, if Pope had already concentrated his own army and Burnside were in fact at Fredericksburg with a whole new force, then Jackson would find himself confronted by a superior enemy in his front, while another dangerous foe operated on his right flank and rear.[81]

"It was to save you the abundance of hard fighting," Lee wrote pointedly, "that I ventured to suggest for your consideration not to attack the enemy's strong points, but to turn his position at Warrenton, &c., so as to draw him out of them." Plainly, Lee was trying to impress on Jackson his own determination to rely as much as possible on maneuver and to husband meager Confederate manpower. "I would rather," he wrote, cutting to the heart of the matter, "you should have easy fighting and heavy victories." But, since Lee always assumed that a subordinate at a distance must make his own decisions, he acknowledged, characteristically, "I must now leave the matter to your reflection and good judgment." Still, he could not resist reminding Jackson of the wider implications of his action by concluding, "Make up your mind what is best to be done under all of the circumstances which surround *us*, and let me hear the result at which you arrive."[82]

The following day, August 8, Lee received a dispatch from Jackson dated the 7th, which contained a new, more modest proposal.[83] Apparently, Stonewall had received information that Pope was slowly concentrating his army at Culpeper, and he saw the opportunity to smash the enemy vanguard before supporting units arrived. Lee probably liked this plan better, because it did not carry Jackson so far north; and he approved it as "judicious," so long as the "information is correct." But, once again, he cautioned Jackson by writing, "I hope you may be able to strike him moving, or at least be able to draw him from his strong positions." At the same time, he ordered Hood's division forward fifteen miles to Hanover Junction, where it would be in position to afford some protection to Jackson's flank.[84]

Events justified Lee's cautious approval. Pope was not concentrating his army at Culpeper. He had established his five divisions along a twenty-mile defensive line that Franz Sigel's corps anchored at Sperryville and that ran southeast to Culpeper. The Federal commander was centrally located to respond to any initiative Jackson might undertake. When Federal scouts reported Jackson crossing the Rapidan, Pope correctly divined Culpeper to be the Confederate destination and only then did the Federal general begin to concentrate his own army at that point. By August 9, when Jackson reached Cedar Mountain, eight miles south of Culpeper, the Confederate encountered Banks's corps advancing to meet them. Only Sigel's inability to march his corps efficiently saved Jackson from facing superior odds. As it was, although Stonewall enjoyed a slight numerical advantage, it was all he could do—in a poorly managed but hard-fought battle—to push the stubborn Federals from the field.[85]

Jackson met Lee's minimal expectations by not attacking the enemy in his "chosen position," but he accepted battle in such an unfavorable setting that he could not pursue his victory for any advantage. Although he held the battleground itself, he now confronted Pope's united army with odds of about two to one against him, and so on August 11 he retreated southward to Gordonsville. In one sense also, Jackson did achieve the strategic results that had brought him north. After the check at Cedar Mountain, Pope would abandon any thought of advancing on Charlottesville and thus end the threat to the Confederate supply line from the Shenandoah Valley.

On another level, however, the results were unsatisfactory. When the Federals hunkered down defensively behind the Rapidan, Pope created a stalemate on the northern flank similar to the one that already existed on the James. This put Lee in an intolerable strategic predicament. By conventional wisdom, the Confederate commander was too weak to shift enough troops to either wing to break the impasse, while, at the same time, neither could he defend his exposed center from a thrust from Fredericksburg. Strategically speaking, Lee was spread-eagled to a wagon wheel.

CHAPTER FIVE

"Richmond was never so safe"

Lee Evolves a Border Strategy, August 9–26, 1862

EVEN BEFORE THE guns had opened on the slopes of Cedar Mountain, Lee decided upon a desperate course of action to end the deadlock and gain a measure of control over the operations in the Eastern theater. Frustrated with Jackson's lack of progress and unwilling to continue longer in a defensive posture that yielded more danger than security, he turned once again to maneuver and the offensive-defensive. Before he could have had any knowledge of the results of Jackson's battle against Pope, Lee decided to send Longstreet north to break the stalemate.[1]

On August 9 Lee ordered McLaws's division to replace Longstreet in the defensive line from Chaffin's Bluff on the James to the Darbytown Road.[2] At the same time, Longstreet himself ordered all six brigades in his own division to cook three days' rations and to march the following day into Richmond to board the Virginia Central Railroad for Gordonsville.[3] During the next two days, similar instructions were issued to the two small divisions of Evans and D. R. Jones, while Longstreet's artillery was ordered to set out by road for the same destination.[4] All of the units were ordered to report to Jackson on their arrival, and in spite of delays due to congestion on the railroad, the first arrived early the evening of the 10th.[5] Longstreet joined his troops and took command of the combined forces at Gordonsville on the 12th.[6]

The Longstreet Gamble, August 9–14

The sudden appearance of Burnside at Fredericksburg finally caused Lee's dammed impatience to break. He knew he could not successfully contend against a three-pronged pincers movement. He must choose from among McClellan, Pope, and Burnside, who represented the most immediate danger but at the same time appeared to be most vulnerable. No longer could he remain inactive and on the defensive. He must seize the initiative, no matter the risk, and by maneuver juggle the odds sufficiently in his favor to destroy the noose slowly tightening around Richmond. For the second time in his field career of barely two months, Lee faced a decision on which the fate of his country hinged, and he had to make it based on sketchy and contradictory knowledge of the enemy. He observed once during the war that "he sometimes applied himself so closely to a problem that he found his ideas running around in a circle" and could not "find a tangent." For about five weeks this had been one of those "times."[7]

The "tangent" Lee found on August 9 was to reduce significantly his forces on the James and to launch an offensive northward. It was a startling decision to discount—even temporarily—the largest enemy army and the one that was both nearest to Richmond and best situated to capture the capital. Yet, Lee knew he could not attack the Army of the Potomac in its stronghold, and he judged that the shifting of Burnside from Fort Monroe, coupled with McClellan's sudden retreat from Malvern Hill, suggested the possibility of a short breathing space on the James.[8] On the other hand, the potential for maneuver did exist against the Federal forces in the north. And the convenient route of the Virginia Central offered Lee the possibility to exploit his interior position by shifting troops quickly northward, striking a lightning blow to disrupt the plans of both Pope and Burnside, and still returning to the James in time to fend off any countermove by McClellan.

In selecting Longstreet's entire command of three divisions, Lee determined that he would send 20,000 men north to swell the left wing to 40,000, a force representing almost half of the Army of Northern Virginia and approximately equal to Pope's strength.[9] In sending Longstreet along with his command, Lee knowingly sent an officer senior to Jackson. Since Lee did not plan to travel to Gordonsville himself, he must have intended to supersede Jackson as commander of the operations against Pope. Lee had returned Jackson to independent command and dispatched him northward to duplicate the dazzling maneuvers of the spring Valley campaign and not to reach an impasse with Pope. Now, the increased risk of weakening Confederate forces on the James made it imperative that operations in the north be pushed more vigorously than they had been during the previous three weeks.[10]

Whether or not Lee consulted with Longstreet before making the decision—and while his thinking was still "running around in a circle"— is uncertain. But Lee did meet with his chief subordinate prior to the latter's departure for Gordonsville. And, plainly, he gave him general instructions for conducting an independent campaign against Pope. Longstreet was to find a way to turn Pope's flank, while Stuart would "sweep by the enemy's rear and cut his communications" with both Fredericksburg and Washington. Although Lee granted Longstreet the customary discretion to shape the turning movement in accord with an assessment made on the scene, Lee himself seems to have favored a move around Pope's left flank. Moving to the east, it would be easier for Longstreet to cooperate with Stuart and to drive a wedge between Pope and Burnside to prevent the two from uniting. Also, an offensive to the east would not carry Longstreet as far away from Richmond as would one to the west.[11]

Undoubtedly, Lee discussed his risky move with Davis and gained the president's approval in advance. Davis had never "preferred defensive to offensive war" and believed opportunities had been missed in the past. His commanders had either concocted grandiose schemes or demanded resources he could not provide. He must have found it a welcome change to have a general willing to shoulder responsibility, use the forces at hand, and seek permission to launch an unfanciful offensive. It helped, of course, that the general was one in whom he repeatedly avowed his "entire confidence."[12]

In staying behind to confront McClellan, Lee signaled the importance he attached to defending the James with a weakened force, but he also manifested a preference he would exhibit throughout the war for remaining with the main body and entrusting the command of a striking column to a subordinate. As Longstreet set out for Gordonsville, Lee did what he could to secure Richmond during the absence of nearly half the Army of Northern Virginia. He shifted McLaws's division from the Nine Mile Road to replace Longstreet, whose command had run from Chaffin's Bluff on the river to the Darbytown Road with a brigade thrown forward to New Market. With D. H. Hill and R. H. Anderson still south of the James, the first line of defense against any advance by McClellan now fell to two divisions, McLaws's and Ripley's. Lee ordered the Artillery Reserve under Pendleton—which had been on the south side to support the harassment of Harrison's Landing—to reconcentrate behind McLaws. And he named G. W. Smith, who had just returned from sick leave, to command the five brigades that had been under Roswell Ripley, their senior brigadier, since D. H. Hill had replaced Holmes at Petersburg. There was little more he could do.[13]

As Lee waited for the unfolding of events beyond his control, one alarm arose to test his nerves. Either late on the night of the 11th or very early on the morning of the 12th, word arrived at headquarters that once again "the enemy is advancing by way of Malvern Hill." By this time all but two of Longstreet's brigades had withdrawn from the line for the journey to Gordonsville, but Lee seems not to have considered their recall. Instead, he alerted McLaws to the danger and ordered G. W. Smith to march his division to New Market and "to oppose the enemy and drive him back." The rumored Federal advance proved false, and the remainder of the 12th passed quietly.[14]

Fortunately, Lee did not for long have to endure such anxious suspense. And, perhaps even more happily for the Confederates, he would never know whether or not his Longstreet gamble would have profited. On Wednesday,

August 13, the six-week-old stalemate that had taxed Lee's patience, strained his resources, and stymied his scheme to pursue an intensive offensive-defensive strategy to win the war began to dissipate. Two pieces of intelligence dramatically altered the equation that Lee had been struggling to solve. By far the more important news was the report from an "English deserter of the embarkation of a part of McClellan's army" from the Peninsula. Lee wrote immediately to D. H. Hill at Petersburg, "It is of the first importance that I should be advised positively on this point, as our own movements must be in a measure regulated by those of that army." Harvey Hill must send his "most reliable and intelligent" scouts down the south bank to watch the enemy "narrowly and unceasingly, and report immediately anything of importance that should occur."[15]

It was incredibly good luck that—almost at the same time—Lee received information indicating Burnside's forces had left Fredericksburg to march west and join Pope at Culpeper. The Confederate commander at once ordered Jeb Stuart, stationed near Hanover Junction, "to ascertain the truthfulness of this report."[16] If either account, but especially if both, were accurate, the enemy was presenting Lee a rare opportunity to employ maneuver to great advantage.

Overripe with frustration, Lee did not await confirmation from his sources. He ordered Hood's division to march from Hanover Junction to join the gathering forces at Gordonsville, where he was to report to Longstreet. Lee also ordered Stuart with the main body of cavalry to Gordonsville. And, significantly, he added to Stuart's dispatch that Jeb was to report to Longstreet "in the event of his [Lee's] absence."[17] By the evening of the 13th, it must have occurred to Lee there were diminishing reasons for him to remain in Richmond. He would have to make certain arrangements for the capital's defense, and he might look for other troops that could now be spared, but after that he was free to go north himself.[18]

On Thursday, August 14, the race for the Rapidan began. On that day, McClellan's troops started their march from Harrison's Landing to Fort Monroe, where men, guns, horses, and accoutrements would be loaded onto ships for a 160-mile journey up the Chesapeake Bay to Aquia Creek near Fredericksburg. After disembarking they must travel forty miles overland to join with Pope and his army. It was a race the Federals were fated to lose, unless the Confederate commander and his army, like Aesop's hare, stopped to nap. Nearly half of the Army of Northern Virginia had already gathered at Gordonsville within twenty-five miles of Pope, and whatever troops Lee would now feel free to pull from Richmond could travel by rail to join the striking force.

During the morning, Lee received a dispatch from Longstreet that clinched his decision to take the field personally. Apparently, Longstreet's study of the terrain and the enemy's troop dispositions led him to believe the Confederates should maneuver westward toward the mountains and operate against Pope's right flank. Longstreet hesitated to modify the plans on his own authority, however, and he not only sought Lee's advice but urged his chief to come to Gordonsville. Although Lee declined to issue peremptory instructions from a distance, he reminded Longstreet of the theoretical advantages of operating against Pope's left flank and the desire for Stuart to descend on the Federal rear and cut communications with Washington. Still, in the end, the imperative was speed, and Lee concluded, "It is all-important that our movement, in whatever direction it is, should be as quick as possible." Affirming he would leave before dawn on the morrow for the front, he urged Longstreet to press forward with preparations in the meanwhile and to arrange a three-way conference that included Jackson.[19]

Lee spent the rest of a hectic 14th—he was too busy even to visit home and had to send a farewell note to his wife and children—supervising all of the details attendant upon his leaving Richmond and taking the field.[20] He named G. W. Smith to command the Richmond "wing" of the Army of Northern Virginia and assume the responsibility for the defense of the capital in his absence. Initially, this third wing would be composed of Smith's division and those of McLaws, R. H. Anderson, and D. H. Hill, the cavalry brigade of Wade Hampton, and the four battalions of the Artillery Reserve under Pendleton. Because Lee was yet uncertain whether McClellan's withdrawal was total or partial, Smith was to keep a close watch on the enemy on the James. As McClellan's forces diminished, reenforcements were to be sent to Gordonsville.[21]

As the day progressed evidence accumulated of the lessening threat posed by McClellan. The scouts sent out by D. H. Hill reported "[T]here can be no doubt . . . Porter's corps has left" Harrison's Landing, and Lee would write to Secretary Randolph, "From every indication it appears that General McClellan's forces on the James are being withdrawn and sent to re-enforce Pope." Under these circumstances, Lee decided it would be safe to strengthen his column for the offensive on the Rappahannock, and he ordered R. H. Anderson to prepare his division to take the field as soon as rail transportation could be arranged to carry it to Gordonsville. He also ordered two green North Carolina regiments to replace Anderson at Drewry's Bluff and two newly arrived units from South Carolina to proceed directly to join Longstreet. And, as if in a frenzy to nail down every loose detail, he repeated for a third time his order to Hood to hasten his division's march westward.[22]

Finally, a weary Lee sat down and wrote to Davis, "I have made all arrangements for the well being of the troops around Richmond." He took pains to calm any apprehensions the president might feel by painting the situation in the rosiest possible colors. He was leaving behind an aggregate of 72,000 men under the command of a senior officer to confront a retreating enemy. (Lee did not feel it necessary to mention that only some 40,000 of the men were present for duty; that their commander, G. W. Smith had just returned from a nervous breakdown caused by the strain of battle at Seven Pines; or that the extent of McClellan's withdrawal was not yet established.) Recognizing that distance would now interrupt their frequent and intimate consultations, he promised, "I will keep you informed of everything of importance that transpires." But the president should not worry, he wrote: "When you do not hear from me, you may feel sure that I do not think it necessary to trouble you." In order that he might not be misunderstood, however, he was quick to add, "I shall feel obliged to you for any directions you may think proper to give."[23]

The Rapidan Stall, August 15–20

At four o'clock in the morning on August 15, Lee left on the cars for Gordonsville and the start of a new campaign to shift "the scene of operations" to the Rapidan frontier and in hopes "the war will for a season at least be removed from Richmond." It is a measure of Lee as field commander that he left the capital several days before most other generals would have accepted the information about the enemy as being solid enough to justify decisive action. Not until the 16th would spotters along the James, who counted 108 ships going downriver and only 8 coming up, and corroborative news in the *Philadelphia Inquirer* positively confirm "the enemy has evacuated the James River country. . . ."[24]

Beyond doubt, Lee acted boldly during the days from August 9 to the 15, especially in deciding to send Longstreet to Gordonsville before knowing of McClellan's withdrawal. But his was boldness born of desperation and not of derring-do. Since the close of the Seven Days, the Army of Northern Virginia—the army that Lee believed would decide the fate of the Confederacy—had been locked in a virtual strategic stalemate. Encircling enemy columns had pinned it to the doorstep of the capital. Lee had been reduced to patient watchfulness, unable either to resume the offensive campaigns necessary to wear down the North's material superiority and its will to continue the struggle, or to draw upon some of the Confederacy's richest regions to sustain his own army. Any move he might have made would have given the enemy an opening to destroy his army and capture

Richmond. With the appearance of a new threat, against which he could muster no defense, nothing remained to Lee except boldness.

Then, even as he launched his gamble with Longstreet, the Federal noose around Richmond had begun to unravel of its own accord. Before Lee's grateful eyes, two of the threats united, while the third traveled by a circuitous route to join them. Unaccountably, the enemy had returned the initiative to him.[25] Lee understood that his opening existed for a limited time. He continued to believe that McClellan and the Army of the Potomac—wherever they might be—represented his greatest danger. He speculated that McClellan would either "ascend the Rappahannock, occupy Fredericksburg, and threaten Richmond from there," or unite with Pope. In either case, Lee knew he had to strike Pope before McClellan was in place.[26]

Anxious to get his offensive under way, Lee conferred with Longstreet and Jackson shortly after his arrival on the morning of the 15th. After studying a map prepared by "Jed." Hotchkiss of Jackson's staff, Lee listened to such intelligence as Stonewall was able to provide. Once again Longstreet recommended moving to the west, crossing the fords of the upper Rapidan, and turning Pope's right flank. Lee remained determined, however, to maneuver to the east by crossing the lower Rapidan and turning Pope's left flank, in order to drive a wedge between the Army of Virginia and any reenforcements from McClellan coming from either Washington or Fredericksburg. At the same time, Stuart was to sweep behind Pope and cut his supply line at Rappahannock Station, where the Orange and Alexandria Railroad bridge crossed the river.[27]

While there is no reason to question the soundness of Lee's campaign strategy, the tactical orders he issued the next day to carry it into effect seem to have been based on faulty and perhaps outdated information. He planned for Jackson's command of three divisions (Ewell, Taliaferro, and A. P. Hill) to cross the Rapidan at Somerville Ford, while the four divisions now under Longstreet (Longstreet, D. R. Jones, Evans, and Hood) passed the river at Raccoon Ford on the right, two miles to the east. Lee instructed Stuart to use Mitchell's Ford—eight miles even farther east—and take the route through Stevensburg to Rappahannock Station. The infantry was to advance in the direction of Culpeper with Longstreet remaining on Jackson's right. Stuart was to destroy Pope's telegraph lines and the railroad bridge across the Rappahannock and then turn back to Culpeper, taking position on Longstreet's right.[28] To complete his plans, on the 15th Lee requested Davis to start R. H. Anderson's division toward Louisa Court House, where orders would await it.[29] With the addition of Hood and Stuart, Lee's force numbered about 50,000, and, if Anderson were to arrive in time, he would have another 6,000. He estimated Pope's numbers at between 65,000 and 70,000.[30]

It is not likely that these dispositions would have achieved the results Lee sought. They might have worked, if Pope remained in the position he had taken immediately after the Battle of Cedar Mountain. On August 10 the Federals had formed a line perpendicular to the Rapidan, facing east and running from the Cedar Mountain battlefield to Culpeper. Lee's infantry could then have aimed to interpose between Culpeper and the Rappahannock. Capt. J. Keith Boswell, Jackson's chief engineer, had carefully studied these enemy dispositions on August 13 from the top of Clark's Mountain. In response to Stonewall's request for a route to turn Pope's flank he had suggested crossing the Rapidan at Somerville Ford. It seems probable that Lee based his plans on Boswell's report.[31]

Unfortunately for the Confederates, Pope had decided to defend the line of the Rapidan. On August 14 he had pivoted to face south, advancing his army forward and parallel to the river. His line was now anchored by Sigel's corps in the west at Robertson's River; McDowell's corps held the center at Cedar Mountain; and Jesse Reno's two divisions from Burnside extended the line on the left to Raccoon Ford. Banks was in reserve at Culpeper. With the addition of Reno and King's division of McDowell's corps from Fredericksburg, Pope's Army of Virginia numbered about 57,000.[32]

The flaw in Lee's plans was that his infantry would run directly into Pope's left and left-center by crossing at Somerville and Raccoon fords. It is true that Stuart's raid would constitute a turning movement; there is every indication Stuart's move was to be conducted concurrently with the infantry fording the Rapidan. But it would not likely have saved Lee from a bloody battle on the near bank of the river, or possibly from having to fight his way across the stream. It is probable that Lee's projected turning movement—just as the ones at Beaver Dam Creek and Gaines' Mill—would have translated into a costly frontal assault.[33]

Lee's plans would never be tested in action, however, as once again he experienced the painful truth known eventually to all military commanders and ignored only by armchair strategists. Men and equipment cannot be moved over roads and rivers as easily as pins on a map. Lee came to Gordonsville frustrated by the delays of his lieutenants and determined to execute a rapid offensive. Yet, his council of the early 15th did not yield orders until the following day, and those orders would not call for movement to commence until the 18th—four days after his arrival. Worse yet, on the 18th the Confederates still were not ready. The movement had to be postponed until the 20th, and by that date Pope had retreated to an even stronger defensive line behind the Rappahannock.

All manner of hobgoblins played havoc with Lee's plans. "Fitz" Lee's cavalry brigade, one-half of the force designated for the raid on Pope's rear, meandered out of its way from Hanover Junction to stop at Louisa Court House for provisions. It arrived on the Rapidan on the night of the 18th, a day late, and with horses too fatigued for service the following day.[34] Unexpected logistical problems also delayed the army's advance. For a brief period Lee faced a crisis in feeding his army, while he struggled to establish a depot at Orange Court House. The rapid rail journey by Longstreet's troops left their subsistence wagons far behind, and rations, even hard bread, were running dangerously low.[35] Finally, the seemingly simple task of bringing the columns together on the two country roads leading to Somerville and Raccoon fords could not be accomplished in the time allotted. "The process," Lee observed, "is slow and tedious."[36]

Finally, after resigning himself to a further two-day delay, Lee climbed to the top of nearby Clark's Mountain for a personal reconnaissance, only to witness through his binoculars Pope's army strike their tents, break camp, and withdraw northward. While the Confederates were fumbling their way through their preparations, chance had intervened in the form of the first of three lost documents that would dramatically alter Lee's campaigns during the summer of 1862. A Federal cavalry patrol captured Stuart's adjutant carrying dispatches that sufficiently detailed Lee's numbers and aggressive intentions to convince Pope the Federals must abandon the Rapidan. Since Pope was merely awaiting the arrival of McClellan's troops, he decided it would be prudent to wait a little closer to Fredericksburg. He started his withdrawal on the morning of the 18th, and by the following day he had formed a new line behind the Rappahannock from Kelly's Ford to a point three miles above Rappahannock Station.

Lee watched for a long time from the summit of Clark's Mountain as the dust clouds of the retreating Federals approached the horizon and "melted into the bright haze of the afternoon sun." Finally, he dropped his glasses, and "with a deeply-drawn breath, expressive at once of disappointment and resignation," he turned to Longstreet at his side and said, "General, we little thought that the enemy would turn his back upon us thus early in the campaign."[37] Masked behind the playful reference to Pope's bombastic proclamation was deep disappointment, for it was Lee's first impression that Pope would fall back to a point much nearer to Washington. The Federal commander would then be much closer to the reenforcements on the way from the Army of the Potomac. Now, even if Lee could catch up with Pope before McClellan's arrival, the defenders of Richmond would necessarily have to deliver battle at a considerable distance from the Confederate capital. How far north did Lee dare go in pursuit of Pope?

Lee's original intent had been to transfer "the scene of operations" to the Rapidan frontier to protect the Virginia Central Railroad and his supply line with the Shenandoah Valley, and also in the hope that the war would "for a season at least be removed from Richmond." He believed that retaining the resources of the capital and the Valley were the bare minimum achievements necessary to sustain his army in Virginia. He had not traveled to Gordonsville to assume the defensive, however, but to strike a blow that would baffle the enemy's offensive plans and undercut the will of the Northern people to prosecute the war.

Jefferson Davis understood and supported Lee's strategy, and in most matters he undertook to carry out Lee's wishes. He had endorsed the order sending R. H. Anderson's division from Drewry's Bluff to Gordonsville with the imperative "let it be done immediately," and within twenty-four hours Armistead's brigade had reached Louisa Court House.[38] As soon as Lee suggested the reports on McClellan's retreat were sufficiently conclusive to free additional forces from Richmond's defenses, the War Department quickly asked if McLaws's division should be moved "toward the railroad" to be ready to be transferred. When Secretary of War Randolph discovered McLaws's to be occupied with a reconnaissance in force, he ordered G. W. Smith to send his own division "with the least delay practicable to re-enforce General Lee" and also to prepare the other divisions of his command to go forward. And on the following day, Randolph ordered William N. Pendleton to report to Lee with the Artillery Reserve battalions.[39] Finally, when Lee confided to Davis that D. H. Hill had proven inadequate to the independent role of district commander, the president sent Hill back to head his old division in the field.[40]

There is no indication, however, that Lee at first intended, or that Davis had agreed, for the Army of Northern Virginia to operate much beyond Culpeper and the Rapidan frontier. Regrettably, at the same time that Pope's army receded into the distances of northern Virginia, Federal ghost armies began to appear to remind both the Confederate commander and the administration of the vulnerability of Richmond. Even though intelligence satisfied the Confederates that McClellan's army was embarking at Fort Monroe, it could not confirm he was destined for Fredericksburg. One persistent rumor had the Army of the Potomac sailing up the York River to the White House and once again advancing on Richmond from the Chickahominy.

Then, on the 19th, Lee himself heard that "a body of the enemy is moving from Fredericksburg toward Hanover Junction." As badly as he wanted reenforcements, under the circumstances Lee could not justify stripping Richmond of the third wing of the Army of Northern Virginia, which comprised its last defenders. He suggested to Davis that the two infantry divisions and Artillery Reserve not be sent to him immediately. Instead, for the time being they should be massed behind the North Anna River, where they would be centrally located to defend Hanover Junction, threaten the flank of an enemy on the Chickahominy, or advance to his own support when events warranted.[41]

Thus, when Lee crossed the Rapidan on August 20 to follow Pope and develop Federal intentions, he knew that for the immediate future he would not be able to unite all of his own army in the field. He adhered to his original plan and crossed Jackson at Somerville Ford and Longstreet on his right at Raccoon Ford. Meanwhile R. H. Anderson followed as reserve behind Jackson, and Stuart with the cavalry swept around to the east to try to get in front of Pope. By the morning of the 21st, it became certain that Pope had successfully crossed his army over the Rappahannock, and it seemed to Lee that the Federal force had then divided into columns for its retreat. He informed Davis, "Burnside, Stevens and King appear to have gone toward Fredericksburg. Pope, Banks, Sigel, &c., toward Warrenton."

The splitting of the Union army must have excited Lee, for it offered the possibility of engaging and defeating it in detail. It also beckoned to Lee to push back even farther the frontier for operations and free another area of the Old Dominion from the foe's occupation. But did he dare advance farther north? On the other hand, could he afford to miss the opportunity? He telegraphed at once to the president, "Can Richmond be held if followed?"[42]

The Rappahannock Waltz, August 21–24

Lee's telegram caught Davis by surprise. No more than Lee had the president anticipated that the enemy would retire so far north without giving battle, and he wrote back, "The retreat presents a case not originally contemplated." Still, without forthrightly stating it, Davis gave Lee implicit permission to pursue Pope farther from Richmond. His approval was contingent, however, on Lee's plan to retain temporarily the infantry divisions of McLaws and D. H. Hill and the Artillery Reserve, some 18,000 men, at Hanover Junction to forestall a threat from Fredericksburg. The president also made it clear that the 13,000 men on loan from North Carolina would remain at Richmond under G. W. Smith until the enemy's intentions were better understood.[43]

This telegraphic exchange between Lee and Davis is critical to understanding the development of Lee's strategy during the summer of 1862.

Although a similar conclusion can be read between the lines in most of the correspondence between the two during August, nowhere is it plainer than in this exchange that neither the president nor the general anticipated the great success the Army of Northern Virginia would achieve so quickly. In consequence, they had not determined in advance the limit to which victory might be pursued. Although neither balked at the abstract notion of entering Maryland, neither had they set the crossing of the Potomac as the goal of the summer's campaign. Both men, quite properly, were taking success one step at a time.

In any case, before Lee could have received Davis's reply, he discovered his question had been premature. Pope was not retreating to either Fredericksburg or Warrenton. When Fitz Lee's cavalry at the head of Longstreet's column encountered the enemy at Kelly's Ford late on the twentieth, Lee assumed it was the rearguard of the Army of Virginia. But, when Beverly Robertson's horsemen followed by Jackson's command ran into a strong Federal force at Beverly's Ford six miles upstream on the afternoon of the 21st, Lee realized that Pope had formed a line on the high ground along the north bank of the Rappahannock. Initially, this must have seemed like good news, as it meant a blow could be struck without traveling so far from Richmond.[44]

Reconnaissance quickly determined that Pope was in force on the higher north bank and commanded the approaches from the south. For the Confederates to attempt crossing anywhere between Kelly's and Beverly's fords would be certainly bloody and perhaps futile. It did not take Lee long to decide on a turning movement and to reject trying one to his right, as going east would carry him into the narrow V of the forks of the Rapidan and Rappahannock and away from Pope's communications. Upstream were numerous fords and the opportunity for a turning movement against the Orange and Alexandria Railroad. Lee ordered Longstreet to abandon Kelly's Ford and to march west to replace Jackson at Beverly's Ford, thus freeing Stonewall to move farther to the left and cross beyond Pope's flank. As Longstreet pulled back from Kelly's Ford, a Federal force crossed the river and assaulted his rear. Although Featherston's brigade beat off the attack, it was a signal to Lee that the pesky Pope might not be easy to "suppress."[45]

Apparently, Lee decided from the first that Jackson would lead the turning movement. Otherwise, he would have marched Longstreet behind Jackson to go farther to the west. Instead, Longstreet took over at Beverly's Ford on August 22, and Jackson headed upstream five miles to Freeman's Ford. Before Stonewall got there, Stuart discovered the unwelcome news that Pope—who seemed to be parrying every thrust—was already strongly posted at Freeman's Ford. Lee was beginning to run out of room before he would find Pope's flank anchored on the Bull Run Mountains. Anxious to strike Pope before McClellan's reenforcements arrived, but equally anxious to rely on maneuver, Lee resorted to more drastic measures. He ordered Jackson to continue on past Freeman's to Sulphur Springs Ford eight miles even farther west. Meanwhile, he approved Stuart's plan to sweep behind the enemy's rear and sever Federal communications.

On the afternoon of the 22d, Jackson arrived to find Sulphur Springs Ford unguarded, and he crossed Jubal Early's brigade to secure a foothold while the rest of the command arrived. During the evening an unusually heavy thunderstorm freshened the Rappahannock and trapped Early on the north bank for most of the following day. Late on the 23d, Early was able to escape back across a hastily constructed bridge, just as enemy forces were approaching his position. In the meantime, Stuart had crossed the river at Waterloo Bridge at the foot of the mountains and ridden through Warrenton twenty-five miles to Catlett's Station. The rainstorm prevented him from firing the railroad bridge over Cedar Run near the station, but a captured black who had known Stuart at Berkeley provided the whereabouts of Pope's headquarters. Although Pope himself was absent, Stuart captured several members of the Federal general's staff and numerous dispatches detailing the enemy's strength, location, and plans. Stuart did not this time ride a complete circuit but returned to his point of departure on the 23d.[46]

On Saturday, August 23, after a week of fast-paced events, Lee paused to take stock. Thus far, Pope had checked every attempt to turn the Federal flank. After Jubal Early scrambled back to safety, enemy forces had appeared opposite Sulphur Spring and closed this avenue for advance. Even Stuart's raid on Pope's headquarters had not caused the Federal commander to abandon his naturally strong position. Indeed, Lee had advanced so far to the west that his own right flank and his communications with Gordonsville were now exposed. Pope had perhaps sensed this opportunity, for on this very Saturday Longstreet had been required to hasten back to Rappahannock Station to drive back an enemy force that had crossed the river. If the "miscreant" Pope had proven a surprisingly adept foe, Lee had demonstrated his own determination to retain the initiative and aggressively press his offensive, no matter how often balked.

In the midst of his considerations, Lee sat down and wrote at length to Davis for the first time in nearly a week. After reviewing the frustrations of the past five days, he told the president that his attempts to find a way to turn Pope's flank had been interrupted by the heavy rains that had put the rivers in a "swimming condition."[47] He also noted that information from a captured dispatch and from Pope's quartermaster, who had been taken prisoner by Stuart, indicated that substantial forces were being withdrawn from Jacob Cox's command in the Kanawha Valley to join Pope. Lee urged that William Loring, the Confederate commander in western Virginia, seize the opportunity to undertake an offensive northward and "destroy several links in the Baltimore and Ohio Railroad." Lee not only hoped such a move would check Cox's reenforcements from ever reaching Pope, but it might also interfere with the Federals' ability to transfer troops from their Western armies—a fear which continued to preoccupy him throughout the summer.[48]

The heart of Lee's letter, however, concerned his own immediate problem on the Rappahannock. He had been compelled to conclude that "heavy rains in the mountains at this time . . . will no doubt continue the high water and give the enemy ample time to re-enforce General Pope with McClellan's army." And his thoughts immediately turned to reenforcements for his own army, as he regretted he could "get no news of our troops on the North Anna." Undoubtedly, this was Lee's gentle way of prodding Davis, and he went on to point out that if McClellan were joining Pope and not halting at Fredericksburg, then the Confederates' forces were wasted at Hanover Junction. Without yet having a specific operation in mind, Lee was clearly searching for a way to baffle the enemy's plans and to shift the military frontier even farther north. "If we are able to change the theater of the war from James River to the north of the Rappahannock we shall be able to consume provisions and forage now being used in supporting the enemy," he wrote. Lee gave no clue as to how this might be accomplished, but he was certain it would require "all available re-enforcements be sent here."[49]

During the next twenty-four hours, Lee had time to evaluate more of the dispatches that Stuart had captured at Pope's headquarters. One was so important as to deserve notoriety as the second lost document of the summer of 1862. About seventy-two hours after it had been sent, Lee was able to read Pope's August 20 report to Halleck on the strength and location of the Army of Virginia, and the Federal commander's plans for the next several days. Lee learned that McDowell's corps numbered 18,000, Sigel's 12,000, Banks's 7,000, and Reno's 8,000, "making 45,000 men for duty." Since Lee believed this figure to be "independent of Burnside," and since it did not in fact include cavalry, he assumed it confirmed his earlier estimate of Pope at approximately 65,000.[50]

Pope's revealing dispatch also told Lee that because the Federal commander believed Kelly's Ford the best crossing on the Rappahannock, he would keep Reno's corps there to prevent his left from being turned. The remainder of the Army of Virginia he was concentrating in front of Warrenton and behind the fords of the upper Rappahannock. Lee's latest intelligence on the 24th established that Pope had in fact carried through with this intention, and this meant it would now be difficult if not impossible for the Confederates to slip between the Federal flank and the Bull Run Mountains, even though the high waters had begun to recede. In his own words, Pope believed his "position here is regulated by the arrival of McClellan's forces on the Lower Rappahannock." And Lee correctly interpreted that this meant Pope's "plan to be to hold us in check until McClellan can join him from the Lower Rappahannock." Undoubtedly, Pope's most startling sentence, however, was his last. "I suggest," he had written Halleck, "that General Porter be pushed up at once to Barnett's Ford." This indicated that Fitz John Porter's Fifth Corps, the vanguard of McClellan's Army of the Potomac, was already on the Confederate right flank.

Certainly, there was bad news for the Confederates in Pope's dispatch. The chance to turn Pope's right flank by crossing the upper Rappahannock had disappeared. Worse yet, with the leading unit of McClellan's 100,000-man army now at hand to combine with Pope, plus Cox's division from the Kanawha, Lee—according to the figures as he reckoned them—faced the imminent prospect of confronting nearly 200,000 of the enemy united against him. Lee's quandary on August 24 was in microcosm the predicament of the Confederacy in its war for independence. The preponderant strength of the Union must in time overcome him. No defensive strategy could prevent eventual defeat. The only possible path to victory lay in frustrating the enemy's plans, raising their costs in men and money, and attacking their will to continue the struggle. As Lee saw it, it was more imperative than ever that he press the offensive. But, he must find a way to attack that minimized his own losses, while inflicting maximum punishment on the enemy.

When Lee sat down to write to Davis for the second day in a row, he did not attempt to gloss over the inexorable realities as he perceived them, but in his customary fashion he focused his primary attention on the positive aspects of his situation and on the options open to him. He used Pope's dispatch to prove to the president that "McClellan's destination is to join Pope," and that the whole Confederate army should be united at Culpeper "as soon as possible."[51] Then, rather than asking for permission in advance, he told Davis he intended to order up all three remaining infantry divisions (including the North Carolina troops now under John Walker), as well as the Artillery Reserve and Hampton's cavalry brigade. The defenses of Richmond "must be perfected and completed by hired labor" and manned by artillerymen alone. "Should you not agree with me in the propriety of this step," he wrote, "please countermand the order and let me know."

Having decided what was both correct and absolutely necessary, Lee was willing to shoulder the responsibility for the provocative action. On one level this reduced the president's burden, but on another it forced his hand. While Davis could later blame Lee if the move led to disaster, he was being compelled to accept the stripping of his capital's defenses unless he overruled his most successful commander and the friend in whom he had so frequently expressed confidence.

It is not certain whether Lee had fully developed his new plan of operations by the time he wrote to Davis. By this point, he must have glimpsed at least its outline, for he was ready to expand Loring's mission to include a descent into the Shenandoah Valley. More revealingly, when asserting that his own army could increasingly subsist on the supplies found at hand, he almost casually noted, "[A]s we advance, . . . we shall relieve other parts of the country and employ what would be consumed and destroyed by the enemy." But, if Lee did know more when he wrote, he did not share the details with Davis. He simply reiterated, "The theater of war will thus be changed, for a season at least," although he felt compelled to add, "unless we are overpowered."[52]

Lee Plots a Wider Turn, August 24

On the afternoon of August 24, Lee rolled the die. Not surprisingly, he once again relied upon a turning movement to resolve a strategic deadlock and achieve a heavy victory with easy fighting. Since he was unable to get around Pope's flank near at hand, he decided to send a part of his army on a wide sweep behind the Bull Run Mountains to emerge far in Pope's rear and cut the Orange and Alexandria Railroad. In the meanwhile, the remainder of the Army of Northern Virginia would attempt to distract Pope on the Rappahannock. This time, Lee initiated only the broad outline of his plan, leaving the details to be filled in by subordinates and allowing for modifications to be made in response to the enemy's reactions.

In spite of its flexibility, Lee's strategy is open to serious, critical questions. How much could he hope to accomplish by severing the Orange and Alexandria Railroad? Granted, it served as Pope's only supply line with Washington, but, so far as Lee knew, all of the reenforcements from McClellan were coming from Fredericksburg. The interruption of the flow of food and supplies from Washington would be an inconvenience, but the enemy could draw materiel as well as men from Fredericksburg—in other words, by effecting another change of base.

Pope might respond by simply pulling his army back behind the Bull Run River. In this case, not only would the isolated turning column be vulnerable to destruction, but the scene of fighting would be transferred to the front of Washington, a most inhospitable battleground for the Con-

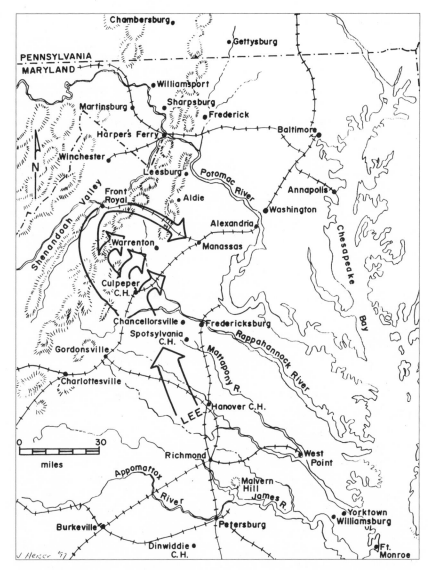

Lee's second turning movement, August 1862. Lee broke the strategic stalemate by concentrating his army against Pope. After a series of unsuccessful small-scale attempts to turn Pope's line, Lee sent Jackson on a wide march through Thoroughfare Gap.

federates. Did Lee count on striking the rear of the Army of Virginia as it left the Rappahannock and came out into the open to defend its communications? If he did, would he have enough strength remaining with him to ensure a reasonable chance of success, because his turning column would be too far distant to participate in the battle?

What would Lee do if Pope became the aggressor and attempted to take advantage of the diminished capacity of the Army of Northern Virginia? Could Lee resist a determined attack from north of the Rappahannock? His distant turning column would be in no better position to come to his aid than he was to help it. Would he not have been better off on all counts to await the arrival of the 30,000 men in his third wing from Richmond and Hanover Junction?[53]

Whether or not all of these questions occurred to Lee, and, if so, how he answered them in his own mind cannot be known. Nonetheless, it is possible to ask what *could* Lee have done on Sunday, August 24? Speaking in broad categories and ignoring operational details, he had six options before him. Two were defensive and four offensive.

Lee's first defensive option was to remain where he was and dig in to protect the Rappahannock frontier. The sole benefit to be derived from this choice was the possibility of retaining for a slightly longer period—perhaps no more than a few weeks—a rich agricultural region of central Virginia and the railroad that brought supplies from the even richer Shenandoah Valley. Otherwise, all military considerations argued against staying in his present position. The enemy commanded his line from the higher north bank of the river; both of his flanks were exposed; and a Federal turning movement against his right would threaten both his communications with Richmond and the capital itself.

If Lee were to remain on the defensive, he must necessarily pursue the second option and withdraw south to a stronger position nearer Richmond. Probably, pulling back to a line behind the North Anna River would have been the soundest tactical move. But in so doing he would abandon central Virginia and its railroad connection with the Valley. He would also be taking a first, long step backward toward a siege of Richmond and the box from which he had just escaped.

There is no indication Lee contemplated adopting a defensive strategy in any of its forms on August 24. He did not believe the South could achieve independence by relying on defense. He had from the moment he took field command determined to do everything in his power to win the war in spite of the odds he faced. In order for the South's resources to out last the North's will to wage the war, Lee must simultaneously press the offensive to discourage the enemy and husband Confederate manpower and supplies. He believed he had no choice but to pursue the offensive.

Nor, in this case, could he choose the first and simplest offensive option open to him. A frontal assault on a foe who was numerically superior (so Lee believed) and who held the higher ground behind a river would repeat the costly mistakes of Beaver Dam Creek, Gaines' Mill, and Malvern Hill. The second option, to try to get around Pope's flank on the Rappahannock, had been Lee's unsuccessful goal for a week, and now the enemy's right flank rested on the mountains and his left flank was secured by the approaching columns of the Army of the Potomac. A third possibility, a wide turning movement to the east, would carry the Confederates away from Pope's communications, nearer to the rivers dominated by Federal gunboats, and squarely into the teeth of McClellan's main force. Thus, finally, after Lee had eliminated the impossible, that which remained, however improbable, had to be his answer.

It is interesting that Lee neither issued written orders nor provided detailed instructions for such a hazardous operation. Probably to secure secrecy, he relied upon verbal orders to his two chief subordinates. In addition, he trusted in their ability to understand his basic intentions, kept his directions to a minimum, and allowed them wide latitude in filling in the details. His attempt to impose a complicated plan with intricate timing had failed in the opening of the Seven Days and again just a week earlier on the Rapidan. This new approach would permit flexibility and adaptability in new situations as they might arise. But, as he would discover, flexibility carried too far in the opposite direction would create the potential for subordinates—while innocently pursuing their discretionary authority—to commit his army to actions contrary to Lee's overall strategy.

Lee met with Jackson, Longstreet, and Stuart on the 24th and explained the outline of his plan.[54] In the absence of any written contemporaneous record of Lee's instructions, it is worthwhile to note what the participants recalled after intervals of two to ten months as their understanding of what was said. "In pursuance of the plan of operations determined upon," Lee reported starkly in June of 1863, "Jackson was directed on the 25th to cross above Waterloo and move around the enemy's right, so as to strike the Orange and Alexandria Railroad in his rear." With equal simplicity, Jackson stated in April 1863, "Pursuing the instructions of the commanding general, I left Jeffersonton on the morning of the 25th to throw my command between Washington City and the army of General Pope and to break up his railroad communications with the Federal capital." The two statements agree on several points: first, that the plan was Lee's; second, that no exact destination was named; third, that no precise route was directed; and, fourth, that nothing was said about what Jackson was to do after cutting the railroad.[55]

Jackson's freedom to select his line of march is confirmed by the fact that immediately after his meeting with Lee, he ordered his chief engineer to propose the most direct but "covered route to Manassas." And Jackson's discretion in picking the point to cut the railroad is strongly suggested by his calling for the route to Manassas but deciding later to strike Bristoe Station first.[56] Lee's failure to provide Jackson with direction to guide his actions after destroying Pope's communications must remain conjecture, but it is suggested by Stonewall's withdrawal from Manassas toward Centreville and his precipitous assault on part of Pope's army.

Such evidence that exists suggests that Lee did not intend to seek a major battle in the Manassas or Bristoe Station area. He probably understood that a victory gained there offered scant prospects for exploitation. With Washington's fortifications looming in the enemy's rear, there would be little room for further maneuvering or to pursue a defeated foe; and, as Johnston's experience had demonstrated, a Confederate force at Manassas was vulnerable to being turned on either of its flanks. It is likely that Lee's original strategy was to cut Pope's communications and then fall back to the Shenandoah Valley to threaten the upper Potomac. He would pull the enemy farther from Washington—and simultaneously from Richmond—and then attempt with further maneuvering to crush whatever Federals pursued him.[57]

Either Lee did not make clear to Jackson that his operation was basically a raid and that he was not to get mired in serious fighting with the enemy at Manassas, or else Jackson violated the spirit of his instructions. The former is more likely the case, and Lee may have miscalculated because he did not anticipate the serious possibility of battle occurring before he arrived on the scene. Perhaps he underestimated Pope's ability to concentrate the Federal army in the vicinity of Manassas and overestimated his own ability to join Jackson with the rest of the Confederate army in a timely fashion.

Lee's directions for the remaining part of the operations were equally simple. "Longstreet in the meantime," he would recall later, "was to divert [Pope's] attention by threatening him in front and to follow Jackson as soon as the latter should be sufficiently advanced." When Longstreet wrote his report, just two months later in October, he mentioned no special instructions, merely stating, "On the 25th we relieved a portion of General Jackson's command at Waterloo Bridge. There was more or less skirmishing at this place," he noted, "until the afternoon of the 26th, when the march was resumed, crossing the Rappahannock at Hinson's Mill Ford, six miles above Waterloo." It should be noted that neither Lee nor Longstreet even hinted that a battle was to be fought along the Rappahannock or with the rear of Pope's retreating army. Indeed, the implication is that Longstreet was to follow virtually on the heels of Jackson.[58]

By definition a turning movement is always undertaken to dislodge an enemy from a strong position, and such was Lee's aim. Frequently, the maneuver is also intended to expose the enemy to a crushing blow while in motion, as was Lee's plan at the beginning of the Chickahominy campaign. This time, however, Lee had no such intention. He meant only to compel Pope to fall back a considerable distance northward, thus freeing a large region of occupied Virginia and opening the door for a new campaign of maneuvering employing pressure on Washington as leverage.

Apparently, Lee expected he would need to "divert" Pope's attention on the Rappahannock for several days, and he was surprised to discover less than thirty-six hours after Jackson's departure that Pope was pulling back from the river. Deciding the opportunity had quickly come to unite his army, Lee asked Longstreet whether he would "prefer" to cross the Rappahannock and take the most direct route north by following in Pope's footsteps, or to pursue the more circuitous path taken by Jackson. Longstreet advised the longer route behind the mountains, because there "were numerous strongly defensive positions" on the road to Warrenton where Pope might delay him with a "small force" for "an uncertain length of time."[59] This incident makes certain that Longstreet's role was to hold Pope and then unite with Jackson, and it was not to catch Pope off balance, nor even to harass the Federal retreat.

One final curiosity remains about Lee's plan, and it demonstrates that the Confederate commander still had much to learn in the effective deployment of his cavalry. Initially, he assigned far too few horsemen to Jackson's column. On the first day of the march, Stonewall would have available only Thomas Munford's 2d Virginia Cavalry and a handful of "guards" from a company of the 6th Virginia to scout his advance and to screen his move from enemy patrols. No doubt Lee had apprised Stuart of the plan, but for reasons never explained Jeb did not report to headquarters until the night of the 25th for his "final instructions to accompany the movement of Major-General Jackson, already begun." Lee then overcompensated for his negligence by directing Stuart to take both brigades of his division to follow after Jackson, leaving no cavalry for himself to probe Pope's position or to protect Longstreet's column when its turn came to march.[60] This is another indication Lee did not intend to attack or harass Pope as the Federals withdrew, as he certainly would have retained some horsemen for the purpose.

The Turning Movement Launched, August 25–26

Lee understood that in order to succeed, the turning movement had to be carried out rapidly; it had to be completed before McClellan joined Pope. The difficulty of concealing the movement of a large body of troops in the near presence of the enemy was an additional reason for haste. For these reasons, the Confederates set out briskly to turn Pope's position on the Rappahannock.

Jackson spent the waning hours of the 24th preparing his three divisions for an early departure, and around midnight Longstreet's artillery replaced Stonewall's guns opposite Waterloo Bridge. In the gray predawn of a "bright and beautiful" morning, Ewell's division, followed by A. P. Hill's and Taliaferro's, broke camp and marched for Amissville five miles to the west. Jackson's column then swung to the right and headed north behind the Bull Run Mountains, reaching the village of Salem on the road to Thoroughfare Gap by nightfall. In a textbook example of efficient logistics, Jackson justified the proud sobriquet of "foot cavalry" for his command by marching his 23,000 men twenty-five miles in fourteen hours. Setting out early the next morning, he then turned east and covered an equal distance in the same number of hours to reach Bristoe Station on the Orange and Alexandria by sunset. He had executed the first part of Lee's plan flawlessly.[61]

Jackson's march had not gone unobserved, however, and by noon of the 25th reports were flowing into Pope's headquarters about the dust clouds raised by the long columns of men and wagons moving northward behind the mountains. Lee would have been gratified—had he known—that the first Federal reports concluded the Confederates were "moving upon the valley of the Shenandoah . . . with designs upon the Potomac, possibly beyond." Pope had perceived that Lee might make a move of this kind and had the day before ordered Franz Sigel to send scouts beyond the mountains to watch for enemy troops.

Pope did not believe such a Confederate movement likely, however, and he was in the midst of plans to shift his line southeastward to Rappahannock Station, fifteen miles nearer to both Fredericksburg and Richmond.[62] By the 25th, Heintzelman's Third Corps of the Army of the Potomac, some 16,500 men, had already arrived at Warrenton Junction by train from Alexandria. And Fitz John Porter with another 19,500 men was approaching Bealton Station after marching overland from Fredericksburg.[63] Had Lee waited a day or two longer to start the campaign, Pope's army of 100,000 men would have been so near its communications and so threatening to Richmond that the Confederate commander might have had to react to that danger instead of launching his own offensive.

With Jackson's timely march, Lee seized the initiative, compelling the Federals to react. By 9:30 on the evening of the 25th, Pope became convinced that no enemy remained in front of him on the Rappahannock, but that Lee with his "whole force" had "marched for the Shenandoah Valley by way of Luray and Front Royal."[64] He lost sight of Jackson, however, when the Confederate column turned east through Thoroughfare Gap. Not until the night of the 26th, when his trains came back from Bristoe

Station after being attacked, did Pope realize the enemy was in his rear and had cut his communications. Initially, the Federal commander was uncertain whether the enemy was still behind the mountains and only a cavalry force was raiding Bristoe, or if the whole Confederate army had reached the Orange and Alexandria Railroad.

After reconnaissance during the day revealed that a strong enemy force remained in his front across from Waterloo Bridge, Pope now knew the Confederates had split into two—or perhaps three—columns.[65] Sometime during the next twelve hours, Pope decided that Jackson was in the Manassas area and that the Confederates could be punished for dividing their forces to undertake the raid on his supplies. On the morning of the 27th, he issued orders aimed at blocking Jackson's retreat to the west by sending McDowell and Sigel to Gainesville, supported on their right at Greenwich by Heintzelman and Reno. Porter was to remain at Warrenton Junction until relieved by Banks. By late afternoon, Pope had established his own headquarters at Bristoe Station.[66]

In the meanwhile, Lee had spent the 25th quietly at Jeffersonton after the departure of Jackson. He opened a letter to his wife somewhat wistfully, "You see I am getting farther & farther from you my dear Mary." Without mentioning the dangerous game he had afoot, he told her, "I think we shall at least change the theater of war from James River to north of the Rappahannock." And, he added, "If it is effected for at least a season, it will be a great gain."[67]

The remainder of Lee's correspondence was more indicative of the strain he felt while waiting for his movement to develop; it also reflected the miscellaneous concerns that occupied his mind. He wrote Jeremy Gilmer, chief engineer of the Army of Northern Virginia on detached service at Richmond, "to use every exertion to perfect and complete the defenses" of the capital, so that all of the remaining troops could be safely forwarded north. He also sent a batch of the dispatches captured from Pope's headquarters to Secretary Randolph, calling especial attention to the intelligence that the Kanawha Valley was being stripped to send reenforcements to Pope. He asked that Loring, the Confederate commander in the region, be directed to "join me in the valley of Virginia."[68]

At some point during the day, Lee received the disturbing intelligence that "a portion of McClellan's army" had already joined Pope, although it is not certain if he understood it was Heintzelman's corps that had arrived or if he had an estimate of its size. Even without specifics, this was bad news, for it meant the increased disparity in numbers he had feared was now reality. It was even worse news, if he learned—and it is not clear whether he did or not—that the Third Corps had arrived from Alexandria.

Lee's plan was based in part on the assumption that the Army of the Potomac was disembarking at Fredericksburg, so that pulling Pope northward was drawing him away from Federal reenforcements. In fact, only Burnside and Porter had landed at Aquia above Fredericksburg. The remainder of McClellan's corps (Heintzelman, Sumner, and Franklin) had been sent to Alexandria on the Potomac. Thus, not only would Pope be carried closer to his reenforcements by traveling north, but also a portion of McClellan's force would be on the left flank of the Confederates at Manassas or Bristoe.[69]

Whatever Lee knew at this point was enough to cause him to send a courier to Rapidan Station with a one-sentence telegram begging Davis "to expedite the advance of our troops."[70] He was no doubt worried that he might have to move before any of the reenforcements from Richmond had reached him. Indeed, because he had not received a response from the president to his initiative of the previous day in ordering up all of the remaining troops from the North Anna and the James, Lee could not be sure how many, if any, additional men were on the way.

Later in the day, he may have received a telegram from Davis that quieted his concern somewhat. The president told Lee, "General Smith will comply with your request," but he referred ambiguously to "the force retained" and cautioned, "You know the condition here." Lee might only safely assume from the wire that D. H. Hill's division (formerly Ripley's) was on its way to join him. But he was too far committed to turn back. When Stuart arrived at army headquarters after dark, Lee gave him "final instructions" for the cavalry role in the turning movement. And, at two in the morning, Jeb set off with both Robertson's and Fitz Lee's brigades to follow the route taken by Jackson.[71]

Thus, at dawn of Tuesday, August 26, Lee confronted Pope on the Rappahannock with fifteen infantry brigades, two artillery battalions, no cavalry (a force totaling about 28,000), and uncertain prospects for reenforcements. It is not clear whether the Confederate commander expected to remain on the Rappahannock only long enough that Jackson's column "should be sufficiently advanced" to clear the roads for new traffic,[72] as his report later stated—or, whether he intended to wait until he knew Pope was pulling back from the river, as his actions suggested. As it turned out, both conditions seemed to occur simultaneously. During the morning and scarcely more than twenty-four hours after Jackson's departure, Lee perceived the enemy was no longer in force opposite Waterloo Bridge. He assumed his strategy was succeeding. Pope had discovered Jackson's movement and was retiring to fight for his communications.

Lee was mistaken, however. Pope spent the 26th puzzling over Confederate intentions. Not until that night did he decide to send his army northward, and he did not issue his orders until the following morning. It was the action of a panicky subordinate, Franz Sigel, that freed Lee prematurely from the watch on the Rappahannock. Sigel with the First Corps held the far right of Pope's line. He not only faced the bulk of the Confederates in his own front, but it was his scouts who reported the dust clouds behind the mountains, and it was his flank that Jackson had turned. Feeling threatened, isolated, and abandoned, he had almost decided to retreat on his own authority, when he received—or so he would later claim—an order from Pope to retire to Warrenton.[73]

Apparently, Lee had been anxious from the start to be off after Jackson. Lacking the cavalry for a thorough reconnaissance, he permitted himself to be satisfied by the disappearance of the enemy from his immediate front. He conferred with Longstreet and decided against crossing the river to follow on Pope's heels—which was fortunate, since Pope was showing only part of one heel—but in favor of leaving immediately to pursue the route taken by Jackson. Leaving only R. H. Anderson's division behind at Waterloo, Lee took Longstreet's twelve brigades and set out for Amissville in the afternoon. By nightfall he established his headquarters at Orleans west of the Bull Run mountains on the road to Salem.[74]

It was likely that, at some point during his busy August 26, Lee received an extraordinary telegram from Jefferson Davis.[75] The president had decided to allow nearly all of the troops defending Richmond to join the Army of Northern Virginia. The five brigades under D. H. Hill and the four under McLaws would be coming from Hanover Junction, as would the four battalions of the reserve artillery. Hampton also was being sent to add a third brigade to Stuart's cavalry division. Somewhat surprisingly, Davis had even ordered forward from Petersburg the two strongest and most seasoned brigades (Walker and Ranson) from the district of North Carolina.

Then, perhaps to guard his place in history in case something should go terribly wrong, Davis briefly reviewed the vulnerable position of Richmond. He noted the overland route from Fredericksburg was now entirely uncovered, that the "York and James Rivers are open to the enemy's fleets," and that there were rumors of new troops arriving at Fort Monroe. Except two half-sized brigades, Wise's at Chaffin's Bluff and Daniel's at Drewry's, the only infantry remaining to defend the Confederate capital were the raw recruits at Peterburg and in North Carolina. In spite of all this, the president concluded, "Confidence in you overcomes the view which would be otherwise taken of the exposed condition of Richmond, and the troops retained for the defense of the capital are surrendered to you on a renewed request."[76]

Davis's support for Lee stands in striking contrast to the position taken by Lincoln in the first three years of the war in regard to the Northern capital, and it helps to explain in part Lee's success over his early opponents. Lee possessed the genius to take advantage of his splintered foes, and the unstinting support he enjoyed from his government permitted him to exercise that genius. By August 26 Davis's confidence in Lee was beginning to yield profit. While exercising unilateral authority over Confederate troops in the Eastern theater and pursuing the freedom to explore strategic theories, Lee had discovered the surest path to prolong the struggle and afford the South a chance to win the war. Aggressive offensive maneuvering had relieved the capital and recaptured the resources of most of Virginia for the sustenance of his army.

After the close of the war, Charles Marshall would remember, "It was a saying of General Lee that Richmond was never so safe as when its defenders were absent."[77] Marshall did not record when Lee first uttered the saying, but doubtless the Confederate commander first discovered its truth during August of 1862.

CHAPTER SIX

— ❧ —

"If we expect to reap advantage"

Lee Pursues Total Victory,
August 27–31, 1862

IN THE ABSENCE of convincing evidence to the contrary, it is difficult to believe that Lee expected Jackson's detached column of 23,000 men— on its own strength—to engage in serious fighting with the vastly superior numbers Pope might bring against it. Lee may well have given Stonewall the discretion to attack if the opportunity arose to inflict great injury on the enemy, but it is doubtful the Confederate commander wanted the turning column to initiate a major battle in the Manassas area that would commit the entire Army of Northern Virginia. On the Chickahominy, Lee had broken McClellan's communications in order to force the Federals into combat outside of their entrenchments. On the Rapidan, he had planned to catch Pope's army in the open. On the Rappahannock, however, he apparently pursued a variant of the turning movement. Although there is no extant record of any understanding reached by Lee and Jackson on the ultimate object of the campaign, on August 30 Lee would write bluntly to Davis, "My desire has been to avoid general engagements" and to achieve success "by maneuvering."[1]

If, indeed, Lee hoped to draw the Federals into the lower Shenandoah Valley—as Marshall remembered and Lee indicated by asking that Loring join him there—then Jackson's turning movement may well have been the first step in a more complicated plan. After all, the Confederates could not simply march into the Valley and expect Pope to follow them. Had Lee moved directly from Jeffersonton due west toward Luray and New Market, he would have exposed his communications under the very nose of the enemy. He would also have left an open road to Richmond without any countervailing offensive threat to prevent the enemy from taking advantage of the opening. It made sense, as a preliminary, to pull Pope northward, well away from Gordonsville and Richmond. Then, by threatening the upper Potomac, Lee could safely lure the Federals into the Valley.

Certainly, the true strategic threat to the Northern capital lay not along the Manassas-Centreville-Fairfax line that led directly to the front of Washington's strong fortifications and ran too near the navigable lower

Potomac on the east. Washington was most vulnerable on its western flank on a line that menaced the upper Potomac and the Baltimore and Ohio Railroad and threatened both Pennsylvania and the capital's tenuous communications with the North through Baltimore. Davis and Johnston had understood this truth, and thus briefly considered an offensive in September of 1861. McClellan understood it when he made his dispositions to secure Washington before leaving for the Peninsula. And Lee and Jackson had exploited it when they disrupted McClellan's plans with the Valley campaign in the spring. It is unlikely, then, that Lee had forgotten or that he would choose to ignore this plain fact of military geography, when he mapped his strategy for the turning movement.

On the other hand, it would have been uncharacteristic of Lee to plan too specifically, too far in advance. First, let Jackson break Pope's communications and compel the Federals to fall back toward Manassas. Next, let the Army of Northern Virginia be reunited. Then, depending upon the positions of the opposing armies, the final stage of the campaign could be plotted. Such a flexible, open-ended campaign strategy would also have incorporated the customary discretion that Lee granted to subordinates operating independently. An understanding between Lee and Jackson—expressed or unstated—that Jackson would not let pass an opportunity to crush an isolated, vulnerable column of the enemy would have fitted well with such a scheme. The chances this plan would yield unwanted results were probably no greater than for any other plan Lee adopted during the war.[2]

Jackson the Raider, August 26–27

Jackson's actions early in the campaign argue that he understood the first part of his mission quite well. His speed was exemplary, and he did what he could to guard the secrecy of his march. He threw out pickets from the 2d Virginia Cavalry on every road leading to the east and kept them there until the entire column had passed. Col. Thomas Munford of the 2d, who led the vanguard, did not encounter any Federals until reaching Haymarket on the other side of Thoroughfare Gap, and the handful of stragglers he captured seemed surprised at their enemy appearing out of nowhere. Jackson also decided wisely in selecting Bristoe as the point for interdicting the Orange and Alexandria Railroad. A mere handful of structures collected around a small wooden station, it would not likely have much in the way of stores, but neither would it be well defended, and closeby was the railroad bridge over Broad Run. Pope would need much longer to replace the bridge than simply to replace torn up track.[3]

Although Munford had only a hundred troopers remaining after picketing the roads along the march, the cavalry commander charged the station, scattered a company of Federal horsemen, and drove a company of infantry into a small hotel, where they were captured. It was at this point that perfect discipline started to break down, as the men themselves began to think of loot, and Jackson's mission began to veer from the spirit of its purpose. Munford and the brigade of Louisiana infantry that had arrived for his support undertook a game of violent hide-and-seek with trains arriving from Pope's army to the south. Two trains forced their way through bullets and obstructions on the rails to spread the alarm up the line toward Manassas, before torn up rails wrecked two others just beyond the station. The engineer of a fifth locomotive saw the pileup in time to reverse direction and carry word of the raid back to Pope.[4]

Thus, on the evening of August 26—and within hours of the Confederates reaching Bristoe—the news of Lee's risky move spread north and south along the railroad, and the clock started running on Jackson's operations. When Jackson should have turned immediately to the destruction of the bridge over Broad Run, he was instead listening to local citizens report that "stores of great value" had been collected by the Federals at Manassas Junction, seven miles up the line. He later wrote, "I deemed it important that no time should be lost in securing them." By nine o'clock Isaac Trimble and two regiments of his brigade were marching in pitch blackness—"the night being very dark"—north toward the beckoning supply depot. Joined by Stuart on the way, Trimble captured two batteries at the edge of town before deciding to await dawn.[5]

First light on the 27th revealed few Federal defenders of Manassas, but the presence of an "immense quantity" of "promiscuous army supplies," including such delicacies as lobster salad and French mustard. Jackson arrived at the junction early in the morning with the divisions of A. P. Hill and Taliaferro, leaving Ewell as a rear guard at Bristoe Station with the task of destroying the bridge over Broad Run. Although Stonewall made an attempt to guard the supplies, he fell well short of success. The scene of plunder that ensued became legendary in the Army of Northern Virginia.[6]

Early in the morning, before the discipline had deteriorated too far, Stuart ordered Fitzhugh Lee on a reconnaissance toward Fairfax Court House with the 3d, 4th, and 9th Virginia Cavalry of his brigade. The Confederates had learned at Bristoe that a sizable body of McClellan's troops (Heintzelman's Third Corps) had just passed down the railroad from Alexandria to join Pope, and they needed to discover if more enemy troops were on the way. Fitz Lee had not gotten far before he learned that a large Federal force—later determined to be Taylor's New Jersey brigade of Franklin's Sixth Corps—had that very morning been rushed by rail from Alexandria to defend the Bull Run Bridge against what was thought to be "a party of guerrillas." The Confederate cavalry commander determined that "Taylor was not supported by other troops" and recommended that the Federal force of some 2,500 infantry—which had been advanced without artillery or cavalry—be allowed to march into a trap at Manassas. Jackson agreed and diverted four brigades of A. P. Hill's division on their arrival at Manassas Junction to maul the Federals and send them back in confusion toward Fairfax Court House.[7]

In one sense, by the close of the small action at Bull Run Bridge around eleven o'clock on the morning of August 27, Jackson was in good shape. Ewell guarded his southern flank several miles below Bristoe, and Fitz Lee's cavalry swept toward Washington affording protection from the north. Stonewall sat squarely on Pope's communications and had captured an immense quantity of Northern supplies. His main body was near the road to Gainesville for a rapid retreat toward Thoroughfare Gap, should retreat become necessary, and his men—who had traveled on short rations for over a month—were indulging themselves at the expense of the enemy.

Looked at differently, however, Jackson was in such precarious shape as to be in danger of failing his mission. At any moment, Federal authorities in Washington, who had been quick to react the night before, might hurl more of McClellan's army down the railroad from Alexandria. And, at this very moment, the corps of McDowell and Sigel had started their march northward to Gainesville, where they would be in Jackson's rear. Moreover, Stonewall had taken almost no action to secure his retreat route to Thoroughfare Gap, which was also the route being taken by Longstreet and Lee to join him. Meanwhile, he had allowed the majority of his men to become engaged in an orgy of plunder; many were drunk, and the fighting effectiveness of all had been impaired at least temporarily.

Why a disciplinarian such as Jackson should have allowed himself to become involved with the supply treasure house at Manassas is a mystery. He had virtually no wagons of any kind with him to haul away goods, and before leaving Bristoe he had learned from his chief engineer that the captured trains were wrecked beyond quick repair and could not be used to transport booty westward on the Manassas Gap Railroad. Surely the very richness of the spoils ought to have convinced him the Northern larder was virtually inexhaustible. He was right to destroy the depot for the temporary inconvenience it would cause Pope; there was time enough for that. But he should not have allowed his army to become mired in personal gratification. Fortunately, Jackson did remember to destroy the railroad bridge over Bull Run, a loss that would be crucial to Pope once the Northern army had fallen back on Manassas as its base.[8]

As the afternoon of the 27th passed in Confederate feasting and celebration, Federal forces began to close around Jackson and restrict his options. "Heavy columns" from Heintzelman's corps appeared at Bristoe, and the vanguard of McDowell approached Gainesville. While Early's brigade played a game of bluff to delay the enemy at Bristoe, Ewell withdrew the rest of his division to Manassas. Jackson came to realize he could not afford to wait until the next morning to move. He could not, however, retire to the most logical fall-back point at Haymarket, just west of Gainesville, where the road from Thoroughfare Gap joined the road from Aldie Gap, the nearest major crossing of the mountains to the north. The presence of McDowell at Gainesville closed this route. Hence, Jackson must move farther north and away from Longstreet's reenforcements on the way to join him.[9]

Sudden night movements—difficult under the best of circumstances— were made doubly complicated amidst the disarray that reigned in the ranks. Written orders, if any ever existed, have disappeared, and the reports written months after that confusing night add little enlightenment. It is likely that Jackson did not know at first exactly where he wanted to concentrate his army, and he sent couriers to lead each division to an interim position to bivouac for the remainder of the night. Taliaferro went first to Sudley Springs and then on to Groveton on the Warrenton Turnpike, only four miles north of Gainesville; A. P. Hill marched all the way to Centreville, nine miles farther north; and Ewell's division, after a short rest for provisions, moved toward Centreville but did not quite reach the Bull Run at Blackburn's Ford. The Confederates destroyed the supplies they had not eaten and could not carry as they departed.[10]

Although stomachs were unwontedly full in the Confederate ranks that night, the minds of the commanding officers could not have rested well as the hours wore slowly on to dawn. How near was the enemy? And in what strength? How soon would Longstreet arrive? The wonder is that Jackson did not during the day or night of the 27th send Stuart and part of the cavalry back to keep open the way to Thoroughfare Gap. If Lee blundered in sending away all of his horsemen, Jackson and Stuart also erred in not reaching back to cover his advance. It was not a small mistake, but the kind from which armies and nations might die.[11]

While Jackson's men raided the Federal pantry, Lee passed a long, hot, perilous day trying to unite at least part of his Army of Northern Virginia, which lay stretched over half the length of Virginia. Jackson and Stuart were at Manassas and Bristoe with four divisions of 28,500 men; Longstreet with 23,000 men in four smaller divisions was marching behind the mountains toward Salem; and R. H. Anderson's division of 6,100 was ten miles behind at Waterloo. Therefore, in the immediate area— although scarcely close enough to be called at hand—Lee had nine divisions and 58,000 men. Eighty miles farther south by rail the divisions of D. H. Hill and McLaws, the cavalry of Hampton, and the artillery of

Pendleton were leaving Hanover Junction to bring Lee another 22,000 men. And fifty miles yet farther south, two fat brigades of 6,500 under John Walker had started to board trains at Petersburg. Hence, Lee had almost 89,000 in twelve divisions under his sole authority in his field army, but its tail was nearly two hundred miles—by routes the units would have to travel to unite—from its head. In the entire Maryland-Virginia theater east of the Blue Ridge Mountains, Lee now had all of the Confederate troops available, except for about 10,000 at Richmond and Petersburg, most of whom were recruits.[12]

At the same time, although Lee could have had only the cloudiest notion of the details, the Federals were much better off strategically, both in numbers and the location of their forces. Pope had at hand and subject to his direct orders over 83,000 men in fourteen divisions, or an advantage of roughly eight to five over Lee's immediate force. The corps of Sigel and McDowell, 34,000, were marching to Gainesville, where they would be on the flank of the Confederate advance from Thoroughfare Gap. The corps of Heintzelman and Reno with another 22,500 were moving just to the east toward Greenwich. Banks's corps of 8,000 was marching from Sulphur Springs to Warrenton; and Porter's corps was at Bealton with 12,000 under orders to head north when relieved by Banks.

At a greater distance but intended for Pope's support were another five divisions of 27,300 at or near Alexandria in the corps of Sumner and Franklin and Cox's Kanawha division; and yet another 4,000 were still with Burnside at Fredericksburg. In the greater Maryland-Virginia theater the Federals had an additional six divisions of 61,600 men in the defenses of Washington, the Eighth corps that covered Washington's flanks from the upper Potomac to Baltimore, and in the Fourth and Seventh corps at Fort Monroe and vicinity. These latter forces were not intended for Pope's use, but their presence secured the North's rear areas and permitted the full deployment of the Army of Virginia and the Army of the Potomac in the field. Total Federal strength in Maryland-Virginia reached 175,000, not counting the green regiments that had already started to reach the front.[13]

Even Lee's sketchy perception of this situation justified his decision to follow quickly after Jackson and not to await the enforcements from Richmond—in spite of the fact that they would increase his strength by over 50 percent. With more numerous reserves and better rail facilities, his enemy would grow proportionately stronger with each passing day.

And, indeed, Lee and Longstreet did get off to a good start. The ten miles covered to Orleans during the afternoon and evening of the 26th gave them a good leg up on the march to join Jackson. Nor was the Confederate commander kept in ignorance of events transpiring with his detached column. Lee had the foresight to loan twenty-five members of the Black Horse Troop to Stonewall to serve as couriers and forge a link of communication between the separated wings of the army. Before sunrise Lee received a dispatch from Jackson announcing the capture of Bristoe Station. The courier had reached Orleans by way of Thoroughfare Gap and could attest that the route ahead remained free of enemy obstructions.

This news may have given Lee a misleading sense of security. In any case, Longstreet did not set out at an early hour in the morning, and the 27th yielded a disappointing thirteen miles in a full-day's effort. Burdened with the wagons of the entire army on a hot and dusty day, Longstreet's column did not reach Salem until the late afternoon. And it was here that the danger of marching blindly struck home. The sudden appearance of a Federal cavalry patrol—which almost captured Lee—signaled the first portent of danger to the mission. Lee's mistake in sending away all of his cavalry meant he could not reconnoiter any significant distance to discover additional Federal forces. After Salem the column crept forward even more slowly than before. Finally, Lee bivouacked for the night at White Plains, seven miles short of the gap. Had he possessed a regiment or two of horse he could have easily secured the mountain pass by nightfall.[14]

After making camp, Lee dispatched a telegram to Davis announcing Jackson's success at Bristoe and Manassas. He also revealed he now knew that part of McClellan's army had reached Pope by rail from Alexandria, indicating the march north was possibly carrying Pope nearer and not farther away from Federal reenforcements. Lee asked the president to expedite his own supports, and not surprisingly he mentioned his particular need for Hampton's cavalry.[15] It would be interesting to know Lee's thoughts as he retired on the night of August 27, twenty miles from Jackson and blind to the dangers that lay between them. Was he thinking of alternative routes through Hopewell and Aldie gaps should Thoroughfare be blocked? Did he ask himself if it was enough that Pope had been forced back from the Rappahannock, his communications cut and his supply depot destroyed? Was there any reason for Longstreet to go east of the mountain at all? What could be accomplished that Jackson had not already achieved? Why not have Jackson fall back and join the main body in the Shenandoah Valley? The reunited wings could then threaten Washington from the west and wait for both the reenforcements from Richmond and Loring from western Virginia.

Whatever specific questions Lee posed to himself that night, he apparently decided that no danger great enough to divert him from his original strategy yet existed. He would go forward on the morrow as planned and join with Jackson. Then he would assess the situation and undertake a new campaign of maneuver. Lee was twice mistaken. He underestimated Pope, and he relied too heavily on Jackson's discretion.

Jackson the Aggressor, August 28

Thursday, August 28, dawned cloudy and warm, the weather a perfect reflection of Jackson's strategic situation. Sometime after daylight, Stonewall decided to unite his divisions just west of the Warrenton Turnpike along the line from Groveton to Sudley Springs already held by Taliaferro. Couriers were sent to fetch A. P. Hill from Centreville and Ewell from Blackburn's Ford on the Bull Run.[16] Jackson's selection indicated he did not intend an unforced retreat. Longstreet was less than a day away—at least by Stonewall's own standard of march—and Pope had not yet pushed the Confederates into a corner. Certainly the rapid appearance of the enemy at Gainesville was inconvenient and perhaps ominous. The small village located at the crossing of the road from Thoroughfare Gap and the Warrenton Turnpike would have been the logical place for Jackson to fall back.

Still, the position Jackson selected wisely took the enemy threat into account. His line covered the road from Haymarket to Sudley Springs, so that if Lee found his way blocked the Confederate commander could turn left at Haymarket five miles before Gainesville and advance directly to Jackson's rear. What is more, the position itself was defensively strong, running along a moderately high ridge—part of which included the embankments of an unfinished railroad—and flanking the Warrenton Turnpike, the most important road in the area. And, if the worst came to pass, the road west from Sudley Springs led to Aldie Gap and the Loudoun Valley.

Unfortunately, the rest of the day would not go so well for Old Jack. At an early hour, he formed the erroneous notion that Pope was fleeing precipitously toward the safety of Alexandria. Fearing the Confederates would not be able to land a telling blow before the enemy reached the safety of Washington's forts, Jackson sent orders to A. P. Hill to halt on the march from Centreville and "to move down to the fords" of the Bull Run and "intercept him." Pope was not in "full retreat," of course. The Federal commander had decided Jackson was at Manassas Junction, and he was hurrying all available Union forces to concentrate there. This included the corps of McDowell and Sigel, who were thus pulled away from Jackson's flank and removed as a threat to Longstreet's arrival through Gainesville. Before Jackson's order arrived, Powell Hill had "just seen two intercepted dispatches from Pope to McDowell, ordering the formation of his line of battle for the next day on Manassas Plains." Hill correctly "deemed it best to push on and join" Jackson at Sudley Springs.[17]

At about the same time in midmorning, Bradley Johnson, a brigade commander in Taliaferro's division, forwarded to Jackson orders of Pope that had been captured by cavalry pickets. These described in detail the battle formations to be taken by the corps of McDowell and Sigel and Reynolds's division in attacking Manassas Junction.[18] Jackson then realized that Pope was not fleeing but pursuing—even if in the wrong direction. Stonewall must have also realized that the threat to the juncture with Longstreet had now dissipated. Hence, he extended his line southward to the Brawner farm, within two miles of Gainesville. Also, although belatedly, Stonewall took action to establish a cavalry connection with Lee.

It was Stuart who called Jackson's attention to the portion of the captured dispatch that directed Bayard's Federal cavalry brigade to Haymarket—which would place it on the road to Thoroughfare Gap. Jeb proposed to collect a force of Confederate horse and drive Bayard off, while making connection with Lee at the same time; and Jackson approved. When the Confederate cavalry commander reached Haymarket in the afternoon, however, he became so involved in skirmishing with George Bayard that he made no farther progress toward Lee, except to send a "trusty man with the dispatch." Still, Stuart could see that a battle was in progress at Thoroughfare Gap, and it is inconceivable he did not perceive the grim possibility that the enemy was blocking Longstreet's passage through the mountains and forward this news to Jackson.[19]

In the meantime, Pope had changed his mind, his plans, and his directions once again. Upon reaching Manassas Junction and finding Jackson gone, the Federal commander heard rumors that the Confederates were in Centreville, probably a ghostly reflection of A. P. Hill's earlier detour there. With commendable celerity but without due regard for the difficulty of turning a large army on a dime, Pope interrupted the Federal concentration on Manassas and ordered his columns to march on Centreville. McDowell's corps had already started toward Manassas, but its rear units were still in the vicinity of Gainesville. King's division, some 10,000 strong, was ordered to take the Warrenton Turnpike directly to Centreville. Reynolds's division was ordered back from Manassas on the Sudley Springs Road to strike the turnpike in advance. McDowell saw no reason to worry about his rear guard and rode off to find and confer with Pope. The route of King's division on the Warrenton Turnpike brought its left flank directly across the front of Jackson's line.[20]

Near sunset, probably between 5:30 and 6:00, Jackson personally observed the exposed enemy column as it marched across his front. According to witnesses, Stonewall rode back and forth on the ridge, within "easy musket range" of the Federal pickets, trying to decide how to respond to this gift that Providence had handed him. Finally, he wheeled his horse about and rode back to order an attack. The battle that followed, usually called Groveton, lasted until nine and was bloody and inconclusive. On the Federal side it was fought primarily by John Gibson's brigade of 2,000 Western regiments destined eventually to win fame as the Iron Brigade. Jackson would throw into the fight all four brigades of Taliaferro's division and two of Ewell's, with Ewell himself going down with a shattered knee.[21]

Jackson's decision to attack is a curious one. At that moment, he had either heard from Stuart and knew of Longstreet's check at the mountain gap, or he had heard nothing and should have been concerned over the unaccountable delay in Longstreet's arrival. In either case, he had no reason to believe support was close at hand. Jackson must have seen the potential for a smashing victory to be so great that he was willing to risk not only the failure of his mission but the destruction of his command. He was wrong. He erred in believing the rout of a single division—no matter how complete—was worth irrevocably committing the Army of Northern Virginia to battle before united. His action was bound to limit Lee's ability to maneuver. From this point in the campaign, success would no longer depend upon Lee's strategic genius. Victory would come—if at all—through bloody combat and from tactical blunders by the enemy. There would be no heavy victory from easy fighting.

Lee, too, was culpable for the turn of events on August 28. White Plains lay but seven miles from Thoroughfare Gap. Yet the Confederate column had not covered that scant distance, when Lee decided to call a halt at about three in the afternoon and go into camp within sight of the mountain pass. Even due allowance for the army's long trains and its lack of cavalry eyes do not fully explain Lee's lethargic progress on the 28th. Earlier reports from Jackson attesting to his safety must have beguiled the Confederate commander into a false sense that all was going well. Still, and in spite of reports that Thoroughfare was unoccupied, the brigade of George T. Anderson was advanced to hold the pass for the night. The sound of gunfire from the mountain slopes soon dispelled all lethargy. Reports came back that Federal infantry in significant strength blocked the route to Jackson.[22]

Early in the morning, Union cavalry had reported to Irvin McDowell near Gainesville that a large Confederate force was approaching Thoroughfare Gap. When McDowell had received Pope's orders to concentrate at Manassas Junction, he had violated that order insofar as to send one of his three divisions to dispute the passage of the Confederates. And it was now the 10,000 men of James B. Ricketts that blocked the way to Jackson.[23]

Lee promptly committed 12,000, more than half of Longstreet's men, to securing the gap. He ordered D. R. Jones to advance straight ahead, while Hood was sent to find a flanking path to the left and Cadmus Wilcox directed to Hopewell Gap, three miles to the north.

In the failing light, it turned out that Jones's brigades alone were enough to cause Ricketts to retire. By nightfall, six Confederate brigades went into camp on the eastern slope of the mountains. It should be noted, however, that Ricketts had not detained Lee, who had already halted for the night. If anything, the Federal presence had actually caused Lee to advance several miles farther than he intended. McDowell's breach of orders also had the counterproductive effect of alarming Lee and making certain his march on the following day would be pressed with energy. That night Lee sent a message to Jackson that he held Thoroughfare Gap, but he could not have assured Jackson of his early arrival, as he could not have known for certain what further obstacles lay ahead.[24]

Lee Hesitates, August 29

Around ten o'clock on the night of the 28th, word reached Pope at Centreville that Jackson had been discovered in the vicinity of Groveton and Sudley Springs. The Federal commander rightly calculated that "the prospect[s] of crushing Jackson . . . were certainly excellent."[25] Unfortunately for Pope, those prospects were dimmed considerably by the cloud of confusion resulting from his army's marching and countermarching during the two previous days. He erroneously assumed that McDowell's entire corps (which now included Reynolds's division) still held Gainesville; and that Sigel's corps was within supporting distance of McDowell. Thus, Pope believed some 40,000 men were in position to prevent Jackson's retreat to the west, as well as to threaten the flank of Lee's approach from Thoroughfare Gap. Acting on this belief, Pope laid plans for the next day. He issued orders for the corps of Heintzelman, Reno, and Porter to advance from Centreville and Manassas to attack from the north and east with 36,000 men. Jackson would thus be "sandwiched" between the two wings of the Federal army. On paper, it was an admirable tactical disposition.

About daylight on the 29th, Pope discovered with "great disappointment and surprise" that he was threatening Jackson with a one-pronged pincer.[26] His force at Gainesville was nonexistent. Ricketts's division of McDowell's corps, which had earlier been sent to the mountain gap, could not now be located. Sigel's corps and Reynolds's division had advanced so far toward Centreville that they were now (unknowingly) opposite Jackson's center. King's division had fallen back to Manassas Junction after its fight at the Brawner farm. As the crowning ignominy, Irvin McDowell, the commander who should have sorted out all of this, was nowhere to be found.

Pope once again displayed his ability to react promptly to changing battle-field conditions. He also again revealed his penchant for attempting too much in too short a time, and his revised orders were ambiguous and confusing. Intent on getting a force in place west of Jackson, Pope stopped Porter in his march from Bristoe to Centreville and directed him to pick up King's division and proceed to Gainesville. While Heintzelman and Reno hurried from Centreville, Sigel, supported by Reynolds, was to attack Jackson at Groveton and hold the Confederates in place long enough for the units on either flank to get into place. Again, it was a sound plan on the map, but it failed to account for the distances the Federal troops had to travel, or for the possible untimely arrival of Lee and Longstreet at Gainesville.

After the scare at the mountain pass, Lee made certain of a "very early" start on the 29th. Hood's division took the lead, and in the absence of cavalry "a party of select Texas riflemen" were thrown in advance to act as the eyes of the column.[27] Doubtless Lee was relieved that Hood met only token opposition in his front, but as the march progressed the roar of cannon and musketry from Sigel's attack near Sudley Springs to the north signaled that Pope and Jackson had "locked horns."[28] Stonewall must be heavily outnumbered, Lee believed, and the first priority must be to relieve his embattled command. Events had closed in about the Confederate commander. The campaign of maneuver would have to wait and combat—however costly—be relied upon to extricate them from their predicament.

As Longstreet's column neared Haymarket, a body of horsemen emerged from the woods on its left. It proved to be Beverly Robertson's brigade sent to escort them on the final leg of the journey, and Lee inquired at once for Robertson to report on how affairs were going with Jackson. Shortly after Haymarket, the chief of cavalry himself rode up with his staff, and Lee's first question to Stuart was, "Well, General, what of Jackson?" Upon hearing that Stonewall had fallen back and was defending Sudley Ford, Lee commented, "We must hurry on and help him." He asked if there were no shortcut that would get them out of the dust and heat, but Stuart recommended that they continue forward to Gainesville.[29] By nine o'clock the column had reached the village crossroads and turned north on the Warrenton Turnpike. By ten Hood deployed in a line of battle perpendicular to the road and at a wide obtuse angle to Jackson's right.[30]

• • •

Jackson's flank was now secure, but it was by no means clear that the reunited Army of Northern Virginia was out of danger. There is no indication Lee made any attempt to mask the arrival of Longstreet's wing or that he had any reason to believe his presence was not immediately known to Pope. To the contrary, not only did Hood's men at once run into skirmishers, but nineteen of Longstreet's guns went into battery and opened fire on the Federal flank.

Surprise was not Lee's purpose; relief for Jackson was. He was anxious to launch an attack that would relieve the pressure on Stonewall. Longstreet, however, opposed a hasty assault, pointing out that Jackson had made no urgent pleas for aid, and the Confederate arrival must have been observed, since the enemy in front had fallen back to a strong defensive position. Longstreet argued that ample time allowed them to reconnoiter the ground and to discover the truth of a report of a Federal corps at Manassas Junction on the Confederate right flank. Lee reluctantly agreed to the delay.

Then, before noon, two things happened to cool Lee's ardor for an attack. First, Jackson rode up for a visit and apparently assured his chief that he was not in imminent danger. And, secondly, Stuart reported that indeed a large Federal force was approaching from the right. This column, Porter's corps, preempted Lee's plan to move to the east and turn the Federal left flank. Yet, even after this news, Lee still apparently asked Longstreet and Jackson, "Hadn't we better move our line forward?" Longstreet replied, "I think not."

Considering Lee's continuing desire to avoid needless casualties, his repeated interest in pressing an attack on the 29th, as presented in Longstreet's recollections, seems uncharacteristic and inexplicable. It may be that Lee simply felt a strong moral obligation to reduce the pressure on Jackson's wing. Yet, a more plausible explanation would be that from the first Lee saw better than his subordinate the possibilities of a crushing victory and did not wish the opportunity to slip away. In any event, Lee did not feel strongly enough to overrule Longstreet, and the afternoon passed slowly away.[31]

Finally, after the threat on the right seemed to abate—with McDowell's corps moving away from Porter's—Lee one last time suggested an attack. In an ultimate act of obstinacy, Longstreet protested that the day was now too far advanced and the assault should be postponed until the following morning. The stubborn subordinate did recommend that a "forced reconnaissance" be made to move the "troops into the most favorable positions." Lee's assent was yet another indication that surprise was not part of the Confederate tactical thinking at Second Manassas.

It was after six o'clock and shadows were lengthening, when Hood's two brigades, supported by Evans, moved down the Warrenton Turnpike and ran directly into three brigades of King's division of McDowell. Based on the moderate success gained by Kearny's division against the Confederate left, Pope had concluded that Jackson was retiring. The Federal commander had ordered McDowell to send a force southward to cut off the retreat, and McDowell had sent King's division swinging down the pike with a promise of many prisoners to be captured. Hood and King were evenly matched in size, although after a sharp fight the Federals were forced back in confusion.[32]

This was the only serious fighting undertaken by Longstreet's men during a day in which Jackson had been compelled to beat back continuous—although fortunately uncoordinated—Federal attacks on his front. Ironically, the result of the reconnaissance was entirely negative. After dark, Longstreet ordered Generals Hood and Wilcox to undertake a careful examination of the ground captured by the Confederates and the Federal line beyond. Both generals, although reporting separately, recommended against an attack in the morning "with minute" reasons for the conclusions, which apparently involved "high ground held by bayonets and batteries innumerable." Longstreet hastened to report this to Lee.

Finally, for one last time, Lee allowed himself to be talked out of an attack. He canceled the offensive planned for the morning and abandoned once and for all his readiness to assault the Federals in their "strong position."[33] Historians would be left forever after to puzzle over the undue influence seemingly exerted by Longstreet over Lee on August 29. Considered in the light of Lee's recent experiences, however, his hesitation is not surprising. Attacks against "strong positions" at Beaver Dam Creek, Gaines's Mill, and Malvern Hill had resulted in ruinous casualties incommensurate with the injury inflicted on the enemy or the strategic gains achieved. He had lectured Jackson on the necessity to win heavy victories with easy fighting. There should be little wonder that—faced with an uncertain tactical situation, an unenthusiastic subordinate in Longstreet, and Jackson's apparent ability to hold without relief—Lee should allow himself to be persuaded.[34]

Combat Finds Lee, August 30

Saturday, August 30, dawned hot and bright, the sun rising on the third day of the second battle at Manassas and the sixteenth day of the campaign begun when Lee took the cars for Gordonsville. Daylight found the Confederates in a peculiar situation; one their commander could never have foreseen when he planned the operation at Jeffersonton nearly a week earlier. The Army of Northern Virginia lay in a strong defensive position thirty miles from Washington and invited attack by the combined armies of Pope, McClellan, and Burnside. Even with the arrival of R. H. Anderson's division that morning, Lee knew he was outnumbered. He did not know that Pope was ignorant of Longstreet's presence, but the Federal aggressiveness of the day before led Lee to expect the Federal commander would renew the offensive.

As the forenoon passed quietly away, doubt began to grow in Lee's mind that the Federals would attack. Then, the uncertainty turned to suspicion that Pope was preparing to fall back on the defenses of Washington. The enemy's retreat—unforced and seemingly premature—would be a mixture of good news and bad. On the one hand, it rendered obsolete Lee's plan to draw the Federals into the lower Shenandoah Valley. A simple march westward by the Confederates was not likely to draw such a demoralized enemy away from Washington. Still, this would be a small loss, since the Valley plan had been virtually abandoned with Jackson's initiating battle on the 28th. It was decidedly good news, however, that Pope's army on the move would provide an inviting target for a crushing blow.

Lee held council with Jackson and Longstreet and laid plans for the pursuit. Once again he would undertake a turning movement. He would cross the Bull Run at Sudley Ford and head north—presumably by the Gum Springs Road—to the Little River Turnpike, where he would turn east toward Fairfax Court House and try to "interpose between [Pope] and Washington."[35] But first, however, he needed to confirm that Pope was retreating.

In the brief respite afforded by the inaction, Lee sat down to write his first lengthy communication to Davis since his letter of August 25. In six days there had been time only for several telegrams to announce the success of Jackson's wing. Picking up his narrative where he had left off— waiting at Jeffersonton with Longstreet's command to follow Jackson—he noted that the progress of "this portion of the army" had been "necessarily slow, having a large and superior force on its flank, narrow and rough roads to travel, and the difficulties of obtaining forage and provisions to contend with."[36] He did not feel it necessary to tell the president that his own mistake in sending off all of Stuart's cavalry had been a major contributing factor to the delay. Concentrating on the positives—of which there were many—Lee pointed out that his plan had "succeeded in deceiving the enemy as to its object." Then, Lee reiterated to Davis the "object" of his strategy: "The movement has, as far as I am able to judge, drawn the enemy from the Rappahannock frontier and caused him to concentrate his troops between Manassas and Centreville."

"My desire," Lee continued, "has been to avoid a general engagement, being the weaker force, and by maneuvering to relieve the portion of the country referred to." This was such a perfect expression of the strategy he had pursued for the past month and a half—indeed, of his ulterior aim since taking field command—there was no need to mention that he had almost blown his resolve the day before. Moving quickly on to the bright prospects for the future, he opined, "if not overpowered," he would "be able to relieve other portions of the country" by the same strategy. He probably felt it unwise to mention in a dispatch that might be intercepted that he was already laying plans to cross the Bull Run and advance on Fairfax Court House.

Thoughts of the next phase of the campaign refocused Lee's attention on the problem he had discussed with Davis in the last letter. "The reinforcements seem to be advancing slowly," he noted with some understatement. He had heard only of the two brigades under Ripley, which had barely reached Amissville the day before and were thus still some fifty miles behind. Then Lee cut to the heart of the dilemma he faced as he approached the crux of his summer's offensive campaign. "In order that we may obtain the advantages I hope for, we must be in larger force," he stated bluntly, "and I hope every exertion will be made to create troops and to increase our strength." Pausing to urge the president to exert equally strong efforts to obtain supplies from the "back country," Lee concluded, "We have no time to lose, and must make every exertion if we expect to reap advantage." With more concern for vigorous emphasis than literary grace, Lee repeated "exertion" in each of his final three sentences.

Shortly after Lee completed his letter to Davis, John Pope pulled him back from the future to remind him that there was unfinished business at hand. Lee had underestimated the Federal commander—he would not be the last to do so—by guessing the Northern forces were preparing to retire. Actually, in spite of the almost uniformly unfriendly judgment of history, Pope had performed reasonably well thus far in the campaign.[37] At the Rapidan and the Rappahannock he had baffled Lee—the master "baffler" himself— in an attempt to turn his positions. Pope clearly understood elementary strategy, and he possessed the ability to translate strategy to the map. His plans for catching Jackson were sound and if carried out would have worked. He was a commendably aggressive tactician; he instinctively sought victory through hard fighting, a trait that ought to have endeared him to the Clausewitzian school of armchair generals.

Even the flaws Pope had so far exhibited fell on the side of belligerency. He did not sufficiently take into account the weaknesses of his motley Army of Virginia, which had more than its share of poor officers and units that did not know how to march. His plans sometimes called upon his troops to accomplish too much in too short a time. Yet, on the morning of August

30, the campaign was Pope's to win or lose. He outnumbered his foe nearly 1.3 to 1, and he possessed interior lines for shifting his superior numbers.[38] Lee's line was stretched much thinner, and it would be much more difficult for the Confederates to transfer units back and forth to danger points. Equally important, the opposing armies were so positioned that it would have been exceedingly hard for Lee to break away safely, or even to detach a force to maneuver for a turning or flanking movement.[39]

Pope could have simply outwaited Lee. The Federals had much more to gain in men and supplies than the Confederates.[40] McClellan would probably have done just that, and all things considered, it was perhaps the best plan Pope could have adopted. But Pope's combative temperament decided otherwise. In fact, there is no indication he seriously considered remaining on the defensive. In that case, from the benefit of hindsight, his best offensive plan would have been to refuse his left flank in front of Longstreet and mount a massive assault against Jackson's now sadly depleted line running along the railroad cut to Sudley Springs. Unfortunately for any quick salvation of the Union, on this August Saturday Pope revealed his greatest flaw as a general. Once he got an idea into his head, no stubborn facts could drive it out.

And Pope clung to two fatally erroneous notions in preparing his attack on the 30th. First, he had become convinced that Jackson was pulling back and retreating west to the mountains. Secondly, he believed that no large enemy force existed on his left at Groveton, where Longstreet's command had been in position for nearly twenty-four hours. Hence near midday Pope abandoned plans for another assault on Sudley Springs and ordered Porter's corps to attack what he assumed to be Jackson's unprotected right flank. The point selected was, of course, nearly the center of the Confederate line and about where Longstreet joined Jackson at an obtuse angle. The attacking column would have to march across Longstreet's front to get at Jackson.[41]

Thus came the fine irony that climaxed Second Manassas and gave to Lee the quickest, easiest, and most decisive tactical victory he would ever achieve. As the Confederate commander laid plans to pursue a nonfleeing foe, his opponent in more deadly ignorance exposed the Federal army to a bone-shattering flank assault.

Fitz John Porter assembled an attack column of more than 20,000 men, with his own Fifth Corps in the center, Hatch's division on the right, and Reynolds's on his left. Not more than half of that number would have time to participate in the assault. At three o'clock Porter moved forward to the attack. His column approached the Confederate line from the northeast, and the terrain was such that his men were at first masked from view by woods and undulating ground. But, each step nearer Jackson to the west brought Porter's exposed left flank closer and made it more visible to Longstreet to the south.

Porter's force was strong and Jackson's line was weak, and Stonewall saw that without aid from Longstreet he could not hold. For the first time in the campaign Jackson asked for help, and Lee ordered Longstreet to send a division to support the beleaguered Confederate left. Longstreet, who was watching the attack, realized it would take too long to pull a division from his front and send it by exterior lines to Jackson. He decided to afford quick assistance by opening with artillery on Porter's flank. It is curious but obviously true that at this early stage none of the Confederate commanders grasped the full extent of the opportunity their foe had offered them. Neither Jackson nor Lee asked Longstreet to attack with infantry on the flank, and Longstreet—until asked to give up a division—had been a placid observer. The traditional view of the Confederates springing a carefully laid trap has given credit where little is due.

There are a number of extenuating circumstances that more than explain what might otherwise seem like tactical dullness on the part of Lee, Jackson, and Longstreet. The Confederate generals could not have anticipated Pope's ignorant decision to attack where and when he did. Nor, because of the diagonal direction of the attack—in relation to Longstreet—and the cloaking nature of the ground, could they have instantly perceived the advantage presented them. Suddenly it seemed Porter was on Jackson, and the first Confederate reactions had been reflexive and traditional.[42]

All of this changed in a matter of minutes. Longstreet's artillery blasted Porter's lines into confusion and retreat. Lee perceived the opportunity instantly and ordered Longstreet to attack. Longstreet recognized the opportunity at the same time and was already preparing his attack when Lee's order arrived. Indeed, every Confederate near enough to witness the spectacle understood its potential, and some units moved ahead on their own accord.

Thus Bull Run once again witnessed a great rout. The Federal panic was not so dire this time, and divisions, brigades, and single regiments made heroic stands to cover the withdrawal and delay the enemy's advance. Nor was the Confederate sweeping attack so perfect as is sometimes depicted. Some Southern units lagged behind, others overran, and effective coordination between Longstreet and Jackson was never established. The results were nevertheless impressive. By nightfall Pope had abandoned the battlefield and was retreating to Centreville.[43]

When darkness ended pursuit, most of the jubilant Confederates sank into exhausted sleep on the floor of the valley of the Bull Run. But not all. There were thousands of prisoners to be guarded, wounded to be tended, and badly needed arms and munitions to be gleaned from the battlefield. From a hastily established headquarters in an open field, Lee worked beside a blazing bonfire fueled high to allow for reading and writing dispatches. He heard from subordinates of a complete victory on all parts of the field and of the enemy disappearance in the direction of Centreville. No doubt Lee wished he could push his victory for even further gain. But the "obscurity of the night" and the scattered and uncertain location of his own army "rendered it necessary to suspend operations until morning."[44]

At ten o'clock Lee took time to send a telegram to Davis announcing, "This Army achieved today on the plains of Manassas a signal victory over combined forces of Generals McClellan and Pope." That very morning he had mentioned the possibility that "we shall be able to relieve other portions of the country." The possibility had now become likelihood.[45]

Much later, in reflecting on the victory at Second Manassas in his official report, Lee would write prosaically, "The war was thus transferred from the interior to the frontier." What he would not say in that document—but would make clear in his dispatches written during the campaign—was that he had actually transferred the war to a succession of frontiers. Each frontier had been a distinct step, a goal in itself, beyond which Lee had not planned until it was complete. Each frontier gained, however, had opened new vistas for his developing strategy. First had been the Rapidan frontier, then the Rappahannock, and now, by August 30, the Army of Northern Virginia had cleared the Bull Run.[46] Could Lee *not* have realized that the next major river system that lay beyond was the Potomac, the northern border of the Confederacy and the ultimate frontier? Such questions of grand strategy would have to wait, however, for first Lee desperately wanted to finish the task at hand by destroying the army of the "miscreant" Pope. As he had written Davis, if the Confederates were to win the war, they must "reap advantage" from their victories.

Lee Returns to Maneuver to Finish, August 31

Once before during the summer of 1862, as the Army of Northern Virginia emerged from the White Oak Swamp in pursuit of the Army of the Potomac, Robert E. Lee had fretted over his inability to deliver the coup de grace to his opponent. Now, on August 31, exactly two months later, he faced a frustratingly similar situation. On the plains of Manassas, fortune had presented the Confederate commander with an unexpected chance to deal his foe a crushing blow. But simply sweeping Pope from the fields of

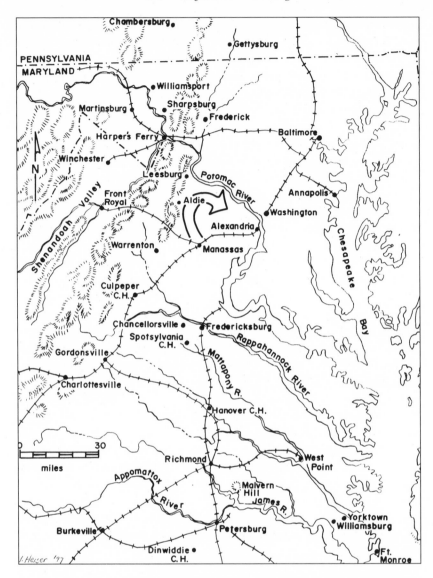

Lee's third turning movement, August–September 1862. Lee's attempt to interpose between Pope and the Washington forts ended in failure at Chantilly on September 1, 1862.

Bull Run was not enough. With its vast reservoir of manpower, the North would soon replenish even the heavy losses incurred in the failing light of the previous day.

Of course, Lee possessed nothing approaching precise figures for either the absolute or relative losses in the battle just concluded. No Civil War general ever did, and Confederate commanders—victims of their sloppy record-keeping system—were usually more ignorant in this respect than their Federal counterparts. In fact, there is some evidence that for several weeks Lee labored under the delusion that he had inflicted 20,000 casualties, while suffering only 5,000 himself.[47] He would have been even less satisfied with the outcome had he known that in the final tallies Confederate casualties would reach nearly 9,500 and Federal losses fall short of 15,000. It is true that causing enemy casualties 153 percent of one's own was an improvement from the Seven Days, where Confederate losses had been 127 percent greater than Federal. Yet Lee's Second Manassas casualties were remarkably high when it is remembered that two of the days' fighting had been defensive and the third had witnessed a rout of the enemy. Moreover, Lee's losses represented a drain on the Confederate manpower pool that was two-and-a-half times greater than that suffered by the North.[48]

This ratio could not be long tolerated, nor could it be justified without commensurate gains in Northern demoralization. To know this plain truth, Lee did not need precise statistics. Nor did he need ciphers to understand that victory must be pursued relentlessly while the enemy was disorganized and vulnerable. Every possible advantage must be harvested. Lee's actions indicate he understood he might never again have the opportunity to achieve a victory so heavy that the demoralized enemy would abandon the war as hopeless. Before daylight he had Stuart's cavalry in the saddle and in pursuit of the Federals.[49]

Unfortunately for the Confederates, a steady rain started to fall during the night, and Sunday, August 31, dawned "nasty and soggy." Henry Kyd Douglas, Jackson's aide, noted with romantic resignation that it seemed "the heavens weep over every bloody battlefield."[50] Poetics aside, the inclement weather severely hampered pursuit of the enemy. A "sharp wind" drove the rain into the faces of Stuart's troopers, obscuring their visibility, while the red-clay country roads had overnight turned into a pasty dough that sucked at hooves and wheels.[51] Moving down the Warrenton Turnpike, Stuart was slowed by the capture of thirty ambulances and hundreds of prisoners he sent under guard to the rear.[52] He also took time to detail Tom Rosser with the 5th Virginia Cavalry and a section of the Washington artillery to return and capture Manassas Junction. When Stuart finally reached Cub Run by midmorning, he found his way blocked by a sizable Federal force, and scouts reported that Pope had concentrated his army in the strong fortifications that Johnston had built around Centreville the previous winter.[53]

Anxious to press the pursuit and receive intelligence at the earliest possible moment, Lee had ridden forward to the vicinity of the ruins of the stone bridge over Bull Run on the Warrenton Turnpike. He dismounted from Traveller to talk with a group of officers, including Jackson and

Longstreet. Emerging suddenly from the gray mist of no-man's land, the prisoners captured by Stuart caused confusion and consternation. The cry went up that Yankee cavalry was at hand. Traveller shied, and as Lee moved to grab the reins, he tripped over the bulky leggings of the rubber overalls he was wearing as protection against the rain. He fell forward, landing heavily on both outstretched hands. He immediately jumped to his feet, but excruciating pain indicated the fall had caused serious damage. While the staff sought a physician among the nearby troops, Jackson's aide, Henry Douglas, poured water from canteens on Lee's bruised and swelling hands to ease his discomfort. The surgeon of the 44th Georgia Infantry, concluding that both wrists were sprained and several bones were broken in the right hand, applied ointment, splints, and bandages and put the right arm in a sling.[54]

Lee necessarily took to an ambulance, since he could no longer hold the reins of his horse, but he did not permit his personal incapacity to interfere with his determination to complete his victory over Pope. The information from Stuart made it clear that direct pursuit would be out of the question, because it would bring the army against the line the Confederates had worked all of the previous winter fortifying. It was not to be another Malvern Hill, however, since Centreville was not located on a river full of gunboats. This time Lee not only had room to maneuver, but he already had at hand his plan from the day before when he prematurely believed Pope was retreating.

Lee ordered Jackson with his three divisions, preceded by Stuart's cavalry, to march northwest from Sudley Springs on the Gum Springs Road to the Little River Turnpike. Jackson would then turn east toward Fairfax Court House and reach Pope's rear. In the meanwhile, Longstreet's command would care for the dead and wounded on the battlefield and press against Pope's front with Pryor's brigade. After the Gum Springs Road had been cleared, Longstreet would follow the route taken by Jackson, leaving R. H. Anderson's division to finish policing the battlefield.[55]

It was the hallmark of Lee's strategic thinking to avoid attacking his opponents "in their strong and chosen positions. They ought always be turned," he had written Jackson just before Cedar Mountain, ". . . and thus force them on more favorable ground."[56] And this is precisely what Lee now attempted. For the fourth time since assuming command, he decided that opportunity lay in a turning movement to the west around his enemy's right flank. The pattern thus emerging in Lee's strategy was probably based simply on the realities of the military situation. If movement straight ahead meant going against the Centreville entrenchments, marching east around the enemy's left flank would have brought Lee under the even stronger forts around Washington. His decision, therefore, was both logical and obvious.

Lee's execution of his plan was as important as the plan itself. So great was his determination to exploit the moment fate had given him that he chose immediate action over a delay that would have increased the strength of his offensive. On the one hand, it was easy to decide not to await the reenforcements from Davis, which seemed to be taking forever to arrive from Richmond. The vanguard of D. H. Hill's division, the brigades of Ripley and Alfred Colquitt, had arrived at Manassas Junction late the day before. But Hill, with his remaining three brigades and the four of McLaws's divisions, was still several days behind at Culpeper. Walker's division was even farther behind at Rapidan Station, and the location of Hampton's cavalry brigade was not known.[57]

On the other hand, Lee's choice of Jackson's command to provide the infantry muscle for the turning movement revealed the full extent of his impatience. It is true Stonewall's three divisions were conveniently at hand. On Stonewall's far left, A. P. Hill's men were in line along the unfinished railroad just in front of Sudley Ford and within a mile of the Gum Spring Road. Yet, Jackson's men alone had fought at Cedar Mountain three weeks before, had carried out the forced march through Thoroughfare Gap, and had just concluded three days of severe fighting at Manassas. Clearly, they were the least battle-worthy of all the troops Lee had at hand. Fresher were any of the units of Longstreet's command, which had experienced easier marches and less fighting. And fresher still were the three brigades of R. H. Anderson's division, which had been acting largely in reserve throughout the campaign, and the two newly arrived brigades under Ripley from D. H. Hill.

Lee's selection of Jackson may also have derived from more than impatience. On every previous occasion the Confederate commander had chosen Jackson to be the striking force for the Army of Northern Virginia. He had picked Jackson to spearhead the turning movement against the White House, to lead the expedition against Pope at Gordonsville, to attempt to turn Pope's flank on the Rappahannock, and to march behind the Bull Run Mountains and gain Pope's rear at Bristoe Station. It was probably a combination of time and personnel that led Lee to select Jackson for his latest turning movement. It may also be that Lee did not fully appreciate the fatigue of Jackson's men. Jackson himself apparently said nothing to alert his commander to his men's condition. Upon receiving his orders, Stonewall was heard to utter the single word "Good!" and depart to form his columns for the march.[58]

Another factor influencing Lee's determination to act quickly undoubtedly was the information brought back by Fitz Lee from the expedition to Fairfax Court House two days earlier. Two additional corps from McClellan's army, Sumner's Second and Franklin's Sixth, as well as Cox's division from western Virginia, were reported to be on the way from Alexandria to form a juncture with Pope. These fresh forces would swell the enemy's numbers by 27,000 men.[59] If Pope were given the time to reorganize his shattered army and incorporate the new forces, the momentum of the campaign could easily and quickly turn against the Confederates.

In actuality, although Lee could not have known it, the Federal commander who had proven so worthy an adversary until the 30th was now a whipped man, begging for reassuring words from Washington and already seeking to shift the blame for his failures. Indeed, the entire Federal high command—both military and political—was fractured with dissent and distrust. The only remaining obstacle to Lee's complete success was the indomitability of the Union soldier.

Having learned his lesson the hard way, Lee this time directed his cavalry to lead the way in the turning movement. Stuart rode to Sudley Ford to take personal charge of the vanguard of what he referred to as "flank movement to the left," and what he apparently saw as the opportunity for another adventure. He personally led Fitzhugh Lee's brigade up the Gum Spring Road until he struck the Little River Turnpike. He then headed east until, near Chantilly plantation, he was joined by Robertson's brigade and a section of the Washington Artillery that had traveled cross-country from the Stone Bridge. Continuing down the pike with Robertson on the right and Rosser on the left, Stuart surprised several Federal patrols. Robertson captured a company of the 10th New York Cavalry, while Rosser captured Capt. Thomas Hight's company of the old 2d U.S. Dragoons.

Emboldened by his success, Stuart pushed forward in the early evening past Ox Hill to Jermantown, about a mile from the Y-shaped junction of the Little River Turnpike and the Warrenton Turnpike that came north from Centreville. Near Jermantown Stuart heard the rumbling of a "continuous roll" of wagons on the Warrenton Turnpike. Turning to the right on a narrow, "difficult" road, he reached a small hill and was able to see the white tops of wagon after wagon of Pope's trains on their way through Fairfax Court House to Alexandria for replenishing. Here Stuart made an error in judgment remarkably similar to the one he had made two months before on Evelington Heights outside Harrison's Landing. He opened fire with several guns, causing much panic and confusion but with little solid results except to alert the enemy to his presence and the potential danger from an unexpected direction. "A few rounds," he later reported, "sufficed to throw everything into confusion, and such commotion, up-setting, collisions, and smash-ups were rarely ever seen."

The cost of Stuart's escapade—just as it had been at Evelington Heights—was the loss of the advantage of surprise for the Confederates. Just as McClellan had been able to seize the vulnerable ridge before Confederate infantry could occupy it, so Pope would now be able to cover his exposed flank once alerted by the exuberant Jeb. Having put in a long, hard day, Stuart retired to make camp two miles north of Ox Hill. But Jeb's irrepressible thirst for romance had not yet been slaked, and he and his staff rode six miles farther north to the plantation of an old friend at Frying Pan, where he spent the remainder of the night serenading the family and talking over old times until dawn.[60] There is no evidence that he sent any intelligence reports back to either Jackson or Lee.

Jackson also got off to a good start. Although the leading division under A. P. Hill did not set out until shortly before noon, the rear of the entire column cleared Sudley Ford on the Bull Run by two o'clock. And, in spite of being limited to "a single track country road . . . through a post-oak forest over quicksand subsoil," he continued to make good progress.[61] Reaching Pleasant Valley on the Little River Turnpike before making camp for the night, he covered a distance of fourteen miles and averaged two miles an hour, a feat that matched the pace of his march one week earlier through Thoroughfare Gap.[62] Marching was one thing, however, and battle quite another. Whether Jackson's men would hold up to hard fighting again so soon remained to be seen.

"The war was thus transferred from interior to frontier"

The Chantilly Fumble, September 1, 1862

MONDAY, SEPTEMBER 1, dawned clear and warm. The first morning of a new and momentous month promised to be a typical summer's day and offered no premonition of the savage thunderstorm already building behind the mountains. Jackson resumed his march down the Little River Turnpike at an early hour with his divisions in reverse order from the preceding day. Jackson's division (under Starke) led the way, followed by Ewell (under Lawton), and last came A. P. Hill. Stonewall had heard nothing from the cavalry about what lay ahead, and necessarily the column moved slowly and cautiously. By late morning he had covered a scant four miles to Chantilly plantation, where he was joined by Stuart, who had just returned from the jaunt to Frying Pan.[1]

Jeb could tell Jackson that nothing but Pope's wagon train and its guards lay ahead, but the information was old and apparently did not satisfy Stonewall, who wisely directed the cavalry to undertake a fresh scout of the ground up to Fairfax Court House. While sending Fitz Lee's brigade directly east to Ox Hill, Stuart accompanied Robertson's brigade in a sweep south of the Little River Turnpike. Although most of Pope's army was now strung out along the Warrenton Turnpike—which because of its acute angle brought the enemy within two miles of Ox Hill—Stuart reported he found "no force but a small one of cavalry was to be found nearer than Centreville."[2]

The sun had long since been overcast with clouds by the time the cavalry chief joined Robertson's brigade at Ox Hill. Here he waited until Jackson covered the two miles from Chantilly and arrived with the van of the infantry at about four o'clock. As towering thunderheads topped the horizon, Stonewall ordered Stuart to push skirmishers ahead to Fairfax Court House. When the Confederate horsemen had advanced about two miles and reached the headwaters of Difficult Run just west of Jermantown and a mile short of the courthouse, they encountered "wooded ridges ... firmly held by infantry and artillery," which "plainly indicated" the enemy intended to "make a stand." Jackson deployed the four brigades of the Stonewall division under William Starke, and then he decided—or at least so was Stuart's understanding—he would wait for the arrival of Longstreet's men before pushing forward. In the meantime, Stuart set out for Flint Hill with Fitz Lee's brigade to uncover and, if possible, turn the Federal flank north.[3]

John Pope—who had been forewarned by the capture of his cavalry patrols and the shelling of his trains on the previous day—had acted in a timely fashion to counter the threat to his rear and right flank. He ordered Joseph Hooker with elements of McDowell's and Franklin's corps into line at Jermantown to cover the retreat to Fairfax Court House. At two o'clock Pope had also ordered Reno's corps to move northward from the Warrenton Turnpike to take an advanced position at Ox Hill.

Shortly after Jackson's arrival at Ox Hill at four o'clock, Confederate scouts reported an enemy force (Reno) approaching on the Confederate right flank from the south.[4] Thus Stonewall was forced to shift his attention from Hooker in his front to the new threat on his right side, and Lee's offensive to turn Pope's position became a defensive battle to protect the exposed flank of the attacking column.

Jackson drew two brigades from his rear division under A. P. Hill and threw them into the thick woods south of the Little River Turnpike. Before they had advanced more than several hundred yards, skirmishers from the brigades of Branch and Field (Brockenbrough) encountered the advancing skirmishers of Isaac Stevens's small division of Reno's corps near the Reid farmhouse. It was a classic meeting engagement in which the two sides discovered each other by running into one another. The ensuing battle was confused and desperate. Eventually all twelve regiments of Reno's small command became engaged, and Jackson committed brigade after brigade of his own until nearly all of his three divisions formed an arc south of the turnpike.

At five o'clock the skies finally gave way and torrents of water drenched the armies. Violent winds drove the rain into the soldiers' faces, while lightning rent the gloomy woods and thunder louder than the artillery shook the trees. At the start of the battle, Jackson outnumbered his foe nearly ten to one, and yet due to fatigue and the storm it was nearly six o'clock before his men began to press Reno from the field. Philip Kearny's division of the Third Corps arrived in time to stabilize the Federal line, and when darkness came early to the stormy field both sides were back approximately to where they had begun. The Union lost both of its major-generals, Stevens and Kearny, killed in the vicious little fight. The Confederates suffered approximately 700 casualties out of 15,000 on the field, while the Federals lost 500 out of 6,000.[5]

In the last half hour of twilight, the head of Longstreet's column approached Ox Hill on the Little River Turnpike, and Old Peter offered his lead brigades to join the fray. He also had the gall to comment to Jackson, "General, your men don't appear to work well today." Considering the extra share of work Jackson's men had shouldered since August 25, Stonewall might have been forgiven a sharp reply. Instead, he said simply, "No, but I hope it will prove a victory in the morning," and declined to commit any further forces to the waning battle.[6] Although Longstreet's barb was ungenerous, it struck close to the truth. As Dorsey Pender, brigade commander in A. P. Hill's division, would confess in a letter to his wife the next day, "None of us seemed anxious for the fight or did ourselves much credit."[7]

Lee's movements on September 1 are not well chronicled. He preceded Longstreet and arrived by ambulance sometime before the battle to establish headquarters in a small farmhouse along the Little River Turnpike between Chantilly and Ox Hill. Here he first discovered the extent to which his injured hands restricted his capacity to command. On foot he was unable to find a vantage from which he could see much or get a feel for the tactical situation.[8] After the fighting started he made no apparent attempt to influence the action. Indeed, untypically, he allowed his mind to drift to other matters.

Around five o'clock, Lee summoned Col. Thomas Munford of the 2d Virginia Cavalry to headquarters for a special assignment. The Confederate commander showed Munford a letter that had just arrived from an old friend in Leesburg. John Janney, who as president of the Virginia Secession Convention had conferred on Lee the command of the Virginia state forces the previous spring, had written asking for protection. The Loudoun Rangers, a company of Union loyalists under Capt. Sam Means, were in the town and threatening to arrest and carry away prominent Confederates on the next day. "We must crush out those people," Lee told Munford, ordering him to leave behind his wagons so that he might travel quickly; "I shall expect to have a good report from you to-morrow." As an afterthought that revealed his concern over his dwindling food supply, Lee added that upon returning Munford should help the commissary department "collect beef cattle for this army."[9]

About 6:30, as an early darkness descended on the waterlogged field, the rain settled into steady drizzle, the temperature began to drop, and the fighting gradually ceased. Both sides broke off the contest and withdrew a short distance to reform. Jackson returned Starke's division to the Little River Turnpike to face east, while the divisions of Ewell and A. P. Hill lay on their arms in the soggy woods south of the road in anticipation of renewing the struggle on the morrow.[10] Stuart in the meantime had ridden north with Fitz Lee's brigade in search of the Federal right flank, only to find it firmly anchored at Flint Hill two miles away. When word of these developments reached army headquarters, the commanding general had to acknowledge that his turning movement had failed. Pope had found time to form a strong defensive line that stretched in a four-mile arc across the front of Fairfax Court House from the Warrenton Turnpike to Flint Hill.

The battle at Ox Hill—named Chantilly by the North—proved the fighting capacity of the Federal army was at least equal to that of the bone-tired Confederates. It also suggested that a frontal assault on the following day would be bloody and perhaps useless. Wisdom—as well as Lee's long-standing strategic policy—dictated that the Confederates should probe the Federal flank at Flint Hill in the morning. Yet, Lee was rapidly running out of room for another turning movement, for seven miles behind Flint Hill lay Fort Buffalo and the perimeter of the forts encircling Washington. On the cold, wet, dreary night of September 1, Lee might have begun to sense the strategic dilemma into which the very magnitude of his successes had carried him. It should not have come as a total surprise, since it was the logical outcome of a victory gained at Manassas.

Lee was now within twenty miles of Washington. He was as near to the Northern capital as McClellan at Harrison's Landing had been to Richmond. "The war was thus transferred," he would later observe in his report, "from the interior to the frontier."[11]

Masked behind the staid prose lay miles of dusty roads, many moments of high anxiety, and excruciatingly large casualties that had in the end yielded final triumph from innumerable uncertainties. Lee must have sensed the even greater opportunity that was unfolding as the summer lengthened. Through chance, risk, and much bloodshed, he and the Army of Northern Virginia were cobbling together the series of rapid victories that might lead to Northern demoralization and Confederate independence.

Yet Lee must also have known he was not going to get much closer to Washington. Even if the morrow should bring the opportunity to deal Pope's army a final blow, what could be accomplished on the day after next? Was he not fast approaching on the Potomac the stalemate he had faced on the James? Were his very victories to render him impotent again? On the other hand, was not the plain lesson of Chantilly that his tired army needed rest?

Heavy decisions lay on the horizon for September 2.

Rudolph Evans's statue of Lee stands in the Virginia Capitol on the spot where Lee accepted command of the state's forces on April 23, 1861. Courtesy of the Library of Virginia, Richmond.

Jefferson Davis, president of the Confederacy, urged the offensive on his generals but allowed them to pursue their own strategies. Courtesy of the Library of Virginia, Richmond.

Known originally as Mechanics' Hall, this building became home to the Confederate War Department. It was destroyed by fire during the evacuation of Richmond. While Lee was adviser to Davis, his office was in the front room on the second floor. Courtesy of the Library of Virginia, Richmond.

The U.S. Customs House became the Confederate Treasury Building. Davis used the entire third floor as his Executive Office, where he hosted strategy sessions. Courtesy of the Library of Virginia, Richmond.

The City of Richmond purchased and donated this house to the Confederacy for the residence of the president. On the second floor of the Confederate White House, or Executive Mansion, Davis maintained an office. Because of his poor health, he conducted much business and some of his strategy conferences here. Courtesy of the Library of Congress/Museum of the Confederacy.

This famous photograph of Lee, the first known full-length portrait of him, was taken in 1862 or 1863. It shows him ready for the field with riding boots, spurs, and field glasses. The statue in the Capitol was copied from this pose. Courtesy of Dementi Studio, Richmond.

This only known wartime photograph of Lee on "Traveller" was taken in Petersburg, Virginia, in 1862. Courtesy of Dementi Studio, Richmond.

The Museum of the Confederacy exhibit of Lee's field tent with cot, saddle, and personal effects. Courtesy of the Museum of the Confederacy

—— ✤ ——

A Working Definition of Strategy

T HE HISTORICAL evolution of the definition of strategy poses a problem in undertaking a study of strategy in the Civil War. Should the historian use the word only as it was understood and employed by Civil War generals? This is an attractive possibility, because it respects historical purity and promotes fuller comprehension of the period under study. The problem is that the term was ambiguously and imprecisely applied by the Civil War generation to military operations from the highest to lowest levels. If the historian honors Civil War usage, the ability to describe analytically is seriously impaired—leading to circumlocutions of long awkward phrases and more than a small risk of creating a new ambiguity.

On the other hand, to impose modern definitions and terminology for the sake of sharper analysis and precision of language is unacceptable on a number of counts. It commits the historiographical error of *presentism*, a particularly obnoxious version of anachronism and justifiably known as one of the deadly sins for historians. It is not only logically fallacious but inherently absurd to use terms the actors themselves would not have understood.

The way out of this impasse would seem to be for the historian to use brief, plain language—which would have been understood by the participants, even if they did not employ it themselves—to describe concepts and distinctions that they made in practice, even if they did not use special terms to describe them. In addition, the historian should write an essay explaining all of this and including a discussion of the terms and their meaning in history. (If this were a map, this is where there would be a bright red dot with the legend: "You are here.")

Below, in italics, are the terms used in the present work with their contextual definitions. An attempt is made to relate the concepts they embody to terms used both in the 1860s and in the twentieth century. References to Jomini and Halleck are to Baron Antoine Henri Jomini, known as the "interpreter" of Napoleon's strategy, and Henry Wager Halleck, the Federal general-in-chief and later chief-of-staff.[1] Both were respected authorities who were widely recognized—if not closely followed—by generals on both sides who had a West Point education.

War aims are the goals that a nation seeks to gain from the struggle. They are by nature political and are exclusively the concern of the statesman. Aims define victory and defeat, and they can change during the course of the war. Jomini recognized this highest level in the conduct of war and referred to it as "statesmanship." Halleck, although admittedly a translator of European military theorists rather than an original thinker, curiously omitted this category altogether. Current military usage would use the term "national objective" here. War aims, or national aims, both as a concept and as a term were understood and used at the time of the Civil War and are a legitimate subject for inquiry and evaluation by the historian.[2]

War policy is the attitudes and programs adopted by the government to achieve war aims. It embraces the mobilization of the economic, physical, and human resources of the nation and includes the political directions and restrictions given for their employment. Policy is also the responsibility of the statesman, but because he must consider not only war aims but also war realities, he should formulate his policy with the advice of experts in economics, military science, diplomacy, and other fields. It is the duty of the statesman to make policy clear and of the general to understand it thoroughly. Both Jomini and Halleck recognized and discussed "military policy," although in a slightly narrower definition; Jomini, for example, expressly excluded diplomacy, which he combined with statesmanship. Current usage would be "national policy." Both the Confederate and Federal governments engaged in the mobilization of economic, physical, and human resources, but neither seemed to comprehend in a fully modern way that these activities should be coordinated with one another or harmonized with war aims. Nor did either side clearly articulate such policies as existed for the guidance of its military commanders. While this failure derived in part from ignorance (that is, lack of historical development), it also resulted on both sides—but particularly in the North—from the political sensitivity of some of the policy questions. Generals who had to execute policy sometimes found it necessary to devise their own.[3]

Strategy, in simplest terms, is the large-scale plan generals devise for the employment of the armed forces within the guidelines of the government's policy for achieving the country's war aims. Strategy exists on several levels, although at this point descriptive terminology can become confusing. *Grand strategy* comprehends the entire war in all of it theaters and all of its forces. *Campaign strategy* involves a particular theater and its army. Grand strategy concerns such broad questions as adopting the offensive or defensive, determining critical points that cannot be lost or must be taken, and the like. Campaign strategy must specifically relate to the current and relative positions of the two hostile forces. In twentieth-century usage grand strategy is simply called "strategy," while campaign strategy is known as "operations." Neither Jomini nor Halleck made a clear distinction between the two levels, nor did the Civil War generals. As some of the thinking and planning in the Civil War did deal with the entire war, however, while others dealt only with theaters and parts of theaters, the distinction is a useful one for historians to make, if done carefully.[4]

Logistics is the moving of armies, except in the presence of the enemy, and the supplying and equipping of armies in all circumstances. It includes all of the military staff functions (adjutant, medical, quartermaster, ordnance, etc.) at both the national and field levels. Both Jomini and Halleck used the term in this sense, and so too is it employed in the twentieth century. Civil War generals dealt with logistics on a daily basis, but they rarely ever used the word. They frequently spoke and wrote of supply lines (or alternatively, of lines of communication) and fully understood their importance both to their own army and to the enemy's.[5]

Tactics is the movements of troops in the presence of the enemy, usually in or preparatory to battle. Jomini divided tactics into two categories: *grand tactics* and *minor tactics*. The former included all those areas for which the commanding general was responsible, such as selecting the ground and posting the line of the army; deciding to stay on the defensive or go on the offensive; determining where to attack, with what force, in what formation; safeguarding the flanks and rear, and the like. According to Jomini, minor tactics covered the deployment of parts of the army (divisions, brigades, etc.) and were the responsibility of subordinate officers. Halleck drew no such distinction, calling tactics everything that happened within the sound of enemy cannon.[6]

Civil War generals did not distinguish between levels of tactics in terminology, but clearly in practice they recognized a difference. Both Lee and McClellan understood their own responsibility for what Jomini called grand tactics, but they realized that once the battle started, much of its guidance was out of their direct control due to the vast amount of rapidly occurring detail and the inability to get timely information or to send timely orders. The distinction is, therefore, not only a legitimate one for the historian, but it is also important for both understanding and evaluating Civil War armies and their commanders.

Notes on Mobilization, Strengths, and Casualties

A. Union and Confederate Mobilization

BECAUSE OF MULTIPLE enlistments and service terms of varying lengths, an accurate head count is not possible for either side. Probably the best approach was taken by Thomas Livermore, who attempted to reduce all of the figures to three-year equivalences. He calculated that the Confederates mobilized the equivalent of 1,082,119 men in three-year enlistments and the Federals 1,556,678.

No one subsequently has studied the question in as much depth as Livermore, but his Confederate total has frequently been challenged as being too high. Admittedly, Livermore was working in reaction to his belief that Confederate writers had propogated the lowest possible figures to further their "lost cause" mythology. In retaliation he may have been guilty of accepting the highest possible numbers. In the preceding text, the figure of 80 percent mobilization of the Confederate manpower pool was derived by dividing 1,197,489 (the total pool as adjusted for loyalty) into 950,000, which allows a moderate discount for Livermore's sum. The figure of 30 percent Federal mobilization was derived by dividing 4,453,114 (the total pool as adjusted for loyalty) into 1,556,678 the number of three-year equivalent enlistments by Livermore, minus some 180,000 black soldiers.[7]

The number of soldiers in the field at any one time was considerably less than the total mobilized for the war. The following table, which refers to aggregate present and absent, gives the figures for the dates known.[8]

Table 1. Comparative Mobilization

DATE	CONFEDERATE	UNION	ODDS
Apr.–July 1861	0–115,000	0–115,000	1 to 1
Dec. 31, 1861	351,448	575,917	1 to 1.64
Apr. 1, 1862	401,395	637,126	1 to 1.59

June 30, 1862	476,891	624,234	1 to 1.31
Dec. 31, 1862	446,622	918,121	1 to 2.06
Dec. 31, 1863	481,160	860,737	1 to 1.79
Dec. 31, 1864	445,203	959,460	1 to 2.16

It should also be noted that the nearly four million slaves, while not counted in the Confederate military pool, contributed labor that freed a high percentage of white males for military service. It should not be assumed, however, that there is a one to one correlation between the total number of slaves and their value as a military resource. Certainly, all slaves who were employed in war industries (such as the Tredegar Iron Works), who built fortifications and railroads, who helped raise foodstuffs and livestock, or who served as servants with the army (performing extra-duty roles as cooks, teamsters, etc.), freed white males to shoulder muskets on the front lines. The question remains, however, how many slaves were engaged in continuing to grow three of the South's largest crops: tobacco, sugar, and cotton. These crops did not materially aid the war effort except to the extent the Confederacy was willing and able to sell them abroad. It might be questioned whether labor thus expended (as well as by all varieties of domestic servants) consumed resources without an equivalent contribution.

B. The Strength of Western Armies, March–April 1862

Tables 2a and 2b summarize the situation in the West from late March through April 1862.[9] While none of the figures are presented as exact, they are useful in determining the approximate ratio of the forces involved.

Table 2a. Confederate Forces

	PRESENT FOR DUTY	PRESENT AND ABSENT
Army of Mississippi *(Johnston)*	49,737	68,752
East Tennessee *(Kirby Smith)*	10,356	25,649
Madrid Bend, Fort Pillow, etc.	5,554	6,781
Army of the West *(Van Dorn)*	21,985	34,035
Alabama, west Florida	8,360	11,000
Totals	95,992	146,217

Table 2b. Federal Forces

	Present for Duty	Present and Absent
Army of the Mississippi		
(Pope)	18,159	26,473
Army of the Ohio		
(Buell)	40,866	61,844
Seventh Division (est.)	7,000	11,000
Army of West Tennessee		
(Grant)	36,544	60,663
Totals	102,569	159,980

C. Strength of the Army of Northern Virginia in the Seven Days

In his memoirs, Joseph Johnston refered to Lee's forces on June 26 as "the largest Confederate army that ever fought." He estimated Lee's reenforcements as follows: 15,000 from North Carolina; 22,000 from South Carolina and Georgia, and 16,000 from Jackson; for a total of 53,000. When combined with the 73,000 Johnston had on May 31, this would have given Lee 126,000 men. Johnston later admitted his figures were too high. For example, he counted Lawton twice (with Jackson and with Georgia); he included forces that did not arrive until July and August; and he overestimated Holmes by 150 percent.[10]

Johnston's claims affronted that plank of the "Lost Cause" myth that insisted the Confederates had always been heavily outnumbered, and his figures were emphatically rejected by Charles Marshall, Jubal Early, Jefferson Davis, the Reverend J. William Jones, and Walter Taylor, who insisted that Lee had 80,000 men or fewer.[11] These defenders of Confederate meagerness indulged in the bad habit of "mixing apples and oranges." They used the figure for their own "effectives," a stripped down statistic, while employing the "present for duty" figures for the enemy. Their 80,000 may be fairly accurate for Lee's combat effectives, but then it should be compared to the approximately 70,000 McClellan had in the same category.

The total of 112,220 present for duty for the Army of Northern Virginia, used in the preceding text, breaks down as follows:[12]

ATTACKING COLUMN NORTH OF THE CHICKAHOMINY:

Army of Northern Virginia

Longstreet	14,291
A. P. Hill	16,411
D. H. Hill	12,318
Stuart	2,109
Total	45,129

Army of the Valley

Jackson	9,604
Ewell	6,353
Whiting	5,537
Cavalry	605
Total	**22,099**
Grand total	**67,228**

Confederate defensive forces south of the Chickahominy:

McLaws	4,915
D. R. Jones	4,503
Magruder	5,671
Huger	6,160
Holmes	9,018
Reserve artillery	1,680
Cavalry	2,000
Richmond defenses	9,136
Petersburg defenses	1,909
Total	**44,992**

D. Union and Confederate Forces in the Virginia Theater, August 27, 1862

The following tables, 3a and 3b, reveal the organization of forces in the Eastern theater and demonstrate the better effort at concentration by Confederates. The tables were compiled from information found in the following sources: Tenney, *Seven Days in 1862*, 133, 188, 196; Allan, "Strengths at Second Manassas," 81, 114, 154, 166–69, 202; J. M. Waddill, "Forty-sixth Regiment," *North Carolina Regiments* 3:66; James A. Graham, "Cook's Brigade," *North Carolina Regiments* 4:502; Jacob Dolson Cox, *Military Reminiscences of the Civil War* (New York: Charles Scribner's Sons, 1900), 1:224–31; and *OR*, vol. 11, 3:367, 645; vol. 12, 3:428–29, 781; vol. 14:575–76; vol. 18:376; and vol. 19, 1:1019.

Note that in Table 3b, McDowell's corps includes Reynolds's division; the Fourth Corps does not include Conch's division, already departed for Alexandria; and the strength of Burnside at Fredericksburg has been estimated.

Table 3a. Confederate Forces

LOCATION	FORCE	DIVISIONS	BRIGADES	STRENGTH (present for duty)
Bristoe/Manassas (Jackson)				
	Ewell	1	4	7,900
	Taliaferro	1	4	6,800
	A. P. Hill	1	6	10,000
	Stuart	1	2	3,500
Total raiding column		4	16	28,200
Orleans/Salem (Longstreet)				
	Kemper	1	3	5,700
	Wilcox	1	3	5,700
	Art (Lee/Walton)			600
	D. R. Jones	1	3	4,800
	Evans (incl. Hood)	1	3	6,900
Total relief column		4	12	23,700
Waterloo (reserve column)	Anderson	1	3	6,100
Total Lee's main body		9	31	58,000
Hanover Junction/Petersburg				
	D. H. Hill	1	5	9,500
	McLaws	1	4	7,700
	Reserve artillery			3,200
	Hampton		1	1,500
	Walker	1	2	6,500
Total reenforcing column		3	12	28,400
Total Army of Northern Virginia		12	43	86,400
Richmond/Petersburg (G. W. Smith)				6,000
	Wise		1	
	Daniel		1	
	Martin		1	
	French		1	
	Richmond defenses			4,000

Total garrison forces	1	4	10,000
Total Confederate forces in Virginia theater	13	47	96,400

Table 3b. Union Forces

LOCATION	FORCE	CORPS	DIVS	BRIGS	STRENGTH (present for duty)
Gainesville	Sigel	1	2	6	9,700
(en route)	McDowell	1	3	11	24,300
Greenwich	Heintzelman	1	2	6	14,100
(en route)	Reno	1	2	4	7,400
Bealton	Porter	1	2	6	12,000
Sulphur Springs	Banks	1	2	5	8,100
	Cavalry			3	6,900
Total Pope's main body		6	13	41	82,500
Alexandria	Franklin	1	2	6	11,200
	Sumner	1	2	6	11,100
	Cox		1	2	5,000
Fredericksburg	Burnside		1	2	4,000
Total reenforcing columns		2	6	16	31,300
Washington	Garrison	1	2	3	27,700
Harpers Ferry/ Baltimore	8th Corps	1	1	3	10,000
Fort Monroe/ Norfolk	4th Corps	1	2	6	14,300
	7th Corps	1	1	3	9,600
Total garrison forces		4	6	15	61,600
Total Federal Forces in Virginia Theater		12	25	72	175,400

E. Confederate Losses at Second Manassas

Two factors complicate determining the comparative losses for the Second Manassas campaign. First is the question of the casualties for each side. John Hennessy has estimated Confederate losses at 8,353 and Union at 13,824, but his figures cover only August 28 to 30 and include no Confederate missing. The figures adopted here, therefore, are those reckoned by the editors of *Battles and Leaders* for August 15 through September 2: Confederate, 9,474; Union, 14,462.[13] Unfortunately, these figures are also misleading for use on August 31, since the casualties for Chantilly ought to be subtracted. They cannot be, however, since they cannot be disentangled on the Confederate side.

The question is further complicated by the changing size of each army during the campaign. It has been decided to use the largest strengths obtained, which would be for August 30: 55,097 officers and men present for duty for the Confederates, and 61,430 for the Union.[14]

For the purposes of an approximate conclusion, therefore, using the *Battles and Leaders* casualties and the strengths for August 30, it is possible to calculate the Confederates incurred 17.2 percent casualties and the Federals 23.5 percent. On this same basis, it can be reckoned that the Confederates suffered a 0.79 percent drain from their military manpower pool, and the Federals 0.32 percent, making a 2.47 times greater drain for the Confederates. While still unacceptably high, this represented a reduction by half from the 4.67 times greater loss for the Seven Days.

Notes on Lee's Strategy

A. Sources of Understanding Lee's Grand Strategy

THE INTERPRETATION OF Lee's grand strategy and his perceptions of the nature of the war presented in chapter 2 is based on three sources: (1) the essay by Charles Marshall titled "General Lee's Military Policy";[15] (2) comments made by Lee at various times throughout the war; (3) and the actions taken by Lee to implement the strategy. The general's own words and actions are cited at appropriate places in the discussion, but the use of Marshall as a source requires extended comment.

Col. Charles Marshall occupied a unique position to know Lee's ideas. He was the staff member charged with drafting the final report of operations for Lee's signature. In discharging this duty he operated as a historian. He had to investigate and understand campaigns, ask questions of Lee and other officers to fill in details, and reconcile conflicts in narratives. He also gained insight into the commanding general's thinking from the changes Lee insisted upon making before signing the final draft. There can be no question, therefore, that Marshall's testimony is of fundamental importance and deserves much greater attention than it has yet received.

At the same time, it must be recognized that Marshall was not a disinterested observer. After the war he was a full-fledged member of the so-called "Lee clique" that sought to memorialize the general.[16] Marshall's partisanship does not disqualify his analysis, however; it simply means his account must be subjected to the same skeptical scrutiny that ought to be accorded all historical sources.

Much of Marshall's evaluation is made credible by the unofficial remarks and "sayings" of Lee he includes. Ultimately, however, the real strength of Marshall's explanation derives from its aptness. The strategy Marshall attributes to Lee reasonably describes Lee's actions and is supported by the occasional official comments the general made during the war.

One weakness in Marshall's account cannot be resolved, however. He implies Lee's strategy was fully developed when the general took the field on June 1—and for this there is no firm evidence beyond Marshall's word. On the other hand, there is no evidence to the contrary. Since it cannot be known which if any parts of Lee's strategic thinking were in embryo when he took the field, and, since Lee's actions indicate any such were developed within a matter of weeks, the account presented herein has taken the risk of some distortion by accepting Marshall's word. Statements Lee made at later dates, which indicated that he did hold a particular view, have been included where possible.

Citing several instances where Lee seemed to violate the policy set forth by Marshall, Alan T. Nolan has dismissed Marshall's views as "rationalization." For the minority opinion that Lee had no grand strategy see J. F. C. Fuller and Thomas L. Connelly. A brief but perceptive evaluation of Lee's grand strategy may be found in an essay by William J. Miller.[17]

B. Lee and the Inevitability of Confederate Defeat

Alan Nolan has suggested that Lee did believe the South could not win the war. He cites two anecdotes to support his case. First is the post–Sailor's Creek comment quoted in chapter 2, above. Lee made the remark to Lt. John Sargent Wise, son of ex-Governor Henry Wise of Virginia, early on the morning of April 7, 1865, just after the last major defeat suffered in battle by the Army of Northern Virginia. Secondly, indeed earlier the same night, in conversation with Gen. William Pendleton, who had brought the recommendation of high-ranking officers to open negotiations for surrender, Lee said: "General, this is no new question with me. I have never believed we could, against the gigantic combination for our subjugation, make good in the long run our independence. . . ."[18]

Both conversations were written down from memory many years after the war, however, and they cannot carry the weight of Lee's words written during the war. Nonetheless, even if Wise and Pendleton recollected Lee's ideas precisely, it must be remembered that both incidents came within hours of the end, and after a worn-down Lee had seen every possible expectation shattered. Under these circumstances, it would scarcely be surprising if he had exaggerated almost no hope into no hope at all.

It might also be noted that in the Pendleton interview, Lee is alleged to have continued: ". . . unless foreign powers should, directly or indirectly, assist us. This I was sure it was their interest to do, and I hoped they would so regard it. But such considerations really made with me no difference."[19] This comment would seem to modify somewhat Lee's statement about expecting no foreign help. Once again, however, it is a conversation recalled after the war versus statements written by Lee during the war. Also, even in Pendleton's memoir, Lee avers that foreign considerations made "no difference" to him.

C. Lee and Northern Morale

Remarks made by Lee during the course of the war support the view that he depended on worsening Northern morale for the South to win the war and that, consequently, he monitored signs of the enemy's martial spirit. The general wrote to his wife on April 19, 1863: "I do not think our enemies are so confident of success as they used to be. If we can baffle them in their various designs this year . . . I think our success will be certain. . . . [N]ext fall there will be a great change in public opinion at the North. The Republicans will be destroyed & I think the friends of peace will become so strong as that the next administration will go in on that basis. We have only to resist manfully." See also, Lee to his son, Custis, February 28, 1863, where he discusses the Federal Congress and its legislation.[20]

On July 10, 1864, when sending a copy of the *New York Herald* with stories about Jubal Early's campaign in Maryland, Lee wrote to Davis: "You will see the people in the U.S. are mystified about our forces on the Potomac. The expedition will have the effect I think at least of teaching them they must keep some of their troops at home & cannot denude their frontier with impunity. It seems also to have put them in bad temper as well as bad humor. Gold you will see has gone as high as 271 & closed at 266 ."[21]

There are two major instances when Lee acted on his belief and put forward proposals that were wholly political in nature. The first was his notion during the Maryland campaign that the time was suitable for an official peace overture to the North. The second came at the start of the Gettysburg campaign and involved control of the Southern press to foster the false impression that the Confederacy would consider opening negotiations to end the war without excluding the possibility of rejoining the Union.[22]

Lee's almost daily use of newspapers, both Northern and Southern, as a source of information on which he based evaluation of situations and planned operations deserves more study in its own right. Several provisional observations might be made. First, his heavy reliance on the press probably derived in large part from the paucity of other sources and the primitive nature of the government information system. Apparently, he even acquired most of his news about other Confederate military operations from newspapers. Secondly, it is curious that in spite of Lee's manipulation of the Southern press to feed false information to the enemy, he seems to have accepted news from Northern newspapers at face value.

D. Lee and the Northern Phobia over Losing Washington

On June 23, 1863, Lee commented on "the well known anxiety of the Northern Government for the safety of its capital. . . ." Two days later, also writing to Davis, he referred to the "apprehension for the safety of Washington and their own territory" by the "Federal Government and people." So certain was Lee of the predictable reaction of the Lincoln government that in the same letter he urged that a force no matter how small—an army "even in effigy"—be pushed forward under Beauregard toward Culpeper.[23]

It might be questioned whether or not Lee's appreciation of the enemy's sensitivity to security of its capital was so fully developed in early June of 1862, but Charles Marshall has asserted:

> General Lee had seen how even the supposed presence of a powerful Confederate army at Manassas, thirty miles from Washington, had detained the strongest army of the United States around the capital. He had remarked with surprise how the Federal Government had neglected for months the easy means of compelling the withdrawal of General Johnston from Manassas by transporting its own army to the vicinity of Richmond, and he had been confirmed in his views of the apprehensions of that Government for the safety of their capital by the advance of Jackson down the Valley, when [it] . . . caused the recall of McDowell from Fredericksburg. These results were utterly out of proportion to the Confederate force employed, and satisfied General Lee that the Government of Mr. Lincoln would provide for the safety of Washington in proportion to the political importance attached to its possession, rather than in proportion to the real danger that threatened the city.[24]

In a private conversation with George B. Davis, president of the Antietam Battlefield Board, Marshall indicated that Lee knew and took advantage of the "well known solicitude for the safety of [Washington], on the part of President Lincoln, Secretary Stanton and General Halleck." Walter Taylor, another member of Lee's staff during the entire war, in referring in his memoirs to early July 1862, wrote of Lee's "just conception of the inordinate fear which possessed the mind of the Federal civil authorities for the safety of their capital."[25]

E. Lee and Davis and Jackson's Valley Campaign

Lee has been perhaps given too much credit for originating Jackson's offensive. While in a number of instances he urged Jackson to strike a blow, there is no reason to believe Lee envisioned a campaign that would reach the banks of the Potomac, or that he anticipated the extreme reaction by the Lincoln administration. See especially the May 16 dispatch, sometimes cited as the origin of Jackson's campaign, wherein Lee wrote to Jackson: "A successful blow struck at [Banks] would delay, if it does not prevent, his moving to either place [i.e., Fredericksburg or the Peninsula], and might also lead to the recall of the re-enforcements sent to Frémont from Winchester. . . ." Yet later in the same dispatch, Lee continued: "But you will not, in any demonstration you may make in that direction, lose sight of the fact that it may become necessary for you to come to the support of General Johnston, and hold yourself in readiness to do so if required."[26]

There is also this intriguing comment in Jefferson Davis letter of May 30 to his wife: "Thank you for congratulations on the success of Jackson. Had the movement been made when I first proposed it, the effect would have been more important. In that night's long conference it was regarded impossible."[27] The editors of the Davis papers speculate that reference is to a meeting between Davis, Lee, and Johnston at the latter's headquarters on May 12. Not only does this date seem a bit late to warrant Davis's comment, however, but the president seems to be responding to his wife's having given him credit for the idea, and, further, that she knows of the long conference he mentions. Varina Davis and the children left for the safety of North Carolina on May 9. The interesting possibility exists, therefore, that Davis: (1) is referring to the war council of April 14; and (2) that he did propose at that time an offensive by Jackson as a diversion for the Federal movement on the Peninsula. Whatever the facts, it would seem Davis played a larger role in Jackson's campaign than heretofore supposed.

The president also took note that "the Northern press and government show panic lest Washington should be captured."[28]

F. Lee's Intentions in the Second Manassas Campaign

Traditionally, it has been assumed that Lee's purpose in sending Jackson on the turning movement through Thoroughfare Gap was to throw Pope off balance and render him vulnerable to a smashing blow in the Manassas Junction area. This, of course, comes near to being the way the campaign worked out in practice. The view presented in chapter 5, however, is that initially Lee did not intend to deliver battle in front of Washington but to draw Pope west into the Valley of Virginia. This interpretation has the merit of harmonizing with Lee's known desire to pursue maneuver over battle whenever possible, to conserve Confederate resources, to free the largest possible area of Virginia from which to draw supplies, and to play upon the Lincoln administration's fear for the safety of its capital.

This interpretation is also supported by Charles Marshall's postwar explanation of Lee's intentions: "His object was to cause General Pope to retreat by cutting the railroad behind him, and at the same time to delay the arrival of reinforcements. By placing his army on General Pope's right flank, he would be able to use the Shenandoah Valley to approach the Potomac and so cause apprehension in the Federal Government for the safety of their capital. This General Lee told me himself."[29] This last sentence—written by the aide who drafted Lee's reports and questioned him on his intentions—makes it impossible to ignore the strong likelihood Lee had the Valley strategy in mind.

Although Douglas Freeman was aware of Marshall's statement, he interpreted it to mean Lee intended to retire to the Valley only as a backup plan. But Freeman overlooked a dispatch by Lee to Randolph of August 25, in which the Confederate commander wrote, "I deem it important that General Loring should be . . . directed to . . . operate northwardly, so as to join me in the valley of Virginia." This would seem to be a forthright statement of intent to operate in the Shenandoah Valley. It was certainly so interpreted by Randolph, who ordered Loring to "clear the valley of the Kanawha, and operate northwardly to a junction with our army in the valley."[30]

Notes on War Councils and Strategy Conferences

A. Partial List of Strategy Conferences Attended by Lee

LEE HAS ACQUIRED the reputation of aloofness, which is probably justified in regard to his avoidance of partisanship and intrigue. He was not aloof when it came to discussing strategy, however. On the contrary, he seems to have been willing to debate strategic questions freely and frequently, even after he assumed field command and did not need to consult his subordinates. Table 4 is meant to be a contribution toward identifying the strategy meetings in which Lee participated from the beginning of the war through August 31, 1862.

Table 4. Strategy Conferences Attended by Lee

DATE	PERSONS ATTENDING	TOPICS / LOCATION
July 14, 1861	Davis, Cooper, Lee, Chesnut	Beauregard's plan
Apr. 14, 1862	Davis, Randolph, Lee, Johnston, Smith, Longstreet	Plans for the Peninsula
May 13	Davis, Lee, Johnston	Johnston's headquarters
June 3	Davis, division commanders	Chimneys
June 7	Davis, Lee	Lee's headquarters
June 16	Lee, Longstreet	Lee's headquarters
June 23	Lee, Longstreet, Jackson, D. Hill, A. Hill	Dabbs House: plans for Seven Days
July 4	Lee, Jackson	Decision to attack
ca. Aug. 11	Lee, Longstreet	Plans for Pope
Aug. 15	Lee, Longstreet, Jackson	Plans for Pope
Aug. 19	Lee, Longstreet	Clark's Mountain: plans for Pope
Aug. 24	Lee, Longstreet, Jackson, Stuart	Jeffersonton War Council

Aug. 29	Lee, Longstreet, Jackson	Whether to attack
Aug. 30	Lee, Longstreet, Jackson	Plans to pursue Pope
Aug. 31	Lee, Longstreet, Jackson	Bull Run Bridge: Plans to pursue Pope

B. Fairfax Court House War Council, October 1, 1862

There is considerable confusion over what was said at this conference, or more correctly what was understood about the number of additional troops requested.[31] Davis asked how many troops would be needed, and Smith replied 50,000, while Johnston and Beauregard said 60,000. It seems certain that the generals were referring to the *total* required, although Davis may have understood them to mean the *additional* men needed.

Johnston's October returns indicate he had 44,000 men present for duty in the forces at Leesburg, Fairfax Court House, Centreville, and Manassas—that is, not including the Valley or Aquia districts.[32] Hence, the Generals were apparently asking for an increase of only 6,000 to 16,000 men. It is difficult to believe that Davis could not have found this relatively modest number of reenforcements. It is impossible to believe, however, that the four men could have discussed a subject of this importance over several hours without realizing they were talking at cross-purposes over whether 16,000 or 60,000 troops needed to be supplied.

The only reasonable explanation is hinted at in Davis's account, where he states—without a specific figure—that the generals requested "twice the number there present for duty."[33] It is possible that Johnston and the others downplayed the size of their forces, a practice common among generals. Perhaps they did not include the Leesburg forces, men on extra and detached duty and the like, and represented the total as around 30,000 (instead of 44,000). In this case, they would have needed 30,000 additional troops to reach the total of 60,000 and would have been asking for "twice their number," a sizable force that Davis believed he could not scrape together.

C. Richmond War Council, April 14, 1862

There is a possible discrepancy in the dating of this conference. Freeman places the war council on April 14. His account, as well as the memoirs of the participants, indicate that at the end of the conference Davis verbally increased Johnston's command to include the forces of Magruder and Huger. The presidential order, signed by Lee, giving Johnston the troops on the Peninsula and at Norfolk appears in the *Official Records*, dated April 12.[34] There are five possible explanations: (1) the order was written on the

14th and back-dated; (2) Johnston knew of his increased command before the conference, and the participants were wrong in remembering it as news to him; (3) Freeman is wrong about the date of the conference; (4) the order in the *OR* is misdated; or (5) although written two days before the conference, the order had not been given to Johnston. The last possibility is the most likely explanation. In any case, since Johnston in practice would exercise only nominal command of Huger, and since he could not have commanded the Peninsula without also commanding Magruder, the increase in his authority was at best a minor technicality.

D. Jeffersonton War Council, August 24, 1862

Henry Kyd Douglas of Jackson's staff is the only source for this four-way conference, and he includes dramatic details, including that it was held in a field away from staff and even trees. Freeman has rightly questioned many of the details, but he goes too far in doubting that the four met together. While it is possible that Lee conferred separately, a joint meeting was logical and possible. Longstreet was at Jeffersonton, and Stuart may have been. The cavalry chief's report that he received "final instructions" on the night of August 25 indicates he knew of the plan earlier.[35]

— ❧ —

Notes on Lee and the Campaign around Richmond, June 1–August 14, 1862

A. Lee and Stuart's Ride around McClellan

J EB STUART'S FAMOUS ride is another mystery from this period. Lee's need for information was obvious. But why did he permit Stuart to take such a large force? And why instruct him to destroy wagon trains and collect grain and cattle? Both actions magnified Stuart's operations and ran the risk of calling the Federals' attention to the danger to their communications. The intelligence gathering could have been accomplished just as well, if not better, by one or more small and much less conspicuous parties of a company or less. And, if Lee did indeed understand McClellan's cautious nature, as some have hypothesized, there was all the more reason not to risk alerting him. It is possible that Stuart's flamboyant execution of his orders somewhat distracted McClellan from its true purpose. Nevertheless, this result could not have been predicted, and the manner in which the intelligence was gathered must seem an unreasonable risk on the eve of operations necessary to save the capital and perhaps the country.

Stuart's written report did not provide the information required, and Lee wryly commented on it: "The General deals in the flowering style." The source for concluding that Lee was satisfied with the information he received is Charles Marshall.[36]

For a classic account of the ride—long on moonlight and rattling sabers and short on intelligence analysis—see Freeman's *Lee's Lieutenants*, a chapter of which has been reprinted in literature anthologies for college freshmen. For the now-standard narrative, see the new Stuart biography by Emory Thomas. In a recent study, Edwin Bearss suggests that Stuart's ride did alert McClellan to the danger to his communications with the Pamunkey and caused the Federal commander to initiate steps to transfer his base to the James as early as June 18.[37]

B. Lee and Federal Reenforcements at Harrison's Landing, July 5, 1862

Lee had been receiving reports from Stuart since July 3 suggesting a Federal move south of the James. On the 5th, he reported to Davis his own obervations.[38]

The enemy troops seen by Lee were two brigades of some 5,000 men under Gen. O. S. Ferry from McDowell's Department of the Rappahannock. Arriving by water (via Alexandria) at Fort Monroe on July 1, they reached McClellan at Harrison's Landing on the 4th and 5th. Ferry's own brigade (39th Illinois, 13th Indiana, 62d Ohio, 66th Ohio, and 67th Ohio) would be made part of Peck's division of the Fourth Corps, while Nathan Kimball's brigade (14th Indiana, 4th Ohio, 8th Ohio, and 7th West Virginia) would remain an independent brigade with the Second Corps, until becoming part of French's newly formed division of the same corps. These two brigades, plus several miscellaneous regiments, were the only reenforcements that actually ever joined the Army of the Potomac after the Seven Days.[39]

C. Lee and the Replacement of Huger, Holmes, Magruder, and Whiting

A traditional assumption has been that Lee found all four generals wanting during the Seven Days' operations and engineered their removal from his army. However, there is no evidence of this in three cases, and only a hint in the case of Huger. A cryptic reference made by Lee to Randolph on June 19 suggests he may have approved if not sought Huger's transfer, although this came before the fighting started. Magruder had been assigned to the Trans-Mississippi on May 23, a week before Lee replaced the wounded Johnston, but the order had been temporarily suspended and was reinstated at Magruder's own request.[40] There is no evidence that Lee sought Holmes's transfer, nor that he was anxious for D. H. Hill to leave a division in the field, which had to be remanded to the hands of its senior brigadier (Ripley) because no replacement thought to be competent could be found. Finally, there is no reason to believe Lee would have removed Whiting, if that general had not taken sick leave. It is probably true, however, that Hood did so well as division commander as to prevent Whiting's ever returning.

In the case of Huger and Whiting it is likely that someone—Davis if not Lee, or perhaps both—believed them unsuited to field command, as one was transferred to staff and the other to departmental assignment. It is also possible that age may have been a factor for Huger, who was fifty-six, and for Holmes, who was fifty-seven.

D. Lee and Pope's Orders

On August 2, at Davis's behest, Lee sent a copy of the Confederate orders proscribing Pope and his men to Halleck, whom he correctly addressed as "Commanding, U.S. Army"—another indication that newspapers kept Lee current on happenings in the North. Halleck refused to accept the letter and returned it because of its "exceedingly insulting" language.[41] So far as is known, no one on either side died as a result of these orders and counterorders. Incidents did occur, however, which were laid at Pope's door.[42] The most famous, Gen. Adolph von Steinwehr's arrest of five hostages in Luray on July 13, actually occurred before Pope issued any of his infamous orders.[43]

Pope attempted at least twice to curb excesses committed under his orders. The whole ugly incident should have been closed on August 15, when Halleck issued orders forbidding the compulsory administration of oaths of allegiance or excessive penalties for refusing to take them.[44] Nevertheless, there is evidence that the Confederates discriminated against prisoners from Pope's army as late as the aftermath of Second Manassas.

Clearly, Lee not only disliked Pope's orders, he also disliked the Federal general. Twice during a four-day period, Lee referred to Pope as a "miscreant" and three times used the word "suppress" to describe what needed to be done to him.[45] Revealing an irrepressible sense of humor—which not all historians have appreciated—Lee also made two playful remarks at Pope's expense. Referring to his nephew Louis Marshall, who had remained loyal to the North, he told his daughter he hoped Jackson would catch both Pope and Marshall: "I could forgive the latter for fighting against us, if he had not joined such a miscreant as Pope." And several weeks later, after Marshall had been seen looking "wretched" after the battle of Cedar Mountain, Lee wrote to his wife, Mary, "I am sorry to hear he is in such bad company. But I suppose he could not help it."[46]

Nine months later, in writing his official report, Lee would telescope and reverse events, by mistakenly recalling that: "To meet the advance of [Pope] and restrain, as far as possible, the atrocities which he threatened to perpetrate upon our defenseless citizens," Jackson had been ordered toward Gordonsville on July 13.[47] Interestingly, throughout this period, while Lee usually refers to Pope without a title, he normally writes of "General McClellan."

E. Coggins Point, July 31, 1862

Douglas Freeman incorrectly concluded that the expedition against McClellan was intended to free up additional troops to send to Jackson, rather than to cover the transfer of A. P. Hill. Freeman's error undoubtedly grew from his more fundamental mistake in reading Lee's dispatches of this period to be "missing" the considerable "tension" that had been observable in his pre–Seven Days letters. Freeman argues that Lee "was beginning to read with more assurance the minds of the men who opposed him. Pope he never took very seriously; McClellan he respected but understood."[48]

It would be fruitless to debate the degree of tension in Lee's letters. Nevertheless, a large measure of worry is palpably expressed in virtually every letter Lee writes to Jackson, Davis, and Randolph during this period; so also is a frank admission of his inability to fathom McClellan's intentions. If Lee was reading Federal minds, he was unaware of it himself.

It is significant to note that Jefferson Davis understood both Lee's worry and the plan for covering the transferral of A. P. Hill to Jackson. In a letter to Kirby Smith, the president wrote, "We hope soon to strike another blow here, so as to hold one army in check whilst we strike the other."[49]

F. Lee and Burnside's Destination

The claim that Lee knew of the Federal indecision regarding Burnside's destination is made by Lee's aide, Charles Marshall, in his postwar writings, but it is not supported by any wartime correspondence or reports. Freeman writes as if Lee knew from July 7, the date of Burnside's arrival at Fort Monroe, but he cites only Federal sources. Lee's letter to Jackson on July 25 makes it clear he knew virtually nothing about Burnside on that date. Hence, Lee's Burnside "watch," if it took place at all, likely was between July 26 and August 4. Even Marshall wrote of it happening "at the end of July."[50]

There is a tradition, apparently started by John Esten Cooke, that the young John S. Mosby, just returned as an exchanged prisoner of war, informed Lee that Burnside was intended as reenforcement for Pope. This incident, even if true, has been exaggerated. First, Mosby could not have spoken with Lee before the late afternoon of August 5 and may not have seen him until the 6th—in other words, at the same time or after the dispatch from Jeb Stuart. Secondly, Mosby at most could have specified that Burnside was going to Aquia Landing. What Lee needed to know at this later time was whether Burnside would be sent overland to Pope, or whether Burnside would form an independent movement from Fredericksburg against Richmond. This Mosby could not have known.[51]

G. Lee's Decision to Supersede Jackson, August 9, 1862

Previously, it has been assumed that Lee did not reach the decision to send Longstreet northward until August 13, on which date Special Orders No. 181 was issued.[52] A series of eighteen orders, however, signed by Moxley

Sorrel, Longstreet's chief of staff, were sent out August 9 to 11, which set the command in motion. Also, diarists of the Washington Artillery and the 17th Virginia (Pickett's brigade) recorded that their units departed for Gordonsville on August 10.[53]

It cannot be known if Lee issued a written order on August 9 which has not been found, or if he simply gave Longstreet verbal orders. In any case, the Confederate commander made the decision before he knew Jackson had brought Pope to battle at Cedar Mountain.

There is additional, second-hand evidence of Lee's unhappiness with Jackson. In his diary entry for March 6, 1863, Jed. Hotchkiss quotes Jeb Stuart as saying, "Gen. Lee came to us at Gordonsville with rather a low estimate of Jackson's ability."[54]

While it would be unjustified to put too much emphasis on Lee's dissatisfaction with Jackson in the absence of direct evidence, it is nevertheless obvious that Lee could have sent reenforcements northward without selecting Longstreet. Indeed, Longstreet's command was located farthest away on the James. Nearer to hand—in order of their nearness to Jackson—were the divisions of Hood, Ripley, and McLaws, all of whom were new to their level of command and much junior to Jackson. Dorsey Pender, a brigade commander under A. P. Hill, believed that Longstreet's replacement of Jackson "does not look reasonable" and assumed it to be temporary until the arrival of Lee.[55] Historians have made the same assumption.

Lee recognized Longstreet's seniority by addressing him as "Commanding, &c., Gordonsville" and in referring to the "portion of the Army of Northern Virginia now under General Longstreet. . . ." Lee's instructions to Longstreet—probably given on August 9 or 10—are reconstructed from his dispatch of the 14th. In the same letter Lee refers to having met with Longstreet before his departure for Gordonsville.[56] This is further evidence Lee did not originally plan to go to Gordonsville himself.

Considering Longstreet's willingness after the war to press his own claims for prominence in the operations of the Army of Northern Virginia, it is curious that he passes over his role in this affair with one sentence. The fact that he misdates the departure of his command on the 15th (five days after the fact) indicates how fuzzy his memory had become by the 1890s. A decade earlier, in an article for *Century Magazine*, Longstreet wrote that he left on the 13th, and "General Lee accompanied me there."[57] This is another example of why Longstreet's postwar writings must be used with care by historians.

It was finally on August 13 that Special Orders No. 181 was issued from Headquarters, Department of Northern Virginia. Why articles 6 and 7 were issued on this date is a mystery. According to article 6, Longstreet and his command were ordered to Gordonsville, but of course they were already there. According to article 7, Hood was ordered to Hanover Junction, but he had been ordered there on August 8. The retroactive issuance of these orders has misled later students to believe Longstreet started for Gordonsville and Hood for Hanover Junction on August 13; and, apparently, after the passing of time, Lee and his staff were misled as well. When the campaign report was written almost a year later, it simply stated that Longstreet was ordered to Gordonsville on the 13th.[58]

This is purely speculation, but the orders may have been originally suppressed (on the 9th) for the sake of secrecy and may have been published later (on the 13th) for the sake of completing the records. If this were the case, backdating the orders would have been kinder to historians.

H. Lee's Knowledge of McClellan's Withdrawal from the Peninsula

Since McClellan had been ordered to withdraw from the James on August 3, the question naturally arises as to whether Lee had any knowledge of the pending enemy move to help him decide to send more troops to Jackson. Certainly, after McClellan started shipping off his sick (about August 5) and sending artillery to Burnside (on August 7) as specifically ordered by Halleck, there was increased naval traffic on the James.[59]

While it is possible Lee was aware of this and weighed it into his decision, there is no surviving evidence to support the theory. The only known reference is a vague remark by Longstreet to a subordinate on July 31: "We have rumors that the enemy is drawing off his forces, but have not been able to learn anything definite."[60] In the first place, "drawing off" could mean anything; and secondly, July 31 was too early for the rumors to have any grounding in fact.

On the other hand, there are several strong indications that Lee had no knowledge of McClellan's withdrawal until well after the 9th. First, on August 17 Lee wrote to Davis, "It is possible that hearing of the advance of our army in this direction it may have been taken advantage of to extricate him from his dilemma under the pretense of defending Washington." If Lee's reference is to the "advance" of Longstreet, which it probably is, then clearly he believed McClellan's withdrawal was ordered after his decision was made. Second, also on the 17th, Lee wrote to his wife, "I learn since I have left that General McClellan has moved down the river with his whole army."[61] This indicates Lee did not remember feeling certain of the news when he left Richmond on August 14.

After McClellan's withdrawal had been confirmed, Lee recognized that nothing he had done since July 2 could account for the Federal movement, and he was somewhat puzzled. He wrote to Davis on August 17, "I feel greatly mortified [at McClellan's withdrawal], for though the material damage dealt him in the battles of the Chickahominy was not as great as I could have wished, he must have been so morally shattered as to have induced the belief that the safety of his army required his retreat and to have caused his abandonment of his present attack on Richmond." Lee could not know that McClellan did not want to withdraw from the James, but had been ordered to do so over his protests by the new Federal general-in-chief, Henry Halleck.[62]

I. Lee's Report to Davis of August 14, 1862

Lee's report to Davis bears a curious resemblance to the paper left behind by McClellan in April just before sailing for the Peninsula.[63] Lee also is somewhat careless with the figures he reports for his capital's defense. He tells Davis he is leaving behind four divisions that total 72,000 men. Two things are wrong with this figure: although Lee hints that R. H. Anderson may be ordered north, he has already made that decision; and the 72,000 represents aggregate present and absent, not only the largest possible category in counting but also a practically meaningless one. Lee may have assumed that Davis, with his military background, would understand the figure; nevertheless, it is one almost never used by the Confederates, and one cannot escape the conclusion that Lee was putting the best face possible on his plans in order to avoid interference from above. In other words, it is not unreasonable to assume he was doing exactly the same thing McClellan had done.

Notes on Lee and the Campaign against Pope, August 15–September 1, 1862

A. Lee's Orders of August 16–19, 1862

In his report, Lee wrote: "The movement, as explained in the accompanying order, was appointed for August 18, but the necessary preparations not having been completed, its execution was postponed to the 20th." The only orders discovered, however, have been Special Orders No. 185, August 19, Headquarters, Army of Northern Virginia, attached to Stuart's report.[64] It is possible that (1) written orders for August 16 have disappeared through mischance; (2) orders for the 16th were verbal and not issued in written form until the 19th, after the movement had been postponed; and (3), with the written orders for both dates being virtually the same, only the latter were retained in the records. Lee's discussion in his report makes the second and third occurrences most likely, and it has been assumed that the details for those of August 16 were nearly identical to those of the 19th, which have survived.

Lee's plans in regard to Stuart's raid are further documented in his letter to the cavalry chief of August 19.[65]

B. Lee's Visit to Clark's Mountain

When Lee viewed Pope pulling back, he initially believed the Federals would retreat all the way to Fredericksburg, which explains why he was especially disappointed. Pope was retiring only to the upper Rappahannock, however[66]

Longstreet dated the visit to Clark's Mountain on August 18, but Freeman is probably correct in putting it on the 19th.[67] Although this means the Confederates were a day late in perceiving the withdrawal, it makes more sense than their being a day late in starting their pursuit.

Lee was playing on Pope's July 14 address, in which the Federal general proclaimed: "I come to you from the West, where we have always seen the backs of our enemies. . . ." That humor at Pope's expense was already current in the Confederate army is attested by Dorsey Pender's comment, "He will take to thinking about lines of retreat yet if he does not mind."[68]

C. Lee's Dispatch to Davis of August 24, 1862

There is no hour given for the dispatch, but internal evidence moderately suggests Lee wrote it prior to his meeting with Jackson on the afternoon of the 24th. It is, of course, entirely possible Lee had already decided on his wide turning movement but did not mention it to Davis for reasons of security. After all, since most of the letter was devoted to a discussion of Pope's conveniently lost dispatch, Lee must have been reminded of the vagaries of long-distance communications. A day earlier, Walter Taylor had written home: "Too many letters have been captured lately (from the enemy) to warrant any one in putting in writing anything appertaining to our position or intentions."[69]

It might be noted in passing that Lee's letter to Davis, although an admirable reflection of his abilities as strategist and diplomat, is nevertheless open to the sort of criticism commonly leveled against McClellan. Not only did Lee exaggerate the enemy's size by counting Burnside twice, he also was guilty of making excuses in advance by adding "unless we are overpowered."

Lee sent a one-sentence telegram to Davis alerting him the dispatch was on the way and that he had "ordered Genl. Smith to join me with all the troops available subject to your approval."[70]

D. Jackson's Route to Manassas Junction

Capt. J. Keith Boswell, Jackson's engineer, suggested passing below the mountains at Amissville, marching north to Salem and then east to cross through the mountains at Thoroughfare Gap, from which a turnpike roughly paralleled the Manassas Gap Railroad and ran directly to Manassas Junction where it intersected the Orange and Alexandria. Freeman believed that either Boswell misremembered his instructions, or that Jackson misled his chief engineer in order to preserve secrecy.[71] But the latter is unlikely, because the essential part of the mission to be kept secret was the march behind the mountains and through Thoroughfare Gap to Gainesville—which Boswell had to know about in order to provide the route. In any case, since both Bristoe and Manassas were on the Orange and Alexandria, both were far at Pope's rear, both were between Pope and Washington, and the two were but five miles apart, it is difficult to see how the distinction mattered in regard to secrecy. Nor, except that Bristoe Station was slightly closer to Pope's army on the Rappahannock, was the difference important in a strategic sense.

E. The Timing of Lee's March To Follow Jackson

The timing of Lee's leaving the Rappahannock with Longstreet and its relationship to Pope's movements have not been fully understood. None of the official reports connect Lee's march with anything Pope did and thus imply that Lee simply left as soon as he could. Freeman depicts Lee observing a Federal withdrawal on August 26 and poses the hypothesis that Pope was going after Jackson. But this is not possible, since it is certain that Pope did not issue his orders or start after Jackson until the morning of the 27th. Freeman, who did not always understand Federal operations as thoroughly as Confederate ones, was misled by Longstreet's erroneous postwar statement that Lee discovered on the 26th, "Pope's army broke away from its strong position to meet Jackson's daring and unexpected move."[72]

It is tempting to dismiss the whole matter as resulting from Longstreet's fuzzy memory and conclude Lee left independently of any move by Pope. But Longstreet's mistake is supported by the usually reliable Marshall, who recalled that "on the morning of the 26th it became evident that the enemy was beginning to move away from the river."[73]

The question then arises: even if Pope did not start after Jackson until the 27th, did something else happen on the 26th that might have misled Lee? The answer would seem to lie in the the heretofore ignored fact that on the night of the 25th the panicky Sigel withdrew his corps from Waterloo to Warrenton and provided Lee the pretext for believing what the Confederate commander wanted to believe.[74]

F. Jackson's Movements on the Night of August 27, 1862

The confusion of the night movements is reflected in the reports of Jackson and his commanders. In *OR*, vol. 12, pt. 2, Jackson (p. 644) makes no mention of Hill's detour to Centreville, or Ewell's to Blackburn's Ford; Boswell (651) claims all three divisions camped one mile north of Groveton; Taliaferro (656) says his division was at Sudley Mill and moved to Groveton at daylight; B. T. Johnson of Taliaferro's division (664) says his brigade reached Groveton shortly after midnight; A. P. Hill (670) says his division went to Centreville, which is confirmed by Walker (674), Lane (675), McGowan (679), and Archer (700); Early (710) says Ewell's division moved toward Centreville and bivouacked between Manassas and Bull Run; Forno

(718) commanded Hays's brigade and admits he could not find the rest of Ewell's division that night and was lost; and Stuart (735) says his men were the last to leave Manassas and guarded the flanks of the army which moved in two columns, one to Centreville and the other to the stone bridge over Bull Run.

G. Campbell Brown, Ewell's aide, wrote an interesting but ambiguous postwar account that raises the possibility the guides were wrong in leading Ewell's division after Hill toward Centreville. His only evidence is the fact that Jackson called them back the next morning, however, and that could have just as easily resulted from Jackson changing his mind, as from a mistake by the courier.[75]

In his biography of Lee, Freeman gives a brief and inaccurate account of Jackson on the night of the 27th. The noted Confederate military historian did not fully address the issue, however, until he wrote his history of the Army of Northern Virginia.[76] In the latter, he assumes that Jackson decided on the line behind the Warrenton pike from Groveton to Sudley before leaving Manassas, but Stonewall's devotion to secrecy, the darkness of the night, and the ineptness of the guides caused the divisions to scatter off their targets. This interpretation is possible, since there is no evidence to contradict it. Neither, however, is there any proof to support it, except the account by Campbell Brown, which is discussed above and is open to a contrary reading. In the absence of proof, reason suggests it is more likely Jackson waited until daylight to examine the ground and determine a sound position, rather than that two of his guides made the same eight-mile error—Hill went to Centreville, and Ewell thought he was supposed to—while one guide understood and followed orders perfectly.

G. The Lee-Longstreet Disagreement on August 29, 1862

The disagreement between the two Confederate generals was confirmed by the testimony of Charles Marshall at the retrial of Fitz John Porter, when in answer to a direct question, he said: "General Lee was desirous to make the attack on the 29th; Longstreet was not." Marshall could not recall any "particular circumstance" but recollected "that Lee was rather inclined to attack." In his testimony—which it should be remembered was in a trial over the credibility of the old archenemy Pope—Marshall went so far as to imply the whole aim of Lee's campaign was to bring Pope to battle at Manassas. Later, when writing his book, Marshall would recall that Lee had told him of his intention to fall back to the Shenandoah Valley after cutting Pope's communications.[77] Lee's inclination to fight on the 29th— after he found himself drawn by circumstances into contact with the enemy—is reconcilable. Marshall's contradictory explanations of Lee's ultimate aims are too far apart to resolve, however, except by concluding that one is wrong.

H. Defects of the Confederate Line at Second Manassas

Freeman partially noted the defects in Lee's troop deployment at Second Manassas when he wrote, "It was an admirable position in which to meet an attack, though not quite so good for hurling quickly the full weight of the army in assault."[78] It may be speculated that Lee's perception of the weaknesses of his concave line may have played a role in his hesitation to attack on August 29.

It may also be asked why Lee placed Longstreet at an obtuse angle to Jackson in the first place, rather than simply extending him in a straight line from Jackson and parallel to the Warrenton Turnpike. The fact that it resulted from Longstreet's lead division (Hood) simply stopping on the pike, and forming line facing in the same direction it had been marching, does not explain why Lee thought this to be wise tactically. Did it derive initially from ignorance of the terrain and the established location of units already on the field? Did it reflect Lee's desire to hold the pike as a route for withdrawal? Or, was it a result of Lee's original intent to attack Pope immediately to relive the pressure on Jackson? If the latter, which seems most likely, it raises the additional question as to why Lee continued to hold the same position during the night of the 29th and the morning of the 30th.

I. Lee's Injury, August 31, 1862

Lee's injury provides an interesting exercise in the historical method. Virtually nothing about the event is free from ambiguity, and the version in the text is an attempt to reconcile thirteen primary sources: Chilton (for Lee) to Davis, Sept. 2, 1862, *OR*, vol. 19, 2:588; Douglas, *I Rode with Stonewall*, 143–44; Lee letter to wife, Oct. 12, 1862, and account by Lee's youngest son, Lee [Jr.], *Personal Recollections*, 78–79; Long, *Memoirs of R. E. Lee*, 206; Longstreet, *From Manassas to Appomattox*, 192; Owen, *In Camp and Battle*, 127; Squires, "Boy Officer," *Civil War Times Illustrated* 14 (1975): 17; Taylor, *General Lee*, 115–16; Stuart to wife, Sept. 4, 1862, Stuart, *Letters James E. B. Stuart*, 264; H. W. Thomas, *History of the Doles-Cook Brigade*, 469; Dr. Samuel K. Jackson, Essays, p. 2, Virginia Military Historial Society, Richmond; and Gilbert Moxley Sorrel, *Recollections of a Confederate Staff Officer*, ed. Bell Irvin Wiley (Jackson, Tenn.: McCowat-Mercer, 1958), 96–97.

There is general agreement the accident occurred on August 31 (only Thomas misdates it as September 2) and that both hands were severely injured.

Only Taylor explains the cause as the sudden appearance of Federal prisoners and Confederate guards, which is, however, the likeliest explanation. Two accounts say that Traveller was spooked by the presence (Long) or reported presence (Longstreet) of Federal cavalry. Three accounts (Douglas, Lee [Jr.], and Squires) report vaguely that "something" caused the horse to shy. And one account (Sorrel) says Lee tripped over his overalls while his horse moved away, but mentions no cause.

Two accounts (Douglas and Lee [Jr.]) specify that Traveller was the horse in question. (Lee himself always used the old English spelling with the double *ll*.) Curiously, Lee's youngest son, Robert E. Lee, Jr., claims his father was "sitting on a fallen log, with the bridle reins over his arm." Walter Taylor confirms this in part by writing that the general "held his horse, with the bridle loosely depending from his arm." If true, this would have been a foolish mistake for a horseman of the elder Lee's experience to commit.

The site as being near the Stone Bridge is established only in Long's version, but Charles Squires of the Washington Artillery remembered the incident as occurring "on the banks of Bull Run." Squires added that Lee fell on a rock. Taylor recalled it happening "near a high railroad embankment and culvert," but his memory may have confused the river banks with a railroad embankment, as it is unlikely Lee would have gone to the unfinished railroad on the Sudley Springs Road to pursue the latest information on the foe fleeing to Centreville.

Thomas remembered the 44th Georgia (Ripley's brigade) as being at the Stewart farm, when its surgeon was summoned to examine Lee. It is unclear whether he is referring to the Centreville or Chantilly area, but the Stuart farms located at both places are well out of consideration as possible sites. Since his date is wrong, Thomas is likely wrong about the location as well. Considering that Ripley's brigade belonged to Harvey Hill's division and that Hill did not report to Lee until September 2, there has been some question about the authenticity of Thomas's entire story, and indeed, Freeman was chary about using it. There is strong evidence, however, that Ripley (with his own and Colquitt's brigade) was ordered up separately and operated in advance of Hill; and that he probably arrived in the Manassas area on August 30.[79]

According to Thomas, Dr. N. S. Walker of the 44th Georgia "dressed his wound and gave him a bottle of liniment, which greatly relieved him, and he returned the bottle at the battle of Sharpsburg, and told Dr. Walker to keep it for the next patient with a sprained or broken finger or hand."

Only Walter Taylor and Henry Kyd Douglas, aide to Stonewall Jackson, specifically claim to have been present, although Squires implies that he was also. The account of G. Moxley Sorrel, Longstreet's adjutant, is so detailed as to suggest firsthand observation. Taylor puts Longstreet on the scene, and this would make Sorrel's presence likely also. It is assumed that Jackson was present, since Douglas would seldom have been with Lee without his chief. All of this makes it probable that Lee was conferring with his two wing commanders about the pursuit of Pope when the accident took place.

Lee's son, a private in the Rockbridge Virginia Artillery, could not have been present. He saw his father briefly on August 29 and not again until September 5 and 17. He may have received a firsthand account of the incident from his father, however, at the first of these meetings.

Regrettably, the rare contemporaneous reference by Jeb Stuart in a letter to his wife on September 4 is brief and adds little: "General Lee fell and bruised his hand the other day."

How quickly news of Lee's injury spread through the ranks is uncertain. The fact that William Miller Owen recorded in his diary on the following day (September 1) that Lee was traveling by ambulance, in itself, proves little. Owen was adjutant of the Washington Artillery. Although on detached duty at the time of the accident, he would have quickly heard the story from his fellow artillerists, who regularly encamped near Lee's headquarters.

According to Sorrel, there was a "widespread report" that Lee had been wounded, which was picked up and embroidered with details in the Northern press.

J. Lee's Movements on August 31, 1862

Accounts of Lee's movements on August 31 are contradictory and subject to conflicting interpretation. Longstreet clearly implies a meeting of himself, Jackson, and Lee at which the orders for the turning movement were issued. He also implies—although perhaps it is merely careless writing—that this meeting occurred very early in the day and before Stuart had been employed to determine that Pope had stopped the Federal flight in the Centreville fortifications. Unfortunately, the official reports of Lee, Jackson, and Longstreet are not helpful in determining either when or where Lee held his council of war and issued his orders.[80]

Heros Von Borcke says that he met Lee and Jackson early in the morning returning from a reconnaissance to the Stone Bridge, where they had come under fire from enemy pickets. But his observation that they had "sustained no injury" would seem to rule out that Lee had yet suffered his accident.[81]

Freeman resolves the dilemma by having Lee issue his orders early and ride to the front several times during the day, including the late afternoon, when the accident with Traveller occurs. The problem with this interpretation is that it assumes Lee manifested critical interest in the Stone Bridge area long after he had ordered the turning movement and that it does not allow for the presence of Henry Kyd Douglas of Jackson's staff.[82]

The hypothesis followed in chapter 6 assumes that Lee's accident occurred near the Stone Bridge in early midmorning (nine to ten o'clock) and resulted from the fright produced by the sudden appearance of prisoners guarded by Stuart's cavalry. This would also harmonize with Squires memory that Lee was offered but declined breakfast. Since Longstreet and Jackson were present, the council of war took place just before or just after the accident. If Jackson received his orders by ten and started his march by eleven, his column would have had "time to stretch out" and have cleared Sudley Ford by two, at which time Longstreet would claim in his report his "command marched to cross Bull Run at Sudley Ford."[83]

Finally, it is almost certain that Jackson must have started his march at least by noon, or he would not have had time—under existing conditions—to reach Pleasant Valley by nightfall. This supposition is supported by Early's report that his division (Ewell's), which would have been the last in Jackson's column, "in the afternoon . . . was ordered to move" and "to bivouac late at night."[84]

Notes

Overture. "The Most Propitious Time": Fate in Lee's Hands,
September 3, 1862

1. Lee to Davis, Sept. 3, 1862, U.S. War Department, *The War of the Rebellion: A Compilation of the Official Records of the Union and Confederate Armies*, 128 vols. (Washington, D.C.: GPO, 1880–1901), ser. 1, vol. 19, 2:590–91 (hereafter cited as *OR*; citations are to series 1 unless otherwise stated); Armistead Lindsay Long, *Memoirs of Robert E. Lee, His Military and Personal History, Embracing a Large Amount of Information Hitherto Unpublished* (Philadelphia: J. M. Stoddart, 1886), 204.

2. According to Armistead Long, "Whenever he appeared among them his approach was announced by 'Here comes Mars' Robert!' and he would be immediately saluted with the well-known Confederate yell, which called forth in other quarters the exclamation, 'There goes Mars' Robert—ole Jackson, or an ole hare." Long, *Memoirs of R. E. Lee*, 229.

3. Walter Taylor of Lee's staff wrote: "Our advance to this place (near Bull Run) was one of the boldest moves of our so-called *timid* General." Taylor to sister, Aug. 30, 1862, *Lee's Adjutant: The Wartime Letters of Colonel Walter Herron Taylor, 1862–1865*, ed. R. Lockwood Tower (Columbia: Univ. of South Carolina Press, 1995), 41.

4. For a discussion of the sources of information on Lee's injury, see appendix 6, section I.

5. Long, *Memoirs of R. E. Lee*, 227–28, which includes a description by Lord Wolseley. Lt. Col. Robert Hall Chilton, who functioned nearly as chief of staff to Lee during the Maryland campaign, on September 25 would seek reassignment on the grounds (at least partly) that "General Lee's habitual attention to the merest detail" reduced Chilton's role to that of clerk and orderly. Chilton to Davis, Sept. 25, 1862, *The Papers of Jefferson Davis*, 8 vols., ed. Linda Lasswell Crist and Mary Seaton Dix (Baton Rouge: Louisiana State Univ. Press, 1971–95), 8:404.

1. "He who makes the assault": Confederate Strategy from Sumter to Seven
Pines, April 1861–May 1862

1. Davis, Address to the Provisional Confederate Congress in Montgomery, Ala., Apr. 29, 1861, in James D. Richardson, comp., *A Compilation of the Messages and Papers of the Confederacy, Including the Diplomatic Correspondence, 1861–1865*, 2 vols. (Nashville: United States Publishing Co., 1905), 1:82.

2. See Alan T. Nolan, *Lee Considered: General Robert E. Lee in Civil War History* (Chapel Hill: Univ. of North Carolina Press, 1991), 62–70; and Grady McWhiney, "Conservatism and the Military," *Continuity* 4 (1982): 93–126, and "Who Whipt Whom? Confederate Defeat Reexamined," *Civil War History* 11 (1965): 5–26.

3. Davis, Inaugural Address as Provisional President, Feb. 18, 1861, in Richardson, comp., *Messages of the Confederacy* 1:34.

4. The count, undoubtedly not exhaustive, was made from "Summary of Principal Events" in *OR*, vol. 1: passim; and "Preliminary Events" in Robert Underwood Johnson and Clarence Clough Buel, eds., *Battles and Leaders of the Civil War*, 4 vols. (New York: Thomas Yoselof, 1956), 1:1–4 (hereafter cited as *Battles and Leaders*). After the capture of Sumter, only three Florida forts remained in Federal possession, Pickens in Pensacola Harbor and Jefferson and Taylor in the remote Keys. In April and May newly seceded North Carolina, Virginia, Tennessee, and Arkansas followed the same course in seizing Federal property within their borders. The only exception was Fort Monroe at the tip of the Yorktown peninsula, a strong position with a large garrison.

5. Jefferson Davis, *The Rise and Fall of the Confederate Government*, 2 vols. (New York: D. Appleton, 1881), 1:292; and Proclamation of April 17, 1862, Richardson, *Messages of the Confederacy* 1:60. Davis never explained how Sumter represented a gun pointed at the Confederate breast. A small, unfinished fort, surrounded by Confederate batteries, it was militarily unimportant for the Federals and no more than a nuisance in Charleston Harbor. From the Northern viewpoint there was no first act of war, because there was no war. The "insurrection" commenced with the secession of South Carolina. Perhaps more important than such technical disagreements was the fact that both sides recognized that in the five days from April 12 to 17 politics were abandoned and the struggle entered its military phase.

6. See Ellis Merton Coulter, *The Confederate States of America*, vol. 7 of *A History of the South* (Baton Rouge: Louisiana State Univ. Press, 1950), 3, 43–54; and Emory M. Thomas, *The Confederate Nation, 1861–1865* (New York: Harper & Row, 1979), 84–90.

7. See *OR*, ser. 4, vol. 1:281–85; also Richardson, *Messages of the Confederacy* 1:104–10, for the Act of War. The United States never officially declared war, but its Congress did proclaim war aims in the Crittenden and Johnson resolutions passed in July.

8. Missouri was admitted on November 28 and Kentucky on December 10, 1861, and the Arizona Territory was created on January 18, 1862. *OR*, ser. 4, vol. 1:757, 780, 853–59. On the Indian Territory, see Coulter, *Confederate States*, 49–51.

9. Congressional joint resolution on Maryland, Dec. 21, 1861, *OR*, ser. 4, vol. 1:805–6; Davis's statement of war aims for the benefit of Great Britain and France in Hunter to Mason and Slidell, Feb. 8, 1862, in U.S. Navy Department, *Official Records of the Union and Confederate Navies in the War of the Rebellion*, 31 vols. (Washington, D.C.: GPO, 1894–1927), ser. 2, 3:333–36; "Proceedings of the First Confederate Congress, First Session," *Southern Historical Society Papers (SHSP)* 44 (1923): 62–64, 97.

10. The lack of comprehensive policy documents has led some observers to conclude the Confederacy had no war policy or grand strategy. For a sampling, see Coulter, *Confederate States*, 342; and Nolan, *Lee Considered*, 71–72. For a discussion of the use of the terms *aims, policy, strategy*, see appendix 1.

11. According to the Eighth Census (1860), the thirteen Confederate States including Missouri and Kentucky, comprised 877,732 square miles, or 48.6 percent of the total for the admitted states. The loyal states, including Maryland and Delaware, equaled 890,976 square miles. These figures have been computed from U.S. Bureau of the Census, *Statistics of the United States (including Mortality, Property, &c.) in 1860; Compiled from the Original Returns of the Eighth Census* (Washington, D.C.: GPO, 1866), 339 (hereafter cited as 8th Census, *Mortality*). They do not correspond exactly to figures found in recent reference works due to state boundary modifications, improved surveying methods, and the fact that the 1860 census did not include "water surface."

12. Agricultural figures are computed from U.S. Bureau of the Census, *Agriculture of the United States in 1860; Compiled from the Original Returns of the Eighth Census* (Washington,

D.C.: GPO, 1864), 184–87 (hereafter cited as 8th Census, *Agriculture*). Manufacturing figures are computed from *Manufactures of the United States in 1860; Compiled from the Returns of the Eighth Census* (Washington, D.C.: GPO, 1865), 729. The 13 percent given for manufacturing represents both percentage of capital invested and annual value of products. Banking and railroad statistics are computed from 8th Census, *Mortality*, 292, 331. All of these figures are unrealistically high, as they include the full resources of Missouri and Kentucky, neither of which held Secessionist majorities. A complete study of Confederate economic and material mobilization, which lies beyond the scope of the present work, is much needed. Frank E. Vandiver's *Rebel Brass: The Confederate Command System* (Baton Rouge: Louisiana State Univ. Press, 1956) is a good introduction; and Richard D. Goff's *Confederate Supply* (Durham, N.C.: Duke Univ. Press, 1969) carries the story forward.

13. The total population of the thirteen Confederate states in 1860 was 12,351,373 (39.8 percent), as compared to the 18,653,506 of the remaining states (territories not included). The population figures in this and the following two notes have been computed from tables in U.S. Bureau of the Census, *Population of the United States in 1860; Compiled from the Original Returns of the Eighth Census* (Washington, D.C.: GPO, 1864), xvii, 500–505, 516–18, 598–99 (hereafter cited as 8th Census, *Population*). They differ slightly from those found in *The American Annual Cyclopaedia and Register of Important Events of the Year 1862* (New York: D. Appleton, 1863), 777–78; and New York Tribune Association, *Tribune Almanac for 1862* (New York: Tribune, 1861), 47–55. The differences probably result from using early, unrefined reports from the Census Bureau. The figures adopted here are slightly more favorable to the Confederacy than comparisons based only on the eleven states of the deep and upper South.

14. The total Confederate figures (see note 13 above) were adjusted to approximate loyalty as follows: the population of the eleven states of the deep and upper South (Alabama, Arkansas, Florida, Georgia, Louisiana, Mississippi, North Carolina, South Carolina, Tennessee, Texas, and Virginia); minus one-fourth of Tennessee and two-thirds of the western counties of Virginia; plus one-third of the border states (Delaware, District of Columbia, Kentucky, Maryland, Missouri) and one-third of the territories (Colorado, Dakota, Nebraska, New Mexico, Utah, Washington) and two-thirds of the Indian Territory. This would yield a total population of 10,089,968. The comparably adjusted figure for the Union would be 21,419,033.

15. From the figures adjusted for loyalty, the total white population for the Confederacy was 6,006,239, and the Union 21,060,932 (in both cases Indian populations are included with the white).

16. From the figures adjusted for loyalty, the Confederate military pool (white males aged eighteen to forty-five) was 1,197,489, and that of the Union 4,453,114. Why the South had a slightly lower percentage of white males from eighteen to forty-five in its general white population than did the North is not known for certain. However, it should be noted that white males aged twenty to forty represented one-third of all immigrants to the United States from 1820 to 1860, and the large majority of these had settled in Northern states. 8th Census, *Mortality* 521.

17. Actually a series of Confederate statutes were involved. See Coulter, *Confederate States*, 313–28; *OR*, ser. 4, vol. 1:126–31, 302, 310, 326–27; and *The American Annual Cyclopaedia and Register of Important Events of the Year 1861* (New York: D. Appleton, 1862), 128. Lincoln also called for a 22,000-soldier increase in the regular army. Regrettably, no comprehensive study of Confederate manpower mobilization exists. Albert Burton Moore's pioneering *Conscription and Conflict in the Confederacy* (New York: Macmillan, 1924) focuses narrowly on the laws and is especially weak on the first year of the war.

18. *OR*, ser. 3, vol. 1:380 (U.S.); and ser. 4, vol. 1:537 (C.S.).

19. Richardson, comp., *Messages of the Confederacy* 1:205–6; *OR*, ser. 4, vol. 1:1094–100; *American Annual Cyclopaedia . . . 1862*, 243; and *Papers of Jefferson Davis* 8:119–20. The original

conscription bill as authored by Lee and submitted by Davis was militarily sound and weakened considerably by politics in Congress. For a convenient discussion of the modifications and opposition, see Coulter, *Confederate States*, 314ff; and Thomas, *Confederate Nation*, 152–53. The "twenty nigger rule," which exempted one white for every twenty slaves owned, was much more significant for the bitterness it aroused between the rich and poor than it was for the numbers it kept from the army. In 1860, there were only 46,282 owners (including females) of twenty or more slaves in the entire fifteen slave states and territories. 8th Census, *Agriculture* 2:247.

20. The percentages were derived for both Confederacy and the Union by dividing the military pools by the enlistments of each. Enlistments were adapted from Thomas Leonard Livermore, *Numbers and Losses in the Civil War in America* (1901; reprint, Dayton, Ohio: Morningside, 1986), 63. See appendix 3.

21. Relatively stable but not static. See appendix 3.

22. The Confederate and Federal figures for December 31, 1861, and April 1 and December 31, 1862, are from Livermore, *Numbers and Losses*, 47. However, his Federal figures for July 1861 have been modified to subtract the men raised under the new call of that month.The Federal figures for June 30, 1862, are from *OR*, ser. 3, vol. 2:185. The Confederate figures for June 30, 1862, are taken from a study by the author that determined there were 577.7 Confederate regiments of all arms (independent battalions and companies consolidated into regiments) in the field by that date. Southern regiments at this time averaged 825.9 officers and men. It should be emphasized that all these figures are in the category of aggregate present and absent, as is appropriate since the discussion is about *total* mobilization.

23. For a perceptive discussion of the evils of the department system, see Richard M. McMurry, *Two Great Rebel Armies: An Essay in Confederate Military History* (Chapel Hill: Univ. of North Carolina Press, 1989), 58–68.

24. See Goff, *Confederate Supply*, esp. 54ff.

25. The impact of states' rights on the Confederate war effort has been much debated by historians, with interpretations ranging from negligible influence to its being the major cause of the country's downfall. A recent cogent discussion may be found in Richard E. Beringer et al., *Why the South Lost the Civil War* (Athens: Univ. of Georgia Press, 1986), 203–35. The only point intended in the present study is that states and areas long accustomed to employing the rhetoric of local rights were quick to use it to hold onto forces when they were—or felt they were—threatened by the enemy. Ample evidence of this exists in dispatches scattered throughout the *OR*.

26. A suggestive essay on the impact of the presence of Federal troops on slavery may be found in Bell I. Wiley's *Southern Negroes, 1861–1865* (New Haven: Yale Univ. Press, 1965), 3–23. Charles Marshall, a member of Lee's staff, noted that prior to June 1, 1862, "repeated and urgent demands" had been made upon Lee by citizens and congressmen" to furnish troops to protect the people along the navigable rivers of Virginia" and that "one of the chief objections to the Conscript Law . . . was that it would deprive the states the means of providing for the safety of its own citizens." And he concludes: "The mere existence of slavery gave the Federal Government a great advantage in the prosecution of the war and imposed additional cares and responsibilities upon those charged with the conduct of military operations in the South." Charles Marshall, *An Aide-de-Camp of Lee, Being the Papers of Colonel Charles Marshall* . . . , ed. Sir Frederick Maurice (Boston: Little, Brown, 1927), 64–65. It might be noted in passing that the strategy of overwhelming that Federal general George McClellan was pursuing in the winter of 1861–62 called for the establishment of footholds on the Southern coast. While there is no evidence that McClellan possessed insight into the South's special vulnerability because of slavery and states' rights, he did intend by these expeditions to pin down Confederate forces and keep them from concentrating large field armies.

27. Historian Douglas B. Ball has written of the guerrilla warfare alternative approvingly. He suggests that slave owners could have been urged to move their slaves into areas that were not threatened by the enemy. See Ball, *Financial Failure and Confederate Defeat* (Urbana: Univ. of Illinois Press, 1991), 273–74. With considerable insight, George M. Frederickson, in the Thirty-fifth Annual Fortenbaugh Memorial Lecture, has concluded that Southern society was unsuited for a strategy of dispersed warfare even as a last resort at the end. See Frederickson, *Why the Confederacy Did Not Fight a Guerrilla War after the Fall of Richmond: A Comparative View* (Gettysburg: Gettysburg College, 1996), 27–29.

28. Intentionally sidestepped here is the question of Confederate deployment in the East versus the West. Firm conclusions cannot be drawn until there is a study of the distribution of regiments as they were raised. A preliminary investigation by Richard McMurry suggests there was no great disparity. McMurry, *Rebel Armies*, 87ff. But, even if it were proven that the Davis administration showed significant partiality to the East and that a greater concentration of troops in the West would have prolonged the war there, it is not certain that the Confederates would have either had a better chance to win the war or even to have lengthened it. It would also have to be demonstrated that either significant reenforcements could have been sent to the West from elsewhere than the East, or that fewer troops in the East would not have lead to an even earlier end to the war.

29. On lacking grand strategy, see John Frederick Charles Fuller, *Grant and Lee: A Study in Personality and Generalship* (New York: Charles Scribner's Sons, 1933), 250–51. On the perimeter defense see Clement Eaton, *A History of the Southern Confederacy* (New York: Macmillan, 1954), 126–27; George Anson Bruce, "The Strategy of the Civil War," in *Papers of the Military Historical Society of Massachusetts*, 16 vols. (Boston, 1881–1918), 13:465–66 (hereafter cited as *PMHSM*); and Coulter, *Confederate States*, 342. On the invasions see McWhiney, "Who Whipt Whom," 18–19; and Nolan, *Lee Considered*, 69–70. On the Celtic influence see Grady McWhiney and Perry D. Jamieson, *Attack and Die: Civil War Military Tactics and the Southern Heritage* (Tuscaloosa: Univ. of Alabama Press, 1982).

30. Of course, it might be argued that the North did not at this period have a grand strategy either, because it was unable or unwilling to follow any of the plans proposed by its military leaders. For a brief overview of early Northern grand strategy, see Joseph L. Harsh, "Lincoln's Tarnished Brass: Conservative Strategies and the Attempt to Fight the Early Civil War as a Limited War," in Roman J. Heleniak and Lawrence L. Hewitt, eds., *The Confederate High Command and Related Topics: The 1988 Deep Delta Civil War Symposium: Themes in Honor of T. Harry Williams* (Shippensburg: White Mane, 1990), 124–41.

31. The mere circumstance that Davis fought under a different constitution would prevent him from ever being included in the surveys; but if he were, the twin facts that he fought to perpetuate slavery and that he lost the war would almost certainly determine that he would be ranked very low by most historians. For a discussion of the methods and results of the first two surveys of the presidents, see Arthur M. Schlesinger, *Paths to the Present* (Boston: Houghton Mifflin, 1964), 104–14.

32. By comparison, Lincoln sent three veto messages, including the one on the Confiscation Act of July 17, 1862, which did not actually reject the legislation. Pocket vetoes are not included. The veto messages may be found in volume 1 of Richardson, *Messages of the Confederacy*; and in Abraham Lincoln, *Collected Works*, ed. Roy P. Basler, 9 vols. (New Brunswick: Rutgers Univ. Press, 1953–55).

33. For recognition that Davis did generally pursue centralization as a military policy and the explanation that it derived from his growing sense of Confederate nationalism, see Nathaniel W. Stephenson, "A Theory of Jefferson Davis," *American Historical Review* 21 (1915): 73–90; and Paul D. Escott, *After Secession: Jefferson Davis and the Failure of Confederate Nationalism* (Baton Rouge: Louisiana State Univ. Press, 1978), 54–67. For the view that Davis's

military ideas were largely shaped by his relationship with Zachary Taylor, see McWhiney, "Conservatism," 120–21. Here and in other of his writings, McWhiney argues that Davis pursued a fully offensive grand strategy. For the contrary view that Davis pursued a defensive grand strategy throughout the war, see Steven E. Woodworth, *Davis and Lee at War* (Lawrence: Univ. of Kansas Press, 1995).

34. Davis to J. E. Johnston, Mar. 6, 1862, *Papers of Jefferson Davis* 8:81–82.

35. Davis to J. E. Johnston, Feb. 28, 1862, ibid., 69.

36. Davis to William M. Brooks, Mar. 15, 1862, ibid., 100.

37. Davis to Braxton Bragg, Oct. 17, 1862, ibid., 448. For a variation see Davis to Kirby Smith, Nov. 19, 1863, *OR*, vol. 22, 2:1072.

38. Davis to A. S. Johnston, Mar. 12, 1862, *Papers of Jefferson Davis* 8:93.

39. In ibid., vol. 8, see the following from the president: to A. S. Johnston, Mar. 12, 1862 (93); to Kirby Smith, July 28, 1862 (305); and to Bragg, Aug. 5 (322) and Oct. 17, 1862 (448).

40. Quoted is Dennis Hart Mahan, cited in McWhiney, "Conservatism," 105. See also, Antoine Henri Jomini, *The Art of War*, trans. G. H. Mendell and W. P. Craighill (Westport, Conn.: Greenwood, 1971), 72; and the paraphrase by Henry Wager Halleck, *Elements of Military Art and Science; or, Course of Instruction in Strategy, Fortification, Tactics of Battles, &c.* (Westport, Conn.: Greenwood, 1971), 39.

41. Whether those seeking to invade the North were a majority or minority has not been determined. Certainly, Southern editors were full of bluster on the subject, as were some politicians. See Toombs to Davis, Sept. 1, 1861, *Papers of Jefferson Davis* 7:316; and John Beauchamp Jones, *A Rebel War Clerk's Diary at the Confederate States Capital* (Philadelphia: J. B. Lippincott, 1866), 1:39 (May 22), 51 (June 12), 66 (July 22). At the peak of the Confederate offensive in the fall of 1862, the Congress was in nearly unanimous support of Lee's entry into Maryland, but a small minority opposed an invasion of Pennsylvania. "Proceedings of the First Confederate Congress, Second Session in Part,"*SHSP* 46 (1928) : 106–7, 120–25. George C. Rable states that "Davis faced steady pressure to carry the war into enemy territory." See Rable's *The Confederate Republic: A Revolution against Politics* (Chapel Hill: Univ. of North Carolina Press, 1994), 81, 136.

42. Davis to his brother, Joseph E. Davis, June 18, 1861, *Papers of Jefferson Davis* 7:203.

43. Davis to William M. Brooks, Mar. 15, 1862, ibid., 8:100.

44. Davis to John Forsyth, July 18, 1862, ibid., 293.

45. Davis to Lee et al., Sept. 7[?], 1862, *OR*, vol. 19, pt. 2:598.

46. Davis used the phrase in reference to Lee's Seven Days campaign. Actually, he reversed Jomini's "defensive-offensive." See Davis, *Rise and Fall* 2:132–33; and Dunbar Rowland, ed., *Jefferson Davis, Constitutionalist: His Letters and Speeches* (Jackson: Mississippi Department of Archives and History, 1923), 5:197. Early appreciations of Confederate strategy, with references to Jomini, may be found in the following works by Frank Everson Vandiver: "Jefferson Davis and Confederate Strategy," in *The American Tragedy*, ed. Bernard Mayo (Hampden-Sydney, Va.: Hampden-Sydney College, 1959), 19–32; *Basic History of the Confederacy* (Princeton: Van Nostrand, 1962), 69–71; *Their Tattered Flags: The Epic of the Confederacy* (New York: Harper Magazine Press, 1970), 88, 93–94. See also Archer Jones, *Confederate Strategy from Shiloh to Vicksburg* (Baton Rouge: Louisiana State Univ. Press, 1961), 33–36. A recent summary of views may be found in Beringer et al., *Why the South Lost*, chaps. 2 and 6–8.

47. Indeed, Jomini defined victory in terms of the offense. His four fundamental principles of war called for maneuvers to engage the enemy with superior numbers at strategic and tactical decisive points. Jomini, *Art of War*, 70.

48. In his chapter on "Strategy," Jomini wrote: "A defensive war is not without its advantages, when wisely conducted. It may be passive or active, taking the offense at times. The passive defense is always pernicious." He added, "An army is reduced to the defensive only by reverses or by a positive inferiority." Jomini, *Art of War*, 73. Emil Schalk's *Summary of the Art*

of War: Written Expressly for and Dedicated to the U.S. Volunteer Army (Philadelphia: J. B. Lippincott, 1862), although Jominian in philosophy, should not be confused with Jomini's work of the same title. It may be doubted that any of the Southern leaders ever read his work, but Schalk's assertion that "purely defensive [wars] will always end with submission" (2) is, nevertheless, interesting as a reflection of contemporary thinking on such strategy.

49. Jomini warned that the general must have "the good sense not to make the defense passive: he must not remain in positions to receive whatever blows may be given by his adversary; he must, on the contrary, redouble his activity, and be constantly on the alert to improve all opportunities of assailing the weak points of the enemy. This plan of war may be called the defensive-offensive." Jomini, *Art of War*, 74.

50. Col. T. J. Jackson had posted Virginia troops on Maryland Heights opposite Harpers Ferry by May 6, 1861. Union regiments did not occupy Alexandria until May 24.

51. *OR*, vol. 3:98ff, 622–23; see also Thomas L. Snead, Jr., "The First Year of the War in Missouri," *Battles and Leaders* 1:270ff; and James Adlebert Mulligan, "The Siege of Lexington Mo.," in ibid., 307–13. The Confederate War Department had, however, given a blank check to McCulloch on July 26, and on August 28 Secretary of War Walker congratulated him for having "liberated" Missouri. *OR*, vol. 3:615–16, 130. The Tennessee troops under Polk occupied New Madrid, but none were present at Wilson's Creek. Although Confederate forces from Louisiana, Arkansas, and Texas fought in this battle, the Missouri State Guard constituted the bulk of the force, and technically it was fighting for and under the authority of the state of Missouri, which was not admitted into the Confederacy until November 28. Richardson, *Messages of the Confederacy* 1:166–67.

52. For the exchange of telegrams and endorsements, see *Papers of Jefferson Davis* 7:325–27. For the letter from Davis to Polk, Sept. 15, 1861, see *OR*, vol. 4:188. For Polk's report see ibid., 180–81.

53. Special Orders, No. 149, Adjt. and Insp. Gen.'s Office, *OR*, vol. 4:405. The Russellville Convention met on November 18, and Kentucky was officially admitted to the Confederacy on December 10. Coulter, *Confederate States*, 46–47. Both Steven E. Woodworth and William C. Davis interpret the September 5 telegram to signify equivocation on the president's part. While the meaning of the brief telegram must remain somewhat ambiguous to modern historians, Davis's defense of Polk as early as the 8th, his incorporation of Kentucky into a Confederate department on the 10th, his second telegram to Polk on the 12th, and especially the letter of the 15th quoted in the text strongly suggest that, although the president may have been caught by surprise, he did not hesitate to put military considerations above political. See Steven E. Woodworth, *Jefferson Davis and His Generals: The Failure of Confederate Command in the West* (Lawrence: Univ. of Kansas Press, 1990), 41; and William C. Davis, *Jefferson Davis: The Man and His Hour* (New York: Harper Collins, 1991), 377.

54. *OR*, vol. 4:93. See also Ray Charles Colton, *The Civil War in the Western Territories, Arizona, Colorado, New Mexico and Utah* (Norman: Univ. of Oklahoma Press, 1959), 13–17, 21–23; and Alvin M. Josephy, Jr., *The Civil War in the American West* (New York: Alfred A. Knopf, 1991), 22–60. The California possibility is asserted as fact in T. T. Teel, "Sibley's New Mexican Campaign: Its Object and the Causes of Its Failure," *Battles and Leaders* 2:700.

55. *OR*, vol. 2:809–10, 814, 832–33. Ironically, it was Robert E. Lee, as commander of the Virginia forces, who ordered Jackson to retire from Maryland Heights.

56. The Confederates evacuated Alexandria under duress, with Federals entering one end of the town as Southerners fled the other. The Federals did not immediately occupy Harpers Ferry, however.

57. Beauregard to Davis, June 12, 1861, and Davis's reply of June 13, *Papers of Jefferson Davis* 7:197–200.

58. Chesnut to Davis, Nov. 2, 1861, and Lee to Davis, Nov. 24, 1861, ibid., 388–93, 425–27. Douglas Southall Freeman is not entirely fair to Beauregard or his plan in *Lee's Lieutenants: A*

Study in Command, 3 vols. (New York: Charles Scribner's Sons, 1942–44), 1:38–44; but see also, W. C. Davis, *Man and His Hour*, 345. The usual explanation is that Davis rejected not only the plan but also the idea of an offensive, although there is no concrete evidence of a rejection of the latter. It is possible that had McDowell's advance not intervened, some form of Confederate offensive might have been undertaken. Supposedly, Davis opposed Beauregard's plan both because it was too intricate and because the president felt bound to await the Federal offensive thrust in light of the defensive posture of Confederate policy. The latter point should be reconsidered, however, considering Davis's consistent willingness throughout the war to initiate offensive actions or to approve retroactively offensives taken by generals in the field. Undoubtedly, he did believe such complicated movements logistically unfeasible at this early stage in the war.

59. Davis to J. E. Johnston, Nov. 3, 1861, and Johnston's reply on Nov. 10, in *Papers of Jefferson Davis* 7:393–94, 407. Also see W. C. Davis, *Man and His Hour*, 351–52; and Long, *Memoirs of R. E. Lee*, 203–4.

60. Davis to J. E. Johnston, Aug. 1, 1861, *OR*, vol. 5:766–67.

61. Toombs to Davis, Sept. 1, 1861, *Papers of Jefferson Davis* 7:316.

62. Letter by Gustavus W. Smith, quoted in George Francis Robert Henderson, *Stonewall Jackson and the American Civil War* (New York: Longmans, Green, 1949), 132–33, 494. See also John Esten Cooke, *Stonewall Jackson* (New York: G. W. Dillingham, ca. 1899), 308. This is one of the several incidents used by James A. Kegel to argue that Jackson was the source of the strategy of invasion later employed by Lee; *North with Lee and Jackson: The Lost Story of Gettysburg* (Mechanicsburg, Pa.: Stackpole Books, 1996), 40–43. Jackson's voice was but one of many calling for similar operations, and there is no persuasive evidence that his views introduced the notion either to Lee or Davis.

63. *OR*, vol. 5:881–82. It would seem as though an important part of the story here has been lost. Johnston's dispatch to Benjamin, who had just become secretary of war, does not read as if he were springing a surprise on the administration, but rather as if were referring to matters already known and agreed upon. It is possible there had been prior discussion, oral or written, that has not been discovered.

64. Benjamin to Johnston, Sept. 29, 1861, *OR*, vol. 5:883.

65. *Papers of Jefferson Davis* 7:352–53. It is not entirely certain whether the meeting was held at Beauregard's quarters, where Davis was staying (and where he had met briefly with Johnston on the evening of the 30th), or at G. W. Smith's quarters in the Union (or Willcoxon) Hotel, immediately across the street from the courthouse. In Virginia, "Court House" is used to signify the county seat, while "courthouse" designates the actual building.

66. Davis to brother, June 18, 1861, *Papers of Jefferson Davis* 7:203.

67. Firsthand accounts of this conference may be found in *OR*, vol. 5:884–87; Davis, *Rise and Fall* 1:445–54; Joseph Eggleston Johnston, *Narrative of Military Operations, Directed during the Late War between the States*, ed. Frank E. Vandiver (Bloomington: Indiana Univ. Press, 1959), 75–76; Gustavus Woodson Smith, *Confederate War Papers, Fairfax Court House, New Orleans, Seven Pines, Richmond and North Carolina*, 2d ed. (New York: Atlantic Pub. Co., 1884), 13–40; and Pierre Gustave Toutant Beauregard, "The First Battle of Bull Run," *Battles and Leaders* 1:221–22. See appendix 4.

68. J. E. Johnston to Davis, Nov. 10 and 22, 1861, *Papers of Jefferson Davis* 7:407, 424.

69. This story may be pieced together from *OR*, vol. 5:737, 978–79, 982, 984–86, 990. When the Army of the Potomac occupied Centreville on March 11, reporters discovered the "Quaker guns" and used them to ridicule McClellan for having wasted so much time to prepare a juggernaut to crush such a flimsy defense. The defenses were actually quite strong, and had the Federals advanced on Centreville before its evacuation, Johnston would have had ample time to return the real guns to their embrasures. If anything, Johnston's prepara-

tion of a flexible defense had made his entire line much stronger than if he had been pinned down in a single place.

70. See Fritz Haselberger, *Yanks from the South! The First Land Campaign of the Civil War: Rich Mountain, West Virginia* (Baltimore: Past Glories, 1987), 9–120; Richard Orr Curry, *A House Divided: A Study of Statehood Politics and the Copperhead Movement in West Virginia* (Pittsburgh: Univ. of Pittsburgh Press, 1964), 55–68; and Douglas Southall Freeman, *R. E. Lee: A Biography*, 4 vols. (New York: Charles Scribner's Sons,1934–35), 1:541–602.

71. Baylor in New Mexico, Price in Missouri, and Polk in Kentucky had outnumbered their Federal opponents, while Beauregard and Johnston combined had roughly equaled the forces under McDowell at Bull Run.

72. Davis, Annual Message to Congress, Nov. 18, 1861, *Papers of Jefferson Davis* 7:413.

73. Davis to Johnston, Sept. 8, 1862, *OR*, vol. 5:833–34. Rather than seeing Davis's views in this dispatch as directed to a particular time and situation, Steven Woodworth reads it as a seminal statement of the president's war-long commitment to a grand defensive strategy. Woodworth, *Davis and Lee*, 53.

74. In July 1861 there were 89,240 men (80 percent) concentrated in the field armies, while 22,800 (20 percent) served elsewhere. In January 1862, 221,982 (63 percent) were with the two Johnstons, Price, and McCulloch, while 129,436 (37 percent) were otherwise occupied. These figures are for aggregate present and absent, and have been computed from the tables in Livermore, *Numbers and Losses*, 42–43.

75. Reference is to Zollicoffer in east Kentucky, Van Dorn and Price in Arkansas, and Sibley in New Mexico. Shiloh and Seven Pines came in April and May and represented the beginning of the third phase, which overlapped with the ending of the second.

76. W. C. Davis, *Man and His Hour*, 396–97. The president gave no hint as to why he believed the timing wrong, or even whether the reasons were military or political. If he were thinking about conscription as early as January, he may have meant it would be necessary to await its effects.

77. All of the strength figures are aggregate present and absent and are from Livermore, *Numbers and Losses*, 43. This category is useless, of course, in terms of effective battle strength, but it reflects troop distribution policy better than present for duty because it screens out such irrelevant factors as uneven regional sickness rates and variations in furloughs by local commanders.

78. Thomas Lawrence Connelly, *Army of the Heartland: The Army of Tennessee, 1861–1862* (Baton Rouge: Louisiana State Univ. Press, 1967), 131–40.

79. W. C. Davis, *Man and His Hour*, 403; *OR*, vol. 8:283; and "Opposing Forces at Pea Ridge, Ark.," *Battles and Leaders* 1:337.

80. Colton, *Western Territories*, 23–95; Josephy, *American West*, 61–92.

81. On the role of such enclaves in Northern strategy, see Harsh, "Lincoln's Tarnished Brass," 133–35. Not only did these amphibious expeditions make more difficult the Confederate task of concentrating forces into central armies, but in at least one instance they caused troops to flow in the wrong direction. Joseph Johnston lost two brigades that were ordered to North Carolina in response to the Burnside threat. See *OR*, vol. 9:450–51.

82. This small but significant battle is well covered in Kim Bernard Holien, *Battle at Ball's Bluff* (Orange, Va.: Moss Publications, 1985).

83. Johnston's early-morning interview is covered in his *Narrative of Military Operations*, 112–13; the expanded conference is covered in ibid., 114–16. G. W. Smith, *Confederate War Papers*, 40–44; Davis, *Rise and Fall* 2:86–87; and James Longstreet, *From Manassas to Appomattox: Memoirs of the Civil War in America*, ed. James I. Robertson, Jr. (Bloomington: Indiana Univ. Press, 1960), 66. The views given here as presented at the conference are either from the memoirs or inferred from references in dispatches written immediately

after the event. See also *OR*, vol. 11, 3:452, 455–56, 458–59, 464, 469–70, 473, 477, 485.

84. From G. W. Smith's version, *Confederate War Papers*, 40–42, which he asserted was based on a memorandum written later in 1862. Douglas Freeman, *Lee's Lieutenants* 1:149–51, argues that Johnston merely used Smith's idea as a foil to advance his favorite option of fighting near Richmond, but a later dispatch to Lee casts serious doubt on this. *OR*, vol. 11, 3:477. If Johnston favored an offensive across the Potomac on April 30, it makes sense to believe Smith's claim that he supported it on the 14th. See note 92 below.

85. Smith noted that before "the President began to take an active part in the conference," it was not evident which side he favored. Smith, *Confederate War Papers*, 44. For the intriguing possibility that during the meeting Davis may have proposed an offensive by Stonewall Jackson in the Shenandoah Valley, see appendix 3, section E.

86. This was certainly an ironic position for Lee to take, but that he so argued is attested by Johnston, Smith, and Davis. Once Lee entered upon field command and came to depend on maneuver for success, he would never have wanted to be caught in such a restricted field. In giving his advice at this time, he must have been thinking that the confined area would operate most to the disadvantage of the Federals, who would not be able to bring the full force of their superior numbers to bear on such a narrow front. Five months later, at Sharpsburg, similar thinking may have permitted Lee to accept battle on an even more constricted field; however, then it would not be his first choice, but rather nearly his last resort.

87. This, too, is a position Lee would not long maintain. As discussed in chapter 2, once Lee took field command, both he and Davis would attempt to wring every possible regiment from the south Atlantic states.

88. No direct written evidence proves this question was discussed, although Davis interrupted the debate at one point to insist that they not underrate McClellan. Longstreet, *From Manassas to Appomattox*, 66. Moreover, it is impossible to believe that an eleven-hour strategy discussion would not have considered the objection. It took Jackson's Valley campaign to demonstrate how sensitive the Lincoln administration was on the safety of Washington—a lesson that would not be lost on Lee.

89. For a possible discrepancy on the date of the conference, see appendix 4, section C.

90. *OR*, vol. 9:458, 459, 462, 467–68, and vol. 14:480, 481, 482. Lee's action may reveal an additional reason he opposed Johnston's northern offensive at the war council. Apparently, in April he still viewed the threat on the Rappahannock to be as great as the one on the Peninsula.

91. *OR*, vol. 11, 3:473; Johnston, *Narrative of Military Operations*, 117–19.

92. *OR*, vol. 11, 3:477. It is not known whether the idea of a simultaneous invasion of Ohio by Beauregard—who had by this time replaced the mortally wounded Albert Sidney Johnston—had been presented at the conference on April 14 or was a later thought.

93. *OR*, vol. 11, 3:485. Four months later, when Lee sat at Leesburg pondering whether to cross the Potomac without the president's express approval, it is possible he remembered conferring with Davis about Johnston's idea and writing this dispatch—or, at the very least, it is likely he retained the general impression of the president's favorable attitude toward such an undertaking.

94. *OR*, vol. 11, 3:458–59.

95. Among the troops collected in May would be Branch's brigade from North Carolina and Ripley's from South Carolina. On May 13 Lee wrote to Holmes, commanding in North Carolina, "Such is the pressure in Virginia that it is imperatively necessary to concentrate our forces to enable us successfully to meet the heavy columns of the enemy." *OR*, vol. 9:471; see also ibid., 470, 472, and vol. 14:509–10, 511–12, 518, 519, 520, 528.

96. Johnston, *Narrative of Military Operations*, 119–28. From this point on, the Confederates would be ever fearful of a concerted Federal advance up the James.

97. Memorandum of the Secretary of War to Bureau Chiefs, dated May 28, 1862, *OR*, vol. 11, 3:557.

98. Jomini continued: "The enemy fall with large force upon fractions of his force; he neither knows where his adversary proposes to attack him nor in what manner to repel him." Jomini, *Art of War*, 73.

99. Of the eleven states that constituted the effective resources of the Confederacy (i.e., not counting Missouri or Kentucky), Virginia and Tennessee contained only 13.8 percent of the land area but possessed 34.4 percent of the white population; produced 32.1 percent of the corn, 55.6 percent of the wheat, 62.6 percent of the oats, 54.6 percent of the rye, 42.7 percent of the barley, and 91.9 percent of the buckwheat; raised 30.5 percent of the horses and mules, 17.2 percent of the cattle, 25.4 percent of the swine, and 36.3 percent of the sheep; and owned 44 percent of the manufacturing (43.6 percent of the capital invested and 44.1 percent of annual production), 26.2 percent of the banking capital, and 33.2 percent of the railroad mileage. See note 12 above for sources.

100. Davis, Inaugural Address, Feb. 22, 1861, and Message to Congress, Feb. 25, 1861, in Richardson, *Messages of the Confederacy* 1:186, 189; Davis to J. E. Johnston, Feb. 28, 1861, and to William M. Brooks, Mar. 15, 1861, *Papers of Jefferson Davis* 8:69, 100.

101. Richardson, *Messages of the Confederacy* 1:205–6. Although the measure may have been under discussion for some time, it must have been drawn up hastily. Charles Marshall of Lee's staff would later remember that Lee asked him to prepare the draft of the original act "about April 1st, or perhaps a few days earlier." Since the bill was reported out of committee on April 1, it must have been earlier. Perhaps Davis submitted the draft on March 28 with his message to Congress. In any case, it could not have been drawn up much before that, since Marshall did not join Lee's staff until March 21. See Marshall, *Aide-de-Camp*, 30–31.

102. Freeman, *Lee's Lieutenants* 1:312ff.

103. Ibid., 330.

104. Ibid., 362–411. For a note on the influence of Lee and Davis on Jackson's Valley campaign, see appendix 3, section E.

105. Connelly, *Army of the Heartland*, 140, 152; and William Preston Johnston, "Albert Sidney Johnston at Shiloh," *Battles and Leaders* 1:549.

106. For tables summarizing the situation in the West from late March through April 1862, see appendix 2, section B.

107. Lee to A. S. Johnston, Mar. 26, 1862, in the Barrett Collection of Johnston Papers, Tulane University, cited in Charles P. Roland, "The Generalship of Robert E. Lee," in Grady McWhiney, ed., *Grant, Lee, Lincoln and the Radicals: Essays on Civil War Leadership* (Evanston, Ill.: Northwestern Univ. Press, 1964), 35–36. See also Connelly, *Army of the Heartland*, 152.

108. Connelly, *Army of the Heartland*, 152–77. The standard study is Wiley Sword's *Shiloh, Bloody April* (New York: William Morrow, 1974), which, however, is much stronger on tactics than on strategy. A newer work, Joseph Allan Frank and George A. Reaves, *Seeing the Elephant: Raw Recruits at the Battle of Shiloh* (Westport, Conn.: Greenwood, 1989), is a groundbreaking attempt to blend cultural and military history and deserves attention.

109. *Papers of Jefferson Davis* 8:184–86. The editors' notes to this dispatch are especially full on the Davis/Johnston relationship at this time. See also Woodworth, *Davis and Lee*, 128–48.

110. Keyes's Fourth Corps crossed on May 23, followed by Heintzleman's Third Corps on the 25th. Remaining north of the river to protect the supply line to White House on the Pamunkey and to cover McDowell's approach were the Second (Sumner), Fifth (Porter), and Sixth (Franklin) corps. See Alexander Webb, *The Peninsula, McClellan's Campaign of 1862* (New York: Charles Scribner's Sons, 1881), 97.

111. Johnston's forces numbered 98,050 aggregate present and absent, and 62,112 present for duty, including the main army at Centreville, Jackson's Valley District, and Holmes's Aquia District, as well as the forces at Leesburg and Manassas. *OR*, vol. 5:1015.

112. On or about April 30, Johnston's army on the Peninsula, including Magruder but not including Huger at Norfolk, totaled 56,183 present for duty (with allowance for reserve artillery) and an estimated 74,723 aggregate present and absent (computed at 133 percent of the present for duty). See tables in *OR*, vol. 11, 3:479–84. For the loss to North Carolina, see ibid., vol. 9:450–51.

113. J. R. Anderson's brigade from North Carolina and Gregg's South Carolinians stationed at Suffolk were sent to reenforce Field's brigade on the Ta River, with Anderson as senior taking command. Branch's North Carolina brigade was sent to Gordonsville to fill the gap left in the center when Ewell joined Jackson in the Valley. See *OR*, vol. 11, 3:458. For the attempt to transfer Longstreet or Smith, see ibid., vol. 11, 3:485, 502–3, 505.

114. *OR*, vol. 11, 3:454–55, 544.

115. On May 31–June 1, Johnston's army numbered 68,740 present for duty and 91,424 aggregate present and absent. Confederate forces in Virginia and North Carolina totaled 119,778 present for duty and 159,266 aggregate present and absent. On the same dates, McClellan's army numbered 98,008 present for duty and 127,166 aggregate present and absent, while Federal forces in Virginia and North Carolina totaled 209,785 present for duty and 275,798 aggregate present and absent. Confederate figures are computed from Leon Walter Tenney, "Seven Days in 1862: Numbers in Union and Confederate Armies before Richmond" (master's thesis, George Mason University, Fairfax, Va., 1992), a study based upon an examination of company and regimental level morning reports in RG-109, National Archives, Washington, D.C. See also Livermore, *Numbers and Losses*, 42–43. Federal figures are from *OR*, vol. 9:381, vol. 11, 3:204, vol. 12, 3:297, 308.

116. Johnston, *Narrative of Military Operations*, 129–33; Webb, *The Peninsula*, 100–102; and Freeman, *Lee's Lieutenants* 1:219–23.

117. Johnston, *Narrative of Military Operations*, 133–39; Webb, *The Peninsula*, 102–17; and Freeman, *Lee's Lieutenants* 1:223–43. The Battle of Seven Pines (the North called it Fair Oaks) is one of the less-studied major Civil War engagements, but its second day is absolutely the least understood of all. Even Freeman covers June 1 in a single, albeit long, sentence (pp. 242–43).

2. "It would change the character of the war": The Ascent of Lee, to June 1, 1862

1. Versions of Davis's journey may be found in: Davis, *Rise and Fall* 2:121–29, 130; Freeman, *R. E. Lee* 2:74; W. C. Davis, *Man and His Hour*, 424–25; G. W. Smith, *Confederate War Papers*, 211; *Papers of Jefferson Davis* 8:208–9 (editorial note); and Fitzhugh Lee, *General Lee* (New York: D. Appleton, 1894), 149.

2. Lee could have been sent to command in the West, where Davis had no general of rank or stature until the arrival from California of Albert Sidney Johnston in September 1861. It is likely, however, that Davis was saving the Western command for Johnston, whom the president (according to the latest Davis biographer) "almost worshipped." See W. C. Davis, *Man and His Hour*, 377, for a discussion of the relationship. More puzzling is why Lee was not employed for active, overall command of the Confederate armies in Virginia.

3. Feb. 27 and Mar. 6, 1862, *OR*, ser. 4, vol. 1:954, 997–98.

4. Freeman, *R. E. Lee* 2:4–6.

5. Richardson, *Messages of the Confederacy* 1:215–16.

6. Davis to Congress, *OR*, ser. 4, vol. 1:1005.

7. Davis to Lee, ibid., vol. 6:400.

8. Ibid., vol. 5:1099.

9. Freeman, *R. E. Lee* 2:4–6.

10. *Papers of Jefferson Davis* 8:203 (ellipsis in original).

11. Davis's letter to Lee says the appointment will "interfere temporarily with" Lee's duties. *OR*, vol. 11, 3:568–69. See also Davis, *Rise and Fall* 2:122ff; and Freeman, *R. E. Lee* 2:73–76. It should also be noted that as of June 1 Lee was the only available full general. Of the original five, Sidney Johnston was dead; Joseph Johnston was incapacitated by his wound; Cooper was incapable of taking the field; and Beauregard was already in command of the Army of Mississippi, although illness would soon force him to take a leave of absence.

12. A perceptive essay on Lee's human qualities is Emory M. Thomas's "Marse Robert at Mid-Life," in Heleniak, ed., *Confederate High Command*, 108–23.

13. An example of Lee's attempt to project his enemy's weaknesses, typical of many such instances during the war, appeared as early as July 9, 1862, following the Seven Days, when he wrote his wife that "Our enemy met with a heavy loss, from which it will take him some time to recover, before he can recommence his operations." Robert Edward Lee [Jr.], *Recollections and Letters of General Robert E. Lee, By His Son,* enlarged ed. (Garden City, N.Y.: Garden City Pub. Co., 1924), 75. Sometimes mistaken for the ability to read his enemy's mind, this trait occasionally led Lee into trouble, as in the Maryland campaign, where he consistently underrated the recuperative power of the Army of the Potomac.

14. Davis to Lee, June 2, 1862, *OR*, vol. 11, 3:569–70.

15. Lee to Davis, June 5, 1862, Robert E. Lee, *Wartime Papers of Robert E. Lee,* ed. Clifford Dowdey and Louis H. Manarin (Boston: Little, Brown, 1961), 183–84. On August 17, after discussing transportation and commissary concerns, Lee made a similar statement to Davis: "I beg you will excuse my troubling you with my opinions, and especially these details, but your kindness had led you to receive them without objections so often that I know I am tempted to trespass." Ibid., 258–59; or *OR*, vol. 51, 2:1075–76.

16. Long, *Memoirs of R. E. Lee,* 167–68.

17. *Papers of Jefferson Davis* 8:254. Davis frequently expressed his cordiality to Lee. After returning to Richmond from spending a prolonged period with Lee in the field during the first campaign, Davis ended a letter thus: "Before closing I will renew my caution to you against personal exposure either in battle or reconnaissance. It is a duty to the cause we serve for the sake of which I reiterate the warning." And he signed himself uncharacteristically, "Very respectfully and truly, your friend." Davis to Lee, July 5, 1862, *OR*, vol. 11, 3:631–32. A day later Davis wrote to Lee of "The entire confidence reposed in you . . . ." Davis to Lee, July 5 [i.e., 6], *OR*, vol. 11, 3:632–33. Davis's most extraordinary expression of confidence came in a letter of August 26, which is discussed in chapter 5.

18. Davis's address to survivors of the Army of Northern Virginia at a memorial meeting on Lee's death, John William Jones, *Personal Reminiscences, Anecdotes, and Letters Of Gen. Robert E. Lee* (New York: D. Appleton, 1876), 339 (emphasis in original). In a letter to Lee, May 31, 1863, in declining Lee's request to be relieved from command of southside Virginia and North Carolina, Davis wrote, "This is one of the few instances in which I have found my thoughts running in the opposite direction from your own." *OR*, vol. 18:1084. For a recent assessment of the Lee-Davis relationship that draws somewhat different conclusions, see Steven E. Woodworth, "Jefferson Davis and Robert E. Lee in the Seven Days," in William J. Miller, ed., *The Peninsula Campaign of 1862: Yorktown to the Seven Days,* 2 vols. (Campbell, Calif.: Savas Woodbury, 1995) 1:1–17.

19. Davis to Lee, June 1, 1862, *OR*, vol. 11, 3:568–69. Davis originally wrote "to withdraw you from" before changing to "temporarily interfere with." *Papers of Jefferson Davis* 8:207.

20. In *OR*, vol. 10, pt. 2, see Lee to K. Smith, June 4, 1862 (p. 584); Lee (per Chilton) to K. Smith, June 5 (590); K. Smith to Lee, June 6 (596); and Lee (per Taylor) to K. Smith, June 7 (597–98). In ibid., vol. 16, pt. 2, see K. Smith to Taylor, June 21, 1862 (pp. 696–97); and K. Smith to Lee, June 26 (708–9). And see Lee (per Long) to Lovell, June 16, 1862, in ibid., vol. 15:756.

21. General Orders No. 15, Adjutant General's Office, Oct. 22, 1861, defined the Department of Northern Virginia to consist of the three districts: (1) the Valley, under T. J. Jackson, comprising the country between the Blue Ridge and the Allegheny mountains; (2) the Potomac, under P. G. T. Beauregard, from the Blue Ridge to Powell's River; and (3) Aquia, under T. H. Holmes, from Powell's River to the mouth of the Potomac, including the northern neck. *OR*, vol. 5:913–14. For non-Virginians, the northern neck refers to the peninsula between the Potomac and the Rappahannock; the middle peninsula to the land between the Rappahannock and the York; and *the* Peninsula to the land between the York and James rivers.

22. Special Order No. 6, Headquarters, Apr. 12, 1862, signed by Lee for the president, said, "Norfolk and the Peninsula are embraced for the present within the limit of operations of the Army of Northern Virginia." *OR*, vol. 11, 3:438, Significantly, Magruder and Huger, "while conforming" to Johnston's instructions, were to continue to report to Richmond.

23. As early as April 22, Johnston complained to Lee of having lost touch with Jackson and commented, "Stationed here, I can obtain no information except from or through Richmond." And on May 8, he wrote, "My authority does not extend beyond the troops immediately around me" and requested "to be relieved of a merely nominal geographical command." *OR*, vol. 11, 3:455–56, 99–500. On several occasions Lee replied somewhat ambiguously that Johnston had authority over Jackson, Huger, and Field (later A. P. Hill) but that dispatches to and from them had to go through Richmond. At the same time, Lee was issuing orders to these generals in his own name. Ibid., vol. 11, 3:500–501, 505, 534–35. For Johnston's request for the Department of Henrico and Lee's refusal in Davis's name, see ibid., 527. For Johnston's postwar observations, see his *Narrative of Military Operations*, 128–29. Interestingly, once Lee took over and was wearing two hats, dispatches flowed freely from field headquarters to North Carolina and the Valley.

24. The phrase "command of the armies in Eastern Virginia and North Carolina" appears, with slight variation, in Davis's letter to Lee of June 1, 1862; in Lee's Special Order No. 22, Headquarters, June 1, 1862, in which he assumes command; and in Special Order No. 126, Adjutant General's Office, June 2, 1862, which announced his assignment to the military establishment. *OR*, vol. 11, 3:568–69, 571. That Davis did indeed think of Lee in terms of theater command is buttressed by his comment one year later, "It has several times occurred to me that it would be better for you to control all the operations of the Atlantic slope . . . ." Davis to Lee, May 31, 1863, ibid., vol.18:1084. Freeman, in *R. E. Lee* 2:75ff (esp. 6n), focuses on Lee's adopting the style "Army of Northern Virginia" while still mired in the Chickahominy swamps as a portent of future achievements, and he misses the fact Lee was never given command of either the Department or Army of Northern Virginia but instead a much broader theater.

25. The Chimneys conference is covered in Marshall, *Aide-de-Camp*, 77–78; and Longstreet, *From Manassas to Appomattox*, 112–13. Slightly different versions by Jefferson Davis may be found in three places: Davis, *Rise and Fall* 2:130–31; Davis, "Robert E. Lee," *SHSP* 17 (1889): 369; and John Warwick Daniel, ed., *Life and Reminiscences of Jefferson Davis by Distinguished Men of His Times* (Baltimore: Eastern Pub. Co., 1890), 407–8. The Lee quote is in the latter two.

26. Davis to Johnston, May 17, 1862, *OR*, vol. 11, 3:523–24.

27. Marshall, *Aide-de-Camp*, 77.

28. This private Lee-Davis meeting is recorded in Davis, *Rise and Fall* 2:131. For Davis's original understanding of the Johnston plan, see ibid., 120–21. Either Davis had never known Johnston's complete strategy or had forgotten portions of it by the time he wrote his memoirs.

29. Lee to Davis, June 5, 1862, *Wartime Papers*, 183–84.

30. As noted in chapter 1, Lee had urged Sidney Johnston to assume the offensive in March, had prodded Jackson to strike in the Valley in mid-May, and had supported Joseph Johnston's intention to attack McClellan in late May. On the other hand, Lee had been the primary factor scuttling the Johnston-Smith plan of mid-April to leave Magruder on the Peninsula and drive north against Washington with the main Confederate army. At that time he had argued for Johnston's adopting delaying defensive tactics at Yorktown. Likewise noted has been Lee's somewhat tardy conversion to the doctrine of concentration. He did not start a serious attempt to collect reenforcements for the defense of the capital until mid-May, and even then he first distributed the new arrivals to Petersburg, Gordonsville, Hanover Junction, etc. Not until the end of May, on the eve of Seven Pines, did Lee help unite these forces with Johnston's army. A more critical interpretation might see Lee's conversion as resulting from self-centeredness, if not selfishness. A muted version of this view may be found in Johnston's *Narrative of Military Operations*, 142, 145–46.

31. Lee to Seddon, Jan. 10, 1863, Lee, *Wartime Papers*, 389.

32. For a discussion of the sources and interpretations of Lee's strategy, see appendix 3, section A.

33. From an interview with Lee in Richmond, on approximately May 5, 1861, John Daniel Imboden, "Reminiscences of Lee and Jackson," *Galaxy* 12 (1871): 628. For a brief corroboration of Lee's views in the war's opening days, see the Johnston interview, "Memorandum of Conversations between Robert E. Lee and William Preston Johnston, May 7, 1868, and March 18, 1870," ed. W. G. Bean, *Virginia Magazine of History and Biography* 73 (1965): 479. And for an instance when Lee refused to speculate on the outcome, see J. W. Jones, *Personal Reminiscences*, 143–44.

34. Lee to Davis, June 10, 1863, *OR*, vol. 27, 3:881.

35. Lee to Seddon, Aug. 23, 1864, Lee, *Wartime Papers*, 843–44. For other evidence on Lee's views on the inexorability of the numbers involved, see Lee [Jr.], *Recollections*, 232–33; Marshall, *Aide-de-Camp*, 68–69; and a brief comment in John Leyburn, "An Interview with General Lee," *Century Magazine* 30 (1885): 167.

36. Lee to his wife, Dec. 25, 1861, Lee [Jr.], *Recollections*, 59; Fitzhugh Lee, *General Lee*, 129; and Lee, *Wartime Papers*, 95–97. For a similar quote, see Lee to G. W. C. Lee, Dec. 29, 1861, ibid., 97–99.

37. Lee to Davis, July 6, 1864, Lee, *Wartime Papers*, 816.

38. Imboden, "Reminiscences of Lee and Jackson," 628. It might also be noted that Herbert C. Saunders, a visiting Englishman, made a memorandum of a conversation with Lee in November 1865, which included the statement "Taking . . . the well-known antipathy of the mass of the English to the institution [of slavery] into consideration, he said he had never expected help from England." Because Lee refused to authorize publication of the memorandum, at least in part because of unspecified errors, it is impossible to know how much weight to give this source. Lee [Jr.], *Recollections*, 232. See also appendix 3, section B.

39. Lee to Davis, July 6, 1864, Lee, *Wartime Papers*, 816.

40. John Sargent Wise, *The End of an Era* (Boston: Houghton Mifflin 1902), 429. For a different interpretation, see Nolan, *Lee Considered*, 112–13; and for further discussion on this point see appendix 3, section B.

41. Lee to Davis, June 10, 1863, Lee, *Wartime Papers*, 507–9.

42. Lee to Davis, June 25, 1863, ibid., 530–31.

43. Lee to Davis, June 10, 1863, ibid., 507–9.

44. The words quoted in this paragraph are not Lee's but were used by Charles Marshall in describing his chief's strategy. The context is as follows: "As it was the manifest policy of the Federal Government to conclude the war speedily, and to feed the growing impatience of the people with successes which would give them assurance of such a result, so on the other hand it became the policy of General Lee to disappoint these hopes and encourage the belief that the war would be of indefinite length." *Aide-de-Camp*, 74 (see also 71–73).

45. On Lee's analysis of Northern morale, see appendix 3, section C.

46. For examples of Lee's suggested use of political ploys, see appendix 3, section C.

47. "Frustrate" is Marshall's term. Marshall, *Aide-de-Camp*, 74. On Lee's use of "baffle," see Lee to G. W. C. Lee, Nov. 10, 1862, and Lee to wife, Apr. 19, 1863, Lee, *Wartime Papers*, 333, 437–38; Lee to H. T. Clark, Aug. 8, 1862, *OR*, vol. 9:478–79. On Lee's use of "mystify," see Lee to Davis, July 10, 1864, Lee, *Wartime Papers*, 817–18. On Lee's use of "embarrass," see Lee to Davis, June 25, 1863, and repeated use in Lee to Davis, Feb. 3, 1864, ibid., 530–31, 666–67.

48. Lee to G. W. C. Lee, Feb. 28, 1863, Lee, *Wartime Papers*, 410–12.

49. Lee to Davis, June 10, 1863, ibid., 507–9.

50. Lee to Davis, June 8, 1863, *OR*, vol. 27, 3:868–69. Two weeks later, Lee wrote to Davis: "So strong is my conviction of the necessity of activity on our part in military affairs, that you will excuse my adverting to the subject again, notwithstanding what I have said in my previous letter of today." June 25, 1863, Lee, *Wartime Papers*, 532–33. Lee's most famous expression of his belief, "We cannot afford to be idle," formed an important part of his thinking in crossing into Maryland and will be considered in *Taken at the Flood*, forthcoming from The Kent State University Press.

51. Lee to Davis, June 10, 1863, *OR*, vol. 27, 3:880–82. The entire quote is "We should not, therefore, conceal from ourselves that our resources in men are constantly diminishing, and the disproportion in this respect between us and our enemies, if they continue united in their efforts to subjugate us, is steadily augmenting."

52. Lee himself used "destroy" (*OR*, vol. 11, 2:497); "crush" (ibid., 3:575, 589, vol. 51, 2:761); "ruin" (Lee, *Wartime Papers*, 389); and "wipe out" (ibid., 188).

53. Lee to Davis, July 6, 1864, Lee, *Wartime Papers*, 816.

54. Lee to Jackson, Aug. 7, 1862, *OR*, vol. 12, 3:925–26.

55. Lee's use of action and activity has been discussed. For "taking the aggressive," see Lee to Seddon, June 8, 1863, Lee, *Wartime Papers*, 504–5.

56. Daniel, *Reminiscences of Jefferson Davis*, 411; Henry Heth, "Letter from Major-General Henry Heth, of A. P. Hill's Corps, A.N.V.," *SHSP* 4 (1877): 156–57. Interestingly, the remarks of both Davis and Heth came in a discussion of Lee at Gettysburg. Neither attempted to explain Lee and his strategy in terms of this one trait, however. Porter Alexander narrated an anecdote that has been much quoted in which Col. Joseph Ives, who had been engineer for Lee before joining Davis's staff, in mid-June said that Lee's "name might be audacity" and predicted that "he will take more desperate chances and take them quicker than any other general in this country, North or South." In recounting the story, Alexander confessed he did not understand how any one could have seen this in Lee at the time. See Edward Porter Alexander, *Military Memoirs of a Confederate: A Critical Narrative*, ed. T. Harry Williams (Bloomington: Indiana Univ. Press, 1962), 110–11.

57. Jomini, *Art of War*, 73; Halleck, *Elements of Military Art*, 43.

58. See Lee to Seddon, June 8, 1863, and Seddon to Lee, June 10, *OR*, vol. 27, 3:868–69, 882.

59. Davis to Lee, May 31, 1863, ibid., vol. 18:1083–84.

60. "He who awaits the attack is everywhere anticipated: the enemy fall with large force upon fractions of his force: he neither knows where his adversary proposes to attack him nor in what manner to repel him." Jomini, *Art of War*, 73.

61. Johnston to Lee, Apr. 30, 1862, *OR*, vol. 11, 3:477. It should also be noted that Halleck had demonstrated the same lesson to Beauregard at Corinth in May.

62. Lee to Davis, June 5, 1862, Lee, *Wartime Papers*, 183–84. In a letter to Jackson, dated June 11, Lee referred to McClellan as "strongly posted on the Chickahominy, and apparently preparing to move by gradual approaches on Richmond." *OR*, vol. 11, 3:589–90. Also to Jackson, on June 16, Lee commented, "Unless McClellan can be driven out of his entrenchments he will move by positions under cover of his heavy guns within shelling distance of Richmond." Lee, *Wartime Papers*, 194.

63. The sharpest expression of this criticism may be found in Thomas Lawrence Connelly, "Robert E. Lee and the Western Confederacy: A Criticism of Lee's Strategic Ability," *Civil War History* 15 (1969): 130–31. Albert Castel ably rebutted the argument in his "The Historian and the General: Thomas L. Connelly vs Robert E. Lee," *Civil War History* 16 (1970): 215–28.

64. One was tried and the other contemplated. Lee was deprived of Longstreet and two of the best divisions in the army for seven months (September 1863 to May 1864), when they were sent to the West. According to John Echols, Davis seriously considered sending Lee to command in the West. J. W. Jones, *Personal Reminiscences*, 182–83. The question remains, however, whether Lee should have paid more attention to Tennessee. Inevitably, the answer must be yes, since the Confederacy lost the war through Tennessee. But the question is meaningless, because it is impossible to see how he could have paid more attention without lessening his attention to his own theater, in which case the Confederacy would have lost the war through Virginia.

65. Excluding Missouri and Kentucky from Confederate totals, but including the western counties in Virginia's figures, Virginia had 7.9 percent of the land area, 19.2 percent of the white population, 32.6 percent of the value of the industrial products produced annually, 17.4 percent of the banking capital, and 19.2 percent of the railroad mileage. In grains, Virginia produced 13.4 percent of the corn, 39.3 percent of the wheat, 51.2 percent of the oats, 42.9 percent of the rye, 31.3 percent of the barley, and 89.2 percent of the buckwheat, for a total of 18.9 percent of all grains by volume. In livestock, Virginia's portion was less impressive but still significant: 13.4 percent of the horses and mules, 9.9 percent of the cattle, 10.3 percent of the swine, and 20.9 percent of the sheep. These figures are computed from the raw statistics of the 8th Census. See chap. 1, nn.11–13. No pretense is made that Lee possessed this 1860 census information. It is cited merely to show that his belief in the importance of Virginia had basis in fact. An extended and well-argued statement of Virginia's preeminence may be found in McMurry's insightful *Rebel Armies*, 25–29. Some of McMurry's statistics differ slightly from those here due to the use of different parameters.

66. Charles Marshall asserted, "In the opinion of General Lee, Virginia presented the most favorable theater of war for [his] plan of operations. He considered that there were circumstances by the judicious use of which he could impart to his army an importance and influence greatly exceeding what was due to its actual strength and numbers." Marshall, *Aide-de-Camp*, 75.

67. Lee to Davis, June 23, 1863, *OR*, vol. 27, 3:924–25. For a further discussion of Lee's appreciation of the Northern sensitivity to the loss of Washington, see appendix 3, section D.

68. Davis to Johnston, May 17, 1862, ibid., vol. 11, 3:523–24.

69. John Henninger Reagan, *Memoirs, with Special Reference to Secession and the Civil War*, ed. Walter Flavius McCaleb (New York: Neale Pub. Co., 1906), 139.

70. Marshall, *Aide-de-Camp*, 71. Joseph Johnston agreed, writing to Davis on May 10, 1862, "If we permit ourselves to be driven beyond Richmond we lose the means of sustaining this army." *OR*, vol. 11, 3:506. A passage in Walter Taylor's memoirs and a verbal comment by Charles Marshall, reported by George Breckinridge Davis (president of the Antietam Battlefield Board), may seem to imply that Davis compelled Lee to defend Richmond against the general's better judgment. Both statements merely demonstrate, however, that Lee believed it imperative to avoid becoming besieged and that Richmond was best defended at a distance. See Walter Herron Taylor, *General Lee, His Campaigns in Virginia, 1861–1865, with Personal Reminiscences* (Norfolk: Nusbaum Book and News Co., 1906), 48–49; and George Breckinridge Davis, "The Antietam Campaign," in *PMHSM* 3:30.

71. Reagan, *Memoirs*, 139.

72. See Robert C. Black, *The Railroads of the Confederacy* (Chapel Hill: Univ. of North Carolina Press, 1952), and Angus J. Johnston, *Virginia Railroads in the Civil War* (Chapel Hill: Univ. of North Carolina, 1961), on Confederate problems in maintaining its railroads and in attempting to construct new ones. Note especially that it took Joseph Johnston four months (one of actual construction) to get an eight-mile spur built from Manassas to Centreville. Lynchburg is discussed as an alternative by Marshall, *Aide-de-Camp*, 71.

73. 8th Census, *Manufactures* 3:578, 616–17, 637. Richmond's statistics are inseparable from its county. All figures are in terms of annual value of products. It has been pointed out that Henrico, if a state, would have ranked sixth among the eleven Confederate states. McMurry, *Rebel Armies*, 26.

74. Marshall, *Aide-de-Camp*, 72. Manifestations of Lee's continuing anxiety over the James River approach would be evident in his actions after the Seven Days in fearing McClellan more than Pope, in his reasoning for entering Maryland, and as a motive for Stuart's October 1862 raid.

75. Marshall, *Aide-de-Camp*, 66–67. For evidence Lee believed his concentration in the summer of 1862 had operated in just this fashion, see Lee to Davis, June 23, 1863, *OR*, vol. 27, 3:924–25.

76. For example, Lee would not have the advantage of interior lines in the battles of the Seven Days, Second Manassas, Chantilly, Chancellorsville, or Gettysburg.

77. Lee to Davis, June 25, 1863, Lee, *Wartime Papers*, 532–33.

78. For example, on June 5, 1862, and Aug. 31, 1863, Lee used the phrase "to bring . . . out" (ibid., 184; and *OR*, vol. 51, 2:761); on June 11, 1862, "forced to come out of his intrenchments" (ibid., vol. 11, 3:589); and on June 16, 1862, "driven out of his entrenchments" (Lee, *Wartime Papers*, 194); and on June 8, 1863, "can be drawn out into a position to be assailed" (*OR*, vol. 27, 3:868).

79. Lee to Jackson, Aug. 4, 1862, *OR*, vol. 12, 3:922–23; or Lee, *Wartime Papers*, 245. For a lengthy and enlightening discussion of the turning movement in the Civil War, see Archer Jones, *Civil War Command and Strategy: The Process of Victory and Defeat* (New York: The Free Press, 1992), 56–74.

80. Chesnut to Davis, Nov. 11, 1861, and Lee to Davis, Nov. 24, 1861, *Papers of Jefferson Davis* 7:391, 426.

81. Jomini, *Art of War*, 70. Interestingly, Henry Halleck did not place the same emphasis on maneuvering against decisive points. In his view, "The first and most important rule in offensive warfare is, to keep your forces as much concentrated as possible." Halleck, *Elements of Military Art*, 40. Had Halleck been more Jominian on this point, he might not have ordered the withdrawal of the Army of the Potomac from the James in August 1862.

82. In referring to his four maxims, Jomini confessed, "This truth is evident; and it would be little short of the ridiculous to enunciate such a general principle without accompanying it with all necessary explanations for its application upon the field." Jomini, *Art of War*, 71.

83. It is possible to make too much of Jomini. It is interesting to see how the actions of commanders exposed to his thinking correlate to his theories, and military theorists might wish to test Jomini's currency. Historians, however, should be chary in reading too much Jominian influence into the Civil War. After all, with one or two exceptions, American generals of the period were neither scholars nor theorists; and if they spent much time thinking about Jomini or trying to apply his lessons to the situations in which they found themselves, there is little evidence of it in the records. The nature and extent of Jomini's influence on Confederate and Federal leaders in the Civil War has been much debated in the last thirty years. Until recently, Jomini was accused of teaching obsolete theories and casting a baleful pall on Civil War strategic thinking. For a convenient summary of the controversy, as well as much common sense on the topic, see Herman Hattaway and Archer Jones, *How the North Won: A Military History of the Civil War* (Urbana: Univ. of Illinois Press, 1983), 12–17; and Beringer et al., *Why the South Lost*, 39–52. The latter is somewhat labored in devoting considerable attention to whether or not Civil War generals also abided by the rules of Karl von Clausewitz, a writer apparently unknown to any of the generals except Carl Schurz.

84. Freeman, *R. E. Lee* 1:295–97, saw the value of the turning movement as but one of seven lessons that Lee learned in Mexico. Several of those seven, however, such as effective use of staff and appreciation of fortifications, are questionable.

85. The argument for the influence of Henry Lee is put forward by John Morgan Dederer, "The Origins of Robert E. Lee's Bold Generalship: A Reinterpretation," 49 *Military Affairs* (1985): 117–23.

86. The text of Janney's speech may be found in Freeman, *R. E. Lee* 1:466–67.

3. "How do we get at those people?" Lee's Strategy in the Seven Days Campaign, June 1–July 2, 1862

1. Lee to Charlotte Lee, June 2, 1862, in John William Jones, *Life and Letters of Robert Edward Lee, Soldier and Man* (New York: Neale Publishing Co., 1906), 184.

2. Davis to wife, June 13, 1862, *Papers of Jefferson Davis* 8:243.

3. Stuart to Lee, June 4, 1862, in James Ewell Brown Stuart, *The Letters of Major General James E. B. Stuart*, ed. Adele H. Mitchell (N.p.: Stuart-Mosby Historical Society, 1990), 255.

4. Lee to Davis, June 5, 1862, Lee, *Wartime Papers*, 183–84.

5. Stuart to Lee, June 4, 1862, Stuart, *Letters*, 254–55; Longstreet, *From Manassas to Appomattox*, 114; and Pendleton to wife, June 4, 1862, in Susan Pendleton Lee, *Memoirs of William Nelson Pendleton, By His Daughter* (Harrisonburg, Va.: Sprinkle Publications, 1991), 187–88. In the same letter, in referring to a meeting of June 2, artillerist William Nelson Pendleton wrote, "I like very much General Lee's tone and bearing in the conference I had with him evening before last. His head seems clear and his heart strong. Few men have ever borne a greater weight than now rests upon his shoulders."

6. Lee was using Seven Pines as an argument against frontal assaults, when he wrote to Davis, "You witnessed the experiment Saturday." Lee to Davis, June 5, 1862, Lee, *Wartime Papers*, 183–84. In fairness to Johnston, it will be remembered that Huger's division, which never got into the battle, had been intended to outflank the Federal line. Nevertheless, Johnston opened the battle with Longstreet's attack on the front of the Federal Fourth Corps.

7. Marshall, *Aide-de-Camp*, 77–78; Freeman, *R. E. Lee* 2:81. Lee also kept his lines out from the city to make the moral point of disputing McClellan's advance. He said at the "Chimneys" conference on June 3: "If we leave this line because they can shell us, we shall have to leave the next for the same reason, and I don't see how we can stop this side of Richmond."

8. It is sometimes mistakenly implied that Lee's strategy for the Seven Days was to "isolate" and "destroy" Porter's "vulnerable" Fifth Corps north of the Chickahominy. However, until June 19—long after Lee had decided and was well into planning the details of his move—half of Franklin's Sixth Corps was also north of the river. In fact, the Sixth Corps division was still there when Stuart made his ride around the Federal army, June 12–15. By June 25 McCall's newly arrived division of Pennsylvania Reserves had replaced Franklin's unit and increased Porter's numbers slightly. As Lee would discover, Porter was neither especially isolated nor vulnerable to direct assault. See William Henry Powell, *The Fifth Army Corps (Army of the Potomac), A Record of Operations during the Civil War in the United States of America, 1861–1865* (New York: G. P. Putnam's Sons, 1896), 73; and Josiah Rinehart Sypher, *History of the Pennsylvania Reserve Corps* . . . (Lancaster: Elias Barr & Co., 1865), 197.

9. Lee to Davis, June 5, 1862, Lee, *Wartime Papers*, 183–84; Davis, *Rise and Fall* 2:131. It should not be assumed, however, that only Davis's partiality to Lee was at work. The changed military situation in the Valley made it more feasible to bring Jackson to the vicinity of Richmond.

10. Lee to Longstreet, June 6, 1862, *OR*, vol. 11, 3:577.

11. In his future operations, Lee would divide his army over wide distances for maneuvering, most notably in the Second Manassas campaign, and conceivably he might have in this case. Whether or not he would have done so in his very first operation and while so near the Confederate capital, however, may be doubted.

12. Davis to Johnston, May 17, 1862, *OR*, vol. 11, 3:523–24; Lee to Johnston, ibid., 523. Lee's fear would continue throughout 1862 and beyond. See his letter to Davis, May 30, 1863, Lee, *Wartime Papers*, 495–97.

13. On the Burnside phantom, see Lee to Holmes, June 18 and 21, 1862, Lee, *Wartime Papers*, 195–96.

14. Boteler's account of three visits to Richmond on Jackson's behalf, which is chronologically confused, rhetorically purple, and not altogether reliable, may be found in Alexander R. Boteler, "Stonewall Jackson in Campaign of 1862," *SHSP* 40 (1915): 162–82. Nevertheless, corroboration of his first visit may be found in Lee to Davis and Lee to Randolph, both June 5, 1862, Lee, *Wartime Papers*, 183–84, 185; and in a later letter by Lee to Jackson on June 16, ibid., 194. Freeman not only accepts Boteler's story in its entirety but quotes it at great length. Freeman, *Lee's Lieutenants* 1:413ff. James Kegel goes even further and argues unconvincingly that Jackson's idea, as presented by Boteler, was the origin of both the Maryland and Gettysburg campaigns. Undoubtedly, Lee would welcome Jackson's support in the former and miss his presence in the latter, but there is no evidence that he appropriated the grand strategy of his subordinate. See Kegel, *North with Lee and Jackson*, 100–102, 104–6, 112–16.

15. Davis to Jackson, June 4, 1862, *OR*, vol. 12, 3:905.

16. Davis to wife, June 11, 1862, *Papers of Jefferson Davis* 8:236.

17. Lee to Davis, June 5, 1862, Lee, *Wartime Papers*, 183–84.

18. Ibid. Some of this is speculative, but it is clear that Lee was enthusiastic about Jackson's offer yet viewed it as supplemental to his own "diversion." For Lee's ambivalent feelings about sending Lawton's brigade of Georgians to Jackson ("I wish they were mine . . ."), see Lee to Randolph, June 5, 1862, ibid., 185.

19. Lee to Randolph, June 5, 1862, ibid., 185.

20. Boteler, "Stonewall Jackson," 164–65; Jackson to Johnston, June 6, 1862, with Lee's endorsement of June 8, *OR*, vol. 11, 3:579. Apparently, the movement of Lawton's brigade was suspended on the basis of Lee's comment.

21. Lee to Jackson, June 8, 1962, Lee, *Wartime Papers*, 187.

22. Lee to Randolph, June 9, 1862, ibid., 188.

23. Lee to Davis, June 10, 1862, ibid., 188.

24. Davis to wife, June 11, 1862, *Papers of Jefferson Davis* 8:236.

25. Lee to Jackson, June 11, 1862, *OR*, vol. 11, 3:589–90. Davis would again endorse Lee's ideas four days later: "Views fully concurred in. J. D." Lee, *Wartime Papers*, 193.

26. Special Order No. 130, Headquarters, Department of Northern Virginia, June 11, 1862, *OR*, vol. 11, 3:594. Lee also sent a telegram to Randolph enjoining him to seek the cooperation of the Richmond press in keeping Whiting's movement a secret. Lee, *Wartime Papers*, 191. Since Marshall and others make much of Lee openly advertising the dispatch of Whiting to distract the enemy's attention away from their York River communications, this telegram is a puzzle. See also, Freeman, *R. E. Lee* 2:95. Either Lee sent the message and then decided that secrecy was impossible, and therefore he would execute the move openly but attempt to disguise its ultimate purpose, or he tried to employ an elaborate double ruse. The problem with the theory that Lee was using a ruse at all is that it depends on the belief that Lee—who very much wanted Jackson to "crush" his opponents before coming to Richmond— would flaunt the news of reenforcements being sent to the Valley. The mystery here still is unsolved.

27. Lee to Stuart, June 11, 1862, Lee, *Wartime Papers*, 192.

28. Ibid. It is interesting that Stuart's instructions were not embodied in formal orders.

29. For Stuart's report, see *OR*, vol. 11, 1:1036–40. For further discussion of Lee and Stuart's ride, see appendix 5, section A.

30. Jackson to Lee, June 13, 1862, with endorsements by Lee and Davis, Lee, *Wartime Papers*, 193.

31. Lee to Jackson, June 16, 1862, ibid., 194. McCall's division of Pennsylvania Reserves had started landing at White House on June 11. Sypher, *Pennsylvania Reserve Corps*, 193. Burnside, without any troops, had arrived on June 8 at Fort Monroe for a conference with its commander, General Dix; on June 10 he paid a short visit to McClellan's headquarters before leaving for Washington. William Marvel, *Burnside* (Chapel Hill: Univ. of North Carolina Press), 92–93.

32. Lee to J. C. Pemberton, May 12, 1862, and to Gov. Henry T. Clark, May 13, *OR*, vol. 11, 3:511–12.

33. As a result of Lee's request, Theophilus Holmes, commanding the Department of North Carolina, took two North Carolina regiments from John Walker's oversized brigade, attached them to two newly arrived Georgia regiments, and sent them under Roswell Ripley to Richmond; however, they did not arrive in time. Holmes also sent Walker's reorganized brigade to Petersburg, where it relieved Lewis Armistead's brigade of Virginians, which did reach Johnston by May 30. Armistead was part of Huger's division, which had evacuated Norfolk and been retained for the defense of southside of the James. Thus, the brigade Johnston gained was not new but technically had been his all along. John Pemberton, commanding the Department of South Carolina, Georgia, and Florida, collected six Georgia regiments under Alexander Lawton, but they would not be ready to leave their home state until early June. In *OR*, vol. 11, pt. 3, see Lee to Johnston, May 23, 1862 (pp. 536–37); Lee endorsement to Johnston, May 27 (552–53); Lee to Johnston, May 28 (555–56); Randolph to Holmes, May 30 (559); and Special Order No. 21, Headquarters (of Lee), May 30 (563).

34. Johnston to Lee, May 28, 1862, ibid., 555.

35. The phrases "in rounded figures" and "regiments of all arms" mean that artillery batteries and partial regiments of infantry and cavalry have been converted into abstract regiments of ten companies. The number of Confederate regiments in the field is for the month of June 1862 and is derived from an ongoing study by the author that traces the organization, distribution, consolidation, mustering-out, etc., of all Confederate units by month. The number of Johnston's regiments is based on a study of the army's composition for June 20, with those units deducted that had not yet arrived on May 31. Tenney, *Seven Days in 1862.*

36. According to such unit returns as are available in the National Archives, on June 20, these same units totaled 68,740, which, with the 6,134 casualties of Seven Pines, would give Johnston 74,874 on May 31. Tenney, *Seven Days in 1862*, 133; "Opposing Forces at Seven Pines, May 31st–June 1st, 1862," *Battles and Leaders* 2:219. Johnston estimated his force to be 73,928. Joseph Eggleston Johnston, "Manassas to Seven Pines," in ibid. 2:209.

37. Once again, according to available returns in the National Archives, the Army of the Potomac totaled 101,444 on June 20; subtracting McCall's division, which did not arrive until mid-June, would give McClellan 92,233 present for duty on May 31. Tenney, *Seven Days in 1862*, 208. The monthly return for May gives McClellan 98,008 but does not satisfactorily separate out 5,000 or more men on detached duty at Yorktown, White House, etc. *OR*, vol. 11, 3:204.

38. Number of units and present-for-duty strengths are for June 20. Tenney, *Seven Days in 1862*, 133. Jackson's figures have been adjusted by adding his 1,150 casualties at Cross Keys and Port Republic and the cavalry and artillery (2,143) he left in the Valley when he came to Richmond. "Opposing Forces in the Valley Campaigns, March 23rd–June 10th, 1862," *Battles and Leaders* 2:301.

39. Davis to Pemberton, June 2, 1862, *OR*, vol. 14:534.

40. See Pemberton to Davis, June 2, 1862, ibid., 535. For June 3: Lee to Pemberton, Pemberton to Randolph, and Gov. Pickens to Davis (twice), *OR*, vol. 14:536, 535, and vol. 53:246 (twice). For June 5: Davis to Pickens, Davis to Pemberton (twice), Pemberton to Davis (twice), Randolph to Gov. Clark of N.C., Clark to Randolph, ibid., vol. 14:538–41; and Pickens to Davis, ibid., vol. 53:246. Also for June 5: Davis to Pemberton (twice), Pemberton to Davis (twice), Pemberton to Lawton (twice), ibid., vol. 14:548–50. For June 7: Pemberton to Davis, ibid., 552–53. For June 9: Acting Mayor George Wylly to Davis, ibid., vol. 53:246. For June 11: Randolph to Pemberton, Pemberton to Randolph (twice), and Pickens to Davis, ibid., vol. 14:558 (twice), 559, and vol. 53:247. For June 12: Davis to Pickens (twice) and Pickens to Davis, ibid., vol. 14:560–61, and vol. 53:247 (twice.) For June 19: Davis to Pickens and Lee to Davis, ibid., vol. 14:568, 569.

41. By June 26, Lee would have received the six Georgia regiments in Lawton's brigade and the two in Ripley's, although one of the latter's regiments had already been sent to North Carolina. Lee would also be able to utilize the 2d South Carolina Rifles, which had arrived on May 31, and the Hampton South Carolina Legion Cavalry, which had returned to the army. The July and August accretions are discussed in chapter 4.

42. One regiment each from Alabama and Mississippi arrived in time for the Seven Days, while two regiments from Florida and two from Alabama came later in the summer. See Cooper to H. R. Miller, June 10, 1862, and Lee [per Taylor] to Joseph Finegan, June 21, *OR*, vol. 11, 3:585, 610–11. Randolph [per Cooper] to Gov. Shorter of Alabama, June 10, 1862, ibid., vol. 51, 2:569. It should also be noted that Lee was helping to concentrate forces for other theaters during this same period. See Lee to Kirby Smith, June 4, 1862, and Lee [per Taylor] to Kirby Smith, June 7, ibid., vol. 10, 2:584, 597–98.

43. Reference is to the brigades of Walker, Ransom, and Daniel, which would constitute a division under Holmes during the Seven Days. See all in *OR*, vol. 11, pt. 3: Randolph to Walker, June 1 (p. 565); Lee to Walker, June 5 (575); Lee to Ransom, June 8 (583); Lee to Holmes, June 18 (607); Lee to Holmes, June 21 (610); Special Order No. 140, Headquarters, Department of Northern Virginia, June 21 (611); Lee to Holmes, June 23 (613); Lee to Huger, June 26 (617); and Randolph to Holmes (twice), June 26 (618, 619).

44. The present-for-duty figures are from Tenney, *Seven Days in 1862*, 133, 208; and the count of regiments is derived from ibid., passim. For further comment on the size of Lee's army, see appendix 2, section C.

45. Confederates present for duty 112,220 divided by 1,197,489 equals 9.37 percent. Federal present for duty 101,444 divided by 4,453,114 equals 2.27 percent.

46. Lee to Stevens, June 3, 1862, *OR*, vol. 11, 3:571–72.

47. Lee to Stevens, and General Orders No. 62, Headquarters, Department of Northern Virginia, both June 4, 1862, ibid., 572–73.

48. Davis to wife, June 11, 1862, *Papers of Jefferson Davis* 8:236.

49. See Freeman, *R. E. Lee* 2:81–82, 86–87; and Marshall, *Aide-de-Camp*, 79–80.

50. Sir Frederick Maurice has written: "Lee's great contribution to the military art was his use of entrenchments as an aid to maneuver. He was the first to perceive the possibilities which improvements in arms combined with entrenchments afforded. In 1815, neither Blücher at Ligny nor Wellington at Waterloo, though both were on the defensive, considered with weapons of their day the use of entrenchments in field warfare. In 1854, the Russians on the defensive at Alma had provided entrenchments for some of their guns, but not for their infantry. The Seven Days, therefore, mark the beginning of an epoch in military history." Marshall, *Aide-de-Camp*, 80n. 3. It is doubtful that Lee's fortifying of Richmond should be considered "entrenchments in field warfare." It was Lee's intention to allow fewer men to defend the capital and thus free a larger force for field operations. McClellan had already done the same thing on a larger, strategic scale by fortifying Washington. The concept was well known in European warfare.

51. Jomini, *Art of War*, 63; Lee to Longstreet, June 6, 1862, *OR*, vol. 11, 3:577; and Lee to Davis, June 5, Lee, *Wartime Papers*, 183–84. Also, on the need for an army being "incessantly" employed in "labor and science" when not fighting, see Halleck, *Elements of Military Art*, 43.

52. Chilton to Davis, Dec. 7, 1874, Rowland, *Jefferson Davis, Constitutionalist* 7:410 (emphasis in original).

53. Davis to wife, June 19, 1862, *Papers of Jefferson Davis* 8:254.

54. Lee to Davis, June 10, 1862, Lee, *Wartime Papers*, 188. In his instructions to Jackson on June 11, Lee varied the phrase slightly by writing, "while this army attacks General McClellan in front." *OR*, vol. 11, 3:589–90.

55. Longstreet, *From Manassas to Appomattox*, 120.

56. Long, *Memoirs of R. E. Lee*, 168.

57. Lee to Jackson, June 16, 1862, Lee, *Wartime Papers*, 194.

58. The details of the June 23 conference come from two regrettably brief firsthand accounts: James Longstreet, *From Manassas to Appomattox*, 120–22; and Daniel Harvey Hill, "Lee's Attacks North of the Chickahominy," *Battles and Leaders* 2:347–48. Past accounts have assumed that all of the details of the operation were settled by the end of the meeting. See especially Freeman, *R. E. Lee* 2:110–12. But there is no firm evidence of this; nor is it certain how many of the details Lee left to the discussion of his generals, except for the date on which Jackson was to launch the movement. According to D. H. Hill, Lee gave only a general outline and left the details to his subordinates; but Longstreet remembered Lee giving full particulars and then leaving the room so the generals could "talk the matter over for our better comprehension." The next day Lee would issue written instructions (which are quoted in the chapter text). See General Orders No. 75, Headquarters, Department of Northern Virginia, June 24, 1862, Lee, *Wartime Papers*, 198–200.

59. For a June 20 breakdown of the present-for-duty figures for the Confederate attacking columns, see appendix 2, section C.

60. General Orders No. 75, Headquarters, Department of Northern Virginia, June 24, 1862, Lee, *Wartime Papers*, 198–200.

61. For a June 20 breakdown of the present-for-duty figures for the Confederate forces defending Richmond, see appendix 2, section C.

62. Davis, *Rise and Fall* 2:132. Douglas Freeman says Lee's confidence in holding Richmond derived from his "knowledge of McClellan" and from the fact that once New Bridge was uncovered and in Confederate hands, Lee's route to Richmond would be as direct as McClellan's. Freeman, *R. E. Lee* 2:106. The latter point did probably play a part in Lee's thinking; the first, however, is fanciful. It is one of several times Freeman would claim some clairvoyant ability of Lee to read McClellan's mind. Lee never asserted any such talent, and no evidence survives to demonstrate he acted upon the assumption he did.

63. In addition to Lee's plain words on this point, which have already been cited, Charles Marshall wrote: "General Lee, in conversing with me about these operations, said, as the orders themselves clearly indicate, that his idea was to compel General McClellan to come out of his works and give battle for the defence of his communications with the White House." Marshall, *Aide-de-Camp*, 89.

64. Branch's report, *OR*, vol. 11, 2:882.

65. A. P. Hill's report, ibid., 835. A. P. Hill's latest biographer admits that Hill made the attack "without permission or support" but insists that Jackson's delay and Branch's failure to communicate were more grievous faults. James I. Robertson, Jr., *A. P. Hill: The Story of a Confederate Warrior* (New York: Random House, 1987), 75–77.

66. It should be noted that Hill's men had come under heavy Federal artillery fire and that Lee's order to Hill by a courier is a matter of some controversy. See Freeman, *Lee's Lieutenants* 1:514.

67. According to Charles Marshall, "General Lee also told me that he did not anticipate a battle at Mechanicsville or Beaver Dam. He thought that Jackson's march turning Beaver Dam would lead to the immediate withdrawal of the force stationed there, and did not intend that a direct attack should be made on that formidable position." Marshall, *Aide-de-Camp*, 89. After the war Lee told his cousin Cassius Lee that "the fight at Mechanicsville . . . was unexpected." Lee [Jr.], *Recollections*, 415.

68. This is the explanation favored by Lee's most renowned biographer, Douglas Southall Freeman, *R. E. Lee* 2:133.

69. Lee to Davis, June 26, 1862, Lee, *Wartime Papers*, 201.

70. For June 26, 1862, see Randolph to Holmes (p. 619), Randolph to Walker (618), and Lee to Huger (617), *OR*, vol. 11, pt. 3; and also Lee to Huger, Lee, *Wartime Papers*, 201–2.

71. Lee's report, Lee, *Wartime Papers*, 213.

72. Lee [Jr.], *Recollections*, 415.

73. "[I]t was not intended that Longstreet and A. P. Hill should advance until the enemy moved to meet Jackson's attack, but their troops found themselves engaged with the enemy as soon as they reached the vicinity of New Bridge." Marshall, *Aide-de-Camp*, 99–100.

74. Neither side broke down their total casualties for the campaign by individual battles. Freeman estimated Confederate losses at 8,000 for Gaines' Mill alone. See Freeman, *Lee's Lieutenants* 1:536. Porter's Fifth Corps suffered campaign losses of 7,601, but the total includes the Artillery Reserve, as well as substantial losses later at New Market Crossroads and Malvern Hill.

75. The conclusions in the text are largely, although not entirely, in agreement with Douglas Freeman's detailed analysis of Lee's thinking, which may be found in *R. E. Lee* 2:159–65.

76. Lee's decision to assault Malvern Hill must also be viewed in light of the fact that he did not know McClellan would find the James too narrow there for a permanent base. Lee would have naturally believed his best hope was to attack before the enemy had time to perfect his entrenchments. As it turned out, he could have moved farther to the east and prepared for an attack on July 2, while McClellan was once again on the move.

77. These usually accepted casualty figures are given in "The Opposing Forces in the

Seven Days' Battles, June 25th–July 1st, 1862," *Battles and Leaders* 2:315, 317. Thus, the Confederates lost 17.9 percent of their present for duty and the Federals 15.6 percent.

4. "The enemy is congregating about us": Lee in Strategic Stalemate, July 2–August 9, 1862

1. Lee's remark is quoted in Freeman, *R. E. Lee* 2:202; Lee to wife, July 9, 1862, Lee, *Wartime Papers*, 230; and Lee's report, dated Mar. 6, 1863, *OR*, vol. 11, 2:497. That Lee may also have vented his frustration to Jefferson Davis in a letter of July 4, 1862, which unfortunately has not been found, is reflected in the consoling remark Davis wrote in reply the following day: "It is a hard necessity to be compelled to allow him time to recover from his discomfiture and to receive re-enforcements, but under the circumstances it must be regarded as necessary." *Papers of Jefferson Davis* 8:276. Lee's dispatch to Davis of the 4th in the Lee-Davis Correspondence, Virginia State Library, Richmond, would not seem to justify this response from Davis. Also, in mid-August, when Lee learned of McClellan's nearly completed withdrawal from the James to Washington, he commented: "I feel greatly mortified . . . he ought not have got off so easily." Lee to Davis, Aug. 17, 1862, *Wartime Papers*, 258–59; or *OR*, vol. 51, 2:1075–76.

2. Lee to Mrs. Jackson, Jan. 25, 1866, Lee Family Papers, Virginia Historical Society.

3. Lee to Davis, July 5, 1862, *Papers of Jefferson Davis* 8:278–79. Lee's three chief worries were: (1) the threat from the James; (2) the weakness of his own army; and (3) faulty intelligence. This letter is misdated July 6 in *OR*, vol. 11, 3:634–35. In his reply to Lee on July 5[6], Davis approved the withdrawal, offered the hope of reenforcements, and commiserated with the problem of confusing information. *OR*, vol. 11, 3:632–33 (not reproduced in full in *Papers of Jefferson Davis* 8:280).

4. Lee to Davis, July 5, 1862, *Papers of Jefferson Davis* 8:278–79. See appendix 5, section B.

5. Alfred Rives to Lewis Harvie, July 11, 1862, *OR*, vol. 11, 3:639. On August 7, Lee ordered D. H. Hill, then commanding the District of North Carolina, to "spare no effort in urging on the works at Drewry's Bluff to a speedy conclusion." Ibid, 666. And as late as August 25, Chief Engineer Jeremy Gilmer expressed dissatisfaction with the James River defenses, as well as with the lines around Richmond and Petersburg in general. A major cause of the delay was the severe shortage of engineering officers. Lee had to assign Gilmer to the task, which temporarily left no engineers with the Army of Northern Virginia. Lee to Gilmer, Aug. 25, 1862, ibid., vol. 12, 3:944–45.

6. An older, traditional interpretation has been that Lee "understood" McClellan so well that he retired to Richmond to start planning his campaign against Pope. Douglas Freeman partially corrected this view by pointing out that Lee gave virtually no thought to Pope or northern Virginia until mid-July. See Freeman, *R. E. Lee* 2:258–59, esp. n. 20.

7. Lee to Davis, July 6, 1862, *OR*, vol. 11, 3:634–35. Lee's commitment to concentration remained unabated during the summer. On July 30, he wrote to Davis: "I deem it inexpedient to divide the army by creating independent commands especially at a time when we require the united efforts of all the forces we can collect at the principal points threatened by the enemy." Robert E. Lee, *Lee's Dispatches: Unpublished Letters of General Robert E. Lee, C.S.A., to Jefferson Davis and the War Department of the Confederate States of America, 1862–1865*, ed. Douglas Southall Freeman; new enlarged edition, ed. Grady McWhiney (New York: G. P. Putnam's Sons, 1957), 40–41. And on August 4, he wrote to Randolph: "I am very reluctant to spare any troops from here at this time while from every quarter the enemy is congregating around us." *OR*, vol. 11, 3:663–64.

8. Cooper to Pemberton, July 5, 1862, *OR*, vol. 14:579. For the dissatisfaction with Pemberton, see in ibid., vol. 53:247: Pickens to Davis, June 11, 1862; Davis to Pickens, June

12; and Pickens to Davis, June 12. See also in ibid., vol. 14: Davis to Pickens, June 12, 1862 (pp. 560–61); Davis to Pickens, June 19 (568); and Lee to Davis, June 19 (569).

9. Drayton's brigade: 50th and 51st Georgia; 15th regiment and 3d battalion South Carolina. Evans's brigade: 17th, 18th, 22d, 23d, and Holcombe Legion South Carolina infantry and Macbeth (South Carolina) battery. Also sent during the summer were the 1st South Carolina (Volunteers), the Holcombe Legion Cavalry Battalion, and the 4th South Carolina Cavalry Battalion. The latter would be united with the Hampton Legion Cavalry to form the 2d South Carolina Cavalry.

10. For the unraveling of this story, see in *OR*, vol. 14: Cooper to G. W. Smith, July 4, 1862 (pp. 578–79); Cooper to Pemberton, July 5 (579); Cooper to Pemberton, July 9 (582); Pemberton to Cooper, July 10 (583); Pemberton to Cooper, July 12 (584); Cooper to Pemberton, July 13 (585 [two letters]); Pemberton to Evans, July 17 (586); Pemberton to Drayton, July 17 (586–87); Pemberton to Cooper, July 17 (587); Cooper to Pemberton, July 19 (587); Pemberton to Cooper, July 20 (587–88); Pemberton to Cooper, Aug. 31 (601); and Special Orders, No. 202, Adjutant and Inspector General's Office, Richmond, Aug. 29 (601). Several of these dispatches are duplicated in ibid., vol. 11, pt. 3.

11. Already in Virginia were the brigades of Daniel, Walker, and Ransom and garrisons at Drewry's Bluff and Petersburg. After the transfer of Martin's brigade, these forces totaled 12,504 present for duty. Remaining in North Carolina were French's brigade and the garrisons at Cape Fear and Kinston. See departmental field returns for July 15, 1862, *OR*, vol. 9:476. The 57th North Carolina was ordered to Richmond in August. See *Histories of the Several Regiments and Battalions from North Carolina in the Great War 1861–1865, Written by Members of the Respective Commands*, ed. Walter Clark (Wendell, N.C.: Broadfoot's Bookmark, 1982), 3:406 (hereafter cited as *North Carolina Regiments*); and Special Orders, No. 182, Headquarters, Dept. of Northern Virginia, Aug. 14, 1862, *OR*, vol. 11, 3:675.

12. Special Orders, No. 165, Secretary of War, July 17, 1862, *OR*, vol. 9:476.

13. Clark's letter has not been found but is reflected in Lee's reply of Aug. 8, 1862, *OR*, vol. 9:478–79. Not mentioned in the text above were two regiments from Alabama (47th and 48th) and two from Florida (5th and 8th), which had been started during June but were not incorporated into the Army of Northern Virginia until July.

14. Lee to James Archer and Lee to Wigfall, both July 26, 1862, *OR*, vol. 11, 3:654–55.

15. Davis to Lee, July 5, 1862, *OR*, vol. 11, 3:631–32. For South Carolina, see Lee to Cooper, Aug. 11, 1862, and Lee to Preston, Aug. 12, *OR*, vol. 11, 3:671–72. Lee expected conscripts from Louisiana, but it is not known whether he got them. See Lee to Jackson, July 26, 1862, ibid., vol. 12, 3:917–18. The results from Tennessee and Texas are also not known. See Lee to Archer and Lee to Wigfall, July 26, ibid., vol. 11, 3:654–55. For North Carolina, see ibid., vol. 9:479. The North Carolina conscripts would not arrive until September and would join the army at Frederick, Maryland. On July 23, Lee complained that "the new levies come in so slowly." Long (per Lee) to Loring, ibid., vol. 11, 3:647–48.

16. Entering the Seven Days, Lee had 106,430 men present for duty, including forces from the Department of North Carolina in Virginia but excluding forces in the defenses of Richmond. Tenney, "Seven Days in 1862," 133. After deducting the 20,135 casualties, he should have had 86,295 present for duty on July 2. Projections based on a report for July 20, however, indicate that only 56,260 were present for duty on July 10. *OR*, vol. 11, 3:645. If the difference of 30,035 is reduced by 2,203 (for Martin's brigade, which arrived from North Carolina on July 5), it will be seen that 27,832 men (32.25 percent) were unaccountably missing on July 10. If, as is likely, several thousand men returned to the ranks between July 6 and 10, then over a third of his men were inexplicably absent when Lee wrote his letter to Davis of July 5.

17. Lee to McLaws, July 25, 1862, *OR*, vol. 11, 3:653.

18. According to Armistead Long's journal, as early as June 3 Lee had observed, "There is a great difference between mercenary armies and volunteer armies, and consequently there must be a difference in the mode of discipline. The volunteer army is more easily disciplined by encouraging a patriotic spirit than by a strict enforcement of the Articles of War." Long, *Memoirs of R. E. Lee*, 166. Another manifestation of the army's lack of discipline that Lee confronted at this time was the "depredation" of private property, especially farmers' crops and livestock. See Special Orders, No. —— [*sic*], July 7, 1862, *OR*, vol. 11, 3:636.

19. General Orders No. 63, Headquarters, Dept. of Northern Virginia, June 5, 1862, *OR*, vol. 11, 3:576–77. There is no indication this force guarded the camps to prevent straggling but only that it arrested and returned those who had straggled.

20. Special Orders, No.—— [*sic*], Headquarters, Dept. of Northern Virginia, July 8, 1862, ibid., 636–37.

21. General Orders No. 77, Headquarters, Dept. of Northern Virginia, July 11, 1862, ibid., 639.

22. General Orders No. 94, Headquarters, Dept. of Northern Virginia, Aug. 11, 1862, ibid., vol. 12, 3:928. Also showing the degree to which the problem was on his mind, Lee addressed the issue again in Special Orders, No. 185, Headquarters, Army of Northern Virginia, Aug. 19: "Straggling from the ranks is strictly prohibited, & commanders will make arrangements to secure & punish offenders." Lee, *Wartime Papers*, 259–60.

23. Long to Semmes, July 15, *OR*, vol. 11, 3:643.

24. Lee to Randolph, July 11 and 12, 1862, and Lee to Northrop, Aug. 4, ibid., 638, 640, 662–63.

25. Lee to Cooper, Aug. 7, 1862, ibid., 666.

26. Lee to Hood, Aug. 8, 1862, ibid., 667.

27. Long to Semmes, July 15, 1862, ibid., 643; Lee to Jackson, July 27, ibid., vol. 12, 3:918–19; and Lee to Longstreet, Aug. 1, ibid., vol. 11, 3:659. Another aspect of the problem of estrays was exhibited in Micah Jenkins's brigade, where individuals and groups attempted to leave the army by claiming they had been recruited in units for service elsewhere.

28. Lee to Davis, July 18, 1862, Lee, *Wartime Papers*, 232–33.

29. Field Return for July 20, *OR*, vol. 11, 3:645.

30. A left wing under G. W. Smith (fifteen brigades in the divisions of Whiting, Magruder, and A. P. Hill) and a right wing under Longstreet (thirteen brigades in the divisions of Longstreet, D. H. Hill, and Huger). Smith departed on sick leave, and Longstreet reverted to division command.

31. Jackson's command (fifteen brigades in four divisions): Jackson already commanded two divisions in the Valley (Jackson and Ewell), and he received Whiting before and D. H. Hill during the fighting. Longstreet's command (twelve brigades in two divisions): Longstreet had A. P. Hill added to his own division (led by R. H. Anderson) during the fighting. Magruder's command (six brigades in three divisions): actually nothing more than Magruder's old division but divided into three small divisions under McLaws, Cobb, and D. R. Jones. The divisions of Huger and Holmes (three brigades each) reported directly to Lee.

32. Jackson's command (ten brigades in three divisions): Jackson lost D. H. Hill. Longstreet's command (fourteen brigades in three divisions): Longstreet gained D. R. Jones's small division from Magruder. The old command of Magruder disappeared: D. R. Jones went to Longstreet and the other two divisions (four brigades) were united under McLaws. The four divisions reporting directly to Lee were Huger, Holmes, McLaws, and D. H. Hill.

33. Special Orders, No. 144, Headquarters, Dept. of North Carolina, July 6, 1862, *OR*, vol. 11, 3:635; and two orders headed Special Orders, No. —— [*sic*], Headquarters, Dept. of Northern Virginia, July 7 and 8, 1862, ibid., 636–37.

34. Special Orders, No. 161, Adjutant and Inspector General's Office, July 12, 1862, ibid., 640; and Special Orders, No. 151, Headquarters, Dept. of Northern Virginia, July 14, ibid., 642.

35. Whiting left sometime after July 25 and before August 13. See Lee to Davis, July 25, 1862, ibid., 654; and Special Orders, No. 181, Headquarters, Dept. of Northern Virginia, Aug. 13, 1862, ibid., 675. See also Freeman, *Lee's Lieutenants* 2:64, 258–59.

36. For Holmes, see Special Orders, No. 164, Adjutant and Inspector General's Office, July 16, 1862, ibid., vol. 13:855; and for Magruder, see Special Field Orders No. —— [*sic*], ibid., vol. 11, 3:630.

37. On Lee and the generals removed, see appendix 5, section C.

38. Lee to Mrs. Lee, July 9, 1862, Lee, *Wartime Papers*, 228–30; Freeman, *R. E. Lee* 2:230; and Samuel J. T. Moore, Jr., *Moore's Complete Civil War Guide to Richmond*, rev. ed. (Richmond: Privately printed, 1978), 177–78.

39. Lee to Davis, July 6, 1862, *OR*, vol. 11, 3:634–35; and Lee to Davis, July 18, 1862, Lee, *Wartime Papers*, 232–33.

40. See Lee to Randolph, June 19, *OR*, vol. 11, 3:609; Randolph to Bragg, June 29, ibid., vol. 17, 2:627; and Lee to Davis, July 18, ibid., vol. 51, 2:1074–75.

41. Lee to Randolph, Aug. 4, 1862, ibid., vol. 11, 3:663–64.

42. Lee knew all of this except the latter point before the Seven Days. According to Longstreet, news of the creation of the Army of Virginia and the appointment of Pope was in Richmond by June 29, three days after its announcement by Lincoln in orders. James Longstreet, "Our March Against Pope," *Battles and Leaders* 2:513.

43. Lincoln to Governors, July 1, 1862, Lincoln, *Collected Works* 5:296–97; *New York Tribune*, July 2, 1862; George Templeton Strong, *The Diary of George Templeton Strong*, ed. Allan Nevins (New York: Macmillan, 1952), 3:236; and *OR*, ser. 3, vol. 2:208. No reference by Lee to the North's "new levies" has been found before his letter to Davis of September 3. Lee, *Wartime Papers*, 292.

44. On July 3 Burnside (North Carolina) and Hunter (South Carolina) were ordered to strip their departments to send reenforcements to McClellan. Burnside arrived with some 8,000 men off Fort Monroe on July 7 and Isaac Stevens with some 4,000 from Hunter July 15. Neither disembarked, however, and McClellan got none of their troops. *OR*, vol. 11, 3:290, 305, 322.

45. Lee to Johnston, Mar. 28, 1862, Lee, *Wartime Papers*, 139.

46. According to the historian of the Laurel Brigade, Turner Ashby's twenty-six companies, which were just then becoming the 7th and 12th regiments and 17th battalion of Virginia cavalry under Beverly Robertson, the only force left behind by Jackson, had joined Stonewall at Richmond by July 10. Company B of the 12th was left behind under Lieutenants Milton Rouss and George Baylor in the Valley. See William Naylor McDonald, *A History of the Laurel Brigade, Originally the Ashby Cavalry of the Army of Northern Virginia and Chew's Battery* (Baltimore: Sun Job Printing Office, 1907), 77. The only other force known at this time was the provost-marshal's post at Gordonsville, commanded by Maj. Cornelius Boyle, a doctor from Georgetown, who served in this same capacity for most of the war. See *OR*, ser. 2, vol. 2:80, 1374; and ser. 4, vol. 3:604–6, 611–13, 615, 624.

47. Boyle to Randolph, July 12, 1862, *OR*, vol. 51, 2:590.

48. Special Orders, No. 150, Headquarters, Dept. of Northern Virginia, July 13, 1862, ibid., vol. 12, 3:915. Jackson's instructions are not in these orders but in Lee to Davis, July 18, 1862, Lee, *Wartime Papers*, 232–33. Because of his encampment on the Mechanicsville Turnpike, Jackson was also nearest at hand. It is also worth noting that Whiting (Hood) was detached from Jackson and retained at Richmond.

49. Lee to Holmes, July 13, 1862, *OR*, vol. 11, 3:641. French's brigade totaled 1,421 on July 15. Abstract of the Dept. of North Carolina, ibid., vol. 9:476. Lee apparently learned of

Burnside's withdrawal in a letter from Holmes dated July 12, which has not been discovered. As late as July 25 Lee would still write that Burnside "is said to have been withdrawn from North Carolina." Lee to Jackson, ibid., vol. 12, 3:917. It is important to distinguish between the withdrawal of Federal troops and their arrival elsewhere. There is no evidence that Lee knew of the arrival of either Burnside (on July 7) or Stevens (on July 15) in ships off Fort Monroe before July 26.

50. From Monday, July 14, to Thursday, July 17, only four documents are known to have been issued from Lee's headquarters, all unrelated to strategy. While Lee's nearness to Richmond allowed meetings with Davis and Randolph, none are known during this period. In any case, the meager output of orders and correspondence was highly uncharacteristic. See Special Orders, No. 151, Headquarters, Dept. of Northern Virginia, July 15, 1862, assigning R. H. Anderson to command Huger's division; unsigned to Rhett, July 15, with instructions on Richmond's defenses; and Long [for Lee] to Semmes, July 15, on estrays; *OR*, vol. 11, 3:642, 643–44. Also, Lee to Fitz Lee, July 15, on prisoners of war, Lee, *Wartime Papers*, 231–32.

51. The reports from Jackson on July 17 and Stuart on the 18th have not been found but are reflected in Lee to Davis and Lee to Stuart, July 18, 1862, Lee, *Wartime Papers*, 232–33. Lee's reaction to the news, as quoted in this and the following paragraph, are from the same two dispatches.

52. Lee to Longstreet; Long [for Lee] to Longstreet; and Special Orders, No. 160, Headquarters, Dept. of Northern Virginia; all July 23, 1862, *OR*, vol. 11, 3:646–47. Also, Lee to Jackson, July 23, ibid., vol. 12, 3:916–17.

53. Lee to Jackson, July 23, 1862, ibid.

54. Long [for Lee] to Loring, July 23, 1862, ibid., vol. 11, 3:647–48. The expression that the "enemy seems to be tottering in his various positions" is a curious one. Nothing else found at this time or for the next two weeks suggests that Lee believed the Federals to be shaky or unsteady in any of their positions. It should be noted that this letter was signed by Armistead Long, rather than Lee, and it is possible that "tottering" was poorly chosen to express the notion that enemy forces were in transition (e.g., Burnside in the East and Halleck in the West).

55. Burnside's presence at Fort Monroe is implied in Lee's letter but not stated. See Lee to Jackson, July 25, 1862, *OR*, vol. 12, 3:917.

56. Lee to Davis, July 25, 1862, Lee, *Wartime Papers*, 237.

57. Lee mentions information about the orders coming from the newspapers on July 27, but his changed attitude toward Pope dates from two days earlier. See Lee to Jackson, July 27, 1862, *OR*, vol. 12, 3: 918–19. Pope's orders are published in ibid. 2:50–52.

58. General Orders No. 54, Adjutant and Inspector General's Office, Aug. 1, 1862, *OR*, ser. 2, vol. 4:836–37. For a further note on the Confederates and Pope's orders, see appendix 5, section D.

59. For a discussion of Lee's views on Pope, see appendix 5, section D.

60. Lee to Jackson, July 25, 1862, *OR*, vol. 12, 3:917. Lee here indicated he was thinking of sending A. P. Hill's division, but that its commander was currently under arrest, or D. H. Hill's division, but that unit was without a commander since Harvey Hill had been assigned to the District of North Carolina to replace Holmes. Powell Hill, apparently chaffing at being put under a fellow division commander, had requested transfer from Longstreet's command, and Longstreet had concurred. While Lee had been sitting on the request, Longstreet had arrested Hill for refusal to obey orders from a staff officer. See A. P. Hill to Lee, July 12, with Longstreet's endorsement of July 14, 1862, ibid., vol. 11, 3:639–40. The vastly more complicated story, which included talk of a duel, may be followed in Robertson, *A. P. Hill*, 96–97.

61. Jackson to Lee, July 23, 1862, has not been found but is reflected in Lee to Jackson, July 26, 1862, *OR*, vol. 12, 3:917–18; and in Lee to Davis, July 26, Lee, *Wartime Papers*, 238–39, both of which are quoted above. In the first letter, Lee lectured the "Hero of the Valley": "I was in hopes your stragglers were coming in to you. . . . Let me know your strength. Have field returns every ten days." Jackson was also having trouble with his estrays. Robert Krick has found morning reports for Jackson's own division (Taliaferro), which indicate for August 14 it had 27 percent of its present-for-duty strength absent without leave. See Robert K. Krick, *Stonewall Jackson at Cedar Mountain* (Chapel Hill: Univ. of North Carolina Press, 1990), 372–73.

62. Special Orders, No. 164, Headquarters, Dept. of Northern Virginia, and Lee to Jackson, both July 27, 1862, *OR*, vol. 12, 3:918–19. In his letter Lee again referred to Jackson's missing men and asked, "What has become of them?" He then continued his lecture on straggling.

63. Lee to Randolph, July 28, 1862, *OR*, vol. 11, 2:936. Interestingly, Lee ordered Hill to give out the story that he was moving on Norfolk as a ruse and suggested to Randolph that a similar notice be placed in the *Richmond Dispatch*. This is one of the relatively rare specific examples of Lee's use of dissimulation to confound the enemy. It is curious that Lee, who himself closely read Northern newspapers and normally relied on the information he found there, seems never to have worried about enemy ruses.

64. Lee to Randolph, July 28, 1862, *OR*, vol. 12, 2:936. For a note on the Coggins Point expedition, see appendix 5, section E.

65. Reports on this affair are found in *OR*, vol. 11, 2:934–46. See also Lee to D. H. Hill, Aug. 3, 1862, ibid. 3:660–61; and Lee to D. H. Hill, Aug. 2, 1862, and Lee to Davis, Aug. 17, Lee, *Wartime Papers*, 242, 258–59.

66. Jackson's letter has not been found but is reflected in Lee to Jackson, Aug. 4, 1862, *OR*, vol. 12, 3:922–23, from which the information quoted in the text is also taken.

67. In truth, nothing in the surviving correspondence and reports suggests that Jackson—even three weeks after being sent from Richmond—had anything more than the most general idea of Pope's size, troop disposition, or intentions. In addition to Krick's admirable new study of the tactics of the Confederate side, *Cedar Mountain*, John Hennessy covers Confederate strategy in his new *Return to Bull Run: The Campaign and Battle of Second Manassas* (New York: Simon & Schuster, 1993), a defining study of the Second Manassas campaign.

68. Lee to Jackson, Aug. 4, 1862, *OR*, vol. 12, 3:922–23.

69. Stuart to Lee, Aug. 5, 1862, ibid., 924–25.

70. Federal reports are in ibid. 2:118–26.

71. Stuart to Lee, Aug. 5, 1862, ibid. 3:924–25.

72. On Lee's knowledge of the movements of Burnside, see appendix 5, section F.

73. Lee to Davis, Aug. 7, 1862, Lee, *Wartime Papers*, 246–47.

74. [Chilton] to Hood, Aug. 7, 1862, *OR*, vol. 11, 3:666. Hood commanded Whiting's old division, which had been detached from Jackson and had remained on the Mechanicsville Turnpike. It was thus nearest the new point of danger from the north.

75. Lee to Davis and Lee to Jackson, Aug. 7, 1862, Lee, *Wartime Papers*, 246–47; and in *OR*, vol. 12, 3:925–26. The five divisions were Longstreet, D. R. Jones, Evans (temporary), McLaws, and Ripley (formerly D. H. Hill).

76. Although R. H. Anderson's division—the three brigades that had belonged to Huger—did not receive immediate marching orders, Lee wrote that he wanted it "liberated" from the defenses at Drewry's Bluff. "It is wanted now," he added with uncharacteristic sharpness. Lee to D. H. Hill and [Chilton] to Hood, Aug. 7, 1862, *OR*, vol. 11, 3:666.

77. Lee to D. H. Hill (twice), Aug. 7, 1862, ibid.; and Lee, *Wartime Papers*, 246. Lee referred to the brigades of Walker, Ransom, and Daniel, which Hill had inherited from Holmes

when assuming command of the District of North Carolina.

78. Lee to Davis, Aug. 7, 1862, Lee, *Wartime Papers*, 246–47. Two days later, in describing the affair to his daughters, Lee would write, "I thought they were going to fight the battle over again." Lee to Annie and Agnes Lee, Aug. 9, ibid., 250–51.

79. Lee to Jackson, Aug. 7, 1862, *OR*, vol. 12, 3:925–26.

80. Ibid. Jackson's letter of the 6th has not been found but is amply reflected in Lee's reply.

81. The Confederate confusion about Fredericksburg is understandable, since both Lee and Jackson were partly right. King's division of McDowell's corps of Pope's army was stationed at Fredericksburg when Burnside arrived on August 3 at Aquia Creek. Ibid., 528–29. Thereafter, King was released to join Pope, while Burnside covered Washington. Burnside had with him about 12,000 men in the three small divisions (two from North Carolina and Stevens from South Carolina) that had been united on July 22 to form the Ninth Corps. Ibid., vol. 11, 3:333.

82. Lee to Jackson, Aug. 7, 1862, ibid., vol. 12, 3:925–26 (emphasis added). On the same day, Lee may have tried to influence Stonewall indirectly as well. In writing to Stuart to congratulate him on severing the communications of the brigades of Gibbon and Hatch, the Confederate commander noted that if this force continued to advance, Jackson might be able "to interpose between them and Fredericksburg," and "they would be annihilated." He urged Stuart to give Jackson "all information and co-operation," perhaps, hoping Jackson would bite on the suggestion. Lee to Stuart, Aug. 7, ibid., 925.

83. Once again Jackson's dispatch has not been found, but it is reflected in Lee's reply of Aug. 8, 1862, in ibid., 926. It is not possible to tell if Jackson had received Lee's critique of the 7th before he wrote, but some of the correspondence was passing between Lee and Jackson within twenty-four hours, so he may have.

84. Lee to Jackson, Aug. 8, 1862, ibid.; Lee to Hood, Aug. 8, ibid., vol. 11, 3:667.

85. In addition to Krick's *Cedar Mountain*, see the reports by Pope, Lee, and Jackson in *OR*, vol. 12, 2:132–36, 176–79, 180–85; and John Pope, "The Second Battle of Bull Run," *Battles and Leaders* 2:449–60. Traditionally, Jackson has been credited with 20,000 men and Banks 17,900 at Cedar Mountain, with losses of 1,418 for the Confederates and 2,403 for the Federals. See Krick, *Cedar Mountain*, 362–76; "The Opposing Forces at Cedar Mountain, Va., August 9th, 1862," *Battles and Leaders* 2:495–96; and *OR*, vol. 12, 2:53.

5. "Richmond was never so safe": Lee Evolves a Border Strategy, August 9–26, 1862

1. On Lee's decision to supersede Jackson in command at Gordonsville, see appendix 5, section G.

2. For McLaws's instructions, see Special Orders, No. 177, Headquarters, Dept. of Northern Virginia, Aug. 9, 1862, *OR*, vol. 11, 3:670–71.

3. Sorrel to Wilcox, Pryor, Posey, Kemper, Moore, and Hunton, Aug. 9, 1862, ibid., vol. 51, 2:604. The brigade commanders were ordered to tell no one of their destination.

4. Sorrel to Evans (twice) and Walton, Aug. 10, 1862, and to Mitchell, Aug. 11, ibid., 605, 606, 607.

5. Sorrel to Kemper, Aug. 9, and to Evans, Posey, Wilcox, and Pryor, Aug. 10, ibid., 605–6; also, George Wise, *History of the Seventeenth Virginia Infantry, C.S.A.* (Baltimore: Kelly, Piet & Co., 1870), 92. D. R. Jones's division, comprised only of Toombs's and George T. Anderson's brigades at this time, did not take the train until the 13th, arriving at Gordonsville the same day. Aug. 13, 1862, Osmun Latrobe Diary, Virginia Historical Society. Nathan Evans, with his own and Drayton's brigades, both recently arrived from the Deep South,

was scheduled to follow Jones, but whether he arrived on the 13th or later is unknown. Sorrel to Mitchell, Aug. 11, 1862, *OR*, vol. 51, 2:607.

6. Sorrel to Wise, Aug. 11, 1862, *OR*, vol. 51, 2:607; and Lee to Longstreet, Aug. 14, ibid., vol. 11, 3:676.

7. Lee made the observation to Longstreet, who does not date its occurrence. It is perhaps significant, however, that Old Peter relates the incident during his discussion of his orders to march to Gordonsville. Longstreet, *From Manassas to Appomattox*, 158–59. Ironically, the predicament perceived by Lee did not exist at all; where the Confederate commander viewed three threats, there were for the moment none. Halleck had already ordered McClellan's withdrawal from the James; Burnside was at Fredericksburg, but only to support Pope and cover Washington; and Pope was even then deciding to remain on the defensive until joined by McClellan and Burnside.

8. On Lee's knowledge of McClellan's withdrawal from Harrison's Landing, see appendix 5, section H.

9. All figures are present for duty. Longstreet had 8,514 and D. R. Jones had 3,724 on July 20, for a total of 12,238; but assuming the continuing return of stragglers, the figure probably approached 15,000 by August 10. Field returns, Army of Northern Virginia, *OR*, vol. 11, 3:645. No specific strengths have been found for Evans or Drayton, but field returns for the Department of South Carolina and Georgia for June 30 indicate that the green regiments in the department averaged about 700, which would give Evans 2,400 and Drayton 3,500, for a total of 5,900. Ibid., vol. 14:575–76. The figure in the text has been rounded down to 20,000. The five divisions remaining with Lee, including the reserve artillery and cavalry, totaled 46,843: Ripley, 9,573; McLaws, 7,720; Anderson, 6,136; Hood, 3,860; D. H. Hill, 12,256; Pendleton, 3,257; and Stuart, 4,041.

10. On Lee's unhappiness with Jackson's performance at Gordonsville, see appendix 5, section G.

11. Lee's instructions to Longstreet—probably given on August 9 or 10—are reconstructed from his dispatch of the 14th. Lee to Longstreet, *OR*, vol. 11, 3:676. In the same letter Lee refers to having met with Longstreet before his departure for Gordonsville. This is further evidence that Lee did not originally plan to go to Gordonsville himself. On Longstreet's role in this affair, see appendix 5, section G.

12. Davis seems to have been in an especially combative mood during July and August, as reflected in the letter to a friend previously quoted in chapter 1. Davis to John Forsyth, July 18, 1862, *Papers of Jefferson Davis* 8:293–95. Considering Lee's close relationship with Davis, especially during his first months in command, as well as his nearness to Richmond, it is well-nigh inconceivable that he would not have informed the president before taking a move so hazardous to the capital. Although no evidence contemporaneous with the decision has been found, an exchange of letters almost two weeks later strongly suggests that Davis and Lee had been of one mind from the start of the campaign. See Lee to Davis and Davis to Lee, Aug. 21, 1862, *OR*, vol. 51, 2:609, vol. 12, 3:938–39.

13. Special Orders, No. 177, Headquarters, Dept. of Northern Virginia, Aug. 9, 1862; Long to D. H. Hill, and Special Orders, No. 178, Headquarters, Dept. of Northern Virginia, Aug. 10, *OR*, vol. 11, 3:670–71.

14. McLaws received his alert at three in the morning on August 12. See Drayton to Wise, Aug. 12, 1862, ibid., vol. 51, 2:607; and Long to Smith, Aug. 12, ibid., vol. 11, 3:672. No evidence of a Federal advance has been discovered. However, at about this time the Irish brigade of Sumner's Second Corps was sent to support Pleasonton's cavalry brigade, which was in place at Haxhall's to cover the retreat from Harrison's Landing; and this movement may have given rise to the rumor of an advance. See Pleasonton's report, ibid. 2:965.

15. Lee to Hill, Aug. 13, 1862, ibid. 3:673–74. That Lee had not ordered such close observation of Harrison's Landing earlier is a strong indication he did not suspect a withdrawal prior to this date. Incidentally, nothing of particular importance occurred on the Federal side on the 13th that would have alerted Lee, had it not been for the deserter's report. The next day, however, two army corps would begin to evacuate Harrison's Landing and march to Fort Monroe. Ibid. 1:89.

16. Lee to Hood and Taylor to Stuart, Aug. 13, 1862, ibid. 3:674. Burnside had indeed started Jesse Reno with two of his three divisions westward to join Pope the day before. Ibid., vol. 12, 3:565, 566, 569.

17. Lee to Hood and Taylor to Stuart, Aug. 13, 1862, ibid., vol. 11, 3:674. Lee took the reasonable precaution to tell Stuart to transfer his command only if his scouting confirmed Burnside's movement; and he added to Hood's orders "unless you know to the contrary."

18. It was also on August 13 that Special Orders, No. 181 were issued from Headquarters, Dept. of Northern Virginia. Ibid., 675. For speculation on the dating of this order, see appendix 5, section G.

19. Longstreet's dispatch has not been found but is reflected in Lee to Longstreet, Aug. 14, 1862, OR, vol. 11, 3:676; and Lee to Davis, Aug. 14, Lee, *Wartime Papers*, 253–54; and Longstreet, *From Manassas to Appomattox*, 159. In a relatively rare case of timed Confederate correspondence, Lee received Longstreet's letter at 9:00 A.M., fourteen and a half hours after it was sent at 6:30 the previous evening. For reasons that are not clear, Lee added, "I fear General Pope can be re-enforced quicker than ourselves." Since he cannot have been referring to McClellan, Lee may have thought it still possible to strike Pope before Burnside arrived.

20. Lee to Custis Lee, Aug. 14, 1862, Lee, *Wartime Papers*, 255–56.

21. Lee to G. W. Smith, Aug. 14, 1862, OR, vol. 11, 3:677. Lee's denomination of Smith's command as a "wing" was no doubt his way of retaining control of these forces, including the District of North Carolina, as an integral part of the Army of Northern Virginia. Smith, who may have liked the idea of being considered part of the field army, on August 15 would head an order "Headquarters, Right Wing." By that date, Lee at Gordonsville was already thinking of Longstreet's command as his right wing, thus briefly giving the Army of Northern Virginia two right wings.

22. See the following for Aug. 14, 1862: Lee to Davis, Lee, *Wartime Papers*, 253–54; Lee to Randolph, OR, vol. 11, 3:675–76; Lee to R. H. Anderson, ibid., 677–78; Special Orders, No. 182, Headquarters, Dept. of Northern Virginia, ibid., 675; Long to Hood, ibid., 676–77. Although Lee issued positive orders to R. H. Anderson, he was somewhat less than forthright with Randolph and Davis by seeming merely to suggest the withdrawal of the division. The regiments referred to were the 42d and 57th North Carolina; and the 1st (Volunteers) and 22d South Carolina.

23. Lee to Davis, Aug. 14, 1862, Lee, *Wartime Papers*, 253–54. For additional comments on Lee's report to Davis, see appendix 5, section I.

24. "On the cars" was a contemporary way of distinguishing a passenger train from a freight train; and it was Chilton, writing for Lee, who referred to the Rapidan as the "frontier." See French to Cooper, Aug. 16, 1862, OR, vol. 12, 3:932; Lee to Davis, Aug. 16, Lee, *Wartime Papers*, 256–57; and Chilton to Corley, Aug. 17, OR, vol. 12, 3:933. On the 17th, Randolph would report to Lee "there is no enemy now on this side of the James River and no indications of his presence on the other side." Ibid., 932–33.

25. For a note on Lee's puzzlement over McClellan's withdrawal, see appendix 5, section H.

26. Lee to Davis, Aug. 17, 1862, OR, vol. 51, 2:1075–76; also Lee to wife, Aug. 17, Lee, *Wartime Papers*, 257–58. At this time, Walter Taylor of Lee's staff wrote: "Our march cannot

be too rapid, as the great desideratum is to strike Pope before 'Little Mac' reaches this section." Taylor to sister, Aug. 17, *Lee's Adjutant*, 39.

27. Freeman, *R. E. Lee* 2:279; see also, Longstreet, *From Manassas to Appomattox*, 159.

28. No orders dated August 16 have been found. See appendix 6, section A.

29. Lee to Davis, with Davis's affirmative endorsement, and Special Orders, No. 150, Adjutant and Inspector General's Office, Aug. 15, 1862, *OR*, vol. 11, 3:678, 679. G. W. Smith, in his capacity as commander of the Richmond wing, responded to the loss of R. H. Anderson by ordering D. H. Hill to extend his lines to cover the entire south side, including Drewry's Bluff. Smith also stationed his own division (formerly Ripley's) by the pontoon bridge so that it could support either Hill or McLaws, who defended the north bank from Chaffin's Bluff.

30. Confederate numbers are from the July 20, 1862, field returns, ibid., 645. Lee had heard numbers as high as 92,000 for Pope but disbelieved them. Lee to Davis, Aug. 16, 1862, and Lee to wife, Aug. 17, Lee, *Wartime Papers*, 256–58.

31. Boswell's report, *OR*, vol. 12, 2:648–49. Boswell suggested the Confederates proceed from Somerville Ford directly to Beverly Ford, cross the Rappahannock, and march on Warrenton. Lee more modestly planned to interpose between Pope and the Rappahannock, perhaps because he was unwilling to advance as far as Warrenton at this early date in the campaign.

32. Pope's report and field returns for July 31, 1862, ibid., 28–29, 53.

33. Stuart recalled the attacks were to have been carried out "simultaneously." Stuart's report, ibid., 725. Douglas Freeman hypothesized that Lee intended to trap Pope in the V formed by the fork of the Rapidan and the Rappahannock. Freeman, *R. E. Lee* 2:279–80. This makes no sense, however, based on Pope's position of either August 10 or 14. In either case, it would be Lee who would enter the narrow neck of the *V* and be in danger of entrapment, while the direction of Lee's attack—if successful—would have pushed Pope out the open end to the west.

34. The cavalry brigade of Jackson's command—under Beverly Robertson—had been added to Stuart's division on August 17. Special Orders, No. 183, Headquarters, Dept. of Northern Virginia, *OR*, vol. 12, 3:933–34. Robertson had then been shifted to the Confederate right to participate in the raid. Fitz Lee's brigade had been the force operating out of Hanover Junction to watch the Federals at Fredericksburg. Hampton's brigade remained with the wing on the James. For the controversy over Fitz Lee's late arrival and a defense of the newly minted brigadier, see Freeman, *R. E. Lee* 2:284–86; and Lee to Stuart and [Chilton] to Stuart, Aug. 18, 1862, *OR*, vol. 12, 3:934.

35. Chilton to Corley (twice), and Lee to Stuart, Aug. 17, 1862, *OR*, vol. 12, 3:933, 934. This is another example of how American armies had yet to decipher the impact of railroads on the conduct of war.

36. Lee to Davis, Aug. 17, 1862, ibid., vol. 51, 2:1075–76.

37. Longstreet, *From Manassas to Appomattox*, 161–62. For a further note on Lee's visit to Clark's Mountain and his humor at Pope's expense, see appendix 6, section B.

38. Lee to Davis, Aug. 16, 1862, Lee, *Wartime Papers*, 256–57; Lee to Davis, with Davis's endorsement, Aug. 15, *OR*, vol. 11, 3:678; [Chilton] to Corley, Aug. 17, ibid., vol. 12, 3:933.

39. Randolph to Lee, Randolph to Davis, and Cooper to Smith, Aug. 17, 1862, *OR*, vol. 12, 3:932–33; and Smith to Pendleton, Aug. 18, ibid., 965. Apparently, Colquitt's brigade of the Ripley/Smith division would have departed for Gordonsville on the 18th had it not been for "want of transportation." Davis to Lee, Aug. 18, ibid., 935. The snarl on the railroads had become so bad that the War Department proposed sending the division by way of Lynchburg, but Lee protested that the remedy would be worse than the problem, as it would "prevent transportation of supplies from that point." He suggested the division simply be marched by foot.

40. Lee to Davis, Aug. 17, 1862, ibid., vol. 51, 2:1075–76; and Davis to Lee, Aug. 21, ibid., vol. 12, 3:938–39. On August 21 D. H. Hill left Petersburg to resume command of the five brigades he had led during the Seven Days and that had been under their senior brigadier (Ripley) and briefly under G. W. Smith. From this point forward this division will be referred to as D. H. Hill's. See Hal Bridges, *Lee's Maverick General, Daniel Harvey Hill* (New York: McGraw Hill, 1961), 89. The District of North Carolina would shortly be given to Brig. Gen. James G. Martin, although the forces in the Petersburg area would be commanded by Brig. Gen. Samuel G. French, and the brigades of Ransom and Walker would later join the Army of Northern Virginia under Brig. Gen. John G. Walker.

41. Lee to Randolph, and Melton to Pendleton, Aug. 19, 1862, *OR*, vol. 12, 3:937, 965. Coincidentally, Randolph suggested the same thing. Randolph to Lee, Aug. 19, ibid., 936–37. On McClellan's reappearance at White House, see in ibid., pt. 3: French to [Cooper?], Aug. 16, 1862 (p. 932); Davis to Lee, Aug. 18 (935); Randolph to Lee, Aug. 19 (936–37); and French to Randolph, Aug. 21 (938).

42. Lee to Davis, Aug. 21, 1862, Lee, *Wartime Papers*, 261. Freeman, ignoring the rest of Lee's telegram, assumed that Lee asked this question of Davis after concluding Pope had formed a line behind the Rappahannock and that his question therefore referred only to the possibility of a Confederate move to cross higher up that river. The normally careful Freeman also implies that Lee decided at this point to halt McLaws and D. H. Hill on the North Anna, but Lee had done that two days before. See Freeman, *R. E. Lee* 2:292.

43. Davis to Lee, Aug. 21, 1862, *OR*, vol. 12, 3:938–39; strengths from July 20 field returns, ibid., vol. 11, 3:645. These figures do not include Hampton's cavalry brigade or the forces permanently garrisoning the capital; and it is not clear whether at this point Hampton had been retained at Richmond or sent to Hanover Junction. Smith's forces included the brigades of Wise, Ransom, Walker, Martin, and Daniel.

44. In *OR*, vol. 12, pt. 2, see the official reports of Lee (pp. 552–53), Longstreet (563–64), Jackson (642), and Stuart (729–30). See also Longstreet, *From Manassas to Appomattox*, 163–64, and "Raid against Pope," 515. On the 20th, Robertson encountered at Brandy Station a body of Federal cavalry that had fallen back across the river. The next day the 5th Virginia Cavalry made a lodgment for several hours on the north bank at Beverly Ford. Pope determined on August 20 to stand behind Marsh Run three miles north of the river, but early on the morning of the 21st he returned to take position directly behind the Rappahannock. See Pope to Halleck, Aug. 20 and 21, 1862, *OR*, vol. 12, 2:56–57.

45. In addition to the reports cited in note 44 above, in *OR*, vol. 12, pt. 2, see the reports of Walton (p. 569), D. R. Jones (578), and Wilcox (595–96). And Stuart confirms that the decision was made "late in the afternoon" (920).

46. In addition to the reports cited in notes 44 and 45 above, see Early's in ibid., 705–7.

47. Lee to Davis, Aug. 23, 1862, ibid. 3:940–41. He had, however, sent the brief telegram on the 21st noted above.

48. On the Kanawha Valley situation, Lee also wrote to Randolph and directly to Loring, both on the 23d. *OR*, vol. 12, 3:941–42. The latter is quoted.

49. Lee to Davis, Aug. 23, 1862, ibid., 940–44.

50. Historians are in the fortunate position of being able to know not only the entire contents of the Pope dispatch Lee believed so important, but also to know something of Lee's interpretation of the intelligence it contained. The captured dispatch, a telegram, may be found in *OR*, vol. 12, 3:603; and Lee's comments on Pope's strengths and plans are in Lee to Davis, ibid., 942. Lee erred in not realizing that Reno's corps of two small divisions was all of Burnside's that were ever intended to join Pope. Burnside would remain with his third division at Fredericksburg and Aquia. In that it gave a detailed view of the strength of his army, Pope's lost dispatch was more useful to Lee than Special Orders, No. 191, would be to McClellan on September 13.

51. Lee to Davis, Aug. 24, 1862, ibid.

52. Ibid. For a further note on Lee's dispatch to Davis of August 24, see appendix 6, section C.

53. Recent historical scholarship has been disinclined to question Lee's basic strategy in the Second Manassas campaign, finding his move bold and brilliant without questioning all of its implications and complications. But, in an earlier day, John Codman Ropes concluded, "It was a dangerous move, [and] . . . the object proposed was not worth the risk." Ropes, *The Army under Pope* (New York: Charles Scribner's Sons, 1882), 44. For a well-informed and thoughtful coverage that gives somewhat different emphases and reaches somewhat different conclusions than the ones found here, see Hennessy, *Return to Bull Run*, chap. 5.

54. Henry Kyd Douglas, *I Rode with Stonewall: Being Chiefly the War Experiences of the Youngest Member of Jackson's Staff from the John Brown Raid to the Hanging of Mrs. Surratt* (Chapel Hill: Univ. of North Carolina Press, 1940), 132–33. For a further note on this war council, see appendix 6, section D.

55. See the reports of Lee and Jackson, *OR*, vol. 12, 2:553–54, 644–45.

56. See the reports of Jackson and Boswell, ibid., 643, 650. See also appendix 6, section D.

57. For further discussion of Lee's original intentions in the Second Manassas campaign, see appendix 3, section F.

58. See the reports of Lee and Longstreet, *OR*, vol. 12, 2:554, 564.

59. Longstreet, "March against Pope," 517.

60. See the reports of Boswell and Stuart, *OR*, vol. 12, 2:650, 733–34. A portion of the cavalry was engaged on August 24 and 25 in repulsing a Federal crossing at Waterloo Bridge, but this does not explain why a full brigade could not have been sent with Jackson at the start.

61. Jackson's march is admirably covered in Freeman, *Lee's Lieutenants* 2:84–91; see also the reports of Jackson and Boswell, *OR*, vol. 12, 2:645, 650.

62. Banks to Ruggles, Aug. 25, 1862 (11:25 A.M.), Smith to Sigel, Aug. 24, and Pope to Halleck, Aug. 24, ibid., 66–67, 65, 64.

63. In *OR*, vol. 12, pt. 2, see the reports of Heintzelman (p. 412), Walker (426), Ward (429), Berry (433), Grover (438), and Carr (453) and the itinerary of the Fifth Corps (465). Present-for-duty strengths for the Third and Fifth corps are from field returns for Aug. 10, 1862, ibid., vol. 11, 3:367.

64. Pope to Sigel and Pope to McDowell, Aug. 25, 1862 (9:30 P.M.), ibid., vol. 12, 2:67.

65. Pope to McDowell, Aug. 26, 1862 (12 m. [which apparently was mistaken for midnight]), and Clark to Pope, Aug. 26 (3:45 P.M.), ibid., 70, 69. At this time Longstreet was pulling out of line, but R. H. Anderson's division remained.

66. Pope's report and General Orders No. —— [*sic*], Aug. 27, 1862, ibid., 35, 70–71.

67. Lee to wife, Aug. 25, 1862, Lee, *Wartime Papers*, 264–65.

68. Lee to Gilmer and Lee to Randolph, Aug. 25, 1862, *OR*, vol. 12, 3:944, 943.

69. Lee to Davis, Aug. 25, 1862, Lee, *Wartime Papers*, 264. It is not clear from surviving evidence when Lee discovered that some of the Federal forces were coming from Alexandria. If he had known it on the 24th, however, his plan to send Jackson to either Bristoe or Manassas would not have been so attractive, as it was sending Jackson into the teeth of a pincer.

70. Lee to Davis, Aug. 25, 1862, Lee, *Wartime Papers*, 264.

71. Davis to Lee, Aug. 25, 1862, *OR*, vol. 12, 3:944. It is not certain that Lee received the telegram from Davis on the same day. Unfortunately, unlike the Federals, the Confederates seldom noted the hours sent or received on their messages. See also the reports of Stuart and Lee, ibid. 2:734, 554.

72. Lee's report, Lee, *Wartime Papers*, 278.

73. Sigel's report, *OR*, vol. 12, 2:263–64. No such order has surfaced and likely did not exist. Pope not only expected Sigel to remain at Waterloo but sent him an order for the following morning to force a passage at the bridge. See Pope's report, ibid., 33–35; and Pope to Sigel, Aug. 25, 1862, ibid., 67. See also Pope, "Second Battle of Bull Run," 461–63.

74. For a discussion of the timing of Lee's decision to abandon the Rappahannock and follow Jackson, see appendix 6, section E.

75. Since Lee's telegram to Davis on August 26 was received on the same day, it may islikely that Davis's did the same. Lee, *Dispatches*, 52. Moreover, the telegram Lee sent to Davis late in the afternoon of the 27th was received and answered by the president within twenty-four hours. Lee, *Wartime Papers*, 265–66; *OR*, vol. 12, 3:946.

76. Davis to Lee, Aug. 26, 1862, *OR*, vol. 12, 3:945. In June, Wise's brigade numbered only 1,901 and Daniel's 1,862. Tenney, *Seven Days in 1862*, 196, 188.

77. Marshall, *Aide-de-Camp*, 73.

6. "If we expect to reap advantage": Lee Pursues Total Victory,
August 27–31, 1862

1. Lee to Davis, Aug. 30, 1862, Lee, *Wartime Papers*, 266–67.

2. For a contrary view that Lee intended battle in the Manassas area, see Hennessy, *Return to Bull Run*, chap. 8.

3. Munford later wrote, "On the evening of the 26th, the advanced guard captured some 12 or 15 Yankees at Hay Market and Gainesville. They seemed entirely ignorant of any movements of our army, and we pressed on toward Bristoe Station." This report—the import of which is ignored by Freeman—seems to indicate that Munford knew his destination by the time the vanguard reached Gainesville. Hence, whether Jackson originally intended Manassas or Bristoe, he likely made up his mind for the former before the main body reached Gainesville. Since Stuart joined the column at the latter place, he would not have been able to influence the decision. See Munford's report, undated, *OR*, vol. 12, 2:747. Also see Freeman, *Lee's Lieutenants* 2:89, including n. 36.

4. Munford's report, *OR*, vol. 12, 2:747.

5. In *OR*, vol. 12, pt. 2, see Jackson's report (p. 643); Lee's report, in which he accepted and repeated Jackson's reason (554); and reports of Trimble (720–21) and Stuart (734, 739).

6. Classic coverage of the plunder scene may be found in Freeman, *Lee's Lieutenants* 2:100–101; see also in *OR*, vol. 12, pt. 2, the reports of Jackson (p. 645), Boswell (651), Taliaferro (655–56), Early (708), and Trimble (721).

7. This affair, known as the engagement at Bull Run Bridge, cost the Federals more than 500 casualties. Fitzhugh Lee apparently missed the fact that other Federal troops, including two Ohio regiments from Cox's Kanawha division, were also present. See Fitzhugh Lee, *General Lee*, 187, 193. In *OR*, vol. 12, pt. 2, see the reports of Scammon (pp. 405–6) and Waagner (401). The reports of A. P. Hill and Archer make it seem likely that Hill's brigades were ordered forward before they had become involved in the looting. Ibid., 670, 699. Taylor's strength is estimated from the Army of the Potomac field returns for August 10, ibid., vol. 11, 3:367. Other sources used for the account in the text, all from *OR*, vol. 12, pt. 2, include the itinerary of the Sixth Corps (p. 537) and the reports of Brown (541) and Stuart (735).

8. The destruction of the Bull Run railroad bridge is confirmed in Herman Haupt, *Reminiscences of General Herman Haupt* (Milwaukee: Wright & Joy Co., 1901), 109ff.

9. See the reports of Early and McDowell, *OR*, vol. 12, 2:709, 335.

10. For further discussion of Jackson's movements on the night of August 27 and analysis of the sources, see appendix 6, section F.

11. As will be developed below, Jackson did keep open communications with Lee. Since couriers were regularly passing through Thoroughfare Gap without incident, apparently neither Jackson nor Stuart felt compelled to return any cavalry to the main body.

12. For the strength and distribution of Confederate forces in the Virginia theater on August 27, 1862, see appendix 2, section D.

13. For the strength and distribution of Federal forces in the Virginia theater on August 27, 1862, see appendix 2, section D.

14. The Black Horse Troop was Company H, 4th Virginia Cavalry, of Fitzhugh Lee's brigade; its members were from Faquier and Loudoun counties. Information regarding the couriers comes from sworn statements by two of them, James Vass and W. H. Lewis, Virginia State Library. See the reports of Lee and Longstreet, *OR*, vol. 12, 2:555, 564; Longstreet, *From Manassas to Appomattox*, 170, and "March against Pope," 517. As always, Freeman can be counted on to capture the drama and stray colorful incidents of the event. See Freeman, *R. E. Lee* 2:308–12.

15. Lee to Davis, Aug. 27, 1862, Lee, *Wartime Papers*, 265–66.

16. Jubal Early establishes the time for Ewell's division, and Hill was already en route when he received the revised order discussed below. In *OR*, vol. 12, pt. 2, see the reports of Taliaferro (p. 656), Early (710), and A. P. Hill (670).

17. A. P. Hill's report, ibid., 670. Jackson wrote in his report, "Dispositions were made to attack the enemy, based upon the idea that he would continue to press forward upon the turnpike toward Alexandria." Ibid., 644.

18. Johnson's report, ibid. Freeman is correct that there is no conclusive proof Jackson received the captured dispatches. Freeman, *Lee's Lieutenants* 2:106n. 41. But Jackson's comment in his report that "there was reason to believe that [Pope's] main body was leaving the road and inclining toward Manassas Junction" is strong presumptive evidence. *OR*, vol. 12, 2:644–45. And Stuart's testimony that he discussed a captured dispatch with Jackson that morning should settle the question.

19. Stuart's report, *OR*, vol. 12, 2:735. The important point here is whether or not Jackson knew Lee had been challenged at the gap before he decided to attack Pope. It is possible, of course, that Stuart sent the news but that it arrived after Jackson was engaged with King. Stuart's report also raises the interesting possibility that the original or a copy of Pope's captured dispatch was sent to Lee.

20. In *OR*, vol. 12, pt. 2, see the reports of Pope (p. 37), McDowell (336–37), and Gibbon (377–78).

21. Freeman, *Lee's Lieutenants* 2:107–8, dramatically recounts Jackson in the act of deciding to attack. The time is established in Doubleday's report, *OR*, vol. 12, 2:369. See the recent admirable tactical study, Alan D. Gaff, *Brave Men's Tears: The Iron Brigade at Brawner Farm*, 2d rev. ed. (Dayton, Ohio: Morningside Press, 1988).

22. Longstreet's report establishes the time at 3 P.M. *OR*, vol. 12, 2:564. And A. L. Long asserts that nothing had recently been heard from Jackson. Long, *Memoirs of R. E. Lee*, 194. See also Longstreet, "March against Pope," 517–18; and Latrobe, Diary, Aug. 28, 1862.

23. See the reports of McDowell and Ricketts, *OR*, vol. 12, 2:336, 383–85. For Ricketts's present-for-duty strength as of August 16, see ibid. 3:580.

24. Freeman gives an excellent tactical coverage of this small encounter in *R. E. Lee* 2:313–16. He closes, however, with the assertion that "Only the open road lay before [Lee] now." This was in fact true, but without cavalry reconnaissance Lee could not have known where Ricketts had gone or what other Federal forces lay in his path.

25. Pope, "Second Battle of Bull Run," 470.

26. Ibid., 470–71; and Pope's report, *OR*, vol. 12, 2:38. The tactical history of Second Manassas is superbly detailed in the sixteen maps by John Hennessy and his meticulous

Second Manassas Battlefield Map Study (Lynchburg: H. E. Howard, 1991), which accompanies them. In this instance see Map No. 3 and pp. 60–61 in the text.

27. Marshall's testimony, U.S. War Department, *Proceedings and Report of the Board of Army Officers Convened by Special Order No. 78, Headquarters of the Army, Washington, D.C., April 12, 1878, in the Case of Fitz John Porter*, 3 vols. (Washington: GPO, 1879), 2:202 (hereafter cited as *Porter Proceedings*); and Hood's report, *OR*, vol. 12, 2:605.

28. William Miller Owen, *In Camp and Battle with the Washington Artillery of New Orleans: A Narrative of Events during the Late Civil War, from Bull Run to Appomattox and Spanish Fort* (Boston: Ticknor and Co., 1885), 114.

29. The version in the text attempts to reconcile the contradiction noted by Freeman between Napier Bartlett and William Owen over whether the dramatic conversation took place between Lee and Robertson or Lee and Stuart. Freeman, *R. E. Lee* 2:318n. 3; Bartlett, *A Soldier's Story of the War* (New Orleans: Clark & Hofeline, 1874), 127; and Owen, *In Camp and Battle*, 114. It is likely there were two meetings: one with Robertson at or before Haymarket and another with Stuart between Haymarket and Gainesville. This is supported by Stuart's report in *OR*, vol. 12, 2:736; and by Robertson's testimony, *Porter Proceedings* 2:216. It also makes more sense to believe that Stuart did not recommend the Haymarket-Sudley Springs Road to Lee because the column had passed it, rather than that Stuart was ignorant of the road.

30. John Hennessy summarizes the testimony on this point that was crucial in the court-martial of Fitz John Porter. See Hennessy, *Map Study*, 76, and *Return to Bull Run*, 224–29.

31. Longstreet, "March against Pope," 519–20. Lee's question was overheard by Owen, but it should be noted that neither it nor Longstreet's reply necessarily refer to an all-out attack. Owen, *In Camp and Battle*, 117. It should also be noted that Owen's account is not, strictly speaking, an independent verification of Longstreet's version, since Longstreet admits elsewhere in his article that he has read Owen's diary and taken it into account. Longstreet, "March against Pope," 518. Also see Longstreet's *From Manassas to Appomattox*, 181–84, for a variant telling.

32. Longstreet, "March against Pope," 520, and *From Manassas to Appomattox* 183–84. Curiously, Hood would write his report less than a month later and refer to an order "to move forward and attack the enemy" without any reference to reconnaissance, forced or otherwise. *OR*, vol. 12, 2:605. On the engagement, see Hennessy, *Map Study*, 202–10, 215–21.

33. Longstreet, "March against Pope," 519–20 (where he uses the phrase "strong position"), and *From Manassas to Appomattox*, 183–84 (where he notes the scout by Hood and Wilcox). Neither Hood nor Wilcox makes any mention of the nocturnal survey in their reports. *OR*, vol. 12, 2:598, 605.

34. See Freeman in *R. E. Lee* 2:325, 347–48, and *Lee's Lieutenants* 2:137–38, where he suggests that the seeds for future disasters, especially at Gettysburg, were sown on August 29. For a further note on the Lee-Longstreet disagreement, see appendix 6, section G.

35. Longstreet, "March against Pope," 520, and *From Manassas to Appomattox*, 186; Marshall in *Porter Proceedings* 2:212. Freeman pieces together accounts by three privates to assume Lee, Jackson, Longstreet, and Stuart conferred at the same time, but Marshall doubted Longstreet and Jackson met with Lee at the same time. Freeman, *Lee's Lieutenants* 2:122; Marshall in *Porter Proceedings* 2:212.

36. Lee to Davis, Aug. 30, 1862, Lee, *Wartime Papers*, 266–67. The hour of the letter is unknown, but clearly Lee wrote it before Longstreet's attack in midafternoon. As Sir Frederick Maurice has noted in editing Charles Marshall's recollections, this letter was not published until years after Marshall's death and therefore was not available to him for reference. It nevertheless confirms the essential elements of Lee's strategy as outlined by his former aide. Marshall, *Aide-de-Camp*, 130n. 9.

37. For many years, Kenneth Powers Williams, a full-time mathematics professor who pursued the Civil War as an avocation, stood all but alone as a defender of Pope in print. Williams's five-volume *Lincoln Finds a General* (New York: Macmillan, 1949–59), a caustic and highly opinionated work, won few converts. A recent biography explains Pope in terms of the difficulties he faced, which is certainly a step in the right direction. See Wallace J. Schutz and Walter N. Trenery, *Abandoned by Lincoln: A Military Biography of General John Pope* (Urbana: Univ. of Illinois Press, 1990).

38. This estimate of the ratio of the two armies is based on a study of the extant regimental and company morning reports in the National Archives, John Owen Allen, "The Strength of the Union and Confederate Forces at Second Manassas" (master's thesis, George Mason University, Fairfax, Virginia, 1993), 154, 166–69, 202. According to Allen, on August 30, John Pope had present for duty 70,082 men, including Banks's corps (pp. 102, 114); and Lee had present for duty 55,097, including R. H. Anderson's division (175). These figures are close to those eventually agreed upon by survivors of the Civil War generation. See William Allan and John Codman Ropes, "Strength of the Forces under Pope and Lee," *PMHSM* 2 (rev. ed.): 211, 218.

39. For a discussion of the defects of Lee's troop dispositions, see appendix 6, section H.

40. While Lee could get no news of his reenforcements, Pope could expect some 31,000 men in the corps of Franklin and Sumner and the divisions of Cox and Burnside. Another 5,000 were on the way from Fort Monroe in Couch's division of the Fourth Corps. Similarly, while the Confederates were short in every category of provisions, the Federals were supplied by the Orange and Alexandria Railroad through Union Mills, and the bridge over Bull Run was being repaired even as the battle was being fought, which would open the road through Manassas Junction. See Haupt, *Reminiscences*, 125.

41. This interpretative summary of the battle is based on Hennessy, *Map Study:* for the Federals, see pp. 226–28, 240–41, 261–62, 271–72; for the Confederates, see pp. 248, 279.

42. See ibid.: for Federals, see pp. 283, 286–90, 293, 294–300; for Confederates, see pp. 303–7, 308.

43. See ibid., 316–451.

44. Freeman, *R. E. Lee* 2:337; Longstreet, "March against Pope," 521; and Marshall, *Aide-de-Camp*, 140.

45. Lee to Davis, Aug. 30, 1862 (twice), Lee, *Wartime Papers*, 266–57; and Lee, *Dispatches*, 59.

46. Lee's report, *OR*, vol. 19, 1:144. Lee's perception of frontiers may be seen in Lee to Davis, Aug. 16, 1862, Lee, *Wartime Papers*, 256–57; Chilton to Corley, Aug. 17, *OR*, vol. 12, 3:933; Lee to Davis, Aug. 23, ibid., 941; and Lee to Davis, Aug. 30, Lee, *Wartime Papers*, 266–67.

47. No overall estimate by Lee of Federal losses in the Second Manassas campaign have been found. He did report, however, the capture of 7,000 prisoners of war and estimate the enemy losses in killed and wounded to be 8,000 for August 29 alone. If he believed the losses in the fighting on the 28th and 30th comparable, he must have reckoned the total to be in excess of 20,000. Lee to Davis, Sept. 3, 1862, Lee, *Wartime Papers*, 269–70. On September 13 Lee wrote to Davis, "I have reason to hope that our casualties in battle will not exceed five thousand men." Lee, *Wartime Papers*, 307.

48. For a discussion of losses at Second Manassas, see appendix 2, section E.

49. Robertson's brigade was at hand, having led the pursuit the night before and clashed with Buford's Federal brigade near Lewis Ford in the largest cavalry battle of the war up to that point. Fitz Lee's brigade, having returned from the reconnaissance to Fairfax Court House, was protecting Jackson's left flank at Sudley Springs. In *OR*, vol. 12, pt. 2, see the reports of Stuart (pp. 737–38) and Munford (749). See also Fitzhugh Lee, *General Lee*, 193–94; and Heros von Borcke, *Memoirs of the Confederate War for Independence* (New York: Peter Smith, 1938), 1:161–62.

50. Longstreet, *From Manassas to Appomattox*, 191; Douglas, *I Rode with Stonewall*, 142. In their official reports, Lee referred to "the prevalence of a heavy rain," and Longstreet to a day that was "stormy and disagreeable." *OR*, vol. 12, 2:557, 566. Douglas commented that it had rained after First Bull Run and Malvern Hill. The artillerist/diarist William Owen made the more scientific observation: "It is raining hard, as it always does after a heavy cannonade." Owen, *In Camp and Battle*, 126.

51. Von Borcke, *Memoirs* 1:161; Longstreet, *From Manassas to Appomattox*, 193.

52. Stuart's report, *OR*, vol. 12, 2:738. The Texas brigade seized the ambulances as "fresh captures." This is probably the origin of the controversy that arose and led to Hood's arrest.

53. The reports of Stuart, Walton, and Rosser, *OR*, vol. 12, 2:738, 743, 572, 751; Charles Winder Squires, "'Boy Officer' of the Washington Artillery—Part I," *Civil War Times Illustrated* 14 (1975): 17. The Federal force encountered by Stuart at Cub Run was most likely Reynolds's division of Pennsylvania Reserves or, less likely, Stevens's division of Reno's corps. *OR*, vol. 12, 2:399.

54. For a discussion of Lee's injury, see appendix 6, section I.

55. For a discussion of Lee's movements on August 31, see appendix 6, section J.

56. Lee to Jackson, Aug. 4, 1862, *OR*, vol. 12, 3:923.

57. For Ripley and Colquitt, whose arrival on August 30 has previously gone largely unnoticed, see *OR*, vol. 12, 3:942, 965; Henry Walter Thomas, *History of the Doles-Cook Brigade, Army of Northern Virginia, C.S.A.* (1903; reprint, Dayton, Ohio: Morningside House, 1988), 469; and William Lord DeRosset, "Additional Sketch Third Regiment," *North Carolina Regiments* 1:223. For the remainder of D. H. Hill (G. B. Anderson, Garland, and Rodes) and McLaws's division, see *OR*, vol. 12, 3:948, and vol. 19, 1:1019; and Bridges, *D. H. Hill*, 89–90. For Hampton's cavalry, see *OR*, vol. 12, 2:744, and vol. 19, 1:822. For Walker's division, see *OR*, vol. 12, 3:948–49; and John George Walker, "Jackson's Capture of Harper's Ferry," *Battles and Leaders* 2:604. The story of the reenforcing column is covered in greater detail in *Taken at the Flood*, forthcoming.

58. Longstreet, *From Manassas to Appomattox*, 191.

59. Fitzhugh Lee, *General Lee*, 193–94. For strengths, see appendix 2, section E.

60. Stuart's report, *OR*, vol. 12, 2:744; von Borcke, *Memoirs* 1:168–69. The distances involved would have put Stuart's nocturnal visit in the vicinity of the crossroads called Frying Pan. It is highly likely, therefore, that the "old friend" was Laura Ratcliffe, to whom Stuart had been writing letters since December 1861. See Thomas Low, "Letters to Laura," *Civil War Times Illustrated* 32 (July 1992): 12ff.

61. Longstreet, *From Manassas to Appomattox*, 192–93, describes the Gum Spring Road.

62. Lee explained Jackson's progress as "retarded by the inclemency of the weather and the fatigue of his troops, who, in addition to their arduous marches, had fought three severe engagements in as many days." *OR*, vol. 12, 2:558. But Lee must have been referring to the net progress of August 31 and September 1, as it is hardly a fair depiction of Jackson's march of the 31st.

Intermezzo. "The war was thus transferred from interior to frontier": The Chantilly Fumble, September 1, 1862

1. Reports of Jackson and Stuart, *OR*, vol. 12, 2:647, 744; neither mentions hours. Stuart tacitly admitted not having reported previously by stating, "Next morning I returned by way of Frying Pan, to connect with General Jackson and inform him of the enemy as far as ascertained." According to two recent historians, the Stuart-Jackson meeting occurred at either eight or nine in the morning, but neither cites any evidence to support his claim. See Joseph W. Whitehorne, "A Beastly, Comfortless Conflict: The Battle of Chantilly, September 1, 1862," *Blue & Gray Magazine* 4 (1987): 17; and Robert Ross Smith, "Ox Hill: The Most

Neglected Battle of the Civil War," in *Fairfax County and the War Between the States* (Fairfax: Fairfax County Civil War Centennial Commission, 1961), 29. On the other hand, von Borcke, who had been with Stuart at Frying Pan, observed that "the morning of the 1st of September passed off quietly enough"—before mentioning that he and his chief rode to join Stonewall. Moreover, the Prussian staff officer states that the orders for the reconnaissance came from Jackson "about noon." Von Borcke, *Memoirs* 1:169–70.

2. Stuart's report, *OR*, vol. 12, 2:744.

3. Ibid. "Jermantown" is the correct historical spelling for the small community, although Civil War maps frequently refer to it as "Germantown."

4. Smith, "Ox Hill," 43–44. There is no existing evidence on how Jackson discovered the approach of Reno, but since Robertson's brigade was patrolling the area, it is reasonable to assume cavalry scouts of his brigade provided the warning.

5. This brief summary is based on the admirable tactical studies by Smith, "Ox Hill," and Whitehorne, "A Beastly, Comfortless Conflict," the latter unfortunately undocumented.

6. Longstreet, *From Manassas to Appomattox*, 194. D. R. Jones led Longstreet's column, as he reported he advanced the brigades of Toombs and G. T. Anderson into the woods in support of Jackson. *OR*, vol. 12, 2:580. This is confirmed in Latrobe, Diary, Sept. 1, 1862.

7. Pender to wife, Sept. 2, 1862, William Dorsey Pender, *The General to His Wife: The Civil War Letters of William Dorsey Pender to Fanny Pender*, ed. William Woods Hassler (Chapel Hill: Univ. of North Carolina Press, 1965), 170.

8. Lee broke up his headquarters at Manassas on the afternoon of the 31st, but it is not clear where he spent the night. See Freeman, *R. E. Lee* 2:342; D. M. Perry, "The Time of Longstreet's Arrival at Groveton," *Battles and Leaders* 2:527; William Willis Blackford, *War Years with Jeb Stuart* (New York: Charles Scribner's Sons, 1945), 135; and Luther Wesley Hopkins, *From Bull Run to Appomattox: A Boy's View* (Baltimore: Fleet-McGinley, 1908), 50.

9. The sole source for this interview is a memoir by Thomas Munford, who fixes its time by recalling that it started to rain just as he left Lee. The account is plausible except for one detail. According to Munford, when Lee uttered the word "crush," he crumpled the Janney letter in his hand for emphasis. This, of course, Lee was incapable of doing on September 1. See Thomas T. Munford, "Lee's Invasion of Maryland," in *Addresses Delivered before the Confederate Veterans Association of Savannah, Ga.* (Savannah: Braid & Hutton, 1893–1902), 3:36–37.

10. The dispositions made after the battle may be worked out from the reports in *OR*, vol. 12, pt. 2, of A. P. Hill (p. 672) and Early (715); and in H. J. Williams's report, ibid., vol. 19, 1:1011.

11. Lee's report, Lee, *Wartime Papers*, 312.

Appendixes

1. This essay is based on Jomini, *Art of War*, esp. 13–14, 38, 66–70, 179, 252; and Halleck, *Elements of Military Art*, esp. 37–38, 88, 114, 135. See also Edward Meade Earle, ed., *Makers of Modern Strategy: Military Thought from Machiavelli to Hitler* (Princeton: Princeton Univ. Press, 1943), 77–92; and Joseph L. Harsh, "Battlesword and Rapier: Clausewitze, Jomini, and the American Civil War," *Military Affairs* 38 (1974): 133–38.

2. Jomini, *Art of War*, 13–15; Halleck, *Elements of Military Art*, 35–36.

3. Jomini, *Art of War*, 38; Halleck, *Elements of Military Art*, 135ff.

4. Jomini, *Art of War*, 66–69; Halleck, *Elements of Military Art*, 37–44.

5. Jomini, *Art of War*, 252ff; Halleck, *Elements of Military Art*, 88.

6. Jomini, *Art of War*, 70, 178–79, 277ff; Halleck, *Elements of Military Art*, 114.

7. Livermore, *Numbers and Losses*, 63. See also the essays on military populations in 8th Census, *Population*, xvii and *Mortality*, xlix.

8. All statistics are from Livermore, *Numbers and Losses*, 47, except for June 30, 1862. In the latter case the Union figures are from *OR*, ser. 3, vol. 2:185; and the Confederate figures are from a study by the author that determined there were 577.7 Confederate regiments of all arms (independent battalions and companies consolidated into regiments) in the field at that date. Southern regiments at this time averaged 825.9 officers and men, present and absent.

9. Sources for Confederate figures are *OR*, vol. 10, 2:377, 378, 382, 476, 491; and Livermore, *Numbers and Losses*, 44. Federal figures are from *OR*, vol. 10, 2:146, 148, 151, including an estimate for Grant's aggregate present and absent as 66 percent larger than the present for duty based on the known ratio of 68.6 percent in Pope's army and 66.1 percent in Buell's.

10. Johnston, *Narrative of Military Operations*, 145–46; and Johnston, "Manassas to Seven Pines," *Battles and Leaders of the Civil War* 2:209, 217–18.

11. Davis, *Rise and Fall* 2:155–58; Charles Marshall, Joseph Eggleston Johnston, and Jubal Anderson Early, "Strength of General Lee's Army in the Seven Days Battle around Richmond," *SHSP* 1 (1876): 407–24; John William Jones, *Army of Northern Virginia Memorial Volume* (Richmond: J. W. Randolph & English, 1880), 343; Walter Herron Taylor, *Four Years with General Lee*, ed. James I. Robertson, Jr. (Bloomington: Indiana Univ. Press, 1962), 49–56.

12. Tenney, *Seven Days in 1862*, 133.

13. Hennessy, *Map Study*, 463, 472; and "The Opposing Forces at Second Bull Run," *Battles and Leaders* 2:499–500.

14. Allen, "Strengths at Second Manassas," 102, 175.

15. Marshall, *Aide-de-Camp*, 63–76. For an earlier and much thinner version, see Marshall, "Strategic Value of Richmond," in Jones, *Army of Northern Virginia Memorial Volume*, 69–88.

16. Thomas Lawrence Connelly, *The Marble Man: Robert E. Lee and His Image in American Society* (New York: Alfred A. Knopf, 1979), 40ff, esp. 49.

17. Nolan, *Lee Considered*, 99–100; Fuller, *Grant and Lee*, 252; Connelly, "Robert E. Lee and the Western Confederacy," 201; and William J. Miller, "Did Robert E. Lee's Generalship Help or Hurt the Confederacy's Chances for Victory?" *The Color Bearer* 1 (1992): 9, 11.

18. Nolan, *Lee Considered*, 112–13; Wise, *End of an Era*, 429; Jones, *Personal Reminiscences*, 297.

19. Jones, *Personal Reminiscences*, 297.

20. Lee, *Wartime Papers*, 437–38, 410–12.

21. Ibid., 817–18.

22. See Lee to Davis, Sept. 8, 1862 (which will be discussed in *Taken at the Flood*), and Lee to Davis, June 10, 1863, ibid., 301, 507–9.

23. Ibid., 528, 531.

24. Marshall, *Aide-de-Camp*, 75–76.

25. Davis, "The Antietam Campaign," 30n. 1; Taylor, *Four Years with General Lee*, 57.

26. *OR*, vol. 12, 3:892–93.

27. *Papers of Jefferson Davis* 8:203.

28. Davis to wife, June 2, ibid., 209.

29. Marshall, *Aide-de-Camp*, 130.

30. Freeman, *R. E. Lee* 2:299; *OR*, vol. 12, 3:943, 946.

31. Firsthand accounts of this conference may be found in *OR*, vol. 5:884–87; Davis, *Rise and Fall* 1:445–54; Johnston, *Narrative of Military Operations*, 75–76; Smith, *Confederate War*

Papers, 13–40; and Beauregard, "The First Battle of Bull Run," *Battles and Leaders* 1:221–22.

32. *OR*, vol. 5:932.

33. Davis, *Rise and Fall* 1:449.

34. Freeman, *Lee's Lieutenants* 1:149; *OR*, vol. 11, 3:438.

35. *OR*, vol. 12, 2:733. For the controversy, see Douglas, *I Rode with Stonewall*, 132–33; Henderson, *Stonewall Jackson*, 432–33; Freeman, *R. E. Lee* 2:300–301, and *Lee's Lieutenants* 2:82–83, including nn. 9, 12.

36. Stuart's report, *OR*, vol. 11, 1:1036–40; Lee to Charlotte Lee, June 22, 1862, John William Jones, *Life and Letters of Robert Edward Lee, Soldier and Man* (New York: Neale, 1906), 184; Marshall, *Aide-de-Camp*, 82.

37. Freeman, *Lee's Lieutenants* 1:275–302; Emory M. Thomas, *Bold Dragoon: The Life of J. E. B. Stuart* (New York: Harper & Row, 1986), 111–29; and Edwin C. Bearss, ". . . into the very jaws of the enemy . . .": Jeb Stuart's Ride around McClellan," in *The Peninsula Campaign of 1862: Yorktown to the Seven Days*, ed. William J. Miller (Campbell, Calif.: Savas Woodbury Publishers, 1995), 1:142.

38. Lee to Davis, July 3, 1862, Lee-Davis Correspondence; and July 5, *Papers of Jefferson Davis* 8:278–79.

39. See Stanton to McClellan and Dix to Stanton, July 1, 1862, *OR*, vol. 11, 3:281, 282–83; and Francis Amasa Walker, *History of the Second Army Corps in the Army of the Potomac* (New York: Charles Scribner's Sons, 1886), 87.

40. *OR*, vol. 11, 3:609; Special Orders, Nos. 113 and 120, Adjutant and Inspector General's Office, May 23 and 26, 1862, ibid., 540, 551; and Magruder to Randolph, July 2, ibid., 630.

41. General Orders No. 54, Adjutant and Inspector General's Office, Aug. 1, 1862, ibid., ser. 2, vol. 4:836–37; Lee to Halleck, Aug. 2, ibid., 328–29; and Halleck to Lee, Aug. 9, ibid., 362.

42. See Sallie A. (Brock) Putnam, *Richmond during the War: Four Years of Personal Observations, by a Richmond Lady* (New York: G. W. Carleton, 1867), 156–57; James Dabney McCabe, *Life and Campaigns of General Robert E. Lee* (Atlanta: National Pub. Co., 1870), 184–88; and Lee to Stuart, July 30, 1862, *OR*, vol. 12, 3:920.

43. McCabe, *General Robert E. Lee*, 182; not found in *OR*.

44. Special Orders, No. 19, Headquarters, Army of Virginia, Aug. 14, 1862, and Ruggles to Sigel, Aug. 16, *OR*, vol. 12, 3:573, 577; General Orders No. 107, War Dept., Adjutant General's Office, Aug. 15, 1862, ibid., ser. 2, vol. 4:393.

45. Lee to Jackson, July 25 and 27, 1862, *OR*, vol. 12, 3:917, 918–19; Lee to Davis, July 26, Lee to Randolph and Lee to daughter Mildred, July 28, Lee, *Wartime Papers*, 238, 240–41.

46. Lee to daughter Mildred, July 28, and to wife, Aug. 17, 1862, Lee, *Wartime Papers*, 240, 257–58.

47. Lee to Cooper, Apr. 18, 1863, *OR*, vol. 12, 2:176.

48. Freeman, *R. E. Lee* 2:267–68.

49. Davis to Smith, July 28, 1862, *Papers of Jefferson Davis* 8:305.

50. Marshall, *Aide-de-Camp*, 122; Freeman, *R. E. Lee* 2:258–59; *OR*, vol. 11, 3:305; Lee to Jackson, July 25, 1862, *OR*, vol. 12, 3:917.

51. John Esten Cooke, *Robert E. Lee* (New York: G. W. Dillingham, 1899), 108–9.

52. See, for example, Freeman, *R. E. Lee* 2:270–73.

53. *OR*, vol. 51, 2:604–7; Owen, *In Camp and Battle*, 99; and Wise, *17th Virginia*, 92.

54. Jedediah Hotchkiss, *Make Me a Map of the Valley: The Civil War Journal of Stonewall Jackson's Topographer*, ed. Archie McDonald (Dallas: Southern Methodist Univ. Press, 1973), 118.

55. Pender to wife, Aug. 14, 1862, Pender, *The General to His Lady*, 167–68.

56. See Lee to Longstreet and Lee to G. W. Smith, Aug. 14, 1862, *OR*, vol. 11, 3:676, 677.

57. Longstreet, *From Manassas to Appomattox*, 158, and "March against Pope," 514.

58. *OR*, vol. 11, 3:675; Lee to Hood, ibid., 667; Lee's report, June 2, 1863, ibid. 2:552.

59. McClellan's report, ibid. 1:84–85.

60. Longstreet to Wise, July 31, ibid., vol. 51, 2:602.

61. *OR*, vol. 51, 2:1075–76; Lee, *Wartime Papers*, 258.

62. Lee to Davis, Aug. 17, 1862, Lee, *Wartime Papers*, 258–59.

63. Lee to Davis, Aug. 14, 1862, ibid., 253–54; and McClellan to L. Thomas, Apr. 1, 1862, *OR*, vol. 5:60–61.

64. *OR*, vol. 12, 2:552, 729. See also Lee, *Wartime Papers*, 259–60, from a file copy in the Museum of the Confederacy, Richmond.

65. Lee to Stuart, Aug. 19, 1862, Lee, *Wartime Papers*, 260.

66. See Longstreet, *From Manassas to Appomattox*, 161–62; and Pope's report, *OR*, vol. 12, 2:29.

67. Freeman, *R. E. Lee* 2:286–87n. 35.

68. *OR*, vol. 12, 3:474. Pender to wife, Aug. 14, 1862, Pender, *The General to His Lady*, 167.

69. Lee to Davis, Aug. 24, 1862, Lee *Wartime Papers*, 263–64; Taylor to sister, Aug. 23, 1862, Taylor, *Lee's Adjutant*, 40.

70. Lee to Davis, Aug. 25, 1862, Lee, *Lee's Dispatches*, 52.

71. See the reports of Jackson and Boswell, *OR*, vol. 12, 2:643, 650; and Freeman, *R. E. Lee* 2:300n. 36.

72. Freeman, *R. E. Lee* 2:306; Longstreet, "March against Pope," 517.

73. Marshall, *Aide-de-Camp*, 134.

74. See *OR*, vol. 12, 2:263–64.

75. Percy Gatling Hamlin, *"Old Bald Head" (General R. S. Ewell): The Portrait of a Soldier* (Strasburg, Va.: Shenandoah, 1940), 125–26.

76. Freeman, *R. E. Lee* 2:320, and *Lee's Lieutenants* 2:103–5.

77. *Porter Proceedings* 2:204, 211; Marshall, *Aide-de-Camp*, 130.

78. Freeman, *R. E. Lee* 2:322.

79. Ibid. 2:340n. 112; H. W. Thomas, *Doles-Cook*, 469; *OR*, vol. 12, 2:553, 3:942, 965.

80. Longstreet, *From Manassas to Appomattox*, 191; *OR*, vol. 12, 2:557–58, 647, 566.

81. Von Borcke, *Memoirs of the Confederate War* 1:165.

82. Freeman, *R. E. Lee* 2:338ff; and Douglas, *I Rode with Stonewall*, 143–44.

83. Squires, "Boy Officer," *Civil War Times Illustrated* 14 (1975): 17; Longstreet, *From Manassas to Appomattox*, 192; Longstreet's report, *OR*, vol. 12, 2:566.

84. *OR*, vol. 12, 2:714.

Select Bibliography

Addresses Delivered before the Confederate Veterans Association of Savannah, Ga. 5 vols. Savannah: Braid & Hutton, 1893–1902.

Alexander, Bevin. *Lost Victories: The Military Genius of Stonewall Jackson.* New York: Henry Holt, 1992.

Alexander, Edward Porter. *Military Memoirs of a Confederate: A Critical Narrative.* Ed. T. Harry Williams. Bloomington: Indiana Univ. Press, 1962.

Allan, William. *The Army of Northern Virginia in 1862.* Dayton, Ohio: Morningside House, 1984.

Allan, William, and John Codman Ropes. "Strength of the Forces under Pope and Lee." *Papers of the Military Historical Society of Massachusetts* 2 (rev. ed.): 195–220.

Allen, John Owen. "The Strength of the Union and Confederate Forces at Second Manassas." Master's thesis. George Mason University, Fairfax, Virginia, 1993.

America: History and Life—A Guide to Periodical Literature. Santa Barbara, Calif.: Clio Press, 1964–.

The American Annual Cyclopaedia and Register of Important Events. 14 vols. New York: D. Appleton, 1862–75.

Amman, William Frayne, ed. *Personnel of the Civil War.* 2 vols. New York: Thomas Yoselof, 1961.

Ball, Douglas B. *Financial Failure and Confederate Defeat.* Urbana: Univ. of Illinois Press, 1991.

Bartlett, Napier. *A Soldier's Story of the War.* New Orleans: Clark & Hofeline, 1874.

Bearss, Edwin C. "'. . . into the very jaws of the enemy . . .': Jeb Stuart's Ride around McClellan." In Miller, ed., *The Peninsula Campaign* 1:71–142.

Beauregard, Pierre Gustave Toutant. "The First Battle of Bull Run." In Johnson and Buel, eds., *Battles and Leaders of the Civil War* 1:196–227.

Beers, Henry Putnam. *Guide to the Archives of the Government of the Confederate States of America.* Washington, D.C.: GPO, 1968.

Beringer, Richard E., Herman Hattaway, Archer Jones, and William N. Still, Jr. *Why the South Lost the Civil War.* Athens: Univ. of Georgia Press, 1986.

Black, Robert C. *The Railroads of the Confederacy.* Chapel Hill: Univ. of North Carolina Press, 1952.

Blackford, William Willis. *War Years with Jeb Stuart.* New York: Charles Scribner's Sons, 1945.

Blosser, Susan Sokol, and Clyde Norman Wilson, Jr. *The Southern Historical Collection: A Guide to Manuscripts.* Chapel Hill: Univ. of North Carolina Library, 1970.

Boatner, Mark Mayo. *The Civil War Dictionary.* New York: David McKay, 1959.

Boritt, Gabor S., ed. *Why the Confederacy Lost.* New York: Oxford Univ. Press, 1992.

Boteler, Alexander R. "Stonewall Jackson in Campaign of 1862." *Southern Historical Society Papers* 40 (1915): 162–82.

Bridges, Hal. *Lee's Maverick General, Daniel Harvey Hill.* New York: McGraw Hill, 1961.

Bruce, George Anson. "The Strategy of the Civil War." In *Papers of the Military Historical Society of Massachusetts* 13:391–483.

Castel, Albert. "The Historian and the General: Thomas L. Connelly vs. Robert E. Lee." *Civil War History* 16 (1970): 215–28.

Clark, Walter, ed. *Histories of the Several Regiments and Battalions from North Carolina in the Great War 1861–1865, Written by Members of the Respective Commands.* 5 vols. Wendell, N.C.: Broadfoot's Bookmark, 1982. Cited herein as *North Carolina Regiments*

Cole, Garrold L. *Civil War Eyewitnesses: An Annotated Bibliography of Books and Articles, 1955–1986.* Columbia: Univ. of South Carolina Press, 1988.

Colton, Ray Charles. *The Civil War in the Western Territories, Arizona, Colorado, New Mexico and Utah.* Norman: Univ. of Oklahoma Press, 1959.

Connelly, Thomas Lawrence. *Army of the Heartland: The Army of Tennessee, 1861–1862.* Baton Rouge: Louisiana State Univ. Press, 1967.

——. *The Marble Man: Robert E. Lee and His Image in American Society.* New York: Alfred A. Knopf, 1979.

——. "Robert E. Lee and the Western Confederacy: A Criticism of Lee's Strategic Ability." *History* 15 (1969): 197–213.

Cooke, John Esten. *Robert E. Lee.* New York: G. W. Dillingham, 1899.

——. *Stonewall Jackson.* New York: G. W. Dillingham, ca. 1899.

Coulter, Ellis Merton. *The Confederate States of America.* Vol. 7 of *A History of the South.* Baton Rouge: Louisiana State Univ. Press, 1950.

Cox, Jacob Dolson. *Military Reminiscences of the Civil War.* 2 vols. New York: Charles Scribner's Sons, 1900.

Crawford, Samuel Wylie. *The Genesis of the Civil War: The Story of Sumter, 1860–1861.* New York: Charles L. Webster & Co., 1886.

Crook, Paul David. *The North, the South, and the Powers, 1861–1865.* New York: Wiley, 1974.

Crute, Joseph H., Jr. *Confederate Staff Officers, 1861–1865.* Powhatan, Va.: Derwent Books, 1982.

——. *Units of the Confederate States Army.* Midlothian, Va.: Derwent Books, 1987.

Curry, Richard Orr. *A House Divided: A Study of Statehood Politics and the Copperhead Movement in West Virginia.* Pittsburgh: Univ. of Pittsburgh Press, 1964.

Daniel, John Warwick, ed. *Life and Reminiscences of Jefferson Davis by Distinguished Men of His Time.* Baltimore: Eastern Pub. Co., 1890.

Davis, George Breckenridge. "The Antietam Campaign." In *Papers of the Military Historical Society of Massachusetts* 3:27–72.

Davis, Jefferson. *Jefferson Davis, Constitutionalist: His Letters and Speeches.* Ed. Dunbar Rowland. 10 vols. Jackson: Mississippi Department of Archives and History, 1923.

———. *The Papers of Jefferson Davis.* Ed. Lynda Lasswell Crist and Mary Seaton Dix. 8 vols. to date. Baton Rouge: Louisiana State Univ. Press, 1971–.

———. *The Rise and Fall of the Confederate Government.* 2 vols. New York: D. Appleton, 1881.

———. "Robert E. Lee." *Southern Historical Society Papers* 17 (1889): 362–72.

Davis, William C., ed. *The Confederate General.* 6 vols. N.p.: National Historical Society, 1991.

———. *Jefferson Davis: The Man and His Hour.* New York: Harper Collins, 1991.

Dederer, John Morgan. "The Origins of Robert E. Lee's Bold Generalship: A Reinterpretation." *Military Affairs* 49 (1985): 117–23.

DeRosset, William Lord. "Additional Sketch Third Regiment." In Clark, ed., *North Carolina Regiments* 1:215–24.

Dornbusch, Charles Emil. *Military Bibliography of the Civil War.* 3 vols. New York: New York Public Library, 1961–72. Vol. 4 (supplement) edited by Robert K. Krick. Dayton, Ohio: Morningside Press, 1987.

Douglas, Henry Kyd. *I Rode with Stonewall, Being Chiefly the War Experiences of the Youngest Member of Jackson's Staff from the John Brown Raid to the Hanging of Mrs. Surratt.* Chapel Hill: Univ. of North Carolina Press, 1940.

Dowdey, Clifford. *Lee.* Boston: Little, Brown, 1965.

Earle, Edward Meade, ed. *Makers of Modern Strategy: Military Thought from Machiavelli to Hitler* Princeton: Princeton Univ. Press, 1943.

Early, Jubal Anderson. *War Memoirs, Autobiographical Sketch and Narrative of the War Between the States.* Ed. Frank E. Vandiver. Bloomington: Indiana Univ. Press, 1960.

Eaton, Clement. *A History of the Southern Confederacy.* New York: Macmillan, 1954.

Escott, Paul D. *After Secession: Jefferson Davis and the Failure of Confederate Nationalism.* Baton Rouge: Louisiana Univ. Press, 1978.

Evans, Clement Anselm, ed. *Confederate Military History.* Vol. 2: *Maryland,* by Bradley Tyler Johnson. Vol. 3: *Virginia,* by Jedediah Hotchkiss. Atlanta: Confederate Pub. Co., 1899.

Ewell, Richard Stoddert. *The Making of a Soldier: Letters of General R. S. Ewell.* Ed. Percy Gatling Hamlin. Richmond: Whittet & Shepperson, 1935.

Fairfax County and the War Between the States. Fairfax: Fairfax County Civil War Centennial Commission, 1961.

Faust, Patricia L., ed. *Historical Times Illustrated Encyclopedia of the Civil War.* New York: Harper & Row, 1986.

Fishel, Edwin C. *The Secret War for the Union: The Untold Story of Military Intelligence in the Civil War.* Boston: Houghton Mifflin, 1996.

Fox, William F. *Regimental Losses in the Civil War, 1861–1865: A Treatise on the Extent and Nature of the Mortuary Losses in the Union Regiments, with Full and Extensive Statistics Compiled from the Official Records on File in the State Military Bureaus and at Washington.* Albany: Albany Pub. Co., 1889.

Frank, Joseph Allan, and George A. Reaves. *"Seeing the Elephant": Raw Recruits at the Battle of Shiloh.* Westport, Conn.: Greenwood Press, 1989.

Freeman, Douglas Southall. *Lee's Lieutenants: A Study in Command.* 3 vols. New York: Charles Scribner's Sons, 1942–44.

———. *R. E. Lee: A Biography.* 4 vols. New York: Charles Scribner's Sons, 1934–35.

Fredrickson, George M. *Why the Confederacy Did Not Fight a Guerrilla War after the Fall of Richmond: A Comparative View.* 35th Annual Fortenbaugh Memorial Lecture. Gettysburg, Pa.: Gettysburg College, 1996.

Fuller, John Frederick Charles. *Grant and Lee: A Study in Personality and Generalship.* New York: Charles Scribner's Sons, 1933.

Gaff, Alan D. *Brave Men's Tears: The Iron Brigade at Brawner Farm.* 2d rev. ed. Dayton, Ohio: Morningside Press, 1988.

Gallagher, Gary W. *Lee: The Soldier.* Lincoln: Univ. of Nebraska Press, 1996.

Goff, Richard Davis. *Confederate Supply.* Durham, N.C.: Duke Univ. Press, 1969.

Gordon, John Brown. *Reminiscences of the Civil War.* New York: Charles Scribner's Sons, 1903.

Goree, Thomas Jewett. *Longstreet's Aid: The Civil War Letters of Major Thomas J. Goree.* Ed. Thomas J. Cutrer. Charlottesville: Univ. Press of Virginia, 1995.

Graham, James Augustus. "Cooke's Brigade." In Clark, ed., *North Carolina Regiments* 4:501–12.

Halleck, Henry Wager. *Elements of Military Art and Science: or, Course of Instruction in Strategy, Fortification, Tactics of Battles, &c.* Westport, Conn.: Greenwood Press, 1971.

Hamlin, Percy Gatling. *"Old Bald Head" (General R. S. Ewell), The Portrait of a Soldier.* Strasburg, Va.: Shenandoah Pub. House, 1940.

Harsh, Joseph L. "Battlesword and Rapier: Clausewitze, Jomini, and the American Civil War." *Military Affairs* 38 (1974): 133–38.

———. "Lincoln's Tarnished Brass: Conservative Strategies and the Attempt to Fight the Early Civil War as a Limited War." In Heleniak and Hewett, eds., *Confederate High Command,* 124–41.

Haselberger, Fritz. *Yanks from the South! The First Land Campaign of the Civil War: Rich Mountain, West Virginia.* Baltimore: Past Glories, 1987.

Hattaway, Herman, and Archer Jones. *How the North Won: A Military History of the Civil War.* Urbana: Univ. of Illinois Press, 1983.

Haupt, Herman. *Reminiscences of General Herman Haupt . . . Giving Hitherto Unpublished Official Orders, Personal Narratives of Important Military Operations.* Milwaukee: Wright & Joy Co., 1901.

Heitman, Francis Bernard. *Historical Register and Dictionary of the United States Army, from Its Organization, September 29, 1789, to March 2, 1903.* 2 vols. Washington, D.C.: GPO, 1903.

Heleniak, Roman J., and Lawrence L. Hewett, eds. *The Confederate High Command and Related Topics: The 1988 Deep Delta Symposium: Themes in Honor of T. Harry Williams.* Shippensburg, Pa.: White Mane, 1990

Henderson, George Francis Robert. *Stonewall Jackson and the American Civil War.* New York: Longmans, Green and Co., 1949.

Hennessy, John J. *Return to Bull Run: The Campaign and Battle of Second Manassas*. New York: Simon & Schuster, 1993.

———. *Second Manassas Battlefield Map Study*. Lynchburg, Va.: H.E. Howard, 1991.

Heth, Henry. "Letter from Major-General Henry Heth, of A. P. Hill's Corps, A.N.V." *Southern Historical Society Papers* 4 (1877): 151–60.

Hewett, Janet B., ed. *Supplement to the Official Records of the Union and Confederate Armies*. 25 nonconsecutive vols. to date. Wilmington, N.C.: Broadfoot Pub. Co., 1996–.

Hill, Daniel Harvey. "Lee's Attacks North of the Chickahominy." In Johnson and Buel, eds., *Battles and Leaders* 2:347–62.

Holien, Kim Bernard. *Battle at Ball's Bluff*. Orange, Va.: Moss Publications, 1985.

Hood, John Bell. *Advance and Retreat: Personal Experiences in the United States and Confederate States Armies*. Ed. Richard N. Current. Bloomington: Indiana Univ. Press, 1959.

Hopkins, Luther Wesley. *From Bull Run to Appomattox: A Boy's View*. Baltimore: Fleet-McGinley, 1908.

Hotchkiss, Jedediah. *Make Me a Map of the Valley: The Civil War Journal of Stonewall Jackson's Topographer*. Ed. Archie McDonald. Dallas: Southern Methodist Univ. Press, 1973.

Imboden, John Daniel. "Incidents of the First Bull Run." In Johnson and Buel, eds., *Battles and Leaders* 1:229–39.

———. "Reminiscences of Lee and Jackson." *Galaxy* 12 (1871): 627–34.

Jackson, Mary Anna. *Memoirs of Stonewall Jackson by His Widow*. 2d ed. Louisville, Ky.: The Prentice Press, 1895.

Johnson, Robert Underwood, and Clarence Clough Buel, eds. *Battles and Leaders of the Civil War . . . Being for the Most Part Contributions Based Upon "The Century Magazine War Series."* 4 vols. New York: Thomas Yoselof, 1956.

Johnston, Angus J. *Virginia Railroads in the Civil War*. Chapel Hill: Univ. of North Carolina Press, 1961.

Johnston, Joseph Eggleston. "Manassas to Seven Pines." In Johnson and Buel, eds., *Battles and Leaders* 2:202–18.

———. *Narrative of Military Operations, Directed during the Late War between the States*. Ed. Frank E. Vandiver. Bloomington: Indiana Univ. Press, 1959.

Johnston, William Preston. "Albert Sidney Johnston at Shiloh." In Johnson and Buel, eds., *Battles and Leaders* 1:540–68.

———. "Memorandum of Conversations between Robert E. Lee and William Preston Johnston, May 7, 1868 and March 18, 1870." Ed. W. G. Bean. *Virginia Magazine of History and Biography* 73 (1965): 474–84.

Jomini, Antoine Henri. *The Art of War*. Trans. G. H. Mendell and W. P. Craighill. Westport, Conn.: Greenwood Press, 1971.

Jones, Archer. *Civil War Command and Strategy: The Process of Victory and Defeat*. New York: The Free Press, 1992.

———. *Confederate Strategy from Shiloh to Vicksburg*. Baton Rouge: Louisiana State Univ. Press, 1961.

Jones, John Beauchamp. *A Rebel War Clerk's Diary at the Confederate States Capital*. 2 vols. Philadelphia: J. B. Lippincott, 1866.

Jones, John William. *Life and Letters of Robert Edward Lee, Soldier and Man.* New York: Neale Pub. Co., 1906.

―――. *Personal Reminiscences, Anecdotes, and Letters of Gen. Robert E. Lee.* New York: D. Appleton, 1876.

―――, comp. *Army of Northern Virginia Memorial Volume.* Richmond: J. W. Randolph & English, 1880.

Josephy, Alvin M., Jr. *The Civil War in the American West.* New York: Alfred A. Knopf, 1991.

Kegel, James A. *North with Lee and Jackson: The Lost Story of Gettysburg.* Mechanicsburg, Pa.: Stackpole Books, 1996.

Krick, Robert K. *Conquering the Valley: Stonewall Jackson at Port Republic.* New York: William Morrow, 1996.

―――. *Lee's Colonels: A Biographical Register of the Field Officers of the Army of Northern Virginia.* 3d rev. ed. Dayton, Ohio: Morningside Bookshop, 1991.

―――. *Stonewall Jackson at Cedar Mountain.* Chapel Hill: Univ. of North Carolina Press, 1990.

Lee, Fitzhugh. *General Lee.* New York: D. Appleton, 1894.

Lee, Robert E. *Lee's Dispatches: Unpublished Letters of General Robert E. Lee, C. S. A., to Jefferson Davis and the War Department of the Confederate States of America, 1862–1865.* Ed. Douglas Southall Freeman. New enlarged ed. Ed. Grady McWhiney. New York: G. P. Putnam's Sons, 1957.

―――. *The Wartime Papers of Robert E. Lee.* Ed. Clifford Dowdey and Louis H. Manarin. Boston: Little, Brown, 1961.

Lee, Robert Edward Lee [Jr.]. *Recollections and Letters of General Robert E. Lee, by His Son.* Enlarged ed. Garden City, N.Y.: Garden City Pub. Co., 1924.

Lee, Susan Pendleton. *Memoirs of William Nelson Pendleton, by His Daughter.* Enlarged ed. Harrisonburg, Va.: Sprinkle Publications, 1991.

Leyburn, John. "An Interview with General Lee." *Century Magazine* 30 (1885): 166–67.

Lincoln, Abraham. *Collected Works.* Ed. Roy P. Basler. New Brunswick, N.J.: Rutgers Univ. Press, 1953–55.

Livermore, Thomas Leonard. *Numbers and Losses in the Civil War in America.* Corrected ed. Dayton, Ohio: Morningside, 1986.

Long, Armistead Lindsay. *Memoirs of Robert E. Lee, His Military and Personal History, Embracing a Large Amount of Information Hitherto Unpublished.* Philadelphia: J. M. Stoddart & Co., 1886.

Longstreet, James. *From Manassas to Appomattox: Memoirs of the Civil War in America.* Ed. James I. Robertson, Jr. Bloomington: Indiana Univ. Press, 1960.

―――. "Our March Against Pope." In Johnson and Buel, eds., *Battles and Leaders* 2:512–26.

Low, Thomas. "Letters to Laura." *Civil War Times Illustrated* 32 (July 1992): 12ff.

McCabe, James Dabney. *Life and Campaigns of General Robert E. Lee.* Atlanta: National Pub. Co., 1870.

McClellan, George Brinton. *McClellan's Own Story: The War for the Union, the Soldiers Who Fought It, the Civilians Who Directed It, and His Relations to It and to Them.* New York: Charles L. Webster & Co., 1887.

McClellan, Henry Brainard. *I Rode with Jeb Stuart: The Life and Campaigns of Major General J. E. B. Stuart.* Ed. Burke Davis. Bloomington: Indiana Univ. Press, 1958.

McDonald, William Naylor. *A History of the Laurel Brigade, Originally the Ashby Cavalry of the Army of Northern Virginia and Chew's Battery.* Baltimore: Sun Job Printing Office, 1907.

McMurray, Richard M. *Two Great Rebel Armies: An Essay in Confederate Military History.* Chapel Hill: Univ. of North Carolina Press, 1989.

McPherson, James M. *Drawn with the Sword: Reflections on the American Civil War.* New York: Oxford Univ. Press, 1996.

McWhiney, Grady. "Conservatism and the Military." *Continuity* 4 (1982): 93–126.

————. "Who Whipt Whom? Confederate Defeat Reexamined." *Civil War History* 11 (1965): 5–26.

————, ed. *Grant, Lee, Lincoln and the Radicals: Essays on Civil War Leadership.* Evanston, Ill.: Northwestern Univ. Press, 1964.

McWhiney, Grady, and Perry D. Jamieson. *Attack and Die: Civil War Military Tactics and the Southern Heritage.* Tuscaloosa: Univ. of Alabama Press, 1982.

Marshall, Charles. *An Aide-de-Camp of Lee, Being the Papers of Colonel Charles Marshall, Sometimes Aide-de-Camp, Military Secretary, and Assistant Adjutant General on the Staff of Robert E. Lee, 1862–1865.* Ed. Sir Frederick Maurice. Boston: Little, Brown, 1927.

————. "Strategic Value of Richmond." In John William Jones, comp., *Army of Northern Virginia Memorial Volume,* 69–88.

Marshall, Charles, Joseph Eggleston Johnston, and Jubal Anderson Early. "Strength of General Lee's Army in the Seven Days Battles Around Richmond." *Southern Historical Society Papers* 1 (1876): 407–24.

Marvel, William. *Burnside.* Chapel Hill: Univ. of North Carolina Press, 1991.

Mearns, David Chambers. *The Lincoln Paper: The Story of the Collection, with Selections to July 4, 1861.* 2 vols. Garden City, N.Y.: Doubleday, 1948.

Miller, William J. "Did Robert E. Lee's Generalship Help or Hurt the Confederacy's Chances for Victory?" *Colorbearer* 1 (1992): 8–11.

————, ed. *The Peninsula Campaign of 1862: Yorktown to the Seven Days.* 2 vols. Campbell, Calif.: Savas Woodbury, 1995.

Moger, Allen W. "General Lee's Unwritten 'History of the Army of Northern Virginia.'" *Virginia Magazine of History and Biography* 71 (1963): 341–63.

Moore, Albert Burton. *Conscription and Conflict in the Confederacy.* New York: Macmillan, 1924.

Moore, Samuel J. T., Jr. *Moore's Complete Civil War Guide to Richmond.* Rev. ed. Richmond: Privately printed, 1978.

Mulligan, James Adelbert. "The Siege of Lexington, Mo." In Johnson and Buel, eds., *Battles and Leaders* 1:307–13.

Munford, Thomas Taylor. "Lee's Invasion of Maryland." In *Addresses Delivered before the Confederate Veterans Association of Savannah, Ga.* 3:35–55.

Munden, Kenneth White. *Guide to Federal Archives Relating to the Civil War.* Washington, D.C.: GPO, 1962.

Murdock, Eugene C., ed. *The Civil War in the North: A Selective Annotated Bibliography.* New York: Garland Pub. Co., 1987.

National Cyclopedia of American Biography. 9 vols. New York: James T. White & Co., 1892–99.

Nevins, Allan. *The War for the Union.* 4 vols. New York: Charles Scribner's Sons, 1959–71.

Nevins, Allan, James I. Robertson, Jr., and Bell I. Wiley, eds. *Civil War Books: A Critical Bibliography.* Baton Rouge: Louisiana State Univ. Press, 1967–69.

Nolan, Alan T. *Lee Considered: General Robert E. Lee and Civil War History.* Chapel Hill: Univ. of North Carolina Press, 1991.

Owen, William Miller. *In Camp and Battle with the Washington Artillery of New Orleans: A Narrative of Events during the Late Civil War, from Bull Run to Appomattox and Spanish Fort.* Boston: Ticknor and Co., 1885.

Parrish, T. Michael, and Robert M. Willingham, Jr., eds. *Confederate Imprints: A Bibliography of Southern Publications from Secession to Surrender.* Austin, Tex.: Jenkins Pub. Co., n.d.

Pender, William Dorsey. *The General to His Wife: The Civil War Letters of William Dorsey Pender to Fanny Pender.* Ed. William Woods Hassler. Chapel Hill: Univ. of North Carolina Press, 1965.

Perry, D. M. "The Time of Longstreet's Arrival at Groveton." In Johnson and Buel, eds., *Battles and Leaders* 2:527.

Pope, John. "The Second Battle of Bull Run." In Johnson and Buel, eds., *Battles and Leaders* 2:449–94.

Powell, William Henry. *The Fifth Army Corps (Army of the Potomac): A Record of Operations during the Civil War in the United States of America, 1861–1865.* New York: G. P. Putnam's Sons, 1896.

Putnam, Sallie A. (Brock). *Richmond during the War: Four Years of Personal Observations, by a Richmond Lady.* New York: G. W. Carleton, 1867.

Rable, George C. *The Confederate Republic: A Revolution against Politics.* Chapel Hill: Univ. of North Carolina Press, 1994.

Reagan, John Henninger. *Memoirs, with Special Reference to Secession and the Civil War.* Ed. Walter Flavius McCaleb. New York: The Neale Pub. Co., 1906.

Richardson, James D., comp. *A Compilation of the Messages and Papers of the Confederacy, Including the Diplomatic Correspondence, 1861–1865.* 2 vols. Nashville: United States Publishing Co., 1905.

Robertson, James I., Jr., *A. P. Hill: The Story of a Confederate Warrior.* New York: Random House, 1987.

————. *Stonewall Jackson: The Man, the Soldier, the Legend.* New York: Macmillan, 1997.

Roland, Charles P. "The Generalship of Robert E. Lee." In McWhiney, ed., *Grant, Lee, Lincoln and the Radicals,* 31–71.

————. *Reflections on Lee: A Historian's Assessment.* Mechanicsburg, Pa.: Stackpole Books, 1995.

Ropes, John Codman. *The Army under Pope.* New York: Charles Scribner's Sons, 1882.

————. *The Story of the Civil War: A Concise Account of the War in the United States of America between 1861 and 1865.* 2 vols. New York: G. P. Putnam's Sons, 1894–98.

Schalk, Emil. *Summary of the Art of War: Written Expressly for and Dedicated to the U.S. Volunteer Army.* Philadelphia: J. B. Lippincott, 1862.

Schlesinger, Arthur M. *Paths to the Present.* Rev. ed. Boston: Houghton Mifflin, 1964.

Schutz, Wallace J., and Walter N. Trenerry, *Abandoned by Lincoln: A Military Biography of General John Pope.* Urbana: Univ. of Illinois Press, 1990.

Sears, Stephen W., ed. *The Civil War: The Best of American Heritage.* Boston: Houghton Mifflin, 1991.

———. "Getting Right with Robert E. Lee: How To Know the Unknowable Man." In Sears, ed., *The Civil War,* 44–53.

Sifikas, Stewart. *Compendium of the Confederate Armies.* 10 vols. New York: Facts on File, 1991–92.

Smith, Gustavus Woodson. *Confederate War Papers, Fairfax Court House, New Orleans, Seven Pines, Richmond and North Carolina.* 2d ed. New York: Atlantic Pub. Co., 1884.

Smith, Robert Ross. "Ox Hill: The Most Neglected Battle of the Civil War." In *Fairfax County and the War Between the States,* 18–64.

Snead, Thomas L., Jr. "The First Year of the War in Missouri." In Johnson and Buel, eds., *Battles and Leaders* 1:262–77.

Sorrel, Gilbert Moxley. *Recollections of a Confederate Staff Officer.* Ed. Bell Irvin Wiley. Jackson, Tenn.: McCowat-Mercer, 1958.

Squires, Charles Winder. "'Boy Officer' of the Washington Artillery—Part I." *Civil War Times Illustrated* 14 (1975): 10–24.

Stephenson, Nathaniel W. "A Theory of Jefferson Davis." *American Historical Review* 21 (1915): 73–90.

Strong, George Templeton. *The Diary of George Templeton Strong.* Ed. Allan Nevins. 4 vols. New York: Macmillan, 1952.

Stuart, James Ewell Brown. *The Letters of Major General James E. B. Stuart.* Ed. Adele H. Mitchell. N.p.: Stuart-Mosby Historical Society, 1990.

Sword, Wiley. *Shiloh, Bloody April.* New York: William Morrow & Co., 1974.

Sypher, Josiah Rinehart. *History of the Pennsylvania Reserve Corps: A Complete Record of the Organization, and of the Different Companies, Regiments and Brigades, Containing Descriptions of Expeditions, Marches, Skirmishes and Battles, Together with Biographical Sketches of Officers and Personal Records of Each Man during His Term of Service.* Lancaster, Pa.: Elias Barr & Co., 1865.

Tanner, Robert G. *Stonewall Jackson in the Valley: "Stonewall" Jackson's Shenandoah Valley Campaign, Spring 1862.* Rev. ed. Mechanicsburg, Pa.: Stackpole Books, 1996.

Taylor, Walter Herron. *Four Years with General Lee.* Ed. James I. Robertson, Jr. Bloomington: Indiana Univ. Press, 1962.

———. *General Lee, His Campaigns in Virginia, 1861–1865, with Personal Reminiscences.* Norfolk: Nusbaum Book and News Co., 1906.

———. *Lee's Adjutant: The Wartime Letters of Colonel Walter Herron Taylor, 1862–1865.* Ed. R. Lockwood Tower. Columbia: Univ. of South Carolina Press, 1995.

Teel, T. T. "Sibley's New Mexican Campaign: Its Object and the Causes of Its Failure." In Johnson and Buel, eds., *Battles and Leaders* 2:700.

Tenney, Leon Walter. "Seven Days in 1862: Numbers in Union and Confederate Armies before Richmond." Master's thesis. George Mason University, Fairfax, Va., 1992.

Thomas, Emory M. *Bold Dragoon: The Life of J. E. B. Stuart.* New York: Harper & Row, 1986.

———. *The Confederate Nation, 1861–1865.* New York: Harper & Row, 1979.

———. "Marse Robert at Mid-Life." In Heleniak and Hewitt, eds., *Confederate High Command,* 108–23.

———. *Robert E. Lee: A Biography.* New York: W. W. Norton, 1995.

Thomas, Henry Walter. *History of the Doles-Cook Brigade, Army of Northern Virginia, C.S.A., Containing Muster Rolls of Each Company of the Fourth, Twelfth, Twenty-first and Forty-fourth Georgia Regiments, with a Short Sketch of the Services of Each Member, and a Complete History of Each Regiment, by One of Its Own Members, and Other Matters of Interest.* Atlanta: Franklin Print. and Pub. Co., 1903.

The Tribune Almanac for the Years 1838 to 1868. 2 vols. New York: New York Tribune Association, 1868.

Trout, Robert J. *With Pen and Saber: The Letters and Diaries of J. E. B. Stuart's Staff Officers.* Mechanicsburg, Pa.: Stackpole Books, 1995.

U.S. Bureau of the Census. *Agriculture of the United States in 1860: Compiled from the Original Returns of the Eighth Census.* Washington, D.C.: GPO, 1864.

———. *Manufactures of the United States in 1860: Compiled from the Original Returns of the Eighth Census.* Washington, D.C.:GPO, 1865.

———. *Population of the United States in 1860: Compiled from the Original Returns of the Eighth Census.* Washington, D.C.: GPO, 1864.

———. *Statistics of the United States (Including Mortality, Property, &c.) in 1860: Compilation from the Original Returns of the Eighth Census.* Washington, D.C.: GPO, 1866.

U.S. Congress. *Report of the Joint Committee on the Conduct of the War.* 3 vols. Washington, D.C.: GPO, 1863.

U.S. Navy Department. *Official Records of the Union and Confederate Navies in the War of the Rebellion.* 31 vols. Washington, D.C.: GPO, 1894–1927.

U.S. War Department. *The Official Military Atlas of the Civil War: Atlas to Accompany the Official Records of the Union and Confederate Armies.* Intro. Richard J. Sommers. New York: Arno Press, 1978.

———. *Proceedings and Report of the Board of Army Officers Convened by Special Order No. 78, Headquarters of the Army, Washington, D.C., April 12, 1878, in the Case of Fitz John Porter.* 3 vols. Washington, D.C.: GPO, 1879.

———. *The War of the Rebellion: A Compilation of the Official Records of the Union and Confederate Armies.* 128 vols. Washington, D.C.: GPO, 1880–1901.

Vandiver, Frank Everson. *Basic History of the Confederacy.* Princeton, N.J.: Van Nostrand, 1962.

———. "Jefferson Davis and Confederate Strategy." In *The American Tragedy.* Ed. Bernard Mayo. Hampden-Sydney, Va.: Hampden-Sydney College, 1959.

———. *Rebel Brass: The Confederate Command System.* Baton Rouge: Louisiana State Univ. Press, 1956.

———. *Their Tattered Flags: The Epic of the Confederacy.* New York: Harper Magazine Press, 1970.

von Borcke, Heros. *Memoirs of the Confederate War for Independence.* 2 vols. New York: Peter Smith, 1938.

Waddill, J. M. "Forty-sixth Regiment." In Clark, ed. *North Carolina Regiments* 3:63–82.

Walker, Francis Amasa. *History of the Second Army Corps in the Army of the Potomac.* New York: Charles Scribner's Sons, 1886.

Walker, John George. "Jackson's Capture of Harper's Ferry." In Johnson and Buel, eds., *Battles and Leaders* 2:604–11.

Wallace, Lee A. *A Guide to Virginia Military Organizations, 1861–1865.* 2d rev. ed. Lynchburg, Va.: H. E. Howard, 1988.

Webb, Alexander. *The Peninsula, McClellan's Campaign of 1862.* New York: Charles Scribner's Sons, 1881.

Wert, Jeffry D. *General James Longstreet: The Confederacy's Most Controversial Soldier—A Biography.* New York: Simon & Schuster, 1993.

White, Henry Alexander. *Robert E. Lee and the Southern Confederacy, 1807–1870.* New York: Haskell House Pub., 1968.

Whitehorne, Joseph W. "A Beastly, Comfortless Conflict: The Battle of Chantilly, September 1, 1862." *Blue & Gray Magazine* 4 (1987): 7–23, 46–56.

Wiley, Bell Irvin. *Southern Negroes, 1861–1865.* New Haven: Yale Univ. Press, 1965.

Williams, Kenneth Powers. *Lincoln Finds a General: A Military Study of the Civil War.* 5 vols. New York: Macmillan, 1949–50.

Winfree, Waverly K., ed. *Guide to the Manuscript Collections of the Virginia Historical Society.* Richmond: Virginia Historical Society, 1985.

Wise, George. *History of the Seventeenth Virginia Infantry, C.S.A.* Baltimore: Kelly, Piet & Co., 1870.

Wise, John Sargent. *The End of an Era.* Boston: Houghton, Mifflin, 1902.

Woodworth, Steven E. *Davis and Lee at War.* Lawrence: Univ. of Kansas, 1995.

———. *Jefferson Davis and His Generals: The Failure of Confederate Command in the West.* Lawrence: Univ. of Kansas Press, 1990.

———. "Jefferson Davis and Robert E. Lee in the Seven Days." In Miller, ed., *The Peninsula Campaign* 1:1–18.

Index

Alabama, 98; secession, 9; second phase of the war, 33; troops from, 84

Alamo (Tex.), 8

Aldie Gap (Bull Run Mountains), 149, 151, 152

Alexandria, Va., 19, 21, 72, 147, 152, 168

Allegheny Mountains, 39, 52, 63

American Revolution, 57, 72

Amissville, Va., 143, 160

Anderson, George Thomas (CSA Gen.), 154

Anderson, Joseph Reid (CSA Gen.), 37

Anderson, Richard Heron (CSA Gen.): Drewry's Bluff, 116; Gordonsville, 123, 125, 128, 129; Petersburg, 121; promoted, 106; Second Manassas, 159, 164, 167; Waterloo Bridge, 143, 149, 182

Appomattox Court House, Va., 55, 57

Appomattox River (Va.), 105

Aquia District. *See* Department of Northern Virginia

Aquia Landing, Va., 197

Arizona Territory: claimed by Confederates, 9–10; first phase of the war, 25; second phase of the war, 34

Arkansas, 43; first phase of the war, 23; secession, 9

Arlington Heights, Va., 21, 72

Armistead, Lewis Addison (CSA Gen.), 128

Army of East Tennessee (CSA), 180

Army of Mississippi (CSA), 180

Army of Northern Virginia (CSA): buildup at Gordonsville, 128; casualties, 96, 163–65; in stalemate, 124; Lee dominates, 1–2; organization, 105–6; Rapidan delay,

126–27; reunited at Groveton, 156, 159; Second Manassas, 145–46; Seven Days, 98; third wing, 123, 124, 128–29, 133–34, 136, 142, 143–44; tool of Lee, 59
—strength: Sept. 1861, 192; April 30, 43–44; June 20, 1862, 88, 89; May 31, 1862, 83 (size); June 26, 1862, 88, 89, 180–81 (size); Aug. 27, 1862, 149–50, 182–83 (location); July 1862, 102–3, 104; Aug. 18, 1862, 125–26

Army of the Mississippi (USA), 180

Army of the North (CSA), 44

Army of the Ohio (USA), 180

Army of the Peninsula (CSA), 35, 44, 83

Army of the Potomac (USA): Harrison's Landing, 99, 195; joins Pope, 127, 128; position on the Chickahominy, 53–54, 75; reoccupies Malvern Hill, 115–17; Seven Days Battle, 91, 180; withdrawal from James, 117, 125
  strength: June 20, 1862, 84; Aug. 27, 1862, 183

Army of the Valley (CSA), 181

Army of the West (CSA), 180

Army of Virginia (USA), 108, 110, 112; created, 107; on Rapidan, 125, 126; strength, Aug. 27, 1862, 132–33, 183

Army of West Tennessee (USA), 180

Artillery Reserve, Army of Northern Virginia, 121, 123, 128, 129, 143, 150, 181, 182

Ashland, Va., 79, 80, 87, 94, 115

Baker, Edward Dickinson (USA Col.), 35

Ball's Bluff, Battle of, 21, 30, 35

CONFEDERATE TIDE RISING

was composed in 10.5/12.9 Bell on a Power Macintosh using PageMaker 6.0; at The Kent State University Press; printed by sheet-fed offset on 50-pound Glatfelter Supple Opaque Natural stock (an acid-free, recycled paper), Smyth sewn and bound over binder's boards in ICG Arrestox B cloth, and wrapped with dust jackets printed in three colors on 100-pound enamel stock by Thomson-Shore, Inc.; designed by Diana Dickson; jacket designed by Will Underwood; and published by

THE KENT STATE UNIVERSITY PRESS

Kent, Ohio 44242